FOREWORD

The financial landscape has changed dramatically in the last two decades, particularly in the OECD area. The Committee on Financial Markets of the OECD keeps track of these changes by discussing on a regular basis structural changes in OECD financial markets. In addition, regular discussions between members of the Committee and representatives of the financial services industry constitute an important forum for understanding developments and trends that shape the financial sector. However, these discussions do not always allow sufficient time for a systematic overview and analysis of all long-term trends and policy issues. For this reason, the Committee decided to hold an *ad hoc* expert meeting in July 1994 for an in-depth discussion of trends and structural changes in, and policy implications for, the financial sector as a whole. A second major objective was to determine the main factors likely to shape the financial services industry in the future.

The present report is based on background documentation prepared by the OECD Secretariat and on contributions by participating experts from Member countries. Where necessary, this material has been up-dated.

This publication has been prepared by Hans J. Blommestein and Karsten Biltoft of the OECD Financial Affairs Division with the assistance of national experts and other members of the Division. It is published on the responsibility of the Secretary-General of the OECD.

TABLE OF CONTENTS

Chapter 1

Structural Changes in Financial Markets: Overview of Trends and Prospects

H.J. Blommestein

Chapter 2

The Changing Borders of Banking: Trends and Implications

Claudio E.V. Borio and Renato Filosa

Chapter 3

Banking Industry Performance in Europe: Trends and Issues

Jukka Vesala

Chapter 4

The Changing Role of Banks in Europe - A German Viewpoint

Dietmar K.R. Klein

Chapter 5

The Evolution of the North American Banking System

Edward C. Ettin

Chapter 6

Structural Changes in Japanese Financial Markets: Trends and Prospects in Banking

Yasuhiro Hayasaki

Chapter 7

Risk Management in National Payment Systems

Bruce Summers

Chapter 8

Centralised Foreign Exchange and OTC Derivatives Clearing Issues to be Considered

Graham M. Duncan

Chapter 9

Trends, Structural Changes and Prospects in OECD Capital Markets

H.J. Blommestein, K. Biltoft

Chapter 10

Structural Changes in the North American Capital Markets

Mary Ann Gadziala

Chapter 1

STRUCTURAL CHANGES IN FINANCIAL MARKETS: OVERVIEW OF TRENDS AND PROSPECTS

H. J. Blommestein, OECD

Introduction

The financial landscape in the OECD area has changed dramatically over the past two decades. This chapter provides an overview of longer-term trends and policy issues in financial markets. The overview consists of an in-depth discussion of the main issues concerning trends and structural changes in, and policy implications for, the financial sector as a whole as well as the main factors likely to shape the financial services industry in the future.

Although financial trends and structural changes have an influence on all segments of the financial services industry, for analytical purposes this chapter as well as the publication itself is divided into three parts :

I. Structural changes in the banking sector;
II. The management of risk in the new financial environment;
III. The role of capital markets in the emerging financial landscape.

I. Structural changes in the banking sector

In most OECD countries, financial systems in general, and the banking sector in particular, are going through a period of major and wide-ranging structural changes. Several factors have been identified as the structural forces shaping the banking industry in the last two decades. Domestic deregulation and external financial liberalisation resulted in increased competition for the banking industry. On both the liabilities side and the assets side, banks faced intensive competition from non-banks. Funding became more expensive for banks, while many banking institutions became more aggressive in the riskier parts of the credit market. The combination of these developments led to

9

pronounced deterioration in the profitability and asset quality of banks in many OECD countries in the second part of the 1980s and the beginning of the 1990s[1]. The banking industry witnessed in the 1990s major bank failures or banking crises in several OECD countries. In most OECD countries with banking problems this resulted in a thorough restructuring of banks and a return to profitability.

Spectacular technological advances in communications and information systems enhanced the capacity of banks and other financial market participants to use the opportunities offered by the liberalised environment. Technological developments have eroded statutory and physical barriers between sectors and countries. New information systems allowed the creation and use of highly complex new financial products. Technological advances and the progressive elimination of official barriers to capital flows have spurred an enormous increase in cross-border financial transactions and activities and rapid growth in international financial markets. As a result, linkages among OECD financial markets have been greatly strengthened and financial conditions in individual countries have become increasingly sensitive to developments in external markets.

The impact of structural changes on the banking sector

These structural trends had important consequences for the functioning of the banking sector and the financial services industry more generally. The most important result has been a strong increase in competition among financial intermediaries, in particular in the banking sector[2]. Due to extensive regulation and controls, banks in many countries had been shielded far longer than other sectors from "harsh, competitive reality". For this reason, some of the structural changes that would revolutinise banking were widely percieved as inevitable. Yet, no one would have been able to predict the events of the past few years and their far-reaching consequences for the working of the financial sector[3]

1. There has been a gradual erosion of the distinction between various types of financial assets. In particular, "money" has clearly become much less distinguishable from other liabilities of financial intermediaries.

2. The demarcation lines between the different types of financial intermediaries have become increasingly blurred. An important consequence is increased competition among categories of institutions which were formerly not direct competitors. More intense competition

and the attendant reshaping of financial institutions' strategies have strengthened the trends towards financial conglomeration.

3. The volume and average size of financial transactions have grown spectacularly. This has put higher demands on the stability and efficiency of clearing and settlement systems for payments (see part II below).

4. Capital market activity has gained ground relative to traditional bank lending. In particular, large corporate borrowers have used the capital markets for an increasing share of their external financing requirements.

5. Off-balance-sheet activities of banks have become very important, in particular the use of derivatives as well as the emphasis put on proprietary trading and asset management. In addition, assets tend to be removed from the balance sheet of the originating institution. This has changed the revenue structure of banks.

6. Off-balance sheet business has created stronger linkages between the various sectors of the financial services industry. This trend makes it increasingly difficult to assess the direct credit, liquidity and interest rate risks of individual banks (see part II below). The size of the indirect risks of these interlinkages for the individual institution are very difficult to measure.

7. Against the backdrop of lower profit margins, banking problems accelerated the process of concentration in the banking sector. Also, banks sought entry into new lines of business to compensate for the loss of traditional business and many of them became more active in the riskier (and supposedly more profitable) segments of credit markets -- *e.g.* lending to LDCs, financing of leveraged transactions, and real estate lending. The resulting "financial fragility" of the banks made them more vulnerable to adverse shocks. In a number of countries, the authorities had to rescue banks (or other depositary institutions) at taxpayer expense.

8. There was a structural change in the sources of funding, especially deposits versus money market instruments. The shift of bank funding sources varied among countries and this has implications for the pressures that have arisen on banks. Some analysts have contended that differences in regulatory and tax regimes had played a large role in determining whether the public decided to redirect assets away from

bank deposits in particular countries. In future years, however, demographic changes may also influence the composition of assets. Other things being equal, deposits can be expected to grow more slowly than assets of institutional investors (insurance companies, collective investment instruments or pension funds); this should have a significant impact on future bank activity. Greater shares of total financial intermediation will probably take place through the capital markets and banks will have to adjust their strategies accordingly.

Differences in the structure of banking systems

Traditionally, there have been important **differences in the structure** of OECD banking systems and in banks' relations with non-financial enterprises[4]

i) In OECD countries with universal banking systems, bank are allowed to engage in the full range of financial activities, including underwriting and dealing in secondary markets, to be members of securities exchanges and to deal directly on stock exchanges[5]. In universal banking systems it is assumed that most of the public's savings will flow through the banking system as deposits or in the form of investment assets or securities.

ii) In OECD countries with non-universal banking systems there are restrictions on banks to engage in the full range of financial services. For example, in the United States there continues to exist a legal separation between commercial and investment banking, although this barrier has been lowered in practice.

iii) In some OECD countries, bank holdings of non-financial enterprises' equity are significant(*e.g.* Germany, Spain, Switzerland) while in other countries there are important severe restrictions on the ownership linkages between banks and non-financial companies (*e.g.* the United States, Australia and Canada).

iv) The role of banks in corporate restructurings differs across OECD countries. For example, through the "house bank" and "main bank" systems, German and Japanese banks are frequently involved in resolving the problems of companies in financial distress. In contrast, banks in the United States and the United Kingdom usually play a more limited role in corporate restructurings[6]

Convergence of banking systems ?

Despite the different starting points, as a result of liberalisation of financial markets there seem to be significant convergence of banking systems[7]. In a number of countries the norm has become for financial institutions to form large groups that offer the full range of financial services (*i.e.* banking, securities, leasing etc.); usually each of these activities is performed in a separate subsidiary. Countries now having such an institutional structure include the United Kingdom, France, Italy and Spain. Japan has authorised banks and securities houses to expand into each others' primary line of business. Although the United States continues to maintain banking/securities legal separation, banks and securities firms are active in offering close substitutes for each others' products and banks' securities powers have been extended significantly in the 1980s. Although the structure of the universal banking system appears to be essentially intact in their home markets, institutions from these countries appear to be moving toward international practices when they operate internationally. Thus, in offshore centres, banks from Germany offer essentially the same products as other institutions while some major German corporations are modifying disclosure practices to conform to international practice. In general, the latter developments imply greater reliance on capital markets than in the past.

It has been acknowledged by many analysts that deregulation, internationalisation and increased competition had led to a narrowing of differences among systems. However, views conflict as to how serious remaining differences are, which systems tend to promote innovation, and whether systems are converging toward a common model. There is also disagreements about whether innovation and competition have come as more of a shock in regimes with universal banking than in regimes with greater separation between banking and securities. It has been argued that under universal banking, a small number of institutions control the great bulk of domestic assets, dominate all facets of intermediation and often oppose the introduction of new products. In segmented systems, by contrast, competition is an inherent element of the system because different categories of institutions constantly seek to innovate in order to attract business from competitors. Even when a new product (for example money market funds, commercial paper or financial futures) is introduced in universal banking regimes, frequently such innovation begins in foreign markets and appears only at a comparatively late stage in the domestic market of the universal banking country. The introduction of innovative techniques then takes the form of new products being offered by the same universal banking institutions rather than in a "competitive process" among different categories of institution. Thus, change is absorbed into the existing institutional framework, giving rise to less active market competition.

Others have contested this entire line of argument by noting that the process of internalising new products can be interpreted to mean that the universal banking system had considerable capacity to accept innovation without excessive disturbance. Countries with universal banking regimes have shown themselves adaptable to, and resilient in the face of, both temporary and permanent shifts in patterns of lending and refinancing. It has also been argued that the universal banking system is more flexible inasmuch it permits but does not require banks to engage in all activities; some institutions under universal regimes may choose to specialise in only a few activities if they so wish. Thus, the actual operative structure of the financial system is basically determined by the preferences and strategies of financial intermediaries rather than the authorities' views about the merits of segmentation. The question of whether any particular regime would come to be dominant seems irrelevant, in the sense that change and adaptation is already in process within each type of system and what will emerge in the end will be essentially market-determined.

Patterns of financing and corporate governance

Concerning **patterns of financing** the following stylised facts emerge[8]:

i) In most (if not all) OECD countries, retained earnings are the most important source of finance. However, there are quantitative differences. For example, companies in the United Kingdom pay out a larger part of their earnings in dividends to their shareholders than German enterprises, giving German firms access to a relatively larger share of the internally generated funds[9].

ii) External sources of finances come primarily from banks, although there are differences across OECD countries. For example, over the last decades, Japanese banks have been contributing a dominant proportion to the Japanese corporation's total sources of finance. In many other OECD countries, banks have been contributing a more modest proportion.

iii) Stock markets are relatively minor sources of finance in most OECD countries. Stock market finance typically amounts to less than 10 per cent of **gross** sources in most countries and in many countries substantially less than that. On a **net** basis, aggregate stock market sources of finance have at times been negative, reflecting an excess of repurchases of shares over new issues. Interestingly, financial market analysts have been unable to detect a consistent relationship between the sizes of stock markets and their significance in raising finance for industrial enterprises[10].

iv) Bond markets are relatively minor sources of finance for corporations in aggregate in all countries other than the United States and Canada. However, it is important to note that, due to domestic capital market restrictions or lower cost-effectiveness, many companies have gone offshore for raising longer-term finance. For example, German and Japanese companies have been important issuers of corporate bonds on the international markets.

v) Banks are the dominant source of external finance for small companies in all countries. Financing patterns of medium-sized enterprises diverge across OECD countries. Banks continue to play an important role in project finance[11].

Differences in **corporate governance structures** in OECD countries are much more pronounced than differences in the financing of corporations. The following criteria can be used for evaluating differences in ownership and control of enterprises[12]: the number of listed companies; the liquidity of capital markets and the frequency with which ownership and control rights are traded; the extent of intercorporate equity holdings; and the depth of the domestic investor community. The nature of cross-shareholdings among companies is also important for a characterisation and assessment of corporate governance systems.

In some OECD countries (*e.g.* the United States, Japan, the Netherlands and the United Kingdom) there are a large number of listed companies which are frequently traded in liquid capital markets while other OECD countries have a relatively smaller number of listed companies which are less frequently traded in less liquid capital markets. Cross-holdings among companies with long-term relationships are much more common in France, Germany and Japan than in the United States and the United Kingdom. The majority of shares of Japanese and German companies is held by either industrial companies or by financial institutions such as banks and insurance companies with long-term relationships[13]. Most Japanese and German companies have close relationships with a bank (or a few banks) for lending and other services. This bank is usually called a "main bank" (Japan) or a "hausbank" (Germany). The Japanese main banks often hold significant equity stakes and sometimes send a director to

15

the board of the company. German "hausbanks" hold 9 percent (and insurance companies 11 per cent) of all domestically listed shares of German companies. However, German banks also act as custodians of bearer shares of investors and they can vote using the shares held in deposit. As a result, nearly one-half of listed shares are broadly under the control of German banks[14]. Consequently, the role of German and Japanese banks in corporate governance is large in comparison with banks in the United States and the United Kingdom[15].

The liberalisation and internationalisation of financial markets have highlighted differences in the financial market structure of OECD countries, including differences in the corporate governance role of banks. This in turn may encourage further convergence of OECD financial systems, including the corporate governance role of banks and other financial institutions.

The future of banking

Since the essence of banking has been on-balance sheet intermediation, the **future of traditional banking** is linked to the prospects for the prevailing pattern of intermediation in OECD countries. It has been argued that there are three natural stages of development in a country's financial system[16]: *(a)* internal finance; *(b)* the intermediation of finance; and *(c)* securitisation. It is important to relativise this development pattern with the observation that, in most countries, internal finance, financial intermediation, and securities markets co-exist simultaneously. In reality, one sees a shift of, or change in, the dominant emphasis[17]. Many bank analysts argue that bank lending is inherently more expensive than securitisation. For this reason, many bank analysts predict a further decline of (traditional) banking[18]. However, others have pointed out that although disintermediation is likely to continue, banks will probably continue to play an important financial market role, albeit in a much-changed shape. Banks are still key institutions for mobilising savings. They are essential participants in the payment system. Banks routinely perform credit analysis and are the major source of information concerning small and medium enterprises. Banks are involved in providing back-up lines of credit to capital market participants. More generally, the scope of banking activities is being broadened by technology and deregulation. For example, banks participated in the development of new products, such as the origination and servicing of securitised assets and derivatives, and improved the efficiency with which they distribute old ones. More of banking's revenues will come from fee-based services. Some banks are specialising in areas where they have a clear comparative advantage and which are more profitable than lending to corporations such as investment banking or risk arbitrage. Other banks are using lending relationships as a means to sell other, more profitable products (*e.g.* advice on mergers and acquisitions, underwriting of equity issues, cash management, foreign exchange transactions, and financial advisory services in general). Another notable trend is that more and more banks are stressing risk management and the more efficient use of capital. Finally, at times of financial crises, the banks act as the intermediate lender of last resort, standing between a systemic financial collapse and the intervention of central banks.

The changing nature of banking means that much of the commentary about the "declining role of banks" is basically misplaced. What is actually occurring is not a contraction in banking per se, but a switch of banks from on-balance to off-balance sheet activities and an increasing involvement of banks in the capital markets. Indeed, recent studies show that the banking sector is not shrinking when banking activities are properly measured[19].

II. The management of risks in the new financial environment

Efficient market-based financial systems require an effective framework for managing risks. Risks in financial markets have changed in the past two decades reflecting the changing nature of financial intermediation. Banks (and other depository institutions) began to engage in activities for which they were sometimes ill-prepared, a problem aggravated by the relatively low level of bank capitalisation in some countries. Simultaneously, other fundamental structural changes occurred in financial markets, including: the abolition of exchange controls in many OECD countries and deregulation of domestic financial markets, more active asset and liability management, changes in the type of financial assets held by households, a more prominent role of institutional investors, and greater importance of the treasury function for companies. Financial liberalisation and advances in information technology increased the integration of financial markets which, in turn, has increased the likelihood that markets in the OECD area will move in similar directions in response to shocks[20].

The need for risk management in the new financial environment

New risks, associated with desegmentation, securitisation, financial innovations, globalisation, and increased competition, have emerged. Increased volatility, greater interdependence, and new risks have also made the structure of the risk exposure of banks and other financial institutions more complex. For banks the traditional activity was "on balance sheet" lending, and the associated risk management technique was credit risk analysis. However, lending now accounts for a smaller share of total activity than in the past for many banks. Newer activities are investment banking, origination, trading (agency and proprietary), mergers and acquisitions and information systems -- where the risks are different. The fact that banks will increasingly hold a wider set of instruments (money market assets, bonds, derivatives, forward contracts) and that some of the risks in these assets will be retained while others are passed on implies that risks must continually be identified and quantified and systems must be set in place to offset risk or to hold sufficient capital against any risk that is retained. Also, OECD capital markets have changed beyond recognition. Domestic deregulation and external liberalisation have resulted in major changes in competitive conditions. Advances in communications and information systems enhanced the capacity of financial market participants to use the opportunities offered by the new financial environment.

There is general agreement that structural changes in financial systems have accentuated the need for a more effective framework for managing risk. In particular, since it is now accepted that financial institutions should have greater leeway to make their own decisions without direct government interference, one is implicitly accepting the eventuality that financial institutions will take more risk and occasionally will suffer losses. It should be noted, however, that although new risks have emerged, the so-called "old" forms of risks -- including "Herstatt risk" (defined as the risk connected with cross-currency settlement) and traditional credit risk -- have not disappeared. Despite the growing complexity of risk, the greatest problems in bank solvency in the past two decades have come from credit risk (mainly associated with traditional lending).

In this context the question arises whether the strains in banking of the 1980s and early 1990s amounted to a one-time shock in reaction to the combined impact of several specific events (deregulation, liberalisation, introduction of new technology) or whether finance fragility is likely to continue. Some market analysts emphasize that change would indeed continue and that the increased fragility it had brought to the banking system would become a more or less permanent state. They hold the view that new categories of risk and higher risk concentration would mean a permanently higher level of financial fragility in the banking sector. However, other market analysts argue that the fragility of the banking system experienced in recent years was still to a very large degree caused by old-fashioned poor credit decisions, rather than the result of more intense competition and increased complexity of operations. At the same time, it could also be argued that to some degree the problem had already been contained in the sense that the initial banking crises had resulted in the exit and/or extensive restructuring of depository institutions, in increased stress on capitalisation and risk control for remaining institutions and in improved techniques for supervision.

Proprietary trading is an increasingly important activity of financial institutions meaning that in addition to the risks regularly assumed in the business of intermediation or "underwriting", banks will have to take operational views about the direction of markets. Meanwhile, the product cycle in financial services is operating at a faster pace. New financial services require constant innovation with constant pressure on margins.

These developments have increased the need for better risk management. Financial institutions must improve their capabilities for defining, managing and pricing risk. The general objective is to build and use systems for the disciplined management of credit risk, market risk and liquidity risk. The primary components of a sound risk management process are: a comprehensive system for **measuring** the different types of risk; a framework for **governing** risk taking, including limits, guidelines, and other relevant parameters ; and an adequate **management information system** for monitoring, reporting and controlling risks.

Policy makers can contribute to these objectives by establishing efficient regulatory and supervisory systems for managing risks. Also, efforts by the authorities to improve clearing and settlement systems for payments and securities -- including those related to cross-border transactions -- are key in encouraging the adoption of risk reducing procedures and practices by market participants.

The measurement of risk

Defining and measuring risk is the key to controlling it. Modern financial analysis indicates that the risks and returns from engaging in particular lines of business, or investing in particular financial instruments, must be assessed in the context of the **entire** portfolios of individual investors, financial institutions, and markets as a whole[21]. This approach implies that the focus of risk management should shift from individual transactions to portfolio exposures. As institutions operate in innovative products, especially in the OTC market, the risks of any given operation becomes more complex. Thus, the recent G30 report "Derivatives: Practices and Principles" advocates an integrated approach to the **measurement** of both **market** and **credit** risks[22]. Financial instruments (swaps, bonds, options, etc.) are defined in terms of different types of risk, including interest rate risk, foreign exchange risk, and equity risk. For example, banks

19

could use this approach to manage better both their : *i)* balance sheet risks (*i.e.* mismatches between the currency, maturity and interest-rate structure of assets and the liabilities funding those assets resulting in interest-rate mismatch risk; liquidity risk; and foreign-exchange risk); and *ii)* transaction risks (*i.e.* credit risks; price risks; and operating and liquidity risks).

Frequent valuation of portfolios (*i.e.* **marking to market**) is judged as important by financial analysts to obtain information about market and credit risks taken in the past; the value of positions today; insights about risks that may have to be faced in the future. For example, the G30 report on derivatives notes in this context that marking to market is the keystone for the proper management of market risk and the basis for the quantification of counterparty risk. In addition, the G30 report argues strongly in favour of the quantification of the sources of current and **potential** market risk as well as current and **potential** credit exposures.

The **value-at-risk** method is a frequently used method for measuring **market risk** exposure -- an estimate of potential changes in portfolio value based on a statistical confidence interval of changes in market prices that may occur some proportion of the time. This statistical measure of riskiness, however, should not be interpreted as a projection or forecast nor be seen as a risk limit. By contruction, it is a measure of likely declines in portfolio value that -- even in a perfectly managed portfolio -- will be exceeded some proportion of the time. Within this statistical framework a prima facie case for the conclusion that risk management is not adequate can only be made when the frequency at which losses exceed the value-at-risk is significantly higher than the confidence level of the value-at-risk (under well-defined statistical assumptions).

Credit risk arises from the possibility that a firm will experience a loss when a counterparty defaults. The magnitude of the credit risk depends on the likelihood of default by the counterparty; the potential value of outstanding contracts; the extent to which legally enforceable netting arrangements allow the value of offsetting contracts with that counterparty to be netted against each other, or the value of collateral held against contracts. Measurement of credit risk is complicated by the fact that both credit exposures and the probability of default can vary over time. Ideally, one needs to integrate current credit exposures (measured as the current mark-to-market value) and potential credit exposures (measured as changes in value due to changes in underlying prices) with the estimated probabilities of default.

By framing risk management in terms of types of risk, it is possible to measure exposures consistently across products. The next step is to aggregate risk across portfolios or counterparty. The bottom-line is that the institution's procedures should accurately measure the multiple types of risks facing the institution. For dealer operations, marking to market is essential to measuring exposures accurately on a timely basis. The ability to monitor credit exposures, trading positions and market activity more general, is of great importance for all institutions active in dealing foreign exchange, derivatives and other traded instruments. Institutions that are primarily in the trading business should have the capacity of monitoring their more actively traded products on a real-time basis. Risk measurement and the risk management process should enable the various personnel at **all** levels of the institution to understand fully risk management standards and actual (*i.e.* measured) risk levels -- from individual traders to the board of directors. An important aspect of risk measurement is the analysis of so-called stress situations. Stress scenarios should include abnormally large market swings and periods of prolonged inactivity. In particular senior management should be aware of the consequences of "worst case" scenarios, preferably on an institution-wide basis.

There is a broad consensus that progress had been made in the understanding and measurement of the different types of risks, although several experts are of the opinion that not all risks are sufficiently understood. It has been noted that the focus should not be on particular products but that risks should be assessed in the context of the entire risk exposures of financial institutions and of the measurement and management of those exposures. In other words, it has been argued that it is not a productive approach to set additional new rules for each category of risk encountered, for this would merely lead to an excessive complexity of rules and set in motion the familiar process of regulatory arbitrage. While a divergence of views (and especially of practices) exists at the level of specific computation methods and assumptions, one can identify the following **common features** in risk measurement as practised by an increasing number of financial market participants:

- a portfolio approach;

- a focus on basis types of risk (*e.g.*, interest rate risk, exchange rate risk, credit risk, etc.), rather than instruments or balance sheet categories;

- a measure of the value of the portfolio that reflects all relevant current market prices;

– a measure of the sensitivity of the portfolio's value to changes in these prices.

The role of derivatives

The development of **derivatives** offers new possibilities for better risk management. They allow market participants to "unbundle" risks. Derivatives can be used as management techniques to assess and adjust risks with greater precision -- in helping institutions decide which risks are best kept and which are best shifted[23]. When used defensively, derivatives offer individual market participants an effective method for reducing certain risks through hedging and scope for "immunising" portfolios through offsetting actions in related markets.

Nonetheless, there are major differences of view on the issue whether the use of derivatives, especially OTC derivatives, may have increased the overall risk and/or uncertainty in the system. It has been noted that derivative instruments strengthen the linkages among markets and market intermediaries. This may increase market uncertainty (and the speed of transmission) when shocks or tensions arising in one market may impact on other markets in ways that are not readily identified and quantified. While some analysts point out that derivatives only transform and reallocate risk, others object to the view that derivatives cannot reduce the overall risk in the system, since derivatives can be used to hedge other risks and, in any case, risk is transferred to those market participants who wish to hold the kind of risk in question.

Regulators and other financial sector analysts in many OECD countries have become increasingly concerned about the risk of a systemic disturbance arising from the derivatives markets, particularly the over-the-counter (OTC) markets. Regulators point out that market participants may not always understand how risk is transformed and reallocated. In particular, there is concern that risk has become concentrated in a small number of major commercial banks and securities houses and that, as a result, the overall risk to the financial system may have been increased[24]. An additional point to be kept in mind is that derivative instruments, together with advanced information technology and financial liberalisation, strengthen the linkages between markets and major market intermediaries in ways that are not readily identified and quantified. Consequently, shocks or problems arising in one market or institution may spill-over into other (cash and derivatives) markets in an unpredictable fashion[25].

Some experts look favourably on the situation that OTC derivatives business tends to be concentrated in well-capitalised financial institutions. Although it is to be recognised that, as recent experience shows, non-financial users of the markets may suffer heavy losses by either failing to inform themselves of risk or by making errors in judgement in playing markets, decisions by non-financial companies to use the markets have relatively few systemic consequences.

The development of off-exchange derivative products has been one of the most striking features of the past few years. In particular, the exchanges that trade financial futures and options have received increasingly stiff competition from the swap market. The shift from trading on exchanges to over-the-counter trading is driven by several factors, in particular the lack of regulatory constraint gives the OTC market a flexibility that is difficult for the exchanges to match. Moreover, OTC derivative products can be tailored to the specific needs of clients with respect to expiration dates, industry composition of equity indices, etc. On the other hand, the derivatives exchanges believe that the specific rules for trading provide significant benefits in terms of transparency, liquidity, and reduced counterparty risk. In addition, the exchanges are seeking to rely increasingly on automation. As a matter of fact, the derivatives exchanges and the swap markets complement each other as well as competing for business. Thus, much of the net risk that is acquired in the swap market is eventually hedged using exchange-traded derivatives. Also, intermediaries can use a mix of exchange-listed contracts and OTC products in creating tailor-made investment instruments. Finally, some exchanges have introduced or are planning more product flexibility. Their objective is to combine the flexibility of the OTC market with the strengths (competitive prices, transparant markets, guaranteed trades and a secondary market) and safeguards of the listed market.

Initiatives to limit risk in the new financial environment

Efforts at limiting risk -- including systemic risk -- can be categorised as follows: *i)* development of adequate, up-to-date risk management practices by banks and other financial institutions; *ii)* more effective oversight of off- and on-balance-sheet activities and related risk control systems by senior management of financial institutions and regulators; *iii)* improved clearing and settlement systems for payments and securities.

The adequacy of in-house control systems

The development of adequate in-house control systems is essential in managing risks in the new environment. Portfolio diversification, "marking to market", improved risk measurement procedures, accurate design of reliable in-house risk-management systems, up-to-date control procedures and more effective oversight by senior management are considered as key elements of efforts to implement improved risk control systems. The G30 report "Derivatives: Practices and Principles" contains suggestions to strengthen risk management practices by financial institutions, as well as proposals to enhance oversight by senior management of derivatives transactions. Some market participants argue that the lessons and disciplines of credit should be applied to a wide variety of new instruments. In particular, that the disciplined management of credit risk today must be integrated with equally disciplined management of market risk and liquidity risk to build a comprehensive risk system of proper controls. Proper controls requires, however, that senior management review the adequacy of risk management policies and procedures and that sufficient resources and staff are allocated to measure, report and control risks. The board of directors or a committee thereof should approve and periodically all policies related to in-house risk control systems. In approving existing policies, the board should also articulate its level of risk tolerance.

Although the need for implementing integrated risk management systems is widely recognised, there are many practical obstacles. Banks and other financial firms are encouraged by supervisors to develop systems that can measure and analyse market and credit risk on a global and consolidated basis, as well as to ensure proper integration of front and back-office systems covering all financial instruments. The challenge in putting in place sophisticated and integrated information management systems is enormous in terms of financial and human resources. Many financial firms are dealing with the legacy of different, disparate systems, each having been developed in response to the needs of the different departments. The global consolidated picture of risk is therefore missing. Institutions face the massive task of bringing together into one system information residing on different technology structures and applications. A major challenge is to develop high-quality software that will connect existing systems with the central data base. According to market analysts, some firms with the right culture, the right timing and clear strategy are at the forefront of implementing sophisticated risk management systems. Analysts point out that these firms will enjoy a competitive advantage. Most firms, though, are thought to be either in the design phase or in the process of integrating systems piece-by-piece. In addition to the technological challenge, there is the important task of designing adequate internal controls at all levels of the organisation. The measurement and management of overall portfolio risk also means that the financial services industry needs to understand how the various risk interrelate. A reflection of this fact is that some financial firms have created new "Risk Management Officer" staff positions and have formed a new body -- called Risk Management Committee -- in charge of the overall internal oversight of risks.

A recent report by the Group of Thirty[26], found that the majority of end-users of financial derivatives lack adequate controls of risks. For example, only 8 per cent of users had adopted the so-called "value-at-risk" method of calculating how much they stood to lose from market movements when buying derivatives. However, the same report found important improvements in derivatives dealers' practices. There was also greater monitoring of derivatives' activities by senior managers of banks. Other survey reports have also found that many corporations have inadequate internal controls, in particular regarding control systems governing their derivatives transactions.

Regulatory and supervisory systems in flux

Efficient regulatory systems constitute a key element of the overall framework for an effective management of risk. Regulatory systems need to be adapted because, in dynamic financial systems characterised by strong competition and financial innovations, the nature of risks may change significantly over time, while new risk and uncertainties may emerge. The interlinkages between credit intermediaries and participants in debt and equity securities markets have changed in many OECD countries. The direct risks of these changes for credit intermediaries are very difficult to assess[27]. In addition, credit risk may shift from the banks, over whom the banking supervisors have legal control, to the nonbank financial sector. In countries where the supervisory umbrella is narrow in scope or highly fragmented, this trend may be a reason of concern to the extent that this implies little or no control over the extent of risk-taking by the nonbank financial institutions. Moreover, oversight mechanisms applied to non-bank financial intermediaries (especially securities houses) have traditionally been concerned with investor protection, thus stressing disclosure by issuers, and proper supervision of trading; broader issues involving the solvency of intermediaries have received relatively less emphasis while systemic issues were seldom considered at all. At the same time, the risk-exposure of banks may have increased because the nonbank financial institutions may have borrowed from the banks to take on credit or market risk[28]. Increased competition as a result of the lowering of barriers between the different segments of the financial sector has also led to the emergence of new links in the form of financial conglomerates. The joint ownership or operational control of banks, insurance companies, securities houses is a significant trend in many OECD countries. The process of financial conglomeration may heighten the relevance of a number of specific risks: concentration of power, conflicts of interests, difficulties in assessing aggregate risk exposures, and a weakening of corporate control in the components of the conglomerate[29].

The trade-off between competition and stability continues to present a dilemma for policy makers. Regulators clearly have an interest in preserving the stability of the financial system and stability is characterised by adequate margins and profitability. On the other hand, competition drives innovation and promotes efficiency through the strategic responses adopted by banks to existing or potential threats to their markets from competitors. In this context, it has been noted that competition among products and institutions had led to a general revitalisation of financial markets. An example is the increased liquidity and efficiency brought to securities markets in some countries through banks' entry into these activities. It remains, however, that banks' solvency can be jeopardised if they fail to maintain appropriate risk premiums in the face of cut-throat competition. On balance, it would seem that the ultimate problem is one of risk management by financial institutions -- and it cannot be automatically assumed that increased competition will always bring effective risk management.

Many of the trends that are changing the role of capital markets can be expected to exert significant **strains on existing supervisory and regulatory systems.** Securities market regulation often was founded upon the assumption that investors were mainly individuals and that the balance of market power favoured the issuers and the intermediaries, thus requiring an officially-supervised, formal framework for investor protection. It was necessary to require those who made public securities issues to provide information at the time of issue and throughout the period during which the security was publicly traded. Additionally, securities regulators (frequently in collaboration with self-regulation by exchanges) have usually sought to establish specific rules for secondary market trading, especially of equities, in order to protect investors from market manipulation. While there clearly remain needs for official supervision of the markets, the traditional concerns of investor protection may seem less urgent than in the past.

These trends have led to (proposed) **changes in the regulatory and supervisory framework**. The emergence of risk and uncertainties associated with new links between the different parts of the financial services industry (including conglomerates) may require the implementation of a system that more closely resembles functional supervision. In practice, "true" functional supervision may be impossible to realise at present[30]. Instead, some form of "advanced" consolidated supervision may be called for. More generally, the view is increasingly gaining ground that, though securities firms and other capital market institutions need not necessarily be fully integrated into the supervisory system for credit institutions, more effective co-operation between the supervisors that are responsible for the different parts of the financial sector is desirable or, indeed, indispensable. This should entail, in particular, procedures that would permit close and rapid consultations in situations of financial stress.

The risks associated with the globalisation of the financial services industry have to be tackled by closer international co-operation between regulators and supervisors. Important progress has been made by the Basle Committee on Banking Supervision. Thus, this Committee released a report, "Minimum Standards for the Supervision of International Banking Groups and Their Cross-Border establishments", which is aimed at[31]:

- strengthening of the principles of consolidated supervision to all internationally active banking groups;

- adding a further element of discipline to practices surrounding the cross-border establishment and maintenance of banking offices; and

- promoting a still higher level of communication and co-ordination among the international community of bank supervisors.

Considerable work on analysing issues in capital market regulation and in international co-operation of supervisors is being undertaken by IOSCO[32]. However, IOSCO is primarily concerned with the traditional activities of securities supervision, especially investor protection. IOSCO is also concerned with assuring a "level playing field" between banks and securities houses competing for the same business. But systemic issues have received relatively less attention. More generally, it would seem that additional attention should be paid to the risks and (potential) problems associated with[33]:

- inadequately supervised financial centres or, more generally, major differences in regulatory regimes;

- the lack of harmonisation of regulatory standards such as those related to cross-border depositor protection;

- legal and practical problems that can arise in connection with the liquidation of banking institutions with multiple cross-border offices;

- the supervision of financial conglomerates;

- the legal uncertainties associated with the application of domestic laws to international financial transactions;

- the effects on the stability of financial systems of the use new financial instruments by financial market participants, including institutional investors such as the (unregulated) hedge funds;

- systemic aspects of clearing and settlement systems for payments and securities.

Efforts to modernise legal and regulatory frameworks must, from a public policy point of view, meet a number of critical tests. The following principles are of particular importance in this regard[34]:

- Promote systemic stability, the ability to deal adequately with financial market problems, and the effective implementation o monetary policy;

- Encourage market discipline to the maximum extent possible, consistent with achieving a safe and sound system;

- Establish a level playing field for all institutions providing the same generic services, whether these institutions are called banks or something else;

- Recognise the public interest in the safety and soundness of financial institutions through consolidated, comprehensive oversight of all providers of financial services;

- Promote greater responsiveness to changing customer needs, provide consumer protection, and be receptive to change on the part of the industry.

Rebalancing official supervision and in-house risk control systems

The balance between official supervision of financial institutions and these institutions' in-house risk management systems needs to be carefully considered.

Since the need to operate in the OTC market is increasingly indispensable for all intermediaries, a high credit rating is essential. Thus, most institutions are increasingly sensitive of the need to use their capital efficiently and maintain high credit ratings, giving them a strong incentive to develop advanced in-house risk management systems. It also has other implications: *1)* regulators may well have difficulties in understanding sophisticated private risk management systems; *2)* the combination of competition driving down margins and only the highest rated surviving means that the number of "players" in world-class "risk arbitrage" will decline -- as is already being observed. Given the importance of counterparty risk and the diminishing number of "key counterparty" players, the failure of any major institution would have proportionately greater consequences than in the past.

The need for private institutions to develop sophisticated risk management systems and the need for supervisors to keep abreast of risk management by private institutions may well be a major parameter of financial regulation in the future. In this connection, Federal Reserve Chairman Greenspan recently suggested that banks should focus on developing their own risk management systems while supervisors emphasise the analysis of the adequacy of those systems. Despite the growing complexity of risk, it is also worth remembering that the great problems in bank solvency in the past two decades have come from credit risk (mainly associated with traditional lending) and not from the more complex risks that have been recently identified. Cases in point are lending to LDCs, energy, agriculture and real estate -- all cases of credit misjudgment and portfolio concentration. Thus, while newer risks must plainly be addressed, it would be wrong to neglect "old" forms of risk.

It is increasingly acknowledged that the need to strike the proper balance between official supervision of financial institutions and these institutions' in-house risk management systems is an important challenge for the authorities. The need for supervisors to keep abreast of risk management by private institutions may well be a major parameter of financial regulation in the future. There seems to be wide support for the view that banks should focus on developing their own risk management systems while supervisors emphasise the analysis of the adequacy of those systems. Issues for risk management that are not fully resolved include: *1)* the proper balance between legislation, regulation, and supervision to achieve reliable official oversight of risk management in financial institutions; *2)* the establishment of a level playing field, given that there are important non-bank and non-financial players which operate in the same financial markets but are subject to differential regulatory frameworks (*e.g.* different capital requirements for credit risk for banks and insurance companies); *3)* protection against individual and systemic risks posed by less (or hardly) regulated market participants; *4)* the resolution of open issues of accounting and disclosure, in particular in the derivatives area; and *5)* the extent to which risk management supervision should be harmonised across different jurisdictions.

Possible needed changes in the regulatory and supervisory systems as part of the overall framework for the management of risk have been discussed recently in several fora. Regulatory systems need to adapt because the nature of risks may change over time, while new risks and uncertainties may emerge. This requires that the authorities themselves need to understand fully the risks associated with new products before contemplating regulatory changes, otherwise newly implemented legislation or regulations may prove counter-productive. A frequently mentioned example in this context is that the Basel capital adequacy rules could become unmanageable if they are extended to cover new products. On the other hand, despite more stringent supervision, the last few years had seen dramatic bank failures, and some officials have expressed the opinion that the only way to instill further discipline into the system would be for the authorities to tighten further capital requirements.

Other supervisors and analysts have argued in favour of a shift from capital to risk management. They are arguing that part of the solution to the increasing complexity in bank risk positions may be to rely less on the writing of rules that apply generally to **all** banks. Instead, supervisors should concentrate more on the development of supervisory procedures that can assess risks on a bank-by-bank basis. The focus of supervision should be the evaluation and stress-testing of each bank's overall risk position, along with evaluation of the current value of individual bank assets.

A final point in this context is that in addition to supervisors, rating agencies also influence the incentives for the adoption of effective in-house risk management systems, particularly for intermediaries operating in the OTC derivatives markets where a high credit rating is essential. The rating agencies now examine in-house risk management systems as part of the rating process. One rating agency has assigned counterparty ratings to financial institutions. Counterparty ratings are different from debt ratings because they reflect overall creditworthiness, not just willingness or capacity to repay debt. If this development takes hold, financial institutions increasingly will have to make an effort to explain their risk management systems to banking supervisors, rating agencies and other institutions.

Public disclosure of risks

In tandem with the development of risk management guidelines by supervisors and rating agencies there is a discussion about the strenghtening of disclosure practices. It is widely felt that the evolution of financial trading and risk management practices has moved ahead of the public disclosures that most firms make of information that is relevant for such discussions. This asymmetry of information can cause a mis-allocation of capital among firms and can also amplify market turbulences. Lack of transparency can contribute to (unjustified) rumours about the financial health of a firm, in particular during periods of market stress. This in turn may impair a firm's market access and funding. The problem may spread because problems encountered by one firm may cause funding or market access difficulties at other firms. Thus, the problems caused by a lack of transparancy affect all market participants. In order to address these problems, market participants need to disclose more meaningful information about their risk exposures **and** risk management performance.

Disclosures about market risk and credit risk should be based on systems firms use internally for assessing their risks. This approach may lead to difficulties in an environment that lacks transparency. A firm that discloses more information about its risks than others may fear that outsiders will erroneously perceive its riskiness to be greater than that of other firms. Such concerns may hamper public disclosure efforts. The ideal solution would be a consensus about a **best practice** for the measurement of risk. This consensus is missing. Recognising that such a consensus, and thus comparability of all the parameters of risk management systems, cannot be achieved immediately, the only practical alternative is an evolutionary approach. To that end, flexibility in disclosure methods is desirable, at least for some time. If in this situation firms with superior risk management systems begin to disclose information from these systems, then a dynamic competitive process could be initiated leading to enhanced disclosure practices and greater market transparency. This competitive process may speed up the process of achieving a consensus about best practice for the measurement of risk. The resulting strengthening of disclosure practices is likely to improve the functioning of financial markets[35].

Scope of official safety net

The frontiers between banking and other forms of financial intermediation are becoming blurred. This raises the issue of whether the responsibilities of the authorities (especially central banks) might now extend beyond the commercial banks, or whether the official "safety net" should be broadened. Banks traditionally enjoy a special status because of their role in the payments system, but other institutions now also play an important role in the payments system. Furthermore, deposit insurance schemes had been introduced to protect small depositors and maintain confidence. Access to central bank credit and to insured deposits meant that banks needed to be subject to official scrutiny and also had critical roles in maintaining the integrity of the entire economic system.

At present, the activities (and risks) of financial intermediaries are more complex and intertwined. Several market analysts believe therefore that in current conditions the responsibilities of central banks should be interpreted to cover the integrity of the entire financial system. In some cases, the central bank might allow a bank to accept a major loss (*e.g.* on trading) that would not impair the systemic soundness of the financial system. In other cases, this might require a central bank to provide support to certain non-bank market participants. However, a decision to support any market participant must be limited to the objective of containing systemic risk and central banks will have to strike a delicate balance between assuring systemic soundness and avoiding "moral hazard."

The management of risks in payment systems

Financial transactions generate a range of risks for counterparties that undertake them, their bankers and other intermediaries that process the transactions, and central banks through which final interbank settlement occurs. These risks are greatest in **large-value interbank funds and securities transfer systems** that support trading in financial markets[36]. A key issue is what the respective roles of the private sector and the public authorities should be in managing and containing risks in the payment system, in particular when financial markets are changing rapidly and fundamentally. The clearing and settlement system for payments and securities is one of the first places where financial stress can manifest itself-- *i.e.* through the inability of one or more participants to meet their payment obligations. There is broad agreement that it is the responsibility of the public authorities to lay out clearly the principles and rules governing the safe operation of the payment system (for example, rules for governing settlement and the irrevocability of payment instructions) and that compliance with these rules is also best supervised by the authorities. Within that framework, the payment system generally works best when run by private agents in a competitive environment. The regulatory structure of the payment system should establish the proper incentives for payment system participants to manage their risks. Of critical importance for the overall stability of the financial system is the supervision and regulation of private clearing and settlement arrangements that support large-value transfers[37]. The interactions between the payment system and securities settlement systems provide a prima facie case for regulation and supervision of securities markets by the authorities -- in particular the possibility that problems in securities settlements might result in losses and liquidity pressures that cannot be managed and contained with existing private arrangements and that, as a result, the stability of the payment system might be endangered[38].

The massive expansion in the value of financial transactions, within and across national and market borders, has made the management of these risks an even higher priority. A large part of the huge daily values passing through payment systems is a result of direct transactions between banks and other financial intermediaries themselves. For example, around 80 per cent of the cross-border assets and liabilities of banks in the BIS area are interbank claims and liabilities[39]. Thus, the credit exposures of financial intermediaries vis-a-vis each other have increased dramatically. In addition, there are exposures related to the structure of settlement systems for payments and securities. In particular, **Herstatt risk** has grown while also the potential for **systemic risk presented by (OTC) derivatives** remains a source of concern[40]. Herstatt risk may be reduced by changes in settlement techniques in the foreign exchange markets when individual banking organisations would offer their correspondents special settlement services, including delivery-versus-payment facilities[41]. Central banks can play an important role in encouraging this development by lengthening the hours of operation of national payment systems and by making available real-time settlement facilities for large-value payments[42]. The application of clearing house methods and multilateral netting arrangements have the potential to reduce some of the risks (including systemic risk) associated with transactions in the foreign exchange, swaps and other "over-the-counter" markets[43]. Another area where central banks can make a significant contribution to reduce systemic risks in financial markets is the reduction of legal uncertainty. For example, by adopting regulations that cover netting contracts that will be legally valid, even in the event of bankruptcy[44].

Some central banks in economies with active financial market provide intraday credit in order to reduce settlement costs in money markets. Counterparty credit risk is controlled by caps and/or collateral. The United States Federal Reserve introduced last year a fee for daylight overdrafts to encourage a price incentive to rationalise the use of intraday credit. The aim of this new policy is to reduce payment system risk[45].

III. The role of capital markets in the emerging financial landscape

In the 1980s, the securities and derivatives markets of OECD countries underwent a period of rapid expansion and structural change[46]. Volumes of new securities issues and secondary market trading soared, equity indices rose, and in all OECD countries securities markets gained in importance as a conduit in financial intermediation. However, the transformation of capital markets consisted of much more than a simple expansion in activity. Structural forces -- similar to those identified above for the banking sector -- changed radically capital market institutions and activities. There was the basic change in the nature of securities business from a highly regulated, tradition-bound activity somewhat at the margin of most financial systems to one which was a leading force in changing the financial landscape in OECD countries. The intensification of competition in an increasingly deregulated environment, combined with the use of sophisticated financial techniques supported by significant advances in information technology, set into motion a process of innovation in which new financial instruments, techniques and strategies are developed at an astounding pace. It is expected by most analysts that these developments will continue in the years ahead and that, therefore, the increase in importance of the role of capital market in the emerging financial landscape will continue.

Widespread deregulation of capital markets reflects the increasing reliance of OECD countries on market principles as opposed to official guidance in the financial sector. An important feature of the liberalisation of OECD capital markets was the growing impact of international competitive forces on products and activities in national financial markets. Offshore financial centres, including several based in OECD countries, were critical in the development of an internationalised, market-oriented financial system. In the early 1980s, an international process of transmission of financial innovation was set in motion, with the United States being the leading exporter of new products and techniques. Through the mid-1980s, financial innovation was frequently undertaken by financial institutions operating in the relatively unregulated environment of the offshore centres. From the mid-1980s onwards, however, development has been relatively faster in domestic securities markets, reflecting the need to preserve the international competitiveness of local markets, particularly in Europe. Wherever it originated, innovation was speedily diffused to all major financial centres. As a result, the average OECD level of financial sophistication rose with astonishing speed.

The growth of **bond markets** was spurred in part by the rise in real interest rates that accompanied the sharp reduction in the rate of inflation of the early

1980s. In addition, the emergence of large government borrowing requirements made it difficult to finance government deficits through the traditional privileged channels. Governments came increasingly to rely on market-based financing of budget deficits and, accordingly, had to relinquish control over long-term interest rates[47]. With the creation of a liquid government bond sector, it became easier to issue paper for other borrowers, including banks and other financial institutions, and ultimately private non-financial borrowers. Growing links among bond market compartments, particularly those provided by the euro-markets and resulting from the abolishment of exchange controls, meant that major national bond markets became increasingly integrated into an internationalised market. Bond yields came to be determined in the context of a "single" world market. Investors -- in particular the larger ones -- became willing to hold "global" portfolios because, if well managed, they would provide better diversification and opportunities to enjoy higher yields. Moreover, more liquid markets and the use of derivatives made it possible in principle to manage the additional risks of an international portfolio.

Equity markets also experienced a revival in the 1980s with higher trading, rising share indices and, in most markets, a significant expansion of new equity offerings as well as issues of equity-related products, such as convertible bonds, bonds with warrants, and equity-related derivatives. Factors behind the growth of equity markets are : (1) the greater weight of equity components in the portfolios of institutional investors; (2) the demand for equity transactions triggered by mergers and acquisitions; and (3) the generation of additional equity operations by privatisation programmes.

By the end of the 1980s, OECD securities markets had been transformed beyond recognition. The volume of new issues of debt and equity as well as secondary market trading had soared. The securities markets proved to be able to draw business away from traditional banking activities. Markets in derivatives grew at a astounding pace and, by the early 1990s, most OECD countries had established exchanges dealing in futures and options. The authorities of OECD countries played an important role in these developments by taking a broad range of actions to facilitate the modernisation and internationalisation of their capital markets. As mentioned above, governments deregulated domestic markets and abolished exchange controls. In addition, most governments took the following measures:

– the organisation reforms of government securities markets in order to deepen money and bond markets and provide for a full yield curve of liquid instruments;

- the development of money markets by removing restrictions on money market instruments such as money market mutual funds, commercial paper and certificates of deposits;

- modernisation of the brokerage profession, securities trading systems and of secondary markets;

- introduction of legislation to permit the formation of financial groups which offer both banking and securities services;

- the introduction of legislation for the creation of futures and options markets;

- modernisation of supervisory and regulatory regimes for securities markets;

- agreements among supervisors of securities and derivatives markets to facilitate cross-border trading while co-ordinating supervisory surveillance over trading and intermediaries.

The growing importance of institutional investors

The importance of **institutional investors** (*i.e.* insurance companies, pension funds, and the different types of investment funds) as the main source of investment in securities markets has increased considerably. Institutional investors play an ever-increasing role as: collectors of savings; investors in securities and other financial assets; operators in the securities markets; cross-border portfolio investors; major owners of publicly-held companies. A strong community of institutional investors seems to be a precondition for the development of deep securities markets with sophisticated financial instruments. Many of the trends that have characterised securities markets in the past fifteen years -- such as securitisation, the increasing growth and sophistication of bond markets, the use of derivatives, highly-leveraged corporate restructurings, the growth of equities markets -- developed in large measure in response to the demands of the institutional investor community. In view of the growing influence that institutional investors exert on the structure and modus operandi of financial systems, it is generally recognised that financial policy makers need to take a closer look at both the functioning and the regulation of these institutions.

Investment strategies of institutional investors are influenced by a variety of factors which may differ widely according to the investment objectives of the different types of institutions, the nature of the products they offer and the liabilities which result, the market environment in which they operate, and regulations and other institutional factors governing the structure of portfolios. Considering the nature of the products as an important factor determining investment strategies, a basic difference exists between investment funds (unit trusts, investment trusts, mutual funds), on the one hand, and long-term contractual savings institutions such as life insurance companies and pension funds, on the other hand. Within the categories of investment funds there is, of course, a wide range of funds with different investment objectives. Hedge funds -- private, closed-end investment funds -- assemble pools of private savings to engage in highly leveraged position-taking. Investment funds of the open-end type need to stand ready to meet at short notice request for reimbursement of potentially large numbers of investment certificates and, therefore, they need to hold a relatively large proportion of liquid assets.

All types of institutional investors are generators of substantial international flows of portfolio capital. The impact of the growing financial muscle of institutional investors on the functioning of financial markets became very clear during the stock market crash of October 1987 and also during the turbulent events in the foreign exchange markets in the late summer and autumn of 1992. Analysts have in this context raised questions whether and to what extent institutional investors as holders of large amounts of financial assets have the potential for triggering shocks to securities markets and other financial markets, which may endanger the stability of the financial system as a whole.

The emergence of institutional investors as major market players has also raised questions as to how patterns of **corporate control and governance** will be changed. Institutions have the potential to exert more effective control over management than a widely dispersed group of portfolio investors. There is growing evidence that, in several countries, institutional investors have adopted a more activist stance. More generally, there appears to be a trend towards greater shareholder demand for more adequate corporate disclosure, more adequate representation for institutions on boards of directors, and greater capability to apply strict performance criteria to corporate management.

The emergence of derivatives products

Since the early 1980s, **derivatives products** (futures, options, swaps, forward rate agreements, and related instruments) have evolved from being the basis of a risk management technique used only by the most sophisticated market participants in the most advanced financial markets to one that is now routinely used by a growing range of participants in nearly every significant market in all OECD countries. The main characteristics of the derivatives markets since the mid-1980s are that :

- the number of exchange-traded contracts has continued to grow;

- financial engineering has made it possible to use derivatives to formulate complex investment strategies;

- the over-the-counter (OTC) market in derivatives is now expanding more rapidly than the traditional exchanges.

The derivative market can be seen as both a complement and a substitute for the underlying cash market. Increasingly, the derivatives market is perceived as indispensable to price formation in the cash market. Indeed, trading volumes in exchange-traded derivatives often exceed volumes on the related cash market and, in many cases, market participants believe that prices in the cash market often reflect trading in the derivatives market - rather than the other way around.

Securitisation

The rise of institutional investors has generated an increasing demand for risk-transfer techniques, which enable the investor to choose a desired position on the risk/return continuum. Such techniques include both derivatives, which make it possible to transfer market risk among market participants, and securitisation, whereby the credit risk as well as the market risk of an asset is transferred. **Securitisation** -- broadly defined as the replacement of traditional bank financing with fund-raising through securities issues -- has been a distinctive financial market trend since the early 1980s[48]. In its earlier phases securitisation was mainly used to denote the issue of debt securities (bonds, commercial paper, medium-term notes) as relatively close substitutes for bank credit. More recently, however, the use of the term has been narrowed to describe operations in which the cash flows from specific assets are converted into marketable securities (mortgage-backed and asset-backed securities). The risks inherent in the underlying assets can be priced and traded on the securities market; and, by using derivatives, risks can be further unbundled. In addition to the inherent cost-savings of direct access to the capital market, which was the main factor underlying the rise in securitisation in the 1980s, the changing competitive balance among financial intermediaries has also stimulated further securitisation. However, although the potential for issuance of securitised assets is present in nearly all OECD countries, legal and regulatory impediments are found in many jurisdictions.

Exchange-based trading versus off-exchange transactions

Traditional exchange-based trading in both cash (especially equities) and derivatives markets is being seriously challenged by **off-exchange (or OTC) trading.** It is likely that this trend will continue in the future. It is worth emphasising that what is at stake is not simply the old issue of technical differences across traditional exchanges, such as trading on floors versus trading on screens or auction systems versus quote-driven systems. A more fundamental issue is the choice between, on the one hand, all of these systems which are characterised by trading procedures which are externally determined by some combination of self-regulation and official regulation and which requires that orders are exposed to the market; and, on the other hand, a "dealer" market organised by the intermediaries themselves, such as those exist in most bond and foreign exchange markets. Dealers will seek to engage in propriety trading for revenue and will normally be allowed to delay reporting trades for some time. Competition among trading systems and the aggressive policies of large institutional investors to direct orders to the cheapest trading systems have put strong pressure on the profitability of brokerage business. As a result, financial intermediaries are putting increasing focus on proprietary trading in both cash and derivative markets as a source of earnings.

One of the consequences of the development of alternatives to trading on the traditional exchanges is that many instruments are now traded in several market simultaneously. As mentioned previously, a similar development is occurring in derivatives markets. The interpretation of this development is a matter of controversy because of the introduction of possible impediments to the price discovery process as a result of these trends. It is argued by some that there is a serious risk of "market fragmentation" whereby an increasing share of transactions is not exposed to the broad market. In addition, some in the exchanges characterise those who trade off the exchange as "free riders", who benefit from the price discovery process of the exchanges while avoiding the costs of supporting the exchanges. In recognition of the broad problems arising from the development of multiple trading systems and the possibly excessive cost of regulation, several proposals have been made to address these issues. For example, the US SEC in 1992 issued a "Market 2000" concept in which the question of the possible fragmentation of markets is examined. The replies to the report have not fully resolved the underlying issues. A number of dealer-operated systems that appear to have some of the characteristics of both securities dealers and exchanges have also developed in Europe, which offer the same potential for "market fragmentation" that can be observed in the United States.

The impact of capital market trends on supervisory and regulatory systems

Many of the trends that are changing the role of capital markets can be expected to exert significant **strains on existing supervisory and regulatory systems**[49]. Securities market regulation often was founded upon the assumption that investors were mainly individuals and that the balance of market power favoured the issuers and the intermediaries, thus requiring an officially-supervised, formal framework for investor protection. It was necessary to require those who made public securities issues to provide information at the time of issue and throughout the period during which the security was publicly traded. Additionally, securities regulators (frequently in collaboration with self-regulation by exchanges) have usually sought to establish specific rules for secondary market trading, especially of equities, in order to protect investors from market manipulation.

One of the key issues under consideration is the following. Recent experience seems to indicate that, in a market basically centred around professional business, there is a declining demand for the kind of investor protection that has been traditionally offered by securities supervisors. At the same time, individual investors are increasing their holdings of equities either directly or via instruments for collective investment. One of the adjustments that regulators have made to accommodate the ongoing changes in financial markets has been to increase the differentiation between retail and institutional investors. However, other problems remain. The fact that large volumes of business are moving away from the traditional exchanges also presents the regulators with many dilemmas.

Even where institutions dominate trading, market participants recognise a need for adequate market supervision which should contain some elements of self-regulation as well as official market oversight. Thus, bond investors apparently feel just as comfortable with euro-market investment (where there is minimal official regulation and self-regulation predominates) as with investment in the US bond market where a well-defined framework for official regulation is found. On the other hand, there seem to be some cases where more extensive official regulation (on a national level) is required. Thus, Germany recently decided that an official regulatory body for the securities industry was needed. Similarly, many market intermediaries who mainly deal with big institutions, often indicate that international investors are deterred from entering some markets by lack of protection for minority investors, lack of strong insider trading rules, incomplete disclosure and excessive anti-takeover defences.

While the traditional concerns of investor protection may seem less urgent than in the past, there clearly remain **needs for official supervision of the markets**. First, there has been several cases of market manipulation and fraud by major market intermediaries, which seem to indicate that significant potential exists for criminal market manipulation, even in internationalised markets dominated by professionals. Second, the large volume of funds being managed by institutional investors also raises issues of prudential supervision, particularly since these institutions are increasingly a major repository for the savings of small savers. Third, as mentioned above, the issue of systemic risk remains serious. In particular, the large-scale trading of OTC derivatives and the potential destabilising impact of certain classes of institutional investors are areas of major concern from a public policy standpoint.

Capital market developments in major OECD financial markets

The expansion of securities market activity and the pace of product development between the 1980s and 1994 had been truly remarkable in all OECD regions. Despite broad similarities, developments had been different in each region. In the **United States**, the volume of operations in every asset category had expanded noticeably. Reflecting large government deficits, the outstanding volume of US government securities has grown rapidly since the early 1980s; innovative products related to the Treasury market continued to be introduced, including coupon stripping, derivatives and automated systems to make the Treasury market more accessible to small investors. Other categories of securities had grown even more rapidly than the government bond market. Since the early 1980s, the outstanding volume of mortgage-backed securities increased ten-fold while that of initial public equity offerings rose 40 times. The assets of mutual funds have risen ten times in the last few years. Secondary market trading has also exploded, with volume on US exchanges rising 290 per cent between 1982 and 1992.

Not only had the volume of operations increased but new products and strategies had arisen, such as index arbitrage, index substitution and dynamic hedging. These new techniques and instruments were often developed to meet user demand for custom-tailored products. In many cases, the over-the-counter

(OTC) market has been used to develop products that meet specific investor needs. The OTC market has had the advantage of greater flexibility to create new financial products with a minimum of regulatory interference.

Although the capital market gained in total intermediation at the expense of bank lending, the banks have by and large been able to participate in virtually all aspects of securities business, despite the Glass Steagall Act, which continues to be an irritant. Securitisation was a major example of securities market activity in which banks have played an active role, as were mutual funds where banks now have sizeable market share.

Another noteworthy feature of the US securities industry has been increasing internationalisation. International mutual funds are increasing rapidly in assets. In spite of remaining accounting problems, foreign shares and ADRs are listed in increasing volumes on US exchanges. US insurance companies and pension funds continue to diversify abroad.

A somewhat different pattern could be observed in **Japan**, which has experienced less "disintermediation" than the United States. During the "bubble period" of the late 1980s and early 1990s, large corporations made use of the capital markets, usually through offshore centres, while small and medium-sized enterprises tended to rely more on the banks or the specialised financial institutions. Meanwhile, deposits at banks and in the postal savings system continued to account for a large share of personal savings while competition from collective investment instruments was less intense than in some other major markets. The decline of the stock market and of the property market has inflicted great damage on many institutions. In response, considerable restructuring is expected in the next few years. With continuing deregulation, the non-government fixed income market will expand and many operations which had taken place in the euro-markets will return to Japan. The securities industry will probably try to serve better the needs of small and medium-sized companies.

In **Europe**, where bank-dominated systems of intermediation were often the norm until the early 1980s, considerable progress had been achieved in developing a modern capital market. Government bond markets were now modern and closely interlinked. Derivative markets added to liquidity and enabled investors to manage multi-currency bond portfolios. Equity markets have become important in corporate finance; and with privatisation they will become even more important in the future.

Notes and Bibliography

1   Banks under Stress, OECD, Paris, 1992.

2   C.E.V. Borio and R. Filosa, *The Changing Borders of Banking: Trends and Implications*, Chapter 2 of this volume.

3   Lamfalussy, A*., The Restructuring of the Financial Industry: A Central Banking Perspective*, SUERF Papers on Monetary Policy and Financial Systems No. 12, 1992; OECD, *Financial Conglomerates*, Paris 1993; OECD, *Banks under Stress*, Paris, 1992.

4   See the reference in footnote (2) for a more detailed discussion. The universal banking system is discussed in International Trade in Services Securities, OECD, Paris, 1987, pp. 14-15. Information on regulations concerning bank ownership linkages with non-financial enterprises can be found in *Banks under Stress*, OECD, Paris, 1992, Chapter 6.

5   See reference in OECD (1987), footnote 4 above.

6   Hoshi T., A. Kashyap and D. Scharfstein (1990), The role of banks in reducing the costs of financial distress in Japan, *Journal of Financial Economics* 27, 67-88; Edwards J. and K. Fischer (1991), Banks, finance and investment in West Germany since 1970, *CEPR Discussion Paper no. 497*; Sheard, P. (1989), The main bank system and corporate monitoring and control in Japan, *Journal of Economic Behaviour and Organization*, 11, 399-422.

7   See reference in footnote 2 above.

8   C. Mayer (1990a), *Myths of the West: Lessons from Developed Countries, Asymmetric information, corporate finance and investment*, Chicago, National Bureau of Economic Research.

9   Mayer C. and Alexander (1990), Banks and markets: corporate financing in Germany and the UK, *Journal of Japanese and International Studies*.

10 C. Mayer (1990a), *Myths of the West: Lessons from Developed Countries for Development Finance*, World Bank Discussion Paper; C. Mayer (1990b), *Financial Systems, corporate finance and economic development*, in: G. Hubbard, *Asymmetric information, corporate finance and investment*, Chicago: National Bureau of Economic Research.

11 C. Mayer (1990a), *Myths of the West: Lessons from Developed Countries for Development Finance*, World Bank Discussion Paper; C. Mayer (1990b), Financial Systems, corporate finance and economic development, in :

G. Hubbard, *Asymmetric information, corporate finance and investment*, Chicago: National Bureau of Economic Research.

12   Franks J. and C. Mayer (1992), Corporate Control: *A Synthesis of the International Evidence*, Mimeo.

13   Mitsuhiro Fukao, *Financial Integration, Corporate Governance, and the Performance of Multinational Firms*, First Draft, September 1993.

14   M. Fukao (1993), ibid.

15   While U.S. banks can hold up to 5 per cent of voting shares of nonfinancial companies through bank holding companies, which is essentially the same upper limit as Japanese companies, they are discouraged from doing so because of the presence of institutional, legal and other obstacles (see Fukao (1993), ibid).

16   J.A. Frankel (1993*), Recent Changes in the financial Systems of Asian and Pacific Countries*, Paper presented at the Sixth International Conference of the Institute for Monetary and Economic Studies, Bank of Japan, on the theme "Financial Stability in a Changing Environment", Tokyo, October 28-29, 1993.

17   See J. A. Frankel, 1993, ibid.

18   The Economist, A Survey of World Banking, May 2nd, 1992.

19   G. G. Kaufman and L. R. Mote, *Is banking a declining industry?* a historical perspective, Economic Perspectives, May/June 1994 Volume XVIII, Issue 3, Federal Reserve Bank of Chicago; The Economist, Recalled to Life, A Survey of International Banking, April 30th, 1994. J.H. Boyd and M. Gertler*, Are Banks Dead? Or, Are the Reports Greatly Exaggerated?* Federal Reserve Bank of Minneapolis, Working Paper 531, June 1994; D. C. Wheelock, *Is the Banking Industry in Decline? Recent Trends and Future Prospects from a Historical Perspective*, Federal Reserve Bank of St. Louis Review, September/October 1993.

20   OECD (1991), *Systemic Risks in Securities Markets*, Paris.

21   Alan Greenspan, Symposium Welcome Remarks at the International Symposium on Banking and Payment Services, Board of Governors of the Federal Reserve System, Washington D. C., March 10-11, 1994.

22   G30 Global Derivatives Study Group, Derivatives: Practices and Principles, July 1993.

23   Dennis Weatherstone, *Major Themes in Changing Banking and Financial Market,* International Symposium on Banking and Payment Services, Board of Governors of the Federal Reserve System, Washington D. C., March 10-11, 1994.

24   International Capital Markets, Part II: Systemic Issues in International Finance, IMF, 1993.

25 International Capital Markets, Part II: Systemic Issues in International Finance, IMF, 1993; Eddie George, *International Banking, Payments Systems and Financial Crises*, International Symposium on Banking and Payment Services, Board of Governors of the Federal Reserve System, Washington D. C., March 10-11, 1994; Public Disclosure of Market and Credit Risks by Financial Intermediaries, BIS, September 1994; Issues of Measurement Related to Market Size and Macroprudential Risks in Derivatives Markets, BIS, February 1995.

26 G30 Global Derivatives Study Group, Derivatives: Practices and Principles; Follow-up Survey of Industry Practice.

27 *Recent Innovations in International Banking*, BIS, 1986; E. G. Corrigan,1992, Challenges facing the International Community of Supervisors, Quarterly Review, Federal Reserve Bank of New York, volume 17 number 3.

28 E. H. Rotberg, *Risk Taking in the Financial Services Industry*, in: Risk Management in Financial Services, OECD, 1992.

29 Financial Conglomerates, OECD, 1993.

30 A. Lamfalussy, *The Restructuring of the Financial Industry: a Central Banking Perspective*, SUERF Papers on Monetary Policy and Financial Systems No. 12, 1992.

31 E. G. Corrigan,1992, *Challenges facing the International Community of Supervisors*, Quarterly Review, Federal Reserve Bank of New York, volume 17 number 3.

32 The International Organization of Securities Commissions (IOSCO) was created in 1983.

33 E. G. Corrigan,1992, *Challenges facing the International Community of Supervisors*, Quarterly Review, Federal Reserve Bank of New York, volume 17 number 3; *Systemic Risks in Securities Markets*, OECD, 1991; *Delivery Versus Payment in Securities Settlement Systems*, BIS, September, 1992; *Financial Market Trends No 50*, OECD, October 1991; *Financial Conglomerates*, OECD, 1993; *Recent Developments in International Interbank Relations*, BIS, October, 1992.

34 William J. McDonough, *Rethinking the Structure and Regulation of Financial Services*, Annual Report 1993, Federal Reserve Bank of New York.

35 International Capital Markets, Part II: *Systemic Issues in International Finance*, IMF, 1993; Eddie George, *International Banking, Payments Systems and Financial Crises*, International Symposium on Banking and Payment Services, Board of Governors of the Federal Reserve System, Washington D. C., March 10-11, 1994; *Public Disclosure of Market and Credit Risks by Financial*

Intermediaries, BIS, September 1994; *Issues of Measurement Related to Market Size and Macroprudential Risks in Derivatives Markets*, BIS, February 1995.

36 Paul van den Bergh and John M. Veal, *Payment System Risk and Risk Management*, in: Bruce J. Summers, ed., The Payment System: Design, Management, and Supervision, IMF, 1994.

37 Bruce J. Summers, *Clearing and Payment Systems: the Role of the Central Bank*, Federal Reserve Bulletin, February 1991.

38 *Systemic Risks in Securities Markets*, OECD, 1991; *Delivery Versus Payment in Securities Settlement Systems*, BIS, September, 1992; Financial Market Trends No 50, OECD, October 1991.

39 Eddie George, *International Banking, Payments Systems and Financial Crises*, International Symposium on Banking and Payment Services, Board of Governors of the Federal Reserve System, Washington D. C., March 10-11, 1994.

40 Susan M. Phillips, Board of Governors of the Federal Reserve System, Remarks at the International Symposium on Banking and Payment Services, Board of Governors of the Federal Reserve System, Washington D. C., March 10-11, 1994; Herstatt risk is defined as follows. During the interval between the settlement of each leg of a foreign exchange transaction, the party that has made the first payment risks losing the full value of the second in the event that the counterparty default on its obligation. This risk at settlement - or cross-currency settlement risk -- is known as Herstatt risk.

41 Tim E. Noel, *Report on Central Banking Payment and Settlement Services with Respect to Cross-Border and Multi-Currency Transactions*, International Symposium on Banking and Payment Services, Board of Governors of the Federal Reserve System, Washington D. C., March 10-11, 1994.

42 Alan Greenspan, Symposium Welcome Remarks at the International Symposium on Banking and Payment Services, Board of Governors of the Federal Reserve System, Washington D. C., March 10-11, 1994.

43 John C. Hiatt, *The Potential for Clearing House Arrangments in the OTC Derivatives Market*, International Symposium on Banking and Payment Services, Board of Governors of the Federal Reserve System, Washington D. C., March 10-11, 1994.

44 H. Rodgin Cohen and Michael M. Wiseman, *Legal Issues Related to Netting*, International Symposium on Banking and Payment Services, Board of Governors of the Federal Reserve System, Washington D. C., March 10-11, 1994.

45 Edward W. Kelley, Jr., *Developments in the Dollar Payment System*, International Symposium on Banking and Payment Services, Board of Governors of the Federal Reserve System, Washington D. C., March 10-11, 1994.

46 *Systemic Risk in Securities Markets*, OECD, 1991; Automation of Securities Markets and Regulatory Implications, *Financial Market Trends 50*, OECD, October 1991; World Securities Markets: Looking Ahead, *Financial Markets Trends 55, OECD*, June 1933.

47 Trends in Government Debt Management and Government Securities Markets, *Financial Market Trends 57*, OECD, February 1994.

48 Securitisation: an International Perspective, OECD, 1995.

49 Securities Markets in OECD countries -- Organisation and Regulation, OECD, 1995.

Chapter 2

THE CHANGING BORDERS OF BANKING: TRENDS AND IMPLICATIONS

Claudio E.V. Borio and Renato Filosa

Introduction*

Imagine that a banker, economist or policy-maker had been away from civilisation for the last fifteen years or so and finally returned. Would he recognise the financial industry that he saw? No doubt our fictitious observer's answer would depend on his specific perspective and on whether he was looking at the industry on a global scale or at a particular sector or country. Yet there is little doubt that the changes in the structure and workings of the industry that have occurred over the period, and those in prospect, have profoundly altered the performance, risks and opportunities of individual enterprises and of the system as a whole in all countries.

The present paper considers these changes from an international perspective. The focus is primarily on the nature of banks' activities, with particular reference to the evolution of institutional linkages between commercial and investment banking, on the one hand, and insurance and non-financial business, on the other. The analytical questions tackled concern the case for and against closer integration between these activities and the

* This paper has previously been published as BIS Economic Paper No. 43 and it is a revised version of a paper originally prepared for the meeting of the Associazione Nazionale per lo Studio dei Problemi del Credito, 1st December 1993, Rome, which was entitled "La nuova legge bancaria: rapporto banca-impresa". Given the focus of that conference, the sections of the paper looking at supervisory and regulatory developments place considerable emphasis on those taking place in the European Community. We would like to thank Franco Cesari, Elmar Koch, Rinaldo Pecchioli and Stephen Prowse for their comments.

implications for prudential regulation and supervision. The emphasis is on the wood, not on the trees. The intention is to provide a general framework and a cross-country background against which the interrelations between the various policy issues can be highlighted. The perspective is that of an economist, rather than of a banker or supervisor.

Section I outlines the evolution of the financial industry over the last fifteen years or so. Particular attention is paid to the characteristics of the deregulatory process, to the common threads and differences across countries. Section II discusses the pros and cons of integration between banking, insurance and non-financial business activities and considers the available evidence. The third section addresses the implications of the linkages between these activities for prudential regulation and supervision, identifying some key issues. The conclusion summarises some of the main points made.

I.   Stylised facts about deregulation and structural trends

The ascendancy of free market philosophy, a propitious macroeconomic environment and an acceleration in the pace of technological change: these have been the three key factors underlying the increased momentum in the transformation of the financial industry since the late 1970s. The end-result of the liberalisation and financial innovation process has been a substantial heightening of competitive pressures in the industry. The scope, timing and speed of this process, however, have not been uniform either across countries or across segments of the industry, reflecting the differing objectives of intervention and diverse initial conditions.[1]

Consider what the industry looked like at the end of the 1970s. Largely with a view to limiting the risk of financial instability - albeit at the expense of competition - significant restrictions on the lines of business and geographical location and operation of financial enterprises still existed in many countries, sometimes supplemented by ceilings on deposit rates and/or official tolerance of cartel-type agreements. Often these sets of restrictions dated back to the inter-war years, when they had been introduced in response to episodes of widespread financial distress. The Glass-Steagall Act of 1933, separating commercial and investment banking in the United States, is a typical example. Another is the Italian Banking Law of 1936, which established the principle of separation between banking and non-financial activities ("commerce").

At the same time, interventionist approaches to the implementation of monetary policy and remnants of credit allocation policies had often resulted in quantitative and, to a lesser extent, interest rate controls on the assets side of the credit institutions' balance sheet and on restrictions on international financial transactions. Compulsory investment requirements and/or constraints on bank loans, to mention just two typical examples, were by no means a prerogative of the Italian financial system. At least one of these elements was present in most countries; Canada, Germany and the United States were the main exceptions.

If we look at the financial industry now, the picture is radically different. It seems fair to say, however, that generally the liberalisation process has tended to proceed more speedily and to go furthest in the area of those restrictions more immediately identified with credit allocation and monetary policy objectives. It has been slower and more cautious as regards constraints historically linked, at least in part, with concerns about financial stability and investor protection.

Restrictions other than on lines of business

The easing of *quantitative, interest rate and price restrictions* has been particularly extensive. None of the main industrialised countries retains ceilings or other major constraints on lending. Compulsory investment requirements are rare and of limited significance. Reserve requirements have been drastically reduced and in some countries abolished.[2] Controls on foreign exchange and international transactions have all but disappeared. So have restrictions on lending rates. The only remaining restrictions on interest rates or prices are those traditionally designed to limit competition, *i.e.* those on some forms of bank deposit and, in exceptional cases, on brokerage commissions. Even then, they either are of limited significance, as in France and the United States,[3] or else are in the process of being dismantled, most notably in Japan (Takeda and Turner, 1992).

The deregulatory process has been just as extensive as regards the *range of products* available in the market, often in response to financial innovation. In 1980 only a handful of countries, essentially the Anglo-Saxon ones, had established markets in short-term securities such as Treasury bills, certificates of deposit and commercial paper; today, only a very few have not. Italy and Switzerland, for instance, are the only industrialised countries where no commercial paper market yet exists, not least for fiscal reasons (Alworth and Borio, 1993).[4] Following advances in information technology and applied finance theory, the last fifteen years have seen the rapid growth of sophisticated instruments such as futures, options, swaps and combinations thereof, not least in the international markets. And alongside the rapid expansion of over-the-counter markets, a growing number of countries have equipped themselves with exchanges for the trading of such instruments. Banks have played a particularly active role in the new markets (BIS 1992a and 1992b).

Restrictions on the *geographical location* of banking activity have been substantially eased, but even purely domestic ones still exist in some large industrialised countries. Several countries, including the United Kingdom, Canada and the Netherlands, have traditionally not interfered with the right of domestic banks to set up branch networks. A good number of European countries lifted restrictions during the 1980s. Limits on branching have been retained in Japan and, though they are being eroded, in the United States, where interstate branching restrictions date back to the McFadden Act of 1927. Barriers to the establishment of foreign banks have also been eased considerably. EC legislation has taken this process to the limit, establishing within the EC the principle of the freedom to provide a wide range of financial services as part of the creation of the single market.[5]

Line-of-business restrictions within banking

The process of liberalisation of the range of activities that banking institutions can engage in, either directly or through ownership stakes in other enterprises, has proceeded at an uneven pace. Generally speaking, the closer the activity is to the traditional "core" of banking business, the greater has been the reduction in existing barriers. Accordingly, at least four different types of compartmentalisation can be singled out: between various forms of credit intermediaries; between commercial and investment banking, or securities business broadly defined; between banking and insurance; and, finally, between banking and non-financial business.

Most countries have proceeded to *decompartmentalise their credit systems* by extending the spectrum of permissible lending and funding activities, harmonising other restrictions on credit institutions' balance sheets and eliminating legal distinctions between them. In a majority of European countries and in Australia the legal and regulatory differences between the various types of banks have been significantly relaxed or abolished. By contrast, a considerable degree of compartmentalisation still prevails in Japan; in the United States differences between, say, commercial banks and thrifts have narrowed but still exist.

The ability of banks to engage in *securities business* has been considerably broadened worldwide, mainly since the mid-1980s. Three groups of countries can be distinguished. In the first, including notably Germany, the Netherlands and several Nordic countries, few if any restrictions have historically existed on the combination of traditional banking and securities business. In the second group, including Canada and most European countries, barriers to or, more commonly, the prohibition on the acquisition of securities firms, and hence access to the stock exchange, have been entirely abolished. Finally, in the third group, consisting of the United States and Japan, the separation between commercial and investment banking has been more rigid. In Japan, it was only in April 1993 that commercial banks were allowed to engage in securities business, through separate subsidiaries.[6] In the United States banking organisations were allowed to underwrite securities, within strict limits, through special non-bank subsidiaries only from September 1986. Together with their Japanese counterparts, however, they have been quite active dealers abroad through their subsidiaries.

Restrictions on banking/insurance

By comparison, deregulation concerning the combination of banking and *insurance* business has been limited, at least until recently.[7] *Except through ownership linkages*, to be discussed below, the two sectors have historically been strictly segregated in most countries. Only licensed insurance companies have been allowed to engage in insurance activities. Conversely, the business of insurance companies has been largely confined to insurance and financial activities closely related to it. These basic principles are still broadly valid today.[8] They have, for instance, been enshrined in the relevant EC directives.[9] The principles, however, are most strictly adhered to in connection with the "production" of services (*e.g.* underwriting) and have been much more flexible in the field of distribution. Thus banks have generally been permitted to act as distributors of insurance products. Even here, however, several countries apply restrictions; in particular, a blanket prohibition is in force in Japan while strict limits exist in the United States.[10] Deregulatory steps in this area include the authorisation granted to French and, under certain conditions, Finnish banks to engage in distribution in 1984 and 1988 respectively. In France, Denmark and, to a far lesser extent, Japan, the scope for the distribution of financial products by insurance companies has also been broadened somewhat.

Restrictions on ownership linkages between banks and insurance companies have generally been considerably less severe than on the in-house provision of underwriting and distribution services. What banks could not do directly, they could often do through appropriate organisational structures. These restrictions have also been relaxed somewhat in a number of countries in the last few years. The information available makes it difficult to draw a precise

53

cross-country picture, a problem which applies also to linkages with non-financial companies: the documentation is uneven and very rarely complete, often relates to legal norms rather than to their practical implementation and is not entirely up to date. Nevertheless, some qualitative elements do emerge.

In most European countries banks are allowed to set up insurance subsidiaries ("downstream linkages"); Finland is one exception, while in Norway a combination of the two activities can be achieved only through a holding company structure. Generally, authorisation from the relevant supervisory authorities is required. The banking authorities also typically reserve the right to authorise the acquisition of participations beyond a certain size. The EC Second Banking Directive, which defines the minimum level of harmonisation for the Community, is less restrictive: credit institutions' participations in insurance companies are treated on a par with those in financial enterprises, and neither specific limits nor prior authorisation are envisaged. Significant deregulatory moves under market pressure have also taken place in several European countries in recent years, most notably in France, Italy, Denmark, the Netherlands and Sweden.

This picture contrasts sharply with the restrictions that exist in some countries outside Europe, most notably in the United States and Japan. With the exception of some state chartered banks, in the United States banks and bank holding companies in general may not own insurance companies, except in the credit life and disability insurance fields. In Japan anti-monopoly laws, which do not differentiate between insurance and non-financial business, limit financial companies' holdings of the equity of domestic enterprises to 5%.[11] A limit of 10% of voting shares also existed in Canada until the passing of new legislation in 1992, when it was lifted.

The cross-country pattern of restrictions on the ownership of banks by insurance companies ("upstream linkages") is not fundamentally different. Most countries that do not in principle set any limits on downstream linkages do not set them on upstream ones either; available evidence suggests that Austria, France and Switzerland are three exceptions. Conversely, upstream linkages are typically restricted where downstream ones are.[12] Thus, separation is again especially strict in the United States and Japan. In particular, in the United States insurance companies may not generally hold shares in the capital of a bank other than as portfolio investments, implying no control. In Japan they may hold a maximum of 10% of the stocks issued by any domestic enterprise, including banks. Separation was also very strict in Canada until 1992, when insurance companies were first allowed to acquire banks.[13] The EC Second Banking Directive does not differentiate between the lines of business of the acquirer of stakes in banks and subjects to authorisation the acquisition of "qualifying holdings"[14] beyond certain thresholds.[15]

The scope allowed by the legislative and regulatory framework has been amply exploited by market participants. Since the mid-1980s link-ups between banks and insurance companies have become increasingly common, both within and across national borders, not least as competition for a typically older private saver, less reliant on state transfers, has intensified.[16] To quote a recent study by Salomon Brothers (1990),

> "Perhaps the most meaningful trend in European banking today is the challenge posed to the insurance sector by banks, some of which even have insurance company shareholders, that are distributing life and pension products to their vast customer base." (p. 6)

The trend has been especially strong in Germany (Allfinanz), France (bancassurance), the United Kingdom, Denmark, the Netherlands and Spain. As a result, financial conglomerates, which had previously been mainly limited to banking and a range of securities activities, have increasingly extended their reach into the insurance sector. For instance, some 200 banking/insurance groups are thought to be operating within the European Community alone.

Restrictions on banking/non-financial activities

Ownership linkages between banks and *non-financial companies* are the most strictly regulated and have generally been least affected by the worldwide deregulatory process. At the same time, considerable differences exist across countries.[17]

Available information indicates that only a few industrialised countries, including New Zealand, Spain, Switzerland and the United Kingdom, do not have any formal statutory limits on banks' participations in non-financial companies. Even then, administrative intervention and penalising prudential requirements discourage them. In fact, while holdings of non-financial companies' equity are significant in Switzerland and Spain, they are negligible in the United Kingdom - a country which is typically classified among those which have historically promoted the separation between banking and commerce.

Otherwise, regulation typically sets limits on the size of the individual participation in relation to the equity capital of the non-financial company and/or of the acquiring bank as well as on the aggregate value of participations in relation to the bank's capital. At one end of the spectrum are those countries that prohibit banks from holding any controlling stakes. These include countries outside Europe, most notably the United States, Japan, Canada and Australia, but within Europe too, such as Belgium, Denmark and Sweden.[18] At the opposite end are those where regulation allows substantial bank involvement, Germany being the best-known example.[19] Other countries, such as France, lie in between.[20,21] EC legislation is quite permissive in this area but not as much as some national frameworks,[22] hence the adoption of a ten-year transition period to allow "over-extended" banks to adjust.

Statutory restrictions on non-financial companies' participations in banks are generally weaker. In fact, only a few countries, including the United States, Italy, Sweden and Spain,[23] have in place explicit strict limits designed to prevent the acquisition of control. Such limits are a clear signal of the determination with which the authorities in the countries concerned pursue the goal of maintaining banks' independence; but their absence elsewhere should not necessarily be read as a sign of complacency. Though attitudes differ, the available evidence suggests that supervisory authorities do not generally welcome the control of a bank by non-financial businesses. Requirements that banks be widely held, such as in Canada, may ultimately help to ensure autonomy.[24] Otherwise, the same objective can be achieved, where deemed desirable, through the general powers of authorisation.[25] EC legislation has reflected this prevailing attitude. As already noted, the prescribed minimum authorisation requirements for participations in banks do not differentiate between the type of business the acquirer is engaged in, but the various "trigger" thresholds for authorisation provide the supervisors with sufficient room for manoeuvre.[26]

II. Implications of linkages between banking, insurance and commerce

Should the public authorities allow firms to combine banking, insurance and commercial activities and, if so, to what extent? The very fact that countries have historically exhibited substantially different approaches to the problem indicates that the answer to this question is not straightforward. Less ambitiously, one may consider the arguments for and against such combinations and the extent to which the available evidence helps to evaluate their strength.

The main argument in favour of combinations is just another version of Adam Smith's famous invisible hand: companies should be allowed to choose freely their size and product mix. This freedom is likely to result in greater economic efficiency in the form of lower production costs, higher output and better products. More specifically, at least two types of mechanism can be highlighted: the exploitation of *technological and organisational* efficiencies, in particular economies of scale and scope, and that of *information/control* efficiencies through specific contractual and less formal arrangements aimed at mitigating asymmetric information and incentive problems.

The main arguments against combinations partly turn the tables on those just mentioned. Such combinations may give rise to monopolistic behaviour. Quite apart from the excessive concentration of economic power, possibly undesirable in itself, monopoly negates some of the economic benefits that unrestrained laissez-faire is expected to yield. Moreover, asymmetric information and incentive problems may in some respects have potentially more disruptive effects when activities are combined under the same roof. In particular, conflicts of interest and large size may help to breed fraud and undermine the safety and soundness of the companies and, indirectly, of the financial system as a whole. These problems are compounded by the fact that the linkages can indirectly extend the benefits of the "safety net" set up by the authorities to prevent systemic crises, thereby blunting the incentives to prudent behaviour.

Technological and organisational efficiencies

Lower average costs at higher output levels ("economies of scale") or reflecting cost complementarities in multi-product firms ("economies of scope") have traditionally been the basis for the economic justification of large size and product diversification.[27] A larger size and range of operations permits a finer specialisation of labour and a more intensive utilisation of inputs. It may, for instance, justify the acquisition of information technologies which become profitable only beyond certain production scales. It can also avoid the wasteful duplication of marketing, research and development and information-gathering efforts.

Such production synergies are clearly more relevant to the combination of relatively similar activities. They are not particularly pertinent to linkages between banking and commerce. By contrast, they have often been invoked to justify linkages between commercial and investment banking. It has more recently been argued that synergies exist for banking and insurance combinations too. No doubt this in part reflects the de facto blurring of distinctions between these types of business. Insurance companies have offered products with increasingly significant important "savings" elements, in direct competition with bank deposits, and have expanded their financial investments and asset management business to the point of becoming a major force in securities markets in several countries. For their part, banks have become more involved in the provision of services with a greater "insurance" component, such as off-balance-sheet contingent claims and derivatives.

The available statistical evidence on production economies is somewhat mixed.[28] US studies tend to suggest that economies of scale are mostly exhausted at relatively low levels of "output", but may also exist for very large banks (Shaffer and David, 1991). There is little evidence of economies of scope, but regulatory constraints prevent their proper consideration beyond the narrow confines of commercial banking activities. Evidence for other countries is very limited but somewhat more encouraging. Significant economies of scale and scope have been detected, for example, in Japan, France and Italy.[29] These studies have relatively little to say about combinations of banking and insurance, but the main avowed rationalisation for the link-ups does appear to have a sound economic basis. It can be seen as combining the insurance companies' well-established comparative advantage in the "production" (underwriting) of insurance products with banks' advantage in their "distribution", gained through extensive branch networks and a consolidated reputation.[30] The link-ups are further underpinned by a certain convergence in the range of products provided: the pure savings component of life insurance products is becoming increasingly important. Potential economies of scope appear to exist.

How much reliance can be placed on the statistical evidence is a moot question. Proponents of greater size, largely focusing on the disappointing US results, have been quick to point out the numerous conceptual and statistical shortcomings of the analysis, not least as regards the appropriate definition and measurement of output.[31] Excessive focus on technological economies also runs the risk of neglecting potential synergies on the demand side. Examples are a possible preference on the part of customers for "one-stop shopping" or joint products (Herring and Santomero, 1990), the consolidation of the customer base and the possibility of reducing the variability of overall demand through imperfect correlation across markets. In addition, it is not clear whether statistical techniques can be applied to a situation where rapid changes in the regulatory and technological environment play such a crucial role as they do today.

At the same time, the linkages have for the most part been too recent to allow a clear view to be formed. There has been some retrenchment among those commercial banks that have extended their activities into the investment banking segment, especially in the international markets. But this has been part of a broader wave following the excessive expansion of the booming 1980s in the wake of liberalisation. As indicated by the experience of long-established universal banks, it is more a reflection of exuberant market dynamics than of any incompatibility between the two lines of business.

No significant track record exists for banking/insurance. To the extent that the more encompassing conglomerate wave of the 1960s in the United States contains a relevant message, there is little ground for optimism: the de-merger wave of the 1980s mainly broke up what had previously been put together (*e.g.* Ravenscraft, 1987). An exaggerated appetite on the part of management for size and organisational diseconomies have been blamed for the conglomerates' failure. Admittedly, elements of this kind could also be playing a role today. The difficulties in marrying the profoundly different corporate cultures of bankers and insurers and in effecting the necessary painful cost adjustments have been amply noted. Nevertheless, the existence of an *a priori* economic rationale for these link-ups is well-founded.[32]

Information/control efficiencies[33]

A complementary line of thought focuses on the efficiencies that may arise from alternative forms of contractual relationship, explicit or implicit, rather than technology. It highlights how such relationships affect the flow of information between economic agents, their incentives and the possibility of influencing or controlling behaviour.[34] This approach seems potentially most fruitful when applied to the relationship between banking and commerce, especially as regards downstream linkages.

This type of analysis points to at least three related observations which are germane to the integration of banking and commerce. Ultimately, they all share a certain scepticism of the efficiency of arm's length relationships, the epitome of open markets.

The first observation highlights the advantages of *concentration* as opposed to *fragmentation* of the claims on the company receiving external finance, regardless of the form that these claims take (debt or equity). Concentration limits the scope for "free rider" problems, *i.e.* the ability of agents to share in the benefits of the actions of others without incurring the costs involved.[35] Free rider problems can act as a powerful disincentive to the costly gathering of information and hinder the effective exercise of control. As a result, individual shareholders of a public corporation may fail to safeguard their interests vis-à-vis the firm's management. Conversely, they may thwart hostile takeover attempts which could potentially increase the firm's value: why should they sell if, by refusing to do so, they can share in the benefits of the new management as long as *others* accept the bid (Grossman and Hart, 1980)? Similarly, individual bondholders or creditors may tend to rely excessively on the monitoring and credit evaluation done by others, with the risk that screening will not be sufficiently thorough. And in situations of financial distress the difficulties in coordinating efforts could be much more severe than would otherwise be the case.[36]

The second observation focuses on the benefits of *long-term relationships and contracts*. Such benefits are especially significant when the exchange of the economic service calls for investments by the parties that are "specific" to the relationship, meaning that they have limited or no value outside it (Williamson, 1985)[37] and when the associated returns take time to materialise. Once the investment is made, the counterparty may take advantage of an improved bargaining position to "expropriate" some of those returns.[38] A longer-term arrangement binding the two parties may then be necessary to secure a sufficient return on those investments and hence make them attractive in the first place. For example, compensation for the costs incurred in credit evaluation and for the risks taken in providing funds to a firm in distress or with distant pay-offs may only be secured if the firm is prevented from threatening to abandon the creditor as its fortunes improve. A standard long-term loan may be useful in this context, but the need for flexibility and control may call for a more elaborate relationship.[39]

Hence, the third, related observation: high marks are awarded to the *simultaneous holding of equity and debt*. Not only does this help to cement long-term relationships and improve the information and control possibilities open to the creditor. It also reduces the scope for conflicts of interest between creditors and equity holders, especially acute in situations of financial distress.[40] The firm is therefore more likely to pursue policies in line with total value maximisation, rather than in favour of one category of claimants at the expense of the other. It would also be less vulnerable to a hasty liquidation when facing only temporary difficulties.

Put these three elements together and you have the basis for the justification of relatively close and unconstrained linkages between providers and users of funds in a context of limited information dissemination and proliferation of non-market transactions. The existence of idiosyncratic information undermines the basis for liquid markets in financial claims. And it is of course credit institutions that are the main providers of non-marketed debt (loans). Since banks generally account for the lion's share of loans,[41] this line of reasoning is commonly seen as providing a justification for close downstream banking/commerce linkages, in the form of both debt and equity.

The more than passing resemblance of these stylised financial arrangements to the German system has not gone unnoticed. In Germany banks have a tradition of significant influence on companies, not only through their lending but also through their equity holdings and the exercise of proxy voting,[42] information disclosure has been limited and capital markets have been comparatively underdeveloped. Despite the constraints on equity holdings imposed by the Anti-Monopoly Law, similar elements can be traced in the Japanese system too. Tightly knit groups of companies ("keiretsus") cemented through cross-shareholdings generally include one bank (the "main bank") that typically has a small equity interest in the various companies of the group and provides a substantial part of the group's overall financing.[43] At the other end of the spectrum are countries such as the United States and the United Kingdom, where banking/commerce downstream linkages are practically non-existent, there is a tradition of wide dissemination of information and capital markets are comparatively large and active.[44,45]

The conceptual significance of the economic benefits of close downstream banking/commerce linkages and, more broadly, of financial systems that rely little on arm's length transactions has not gone unchallenged. Close linkages have historically been seen as impairing the independence of judgement necessary in the screening of credit.[46] The bank may favour certain customers at the expense of others, becoming tied into an ultimately detrimental mutual dependence. More generally, it has been argued that free rider, informational and control problems are not as pervasive as otherwise suggested (Fama, 1980). At least in the longer term they can be overcome through the market for corporate control via takeovers and a competitive managerial labour market, which help to correct conflicts of interest between the various stakeholders in the firm (managers, creditors, shareholders).[47]

Adjudicating between these two opposing views is not simple, not least because the available evidence is generally patchy and indirect.[48] Nevertheless, for present purposes certain points can be made.

First, it would be dogmatic to deny that informational/control efficiencies provide a valid justification for downstream linkages between banking and commerce. For example, as long as the size of the bank's interest in a company is not large relative to the *bank's* capital and overall investments, it is difficult to see *a priori* why the intermediary should be hostage to the company and hence have an incentive to discriminate against other funds users.[49] The real questions are of a more empirical nature. How should the appropriate size of the bank's interest be defined in practice? More generally, do banks actually have the necessasry expertise to perform an active governance function? The answers to those questions are likely to be country-specific.

Second, the theoretical arguments are not so convincing in justifying strong upstream linkages; probably they were never intended to. With upstream linkages the risk that the bank would privilege the interests of its owners as customers is greater. In terms of the theoretical paradigm, the conjunction of shareholders' control with diffuse creditors (depositors) exacerbates the conflict of interest between the two categories of claimant. The controlling group has greater scope to expropriate existing debtholders and may gain an unfair advantage vis-à-vis other potential funds users in the market.

Third, the recent expansion of securities markets in the wake of the easing of legal, regulatory and tax barriers, not least in Germany and Japan, and the consequent erosion of established relationships suggest that the previous arrangements entailed costs.[50] In particular, for the longer-established companies, whose creditworthiness is easier to assess, tie-ups provide fewer benefits. More generally, to the extent that advances in the transmission and processing of information reduce the investments required for its acquisition, they will also undermine one of the economic grounds for longer-term arrangements.

Finally, the analysis indicates that the informational/control efficiencies of banking/commerce tie-ups are determined by a broad range of legal and regulatory factors; attention cannot be limited to the aspects that govern the acquisition of equity participations. Large exposure limits are one obvious example; the formal distinction between debt and equity is only partly relevant to incentives and control possibilities. Accounting rules, disclosure requirements and insider trading legislation affect the availability and use of information. Rules concerning shareholder rights impinge on the possibility of effective collusion to gain control.[51] Rules governing takeover bids influence the balance between internal and market control. Broader aspects of the legal system and bankruptcy law can determine the scope and potential benefits of effective control.[52] These are just some of the more obvious examples.[53] The impact of the relaxation of restrictions on ownership linkages in any specific country, therefore, should be assessed in this broader context, which goes beyond the objectives of this paper.[54]

Monopolistic behaviour

Historically, an important reason for limiting combinations of activities has been the fear that the resulting institutions, by virtue of their size, would gain monopoly power in the market. Concentration of economic power may be undesirable in itself; beyond a certain point it may be seen as having unwelcome social and even political consequences. But even leaving such considerations aside, it can have significant undesirable consequences for economic efficiency. In individual markets, the monopolist will unnecessarily restrict output so as to increase its profits. Across markets, it will be in a position to cross-subsidise products, distorting the allocation of resources and the competitive process (*e.g.* predatory pricing). It may also "force" the consumer to purchase joint products from its various lines of business, *e.g.* a car purchase financed with a loan from the bank that controls/is controlled by the manufacturer or a mortgage loan tied to a life insurance policy.[55] Through its direct or indirect control in companies operating in other markets (*e.g.* through equity stakes), the firm may export collusive practices that rule in its market of origin. For example, there is evidence that in Germany banks promoted the cartelisation of the steel industry in the late 19th century, relying on the influence gained through their lending and equity stakes (Tilly, 1990).

The pros and cons of monopoly have been the subject of animated debate over the years. Countries have traditionally differed substantially in their tolerance of concentration of economic power and collusive behaviour. The United States, for instance, appears to lie at one end of the spectrum, exhibiting an ingrained distrust of any form of concentration. This has been reflected in extremely tough legislation. Other countries, notably Germany, have been less concerned.[56] Ultimately, the importance to be attached to objections based on notions of abuse of economic power is a matter of judgement. Nevertheless, there are reasons to believe that the weight of such considerations need not be as great nowadays as in the past. The reasons are both conceptual and empirical.

Recent analytical contributions have tended to downplay the automatic linkage between concentration and monopolistic behaviour. The mere *threat* of entry may exert a powerful influence on performance, encouraging firms in the market to lower prices and increase output so as to discourage potential competitors from entering the fray.[57] In turn, the effectiveness of the threat depends on the extent to which entry costs can be recovered (are not "sunk"), *i.e.* on the extent to which the investment incurred to enter a market can be redirected elsewhere. Empirical evidence on the issue is still limited; nor does it relate specifically to the financial industry.[58] Nevertheless, the theoretical paradigm has already had a significant influence on anti-trust policies in some countries. It has, for example, shaped the criteria applied by the Federal Reserve to its merger policy (Saunders, 1991).

More importantly, the profound transformations in the financial industry in the wake of liberalisation and technological advances may call for a *redefinition of the "market"* with respect to which concentration is to be measured. This relates to the blurring of distinctions between products, such as between savings deposits and certain insurance policies. But it applies above all to the geographical extension of competition. The creation of the European single market is just the most salient example of the broader international integration process in the industry.

Safety and soundness

The preservation of the safety and soundness of individual financial institutions, especially "banks", and of the financial system as a whole, has probably been the most influential reason for the imposition of limits on combinations of economic activities. Such barriers can help to circumscribe the protection afforded by the public authorities. The type of institution protected (*e.g.* a "bank") will not fail because of its in-house or ownership exposure to non-protected activities (*e.g.* a non-financial firm). Similarly, separation makes any necessary supervision more focused and technically simpler.

The set of activities to be protected, and therefore the location of the barrier, depend partly on the precise goal pursued by the authorities. Two such goals may be singled out, although in practice they have often gone together.

The first is *consumer protection*. This motivation draws the main demarcation line between financial and non-financial activities. A key service provided by financial institutions is the investment of funds on behalf of ultimate savers. By comparison with other exchanges of goods and services, the conjunction of a number of characteristics makes the consumer especially vulnerable: the quality of the service is difficult to assess ex ante and monitor ex post; there is a considerable lag between the time when control over (monetary) resources is given up and the time when the pecuniary counterpart of the exchange is received; above all, in the intervening period the bankruptcy of the provider of the service can cause the consumer a major loss on the contract. The same is true of any form of insurance: payment is made well before it is known whether the service provider will be able to honour its obligations.

Since consumer protection considerations do not apply with the same force to all financial services, they have also been an argument for barriers *within* the financial sector. Their strength is greater when the resources at risk constitute a larger proportion of the consumer's wealth, when his ability to assess risk is limited and his acceptance of the risk less voluntary. This line of reasoning, for instance, was an influential argument behind the adoption of Glass-Steagall in the United States (Chernow, 1990).[59]

The second motivation is *limiting systemic risk*.[60] Systemic risk is a somewhat vague but powerful concept, hard to describe precisely but easy to recognise when it materialises. It refers to a situation in which significant parts of the financial system are affected by defaults and insolvencies. The concern is that the nature of financial systems makes them especially vulnerable: intra-sectoral exposures are very large, leverage (the ratio of debt to capital) is high, and information about direct and indirect exposures is relatively limited. Under these circumstances, localised distress can quickly spread through the system.

On the basis of systemic risk considerations, it is mainly banks that have been singled out for protection. It has been argued that they are "special" on two somewhat different counts.

First, banks are the main providers of *payment services* (*e.g.* Corrigan, 1987). It is on them that payment arrangements concentrate the liquidity and credit exposures connected with the settlement of transactions. The banks' task is precisely that of absorbing liquidity pressures by committing themselves to effect funds transfers at short notice. In the process, they also normally take on credit risks that would otherwise have been borne by their customers.[61] And disruptions to the payment system can have ramifications throughout the economy. Payment arrangements represent the connective tissue of all financial and real activity, as it is the ability to settle transactions, and confidence that the counterparties will do likewise, that underpin it. Inevitably, therefore, payment arrangements can be a key channel for the transmission of shocks across institutions and markets.

Second, banks transform shorter-term, if not instantly redeemable, assets (*e.g.* deposits) into longer-term, non-marketable assets (loans).[62] This *asset transformation* function, which in effect generates liquidity for bank customers, is not without risk. A crisis of confidence in the intermediary, whether justified or not, is likely to lead to a disorderly withdrawal of funds (a "run"). Unable to dispose of its non-marketable assets, the distressed institution could quickly be forced into default and bankruptcy even though ultimately solvent, *i.e.* even though, if allowed to continue operating, it would be able to meet its original obligations with the income stream on its assets.[63] In turn, liquidation would entail real costs for society. Borrowers would see their credit lines cut and might find it difficult and costly to obtain funding elsewhere. Presumably, one reason why loans are non-marketable in the first place is that they contain borrower-specific information, difficult to transfer credibly to other potential funds providers.

Clearly, the extent to which banks are "special" differs depending on the specific function highlighted. Liquidity generation through asset transformation is commonly performed to some extent by a wider range of institutions than those actively engaged in the provision of payment services. Nor is the degree of uniqueness constant over time. The changes in the composition of activities as well as in the range and use of financial contracts over the last two decades have in many respects tended to blur institutional specificity. The authorities' response has been to adapt the framework of prudential regulation and supervision. What has been done and what remains to be accomplished merit closer examination.

III. The challenge for prudential regulation and supervision

The challenge that the authorities face in limiting systemic risk involves several dimensions: prudential regulation and supervision of individual financial institutions, system checks and balances and crisis management. In order to keep the discussion manageable, what follows focuses mainly on policies designed to ensure the safety and soundness of *individual* enterprises, with particular attention being paid to the implications of despecialisation and linkages between financial and non-financial activities.[64] By tackling excessive risk-taking at the source, such policies can go a long way towards dealing with the origin of a systemic disruption. Their design must address a number of issues, including the appropriate coverage, the methodology of supervision, the allocation of supervisory responsibilities and the need to strike a balance between official involvement and market discipline.

Conglomerates

The decision taken in most countries to limit the resistance to, or even encourage, the despecialisation of financial institutions has been a major factor shaping the adaptation of the prudential and supervisory framework to the changing financial environment. A corollary of this general approach has been the growth of financial conglomerates, both within and across national borders, covering hitherto separate activities. As a result, existing highly compartmentalised prudential supervisory frameworks have come under pressure: is it still possible for supervision to be effective if it is performed by considering exclusively individual components of a group (on a so-called *solo* basis)?[65]

The answer depends on whether independent capitalisation of units, possibly combined with operational restrictions on the transfer of information ("Chinese walls") and above all of financial capital ("firewalls") between them, can be relied upon to isolate those units from the rest of the group in times of stress. The issues involved are only partly of a legal nature, and hence to this extent country-specific.[66] Recent experience has tended to suggest that market perceptions and group interdependencies undermine effective separation. In mid-1990 in the United Kingdom the collapse of the British and Commonwealth group brought down its well-capitalised merchant banking unit; the difficulties had originated in an (unregulated) computer-leasing subsidiary. Similarly, in the same year in the United States the failure of the Drexel Burnham Lambert holding company did not spare its broker-dealer unit. When the problems emerged, market participants refused to deal with it despite assurances from the relevant authorities that it was fully solvent. The subsidiary, together with other group units, eventually had to be wound down.

This sort of *contagion* risk indicates that group interdependencies must somehow be taken into account; it also provides an argument against excessive reliance on intra-group operational restrictions: they might not work when they are most needed but they risk undermining any potential "synergies" between combinations of activities.[67]

At a minimum, supervisors should be in a position to *access information* about the various group units, including unregulated ones. This also raises the need for exchanges of information between the regulatory authorities responsible for different parts of the group, if any.

As regards non-financial units, the predominant attitude has been one of caution: yes to the possibility of obtaining information but care in the exercise of this right lest the impression be created that the unsupervised unit is actually supervised. This approach has been enshrined, for instance, in the relevant EC legislation on groups containing credit institutions.

In general, the information exchanged about financial units within a group is greater. Both nationally and internationally, efforts have been made to remove legal and other obstacles to the flow of information between different supervisors, typically related to issues of confidentiality. Yet progress has been somewhat uneven. It is now generally possible for banking, securities and insurance supervisors to have access to the relevant information at national level. Within the European Community, legislation has imposed a duty on these authorities to cooperate;[68] implementation may be more difficult, however. Problems are more severe at the broader international level. The exchange of information has a long tradition among banking supervisors, but is more recent for securities regulators and in its infancy among insurance authorities.[69] In some cases, the barriers arise from limited powers to access information in national markets. Until recently a notable example was that of the Securities and Exchange Commission, which had no right to obtain information concerning the affiliates, subsidiaries and holding companies of registered broker-dealers.

The structure of a particular group, both across activities and across national borders, will thus affect the amount of information available to supervisors. As vividly illustrated by the bankruptcy of BCCI, the globalisation of financial markets has provided ample scope for *opaque corporate structures* even for purely banking organisations, commonly the most closely supervised type of group. This episode has triggered a strengthening of supervisory powers. In July 1992 the Basle Committee on Banking Supervision, which brings together supervisors from the Group of Ten countries, reinforced the Basle Concordat of May 1983, which set out the basic principles for the supervision of international banking groups and their cross-border establishments. The guidelines, which had a "best efforts" character, were turned into stricter minimum standards, in particular setting conditions designed to prevent banks from belonging to excessively opaque groups.[70] At the EC level, a proposed new Financial Supervision Directive follows similar lines. Supervisors of banks, investment firms and insurance companies would be mandated to withhold a licence if the applicant belonged to a group with an unduly opaque structure and could withdraw it subsequently in the light of undesirable changes in that structure. Present legislation refers only vaguely to the "suitability" of shareholders and makes no reference to the group to which they might belong.[71] The Draft Directive contains a provision for the relevant national laws to come into effect on 1st January 1996 at the latest.[72]

Should the relevant authorities go beyond exchanges of information and apply some form of *consolidated supervision*? "Some form" is indeed the right expression, for a great variety of techniques fall under this general umbrella. They range from a mixture of qualitative and more formal quantitative methods to full consolidation combined with an attempt to apply the "same rules" to the "same risks" connected with the "same activities". Consolidation within banking groups going beyond the calculation of capital ratios to incorporate qualitative risk assessment on a group basis has long been a fundamental principle of prudential supervision for bank supervisors. Full consolidation is the main concept[73] adopted in the EC Second Consolidated Supervision Directive, in effect since January 1993, with reference to financial groups that include credit institutions. Insurance units are not covered, however.[74] Insurance supervisors in particular view the extension of consolidated supervision as impractical in the short term and not necessarily optimal, given the specificities of their business. Work is in progress to ascertain the feasibility of a convergence in methodologies. At present, the typical methods applied attempt to limit the risk that the same capital might be used in different parts of the group to support business ("double-gearing"). A common method is to deduct the value of participations in subsidiaries/affiliates from the capital of the supervised unit. Techniques of this kind may also be applied to participations by non-financial companies.

Related to the issue of consolidation is that of the *harmonisation of capital standards*. Conceptually, for example, full accounting consolidation views the financial group as a single unit. Applying a capital standard to the consolidated accounts would imply that the risks incurred would be subject to the same standards irrespective of the unit of the corporate organisation in which they are incurred. This is in fact the principle embodied in the EC Second Consolidated Supervision Directive, which applies the 8% solvency ratio in respect of credit risk (Solvency Ratio and Own Funds Directives) and the market risk standards (Capital Adequacy Directive) to the consolidated unit.[75]

The main advantage of such harmonised standards is that they limit the possibility of "regulatory arbitrage", both within conglomerates and among independent firms: companies cannot reduce the stringency of the standards simply by altering their organisational structure.[76] Such a "level playing-field", far from being just a tribute to the ideal of "fair competition", is an integral element of the overall prudential framework. The problem is that devising standards that are appropriate for institutions performing different ranges of activities has proved to be a very difficult task: the approaches historically adopted by the relevant authorities have been profoundly different. This has added a further layer of complication to the difficulties that normally arise from the considerable range of cross-country experience in the regulation of the same type of activity.

Consider, for example, some of the main stylised differences between the prudential philosophy of banking and securities regulators. The bulk of the assets of a securities firm are marketable, their value is thus "objectively" measured by their market price, observable practically on a continuous basis.

Measured net worth fluctuates with movements in these prices. The limited discretion in valuation and the visibility of net worth mean that companies should be in a position to meet losses quickly. As a result, securities regulators have traditionally focused on market (price) risk and placed considerable emphasis on liquidity, treating illiquid claims conservatively and often allowing certain forms of short-term financing to be counted as capital. By contrast, a major proportion of bank assets, such as loans, has been non-marketable, with less of an objective and readily visible benchmark for valuation. Moreover, the asset transformation performed by banks means that one of their major services is precisely providing liquidity to the rest of the economy: by nature they are, in a sense, illiquid. Consequently, bank supervisors have historically focused primarily on credit risk and on the long-run viability of the institutions. Illiquid positions have not been penalised with higher capital requirements and the regulatory definition of capital has only included financing instruments of a more permanent nature. Even in those countries where banks have historically been allowed to engage actively in securities business, separate treatment has not generally been regarded as necessary until recently. One reason was that these operations made up a relatively small part of their overall business.

The differences in approach are clearly considerably greater between banking or securities supervisors, on the one hand, and insurance regulators on the other. Insurance regulators have essentially focused on underwriting risks: the solvency ratio has traditionally been related to the overall volume of the companies' underwriting business. The risk that failure may result from capital losses on the investment of the premiums has received less attention. This risk has typically been constrained through portfolio restrictions on permissible investments.[77] In a sense, the position resembles that of a number of banking systems prior to deregulation: capital requirements which did not differentiate between the composition of (on and off-balance-sheet) assets were combined with restrictions on banks' balance sheets constraining their risk-taking. The time would now appear ripe for a closer examination of these issues: deregulation in the insurance sector and market innovations have not only reduced the specificity of the insurance business; they have also heightened the incentive to take on risks.[78]

Further progress remains to be made at the broad international level towards the achievement of greater harmonisation of capital standards between banking and securities supervisors. It is not clear whether and, if so, to what extent greater convergence will be achieved also with respect to the insurance sector. As mentioned, at the EC level the minimum capital standards for banks and securities firms have recently been harmonised.[79] In April 1993 the Basle Committee on Banking Supervision issued a set of proposals extending the original 1988 agreement on the treatment of credit risk to the coverage of market risk.[80] But despite the understanding reached with the Technical Committee of the International Organisation of Securities Commissions in early 1992, it has not been possible to issue joint proposals ensuring consistency of minimum standards. As regards insurance activities, there is no unanimity on the desirability of greater convergence.

Conglomeration and the blurring of distinctions between activities also raise the question of the appropriate *allocation of responsibilities* between different supervisors. Traditionally, countries have organised their prudential framework along institutional lines. This has generally been on a tripartite basis (banks, securities firms, insurance companies), except in countries such as Germany and Switzerland which have universal banking systems, where securities business is generally regarded as banking business. Typically, when securities business has been performed by banks, either in-house or through subsidiaries, it has fallen under the jurisdiction of banking supervisors.[81] On the other hand, stand-alone securities firms have often been covered by securities authorities, be these stock exchanges, securities commissions or self-regulatory organisations.[82] In the United Kingdom securities and bank supervisors have shared responsibility for the securities business carried out in-house by a bank.[83] A "lead supervisor", chosen on the basis of the dominant activity of the group, has been responsible for coordinating overall efforts. As regards securities business, Italy has adopted a novel allocation rule based on the objectives of supervision rather than the type of activity or institutional form in which that activity is carried out: the Banca d'Italia has responsibility for the safety and soundness of both banks and securities firms, while the securities supervisor (CONSOB) is in charge of conduct-of-business and disclosure rules.

Over the last few years this general picture has not changed much. However, some countries, such as Denmark (in 1988) and Sweden (in 1991), have followed the despecialisation trend by merging the supervisory authorities for banking, securities and insurance business.[84]

If conglomerate structures in the provision of financial services raise problems, the same is true of *group structures among customers*. The main area of concern is the *concentration of credit exposures*. The same lack of transparency that hinders the supervision of financial organisations can complicate the identification and monitoring of aggregate exposures to customers, for both market participants and supervisors. Indeed, the absence of a supervisory authority over the companies belonging to the group can make access to information more difficult. The existence in several countries, including Germany, France and Italy, of credit information exchanges may be of some use in helping to ascertain the overall exposure of a borrower to banks within particular countries but still presupposes knowledge about group configurations which may not be available.

Upstream and downstream ownership linkages have a bearing on the severity of the problem. On the one hand, to the extent that upstream linkages allow some scope for control or collusion, they may create incentives for banks to consciously exceed prudent exposures. On the other hand, the existence of some formal equity interest, particularly downstream, may help to alleviate informational problems.

Available information suggests that all Group of Ten and EC countries now have in place large exposure limits which apply at group level; it is less clear, however, how implementation has dealt with the lack of transparency of both national and international groups. At the EC level, the Large Credit Exposures Directive sets rather strict limits for individual clients or groups to be applied on a consolidated basis to the credit exposure of the financial group,[85] in accordance with the Second Consolidated Supervision Directive.[86] In order to allow countries to comply with the limits, a phasing-in period extending to December 2001 is provided for - a telling indication of the difficulties that some countries will have in implementing the legislation.[87] Italy, where limits have been significantly more generous, is a case in point.[88]

Balance between official involvement and market discipline

A fundamental issue in the design of the framework of prudential regulation and supervision is the balance between official involvement and market discipline. The drawback of market discipline is that it may be insufficient or may operate in a way not consistent with systemic stability. Historically, the inability of unchecked market forces to avoid major crises was precisely the reason for setting up prudential regulation. More recently, the serious difficulties encountered by some Nordic banking systems have in part reflected the failure to strengthen prudential safeguards sufficiently in a liberalised, more competitive financial environment (*e.g.* BIS, 1992a and 1993). A drawback of the authorities' involvement is that it may be counterproductive if it gives market participants a false sense of security, encouraging them to take on further risks. In economics parlance, this has come to be known as the problem of "moral hazard"; more generally, it is one of rendering agents responsible for their actions (Lamfalussy, 1992).

There are at least two ways in which the authorities' involvement may blunt market participants' incentives to exercise discipline. First, and more damagingly, policy may create the perception that agents will be insulated from the losses that the institutions might incur. Typical examples are deposit insurance or guarantee schemes and, more pervasively, less formal policies which result in the authorities' taking exposures to credit risk in, or absorbing the losses of, failing institutions. Actions that encourage the view that the authorities are, directly or indirectly, responsible for the institutions' fortunes may have a similar effect. Second, monitoring and control by the authorities may make agents less inclined to perform these functions themselves, giving rise to the "free rider" problem discussed in Section II. To the extent that the monitoring and control are effective, however, financial stability is not thereby impaired.[89]

These general arguments suggest that the prudential framework can be extended too far; covering an increasing range of activities and institutions is not without potential costs. This has been a powerful reason for the great caution exercised in allowing financial and non-financial activities within connected organisational structures. It explains the reluctance to adopt a more interventionist approach with respect to non-financial units of financial conglomerates. Together with concerns about the possible negative implications of prudential regulation and supervision for economic efficiency, it has even led some observers to ask whether it might not be appropriate to reconsider the whole approach. Rather than extending the "safety net" further, it might be better to restrict it to what is absolutely necessary by assigning the activities requiring protection to specific institutions and "cordoning them off" from the rest of the system through strict ownership and other operational barriers. The so-called "narrow banking" school, for example, would limit institutions involved in the provision of payment services to investments in "safe" securities.[90]

Whether such extreme proposals are viable or indeed desirable is open to question. As argued above, there is no agreement on what activities should in fact be protected in the first place on systemic risk grounds. Investor protection considerations tend to extend the umbrella more widely. There may be considerable economic costs in attempting to separate payments from the provision of financial services in terms of technological and informational efficiencies. And there may be doubts about the effectiveness of barriers in any case, especially when such potential efficiencies are involved. Nevertheless, these arguments are a healthy reminder of the trade-offs involved in extending the prudential framework.

The room for improvement in the balance between official involvement and market discipline should not be underestimated. The authorities can limit the extension of those forms of intervention that provide protection without commensurate control. In the United States, for instance, changes to the payment and settlement system, a tightening of deposit insurance schemes and a reconsideration of the "too big to fail" doctrine have been moves in this direction. The authorities can also take steps to improve information disclosure, not least about organisational structures and balance sheets. Derivatives, for example, have been singled out as an area for potential action (BIS, 1992b, 1994b and 1994c). And the role that the strengthening of capital standards has played in promoting a better balance has been noteworthy. True, capital requirements are an external constraint on portfolio behaviour, and as such they partly substitute for management's judgement. But in an industry where the authorities' concerns about systemic instability probably blunt incentives to prudent behaviour, the standards are a way of providing capital markets with a stronger incentive, as well as with the means, to enforce financial discipline. The renewed focus of banks on profitability with due regard to risk, rather than growth and balance-sheet size, as a guide to policy and yardstick of performance bears witness to this fact. The standards partly shift the burden of supervision away from the authorities and onto the market.

At the same time, shifting the balance towards market discipline is no simple task. The weight of history cannot be erased effortlessly and without pain. To quote from the BIS Annual Report for 1991/92:

"Above all, reducing incentives to excessive risk-taking will depend on the credibility of the authorities' commitment to limiting intervention to the necessary minimum in the event of turmoil. That credibility is only partly a question of legislation and regulations: in the complex present-day financial environment, it inevitably requires a degree of official discretion. In much the same way as the monetary authorities' anti-inflation commitment, it needs to be demonstrated in consistent action." (p. 212)

IV. Conclusion

The process of financial liberalisation that gathered momentum during the 1980s has profoundly changed the borders of banking. While its scope, timing and speed have not been uniform across countries or segments of the industry, certain stylised patterns can be identified.

Generally the process has tended to occur earlier and go further in the area of restrictions mainly motivated by credit allocation objectives and the implementation of monetary policy, typically in the form of controls on interest rates and quantities. It has taken place later and been more cautious with respect to restrictions on the institutions' lines of business. In turn, the liberalisation of restrictions on banks' lines of business has generally proceeded more speedily and been more extensive for those activities considered closer to the "core" of banking business. Liberalisation has gone furthest in the field of commercial and investment banking; the only significant barriers survive in the United States and Japan. It has made significant inroads in the area of linkages between banks and insurance companies, generally permitted through subsidiaries except in the two countries just mentioned. By contrast, it has been very limited as regards links between banks and non-financial companies.

Underlying the relaxation of restrictions on banks' lines of business has been the growing conviction that economic efficiency is best promoted by allowing companies to choose freely their size and product mix. Efficiency gains may be connected with the exploitation of technological and organisational efficiencies, such as economies of scale and scope. They may also derive from information/control efficiencies, such as those which may be reaped by permitting banks to acquire significant equity stakes in non-financial companies, thereby possibly mitigating some of the asymmetric information and incentive problems that beset the relationship between providers and users of funds. While the empirical evidence on the economic significance of either type of gain remains limited and mixed, the increasing globalisation of markets and heightened competition have allayed concerns about one important factor which could undermine the achievement of economic benefits, viz. monopolistic behaviour.

The main brake on the liberalisation process has been prudential concerns, notably the difficulty of devising appropriate prudential safeguards in the light of the increased freedom. The upgrading of the framework of prudential supervision has been a necessary complement to the liberalisation of the financial industry worldwide: experience indicates that securing the benefits of deregulation in terms of greater economic efficiency calls for a strengthening of prudential safeguards with a view to limiting the risk of financial instability. As banks have become exposed to the risks connected with a broader range of activities, either performed in-house or by connected corporate units, the authorities have had to re-examine the coverage and methodology of existing arrangements, both nationally and internationally.

As the typical traditional compartmentalisation of the financial industry into banking, securities and insurance segments has weakened, the corresponding compartmentalisation of supervision has come under pressure. The recognition that independent capitalisation of different corporate units within a group cannot be relied upon to ensure insulation of those units at times of financial distress has given impetus to the exchange of information between banking, securities and insurance supervisors and to the adoption of consolidated methods of supervision. The risk of regulatory arbitrage within conglomerates and between independent units has encouraged greater convergence in supervisory methodologies, including capital standards. At the same time, how far this general process of harmonisation can, and indeed should, be extended remains a moot question. At the EC level, consolidated supervision applies to banking groups that include securities firms; the legislation also provides for a minimum degree of harmonisation of capital standards. At the broader international level the process has not as yet been taken so far. Moreover, consolidated supervision does not extend to insurance companies, either nationally or internationally; nor is it clear to what extent the distance between supervisory methodologies for insurance and the other sectors can be narrowed given the profound differences in the nature of the activities.

A second fundamental issue has been the search for an appropriate balance between official involvement and market discipline. The broadening of the range of banks' activities within the financial sector and of their ownership linkages with non-financial companies carries the risk of extending the "safety net" generally put in place to prevent systemic crises. Market participants' incentives to prudent behaviour may thereby be blunted. The room for improvement in this area should not be underestimated. One possibility would be to strengthen information disclosure, not least about balance sheets and organisational structures; thorny questions regarding the precise nature and range of information to be disclosed would need to be addressed. A complementary mechanism, effectively strengthened in recent years, is the upgrading of capital standards, seen as a way of providing capital markets with a stronger incentive and with the means to enforce financial discipline. As such, the standards can help to shift the burden away from the authorities and onto the market.

Notes

1   For a detailed description of the deregulation process, see Bröker (1989) and OECD (1992a). A more succinct overview and analysis of these developments is contained in BIS (1991 and 1992a) and Pecchioli (1991).

2   However, they remain comparatively high in Italy and Portugal. Even so, the interest paid on compulsory reserves reduces the value of the implicit tax.

3   For example, in France current accounts may not bear interest. In the United States the same restriction applies to deposits with a maturity of up to seven days.

4   While the development of the Treasury bill markets owes much to the financing needs of governments, the establishment of markets for domestic certificates of deposit and, even more so, commercial paper has almost invariably necessitated *ad hoc* changes in the national legislative and regulatory framework.

5   The Second Banking Coordination Directive (credit institutions) came into effect on 1st January 1993. The Investment Services Directive (investment firms) is due to come into effect in January 1996. As regards direct bank access to stock exchange membership, a transitional period up to the end of 1996 is allowed for these countries still prohibiting it (this period is longer for Spain, Portugal and Greece). The Third Life and Non-Life Insurance Directives came into effect in July 1994 (with special deadlines for Spain, Portugal and Greece).

6   The Ministry of Finance has, however, reserved the right to manage the actual speed of the process through administrative guidance.

7   See OECD (1992b) for a more detailed description of country-specific regulations.

8   There is, however, considerable variation in the precise definition of the insurance field.

9   See Article 8(1) of the First Non-Life Directive (1973) and the First Life Directive (1979).

10   In the United States federally chartered banks and bank holding companies are permitted to distribute insurance products only in very small towns (fewer than 5 000 inhabitants). As many as eighteen states rule out any distribution by their state chartered banks and eight limit it to small towns. Note also that while Delaware enacted very permissive legislation on the production and distribution of insurance products by banks in 1990, the Federal Reserve Bank subsequently prevented member banks from taking advantage of this law.

11 The law was actually tightened in 1987, prior to which the limit was effectively 10%.

12 For Finland and Norway the picture is analogous to that of downstream linkages.

13 Until then they could only own securities dealers.

14 A "qualifying holding" is defined as a direct or indirect holding in an undertaking equal to at least 10% of its capital or voting rights or permitting the exercise of significant influence over its management.

15 The thresholds for prior authorisation are lower in Italy, but otherwise there appear to be no *a priori* limits on upstream linkages with insurance companies. Following the decrees published in June 1993, the triggers for prior authorisation have been set at 5, 10, 15, 20, 33 and 50% or control, somewhat less restrictive than those which had applied since 1990 (Law No. 287).

16 In particular, an ageing population (falling population growth and higher life expectancy) and a decline in the retirement age have put pressure on state-run redistribution (pay as you go) pension systems and favoured recapitalisation systems, based on individual savings. Insurance companies' ability to compete with banks in this sector has been enhanced, inter alia, by significant tax advantages (*e.g.* Alworth and Borio, 1992). For complementary overviews of developments in the insurance industry, see The Economist (1990) and the OECD (1992b).

17 For greater detail on some of the main industrialised countries, see Pepe (1986) and Porta *et al.* (1990).

18 In these countries limits on the size of individual participations, for instance, are generally between zero (Australia) and 10% (Canada). Such stakes may not be "controlling" in Denmark.

19 In Germany 100% ownership is allowed in principle. The participation in, plus any loan exposure to, the company may not exceed 50% of the bank's liable capital. The total of such participations plus shares in other banks may not exceed the capital thus defined.

20 As in Germany, in France 100% ownership is possible. In line with the EC Second Banking Directive, the size of individual participations and their total value are restricted to no more than 15 and 60% of the bank's capital respectively.

21 Within this group, of course, differences exist. For instance, with the introduction of the new norms in 1993, Italy has moved from the "highly restrictive" to the "intermediate" camp, but remains much more circumspect than, say, France. In particular, in line with the reiteration of the basic principle of "separation" between banking and commerce, banks may not normally hold more than 15% of any individual firm's capital.

22   According to the EC Second Banking Coordination Directive, 100% ownership is permitted. Individual and total "qualifying" participations must not exceed 15 and 60% of the acquiring bank's capital respectively.

23   In the United States participations of non-bank companies in banks must be less than 25% of the bank's capital. In addition, following the 1970 Amendments to the 1956 Bank Holding Company Act, bank holding companies' activities are restricted to those "closely related to banking". However, more than forty non-bank companies exist that own "non-bank banks" acquired before the Competitive Equality Banking Act of 1987 came into force. "Non-bank banks" may either make loans or take deposits but may not engage in both activities simultaneously. Among the best-known examples are "captive" finance companies, some of which rival with the largest banks in terms of size. See Saunders (1991) for details. In Sweden majority participations in banks may only be held by banks or insurance companies. In Spain non-financial companies may not hold participations in a bank in excess of 20% of its capital during the initial five years of its existence.

24   Domestically owned Schedule II banks, which are closely held, must become widely held within ten years of their creation.

25   In fact, prior authorisation for the acquisition of participations has not been necessary in some countries. Germany and Austria, for instance, appear to be cases in point. Even in its absence, however, moral suasion may be exercised, while other forms of control may act as a deterrent for potential acquirers.

26   The identity of shareholders must be disclosed when the bank is set up and when individual participations are transferred or reach the 20, 33 and 50% thresholds. The authorities reserve the right to deny authorisation when the quality of the shareholders is deemed to endanger the "safety and soundness" of the bank.

27   Economies of scale have a very long history (Viner, 1932); the formal notion of economies of scope is more recent but has been equally influential (Baumol *et al.*, 1982). Economies of scope extend the notion of the relationship between size and costs to the multi-product firm.

28   See Forestieri (1993) for a review of the literature.

29   For Japan, see Kasuya (1986) and Yoshioka and Nakajima (1987); for France, Dietsch (1990); and for Italy, Cossutta *et al.* (1988) and Conigliani *et al.* (1991).

30   The Italian case is one exception to this more common approach. Partly because of previous branching restrictions, banks are not generally regarded as having a comparative advantage in distribution. Similarly, there has been less concentration on life insurance products and a greater reliance on international linkages than in other countries. See Salomon Brothers (1990) for an overview. Outside Europe another exception is Canada, where, despite being allowed to own insurance companies, banks are prohibited from marketing insurance products through their branches.

31 For an analysis of these questions, see Forestieri (1993).

32 As regards the inroads made by non-financial companies in the financial sector, the experience has been somewhat mixed. In the United States, for example, some companies have been very successful, others less so, and the less successful have recently decided to scale back their activities. See, for example, Koguchi (1993).

33 For the sake of clarity, this sub-section considers the issue on its own merits, abstracting for the peculiarities of the nature of banking activities that suggest that the failure of a bank involves greater social costs than that of a non-financial company.

34 More precisely, the reference here is to a family of conceptually closely related approaches which highlight asymmetric information, transactions costs and contracts. This common thread ties together Coase's (1937) work on the theory of the firm, later developed by Williamson (1985) in particular, more formal work in the area of optimal contracts (Hart and Holmström (1988) and, more specifically on ownership, by Grossman and Hart, 1986) and the application of these and related ideas to the theory of financial structure (*e.g.* Gertler, 1988 and Borio, 1990a (reviews), Stiglitz, 1985 and Mayer, 1988). See also Tirole (1988) and Kreps (1990) for useful overviews.

35 Seen from the alternative perspective, those actions involve (positive) "externalities".

36 See White (1989) and Aghion *et al.* (1992).

37 In economic parlance irretrievable costs are also known as "sunk" costs.

38 In Williamson's terminology, the party that has made the investment is exposed to the risk of "opportunistic" behaviour and "hold-up" by his counterparty.

39 In more technical language, the party at risk may need to have considerable control in contingencies that could not easily be specified ex ante in a contract - a form of influence not dissimilar to what ownership rights in principle confer. These so-called "residual rights of control" as a form of ownership are emphasised by Grossman and Hart (1986). For an application of this concept to the banking/commerce relationship, see Bisignano (1993). See also Hellwig (1991) for a critical assessment of the notion of long-term commitments in this context.

40 In situations of distress there is a strong incentive for shareholders to expropriate existing creditors through a variety of means, including excessive dividend payments, the pursuit of particularly risky strategies and the offer of senior collateral to new creditors. Covenants in debt contracts and hybrid debt/equity instruments can of course mitigate these problems.

41 Note that these theoretical observations abstract from the structure of the liabilities side of the balance sheet of funds providers. As such, they cannot distinguish between banks and other credit intermediaries.

42 The "Hausbank" has traditionally been identified with a bank that accompanies a firm throughout its life cycle, "from the cradle to the grave".

43 The formation of "keiretsus" was a response to shareholding restrictions introduced after the Second World War, when the United States had a major influence on the reshaping of the financial system. The "keiretsus" replaced the pre-war "zaibatsus", family-controlled enterprise groups which often had banks as captive institutions. See Goto (1982).

44 For overviews of these cross-country differences, see Borio (1990a), Prowse (1994) and the references therein. Historical perspectives on the distant origins of the present-day differences can be found in Gerschenkron (1962), Gille (1973) and Tilly (1990).

45 Of course, in practice it may not be easy to place individual countries within this stylised spectrum. Italy has so far been a typical example. On the one hand, there has been little emphasis on wide dissemination of information, the role of capital markets has been limited and ownership and control among the large private sector companies have been tied together through cascading shareholdings in groups, consolidated through shareholder "pacts" ("sindacati di controllo") and cross-shareholdings. On the other hand, downstream banking/commerce linkages in the form of equity have been strictly discouraged, although limits on large exposures, which have been comparatively generous, have not necessarily been a serious obstacle to close linkages through debt in some cases. The main distinguishing feature of the system has been pervasive ownership by the public sector, both in the financial and non-financial sector. Increasingly, this involvement has been viewed as being responsible for a serious distortion of economic incentives, undermining the usefulness of the theoretical paradigms used to assess the potential benefits of alternative governance structures. See, for example, Ciocca (1991), Masera (1991), Barca (1993) and Brioschi et al. (1990).

46 See Schumpeter (1939) (especially p. 118).

47 The wave of highly-leveraged buyouts that swept the United States during the 1980s has been mentioned in this context. For an overview, see Borio (1990a).

48 See Prowse (1994) for a review of recent work and Mankiw's (1988) comments on Mayer (1988). Steinherr and Huveneers (1990) provide a critique of the "German" model.

49 In addition, diversification of the bank's portfolio has an additional benefit. Through the law of large numbers, it makes the income stream produced by the bank more stable and less uncertain. This goes some way towards solving the

"who monitors the monitor?" problem. For a formalisation of this point, see Diamond (1984).

50   On Germany, see, for example, Terrahe (1989) and on Japan, Hoshi *et al.* (1990).

51   In the United States, for example, SEC regulations have prohibited communication between large shareholders, effectively discouraging collusion (*e.g.* Prowse, 1994).

52   In the United States the legal system has discouraged effective control by lenders, whether through debt or equity. If the senior lender is found to exercise significant control over management, its claims on collateral may be ranked on a par with those of junior creditors ("lender liability"). Banks owning direct or indirect equity stakes in companies are particularly vulnerable ("equitable subordination"). See, for instance, Borio (1990b).

53   An interesting assessment of the relationship between legal and financial arrangements can be found in MacNeil (1978) and Bisignano (1992).

54   For an analysis of the Italian experience along such lines, see Barca (1993) and a series of related papers published in the Temi di discussione by the Banca d'Italia. On the structure of controls within corporate groups, see also Brioschi *et al.* (1990).

55   Conceptually similar examples relate to so-called "conflicts of interest" connected with the use of information obtained in one line of business to expand others. To the extent that these are not predicated on some notion of "fairness", they must ultimately rest on the view that this information can be used to gain a monopolistic position in a market or at the expense of the customer ("overpricing"). A typical example is the possibility of "forcing" on investors dubious loans repackaged as securities or the ability to lend them money to purchase such securities (commercial/investment banking combinations; see Chernow's (1990) description of the Pecora hearings that helped pass the Glass-Steagall Act). Clearly, greater dissemination of information (*e.g.* through special requirements) and competition in the service markets can mitigate these problems. Another possibility is the device of "Chinese walls", which restrict the flow of information and control between units in the same organisational structure. For an analysis of such "conflicts of interest" in German banking, see Krümmel (1980).

56   The difference, of course, is one of degree. For example, in Germany the power exercised by banks over industry has often come under attack and has been the subject of official enquiries (*e.g.* Monopolkommission, 1979).

57   This is the theory of so-called "contestable" markets. See Baumol *et al.* (1982).

58   See Baumol and Willig (1986). For a criticism of the theory and of the available evidence, see Schwartz (1986).

59 It is also the basis for the view that markets in which the main players are professionals or large institutional investors need not be as tightly supervised as those in which retail investors are involved.

60 See Bockelmann and Borio (1990) for a more extensive analysis of the nature and implications of systemic risk in the light of structural changes in the financial system.

61 For a succint overview of the nature and management of payment system risk, see BIS (1994a). Borio and Van den Bergh (1993) provide an in-depth analysis.

62 See Goodhart (1987) for emphasis on this point. An influential formalisation is provided by Diamond and Dybvig (1983).

63 The risk is exacerbated by the highly fragmented nature of bank deposits and the fact that depositors are relatively uninformed. This parallel with the broader literature on corporate governance discussed above has recently been stressed by Dewatripont and Tirole (1994).

64 For a succinct overview, see BIS (1993).

65 Of course, the issue also arises within each institutional category (*e.g.* banks, securities firms, insurance companies) when they are themselves organised in group form. For a descriptive overview of the current prudential arrangements concerning financial conglomerates in the European Community, with particular reference to groups including insurance companies, see CEA (1993).

66 Legal issues of this kind have been hotly debated in the United States under the heading of "corporate separateness". For example, according to the "source of strength" doctrine, the Federal Reserve demands that holding companies help their bank subsidiaries in distress. As a result, however, creditors may in turn demand that the bank subsidiary's assets be used to help the holding company in distress, piercing the "corporate veil" (on so-called "estoppel" grounds). The Supreme Court has recently agreed to adjudicate between these competing views. See Black *et al.* (1978) and Saunders (1990) or (1991).

67 The potential problems with firewalls are clearly stated in Corrigan (1987) and (1990), the United States being a country that has made extensive use of them. See also Saunders (1991).

68 The Second Consolidated Supervision Directive.

69 In the spring of 1990 the Basle Committee on Banking Supervision reached an agreement with securities supervisors on the need for the progressive removal of barriers to the exchange of prudential information; the agreement was later endorsed by insurance regulators.

70 In October 1992 the standards were endorsed by over one hundred national supervisory authorities.

71 Other provisions are also envisaged. The proposed Directive states that the head and registered office of a bank or insurance undertaking must be located in the same Member State, extends provisions regarding the exchange of information between supervisory authorities and other bodies (including those responsible for overseeing auditors, liquidators and compliance with company law) and tightens auditors' reporting duties vis-à-vis supervisors.

72 The Council of Ministers adopted a common position on the Draft Directive on 6th June.

73 The Directive leaves some discretion as regards the method to be used and provides for significant exemptions. For example, a credit or financial institution subsidiary need not be consolidated when, in the eyes of the authorities responsible, "it would be inappropriate or misleading as far as the objectives of the supervision of credit institutions are concerned" (Article 3/2).

74 These are not viewed as "financial" enterprises in EC legislation.

75 The rules must also be observed at the solo or sub-consolidated level, but supervisors may grant exemptions. While the Solvency Ratio and Own Funds Directives are already in effect, the Capital Adequacy Directive is due to be implemented by January 1996 at the latest, in conjunction with the Investment Services Directive, which grants the single passport to investment firms.

76 The issue of regulatory arbitrage, of course, is much broader and relates to all forms of prudential safeguards.

77 For a few examples of such restrictions, see Davis (1988) and OECD (1992b).

78 In the United States, for example, at least since the late 1980s, regulators have paid increasing attention to the riskiness of insurance companies' assets, especially in the light of the losses incurred on commercial real estate and of weakness in their junk bond portfolios. In June 1990 the National Association of Insurance Commissioners refined the rating criteria for bond holdings (Carey *et al.*, 1993) and in January 1993 it introduced risk-based capital standards. Similarly, the Japanese authorities are reportedly considering the implementation of risk-based capital standards related to insurance companies' investments (The Economist, 1992). They are already in operation in Norway and Canada.

79 The standards have been developed in cooperation with the Basle Committee on Banking Supervision and the International Organisation of Securities Commissions. In order to take into account future broader international agreements, as well as possible market developments, a provision calls for a re-examination of the Capital Adequacy Directive within three years of the date of entry into force.

80 See also Basle Committee on Banking Supervision (1994).

81 Canada, Spain and the United States have been exceptions, since the securities business of bank subsidiaries has been supervised by securities supervisors.

82 In some countries, however, bank supervisors have been responsible. Examples are Denmark, Finland and Sweden. For details, see OECD (1991).

83 If the securities business was performed through a bank-owned subsidiary it would fall under the securities supervisor's jurisdiction and meet its capital requirements; the bank supervisor, while not consolidating the subsidiary into the banking group, would nevertheless oversee the management of the whole group.

84 Norway had already done so in 1986.

85 A large credit exposure is defined as one exceeding 10% of own funds. Each such individual exposure is limited to 25% of own funds and their total to 800% of the same variable. Member states, however, may set the threshold defining a large exposure and the individual ceiling at 15% and 40% respectively until 1998.

86 The Directive also places a limit (20% of consolidated own funds) on the credit exposures within the financial group containing the credit institution. The limit helps to reduce the risk of contagion.

87 In January 1991 the Basle Committee on Banking Supervision issued guidelines for the measurement and control of large credit exposures which were circulated to banking supervisors worldwide.

88 For ordinary banks ("aziende di credito") a large exposure is defined as a credit in excess of 20% of the bank's capital. Each such exposure and their total may not exceed, respectively, 100% of the bank's capital and between 25% and 40% of total customer deposits depending on the ratio of capital to deposits. Similar, but less stringent, limits apply to medium and long-term special credit institutions.

89 These considerations show that, in fact, it is misleading to use the term "moral hazard" to refer to policies that blunt market participants' incentives to execise financial discipline. "Moral hazard" in economics literature results from the inability to monitor the actions of agents, who may have an incentive to behave in a way that conflicts with the interests of those who entrust them with particular tasks (*e.g.* with funds for subsequent investment). The inability to observe the agents' behaviour allows them to exploit those incentives. A moral hazard problem always exists between the claimants on, and the management of, financial institutions. Government intervention shifts the risks and introduces an additional category of claimant.

90 See Pierce (1991) and Bryan (1991). The proposals differ in terms of their details, notably the permissible investments of payment service providers and the "cordoning off" methods. It is no coincidence that these proposals have been developed in the United States, a country that has relied especially heavily on legal and operational barriers to segment its financial system.

References

AGHION, P., O. HART and J. MOORE (1992), "The economics of bankruptcy reform". *NBER Working Paper*, no. 4097, June.

ALWORTH, J.S. and C.E.V. BORIO (1992), "The linkages between taxation, private saving decisions, and financial intermediation: some international comparisons", in D.E. FAIR and C. DE BOISSIEU, (eds.), *Fiscal policy, taxation and the financial system in an increasingly integrated Europe,* pp. 69-104.

ALWORTH, J.S. and C.E.V. BORIO (1993), "Commercial paper markets: a survey". *BIS Economic Paper*, no. 37, Basle, April.

Bank for International Settlements (1991), 61st Annual Report 1990/91, Basle, June.

Bank for International Settlements (1992a), 62nd Annual Report 1991/92, Basle, June.

Bank for International Settlements (1992b), *Recent developments in international interbank relations*, Basle, October.

Bank for International Settlements (1993), 63rd Annual Report 1992/93, Basle, June.

Bank for International Settlements (1994a), 64th Annual Report 1993/94, Basle, June.

Bank for International Settlements (1994b), *Public disclosure of market and credit risks by financial intermediaries.* Discussion paper prepared by a Working Group of the Euro-currency Standing Committee of the Central Banks of the Group of Ten countries, Basle, September.

Bank for International Settlements (1994c), *Measurement of market size and macroprudential risks in derivatives markets.* Report prepared by a Working Group of the Euro-currency Standing Committee of the Central Banks of the Group of Ten countries, Basle, November.

BARCA, F. (1993), "Allocazione e riallocazione della proprietà e del controllo delle imprese: ostacoli, intermediari, regole". *Temi di discussione*, no. 194, Banca d'Italia.

Basle Committee on Banking Supervision (1983), Principles for the supervision of banks' foreign establishment. Basle, May.

Basle Committee on Banking Supervision (1988), International convergence of capital measurement and capital standard. Basle, July.

Basle Committee on Banking Supervision (1991), *Measuring and controlling large credit exposure.* Basle, January.

Basle Committee on Banking Supervision (1992), Minimum standards for the supervision of international banking groups and their cross-border establishments. Basle, July.

Basle Committee on Banking Supervision (1993), *The supervisory treatment of market risks.* Basle, April.

Basle Committee on Banking Supervision (1994), Basle Capital Accord: the treatment of the credit risk associated with certain off-balance-sheet items. Basle, July.

BAUMOL, W.J., J. PANZAR and R. WILLIG (1982), *Contestable markets and the theory of industry structure.* New York: Harcourt Brace Jovanovich.

BAUMOL, W.J. and R.D. WILLIG (1986), "Contestability: developments since the book". *Oxford Economic Papers*, Oxford, vol. 38, pp. 9-36.

BISIGNANO, J.R. (1992), "Banking competition, regulation and the philosophy of financial development", in Fingleton, (ed.), *The internationalisation of capital markets and the regulatory response.* London: Graham & Trotman.

BISIGNANO, J.R. (1993), "The ownership and control linkages between banking and industry: some theoretical issues, history, and policy concerns", paper presented at the Conference on Banking and Industry, organised by the University of Brescia, Italy, December 1992.

BLACK, F., M.H. MILLER and R.A. POSNER (1978), "An approach to the regulation of bank holding companies". *Journal of Business,* Chicago, 51(3), pp. 379-412.

BOCKELMANN, H. and C.E.V. BORIO (1990), "Financial instability and the real economy", *De Economist,* Leiden, 138 (4), pp. 428-450.

BORIO, C.E.V. (1990a), "Leverage and financing of non-financial companies: an international perspective". *BIS Economic Paper,* no. 27, Basle, May.

BORIO, C.E.V. (1990b), "Banks' involvement in highly leveraged transactions". *BIS Economic Paper,* no. 28, Basle, October.

BORIO, C.E.V. and P. VAN DEN BERGH (1993), "The nature and management of payment system risks: an international perspective". *BIS Economic Paper,* no. 36, Basle, February.

BRIOSCHI, F., L. BUZZACCHI and M.G. COLOMBO (1990), *Gruppi di imprese e mercato finanziario.* Roma: La Nuova Italia Scientifica.

BRÖKER, G. (1989), *Competition in banking.* Paris: OECD.

BRYAN, L.L. (1991), Bankrupt: restoring the health and profitability of our banking system. New York: Harper Business.

CAREY, M., S. PROWSE, J. REA and G. UDELL (1993), "The economics of the private placement market". *Staff Study,* no. 166, Board of Governors of the Federal Reserve System, Washington, D.C.

CEA (1993), "Financial conglomerates", *CEA Info,* special issue no. 1, Comité Européen des Assurances, Paris, July.

CHERNOW, R. (1990), *The house of Morgan.* London: Simon and Schuster.

CIOCCA, P. (1991), *Banca, finanza, mercato.* Torino: Einaudi.

COASE, R. (1937), "The nature of the firm". *Economica,* vol. 4, pp. 386-405. Reprinted in *Readings in Price Theory,* vol. VI, G. STIGLER and K. BOULDING, (eds.), Homewood, Ill.: Irwin, 1952.

CONIGLIANI, C., R. DE BONIS, G. MOTTA and G. PARIGI (1991), "Economie di scala e di diversificazione nel sistema bancario italiano". *Temi di discussione*, no. 150, Banca d'Italia.

CORRIGAN, E.G. (1987), "Financial market structure: a longer view". *Annual Report 1986*, Federal Reserve Bank of New York.

CORRIGAN, E.G. (1990), "The separation of banking and commerce", statement before U.S. Senate Committee on Banking, Housing and Urban Affairs, 3rd May.

COSSUTTA, D., M.L. DI BATTISTA, and C. GIANNINI, G. URGA (1988), "Processo produttivo e struttura dei costi nell'industria bancaria italiana", in Cesarini, F. [*et al.*] (eds.), *Banca e mercato*. Bologna: Il Mulino.

DAVIS, E.P. (1988), "Financial market activity of life insurance companies and pension funds". *BIS Economic Paper*, no. 21, Basle, January.

DEWATRIPONT and G. TIROLE (1994), "The prudential regulation of banks", mimeo.

DIAMOND, D.W. (1984), "Financial intermediation and delegated monitoring". *Review of Economic Studies*, Clevedon, July, pp. 393-414.

DIAMOND, D.W. and P. DYBVIG (1983), "Bank runs, deposit insurance, and liquidity". *Journal of Political Economy*, Chicago, vol. 91, pp. 401-419.

DIETSCH, M. (1990), "Return to scale and return to scope in French banking industry", *Working Paper*, Centre d'Etudes des Politiques Financières de Strasbourg.

European Commission (1973), Council Directive on the coordination of laws, regulations and administrative provisions relating to the taking-up and pursuit of the business of direct insurance other than life assurance, 73/239/ EEC, 24th July.

European Commission (1979), Council Directive on the coordination of laws, regulations and administrative provisions relating to the taking-up and pursuit of the business of direct life assurance, 79/267/EEC, 5th March.

European Commission (1989), Council Directive on a solvency ratio for credit institutions, 89/647/EEC, 18th December.

European Commission (1992), Council Directive amending Directive 89/299/EEC on the credit institution's own funds, 92/16/EEC, 16th March.

European Commission (1992), Council Directive on the supervision of credit institutions on a consolidated basis, 92/30/EEC, 6th April.

European Commission (1992), Council Directive on the monitoring and control of large exposures of credit institutions, 92/121/EEC, 21st December.

European Commission (1993), Council Directive on the capital adequacy of investments firms and credit institutions, 93/6/EEC, 15th March.

European Commission (1993), Council Directive on investment services in the securities field, 93/22/EEC, 10th May.

FAMA, E.F. (1980), "Agency problems and the theory of the firm". *Journal of Political Economy,* Chicago, vol. 88, pp. 288-307.

FORESTIERI, G. (1993), "Economies of scale and scope in the financial services industry: a review of recent literature" in OECD (ed.), *Financial conglomerates.* Paris: OECD.

GERSCHENKRON, A. (1962), *Economic backwardness in historical perspective: a book of essays.* Cambridge, Mass.: Harvard University Press.

GERTLER, M. (1988), "Financial structure and aggregate economic activity, an overview". *Journal of Money, Credit and Banking,* Columbus, Ohio, August, pp. 559-588.

GILLE, B. (1973), "Banking and industrialisation in Europe, 1730-1914", in Carlo M. Cipolla, (ed.), *The Fontana economic history of Europe,* vol. 3. Glasgow: Collins/Fontana Books.

GOODHART, C. (1987), "Why do banks need a central bank?". *Oxford Economic Papers,* Oxford, vol. 39 (1), pp. 75-89.

GOTO, A. (1982), "Business groups in a market economy". *European Economic Review,* Brussels, vol. 19, pp. 53-70.

GROSSMAN, S.J. and O.D. HART (1980), "Takeover bids, the free-rider problem and the theory of the corporation". *Bell Journal of Economics*, Washington, vol. 11, pp. 42-64.

GROSSMAN, S.J. and O.D. HART (1986), "The costs and benefits of ownership: a theory of vertical and lateral integration". *Journal of Political Economy*, Chicago, vol. 94, pp. 691-719.

HART, O.D. and B. HOLMSTRÖM (1988), "The theory of contracts", in Truman Bewley, (ed.), *Advances in economic theory*. Cambridge: Cambridge University Press.

HELLWIG, M. (1991), "Banking, financial intermediation and corporate finance", in A. Giovannini, and C. Mayer, (eds.), *European financial integration*. Cambridge: Cambridge University Press.

HERRING, R.J. and A.M. SANTOMERO (1990), "The corporate structure of financial conglomerates". *Journal of Financial Services Research*, Dordrecht. vol. 4, pp. 471-497.

HOSHI, T., A. KASHYAP and D. SCHARFSTEIN (1990), "The role of banks in reducing the costs of financial distress in Japan". *Journal of Financial Economics*, Lausanne, September, pp. 67-88.

KASUYA, M. (1986), "Economies of scope: theory and application to banking" in *Monetary and Economic Studies*, Bank of Japan, pp. 59-104.

KOGUCHI K. (1993), "Financial conglomeration" in OECD (ed.), *Financial Conglomerates*. Paris: OECD.

KREPS, D.M. (1990), *A course in microeconomic theory*. Princeton: Princeton University Press.

KRÜMMEL, H.J. (1980), "German universal banking scrutinized". *Journal of Banking and Finance*, Amsterdam, vol. 4, pp. 33-54.

LAMFALUSSY, A. (1992), "The restructuring of the financial industry: a central banking perspective". *SUERF Papers on Monetary Policy and Financial Systems*, no. 12, Tilburg.

MACNEIL, I.R. (1978), "Contracts: adjustment of long-term economic relations under classical, neoclassical, and relational contract law". *Northwestern University Law Review*, Chicago, vol. 72, pp. 854-905.

MANKIW, N.G. (1988), "New issues in corporate finance: comments". *European Economic Review*, Amsterdam, vol. 32, pp. 1183-1186.

MASERA, R. (1991), Intermediari, mercati e finanza d'impresa. Bari: Laterza.

MAYER, C. (1988), "New issues in corporate finance". *European Economic Review*, Amsterdam, vol. 32, pp. 1167-1183.

Monopolkommission (1979), "Grundsatzfragen der Kreditwirtschaft" (Gessler Report). *Schriftenreihe des Bundesministeriums der Finanzen*, Bd. 28, Mai.

OECD (1991), Systemic risks in securities markets, Paris.

OECD (1992a), *Banks under stress*, Paris.

OECD (1992b), Insurance and other financial services: structural trends, Paris.

PECCHIOLI, R. (1991), "Policies towards financial markets" in J. Llewellyn and S.J. Potter (eds.), *Economic policies for the 1990s*. Oxford: Blackwell.

PEPE, R. (1986), "Riflessioni e confronti in tema di separatezza tra banca e industria", *Temi di discussione*, no. 76, Banca d'Italia, October.

PIERCE, J.L. (1991), *The future of banking*. New Haven: Yale University Press.

PORTA et al. (1990), "The separation of finance and industry: a comparative analysis", in Angelo Porta, (ed.), *The separation of industry and finance and the specialization of financial institutions*. Milano: E.G.E.A., pp. 205-249.

PROWSE, S. (1994), "Corporate governance in international perspective: a survey of corporate control mechanisms among large firms in the United States, the United Kingdom, Japan and Germany". *BIS Economic Paper*, no. 41, Basle, July.

RAVENSCRAFT, D.J. (1987), "The 1980s merger wave: an industrial organisation perspective", in L.E. Browne and E.S. Rosengren, (eds.), *The merger boom*. Boston: Federal Reserve Bank of Boston (Conference series no. 31).

SALOMON BROTHERS (1990), "Multinational money center banking: the evolution of a single European banking market", New York, September.

SAUNDERS, A. (1990), "The separation of banking and commerce and the shifting frontier between banking and nonbank financial services in the United States", in Angelo Porta, (ed.), *The separation of industry and finance and the specialization of financial institutions*. Milano: *E.G.E.A.*, pp. 107-162.

SAUNDERS, A. (1991), "The separation of banking and commerce: a finance perspective". Paper presented at the Fourth Annual Australasian Finance and Banking Conference, The University of New South Wales, School of Banking and Finance, Sydney, Australia, *Working Paper*, no. 42, 28th-29th November.

SCHUMPETER, J.A. (1939), *Business cycles*. New York: McGraw-Hill Book Co.

SCHWARTZ, M. (1986), "The nature and scope of contestability theory". *Oxford Economic Papers*, Oxford, vol. 38, pp. 37-57.

SHAFFER, S. and E. DAVID (1991), "Economies of superscale in commercial banking". *Applied Economics*, London, vol. 23, pp. 283-293.

STEINHERR, A. and C. HUVENEERS (1990), "Universal banking: a view inspired by the German experience", in Angelo Porta, (ed.), *The separation of industry and finance and the specialization of financial institutions*. Milano: *E.G.E.A.*, pp. 37-78.

STIGLITZ, J.E. (1985), "Credit markets and the control of capital". *Journal of Money, Credit, and Banking*, Columbus, Ohio, vol. 17 (2), pp. 133-152.

TAKEDA, M. and P. TURNER (1992), "The liberalisation of Japan's financial markets: some major themes". *BIS Economic Paper*, no. 34, Basle, November.

TERRAHE, J. (1989), "Das traditionelle Hausbankprinzip hat sich in den letzen Jahren zugunsten des Deal-Based Banking gelockert", *Handelsblatt*, 6th April.

The Economist (1990), "Pieces on the board: a survey of European insurance", 24th February.

The Economist (1992), "Japanese insurance: change in the air", 5th December, pp. 83-84.

TILLY, R. (1990), "La banca universale in una prospettiva storica: l'esperienza tedesca". *Banca, Impresa, Società*, Bologna, vol. 9, pp. 3-21.

TIROLE, J. (1988), *The theory of industrial organisation.* Cambridge: MIT Press.

TRENTO, S. (1993), "Il gruppo di imprese come modello di controllo nei paesi ritardatari". *Temi di discussione*, no. 196, Banca d'Italia.

VINER, J. (1932), "Cost curves and supply curves", *Zeitschrift für Nationalökonomie,* vol. 3, pp. 23-46. Reprinted in *Readings in Price Theory*, vol. VI, G. Stigler and K. Boulding, (eds.). Homewood, Ill.: Irwin, 1952.

WHITE, M.J. (1989), "The corporate bankruptcy decision". *The Journal of Economic Perspective*, Nashville, vol. 3, pp. 129-151.

WILLIAMSON, O. (1985), *The economic institutions of capitalism.* New York: Free Press.

YOSHIOKA, K. and T. NAKAJIMA (1987), "Economies of scale in Japan's banking industry". *Monetary and Economic Studies*, Bank of Japan, September, pp. 35-70.

Chapter 3

BANKING INDUSTRY PERFORMANCE IN EUROPE:
TRENDS AND ISSUES*

Jukka Vesala, Bank of Finland

Introduction

Banks' profitability, even disregarding credit losses, has shrank in most European countries since the mid 1980s. Only the Mediterranean countries represent notable exceptions to this trend. The fall in the underlying profitability has been primarily due to a squeeze in banks' intermediation margins. Hence, one could conclude that the degree of interest rate (or price) competition has increased. While the fall in banks' intermediation margins has been in most countries the most prominent change, also other significant changes in banks' income and cost structures can be distinguished that have had a major impact on banks' performance. Three major underlying forces can be identified behind these developments. Namely, financial liberalization and banking deregulation, internationalization of banks and European financial integration, and finally, rapid technological change.

Deregulation of bank conduct, foremost legal controls on loan and deposit rates and service charges, which was effected in most European countries during the 1980s, has enabled banks to compete effectively in rates and charges instead of using the quality of services produced as the only distinguishing parameter. In addition, a rapid emergence of non-bank rivals after financial liberalization has put strong competitive pressures on banks with the effect of narrowing margins on various financial products. Deepening financial integration and creation of the Single Banking Market in Europe has received a lot of attention

---

*   Paper prepared for the OECD Financial Experts' Meeting, Paris, July 11-12, 1994. The views expressed herein are those of the author and not necessarily those of the Bank of Finland. The author would like to thank Heikki Koskenkylä, Juha Tarkka, Vesa Vihriälä and Jouko Vilmunen, all from the Bank of Finland, for helpul comments and suggestions.

in the literature. However, its impact on competition seems to be overestimated in many cases as foreign penetration in retail banking is still relatively modest and many non-legal barriers to entry seem to be effective in retail banking. Moreover, the banking markets for large enterprises are already significantly competitive as these clients have access to capital markets and international finance, which limits the interest rate domestic banks can charge on them.

In contrast, the impact of the technological progress on banks' competitive conduct and performance is much more seldom commented on. The process has led to a considerable productivity growth in the production of banking services and produced indisputable labour cost savings at many instances, most importantly in payment processing. However, it seems that the new delivery technology, primarily ATMs, has been installed to an important extent due to competitive reasons to extend customer base. This strategic aspect has been largely neglected in the literature.

The goal of this paper is, firstly, to examine the effects of the above underlying forces on banks' performance and, secondly, to investigate how increasing competition and weakening profitability are affecting banks' competitive strategies. The strategies analyzed include: *(1)* pricing of services, *(2)* product range choices, *(3)* cooperative conduct, and *(4)* distribution capacity choices. Finally, we consider the repercussions of these modified strategies on banks' performance and what kind of policy issues they raise with respect to efficient competition, availability of services and stability in the banking industry. In order to meet these objectives, models and concepts taken from industrial economics are used as the primary analytical tool. As we think that the competitive aspects of the technological change have received too little attention, changes in banks' delivery methods and their impact on banks' performance and the availability of banking services are discussed quite extensively.

The paper is structured as follows. We identify first the most salient trends in the performance of the European banking industries by examining changes in banks' income and cost structures, and profitability. Chapter 2 presents a number of comparative industry-level analyses and tables for the period from 1980 to 1992, including 13 EC and EFTA countries. According to the objectives of the paper we then examine the feedback from banks' performance to conduct by studying each of the above mentioned strategy areas in turn in Chapter 3. Finally, in Chapter 4, we discuss the issues of public policy toward the banking industry raised by the changes in banks' competitive strategies. Perhaps the most fundamental policy issue is the likely policy conflict between simultaneously achieving efficient competition and stability in the financial system. We comment on this in the final chapter.

Banks can not be examined, however, in isolation, but rather as a part of the overall financial system in each country. Therefore we start by looking at the broad characteristics and major inter-country differences in the financial systems of the European countries in Chapter 1. In order to characterize the role of banks in the overall economy we present the evolution of the GDP share of banking in the countries included in this study. A simple demand analysis is used to predict the evolution of the banking sector with respect to the other sectors in the economy.

1. Financial structure and banks in the economy

1.1 European financial systems - scope and structure

The variety of financial market structure is great in industrialized countries. In every country the structure has a history of its own, and a number of country-specific institutions and features have developed. It is difficult to identify common features, because for example, different institutions may conduct the same operations in different countries, or vice versa.

In order to display some of the most salient features we constructed four indicators for the years 1980 and 1990 from the national accounts of outstanding financial assets collected by the OECD (see table 1)[1]. *(1)* The *size indicator*, defined as the amount of total financial assets outstanding[2] divided by the GDP, measures the size of the financial system and the depth of the financial markets in each country. *(2)* The *financial intermediation ratio*, the ratio of the combined assets of all financial institutions to total financial assets, gives us a measure of the degree of institutionalized intermediation in the financial process. One minus the value of this indicator measures the degree of securitization in the broadest sense (the *disintermediation-type of securitization)* by displaying the substitution of direct finance from capital markets for funds intermediated by financial institutions. *(3)* The *bank intermediation ratio* is the share of banks, including all deposit taking credit institutions, in the total assets of financial institutions. It depicts the standing of banks among financial institutions. Finally, *(4)* the *internationalization ratio* is the ratio of outstanding external assets to total financial assets, which measures the degree of international openness. Data on outstanding stocks of assets are limited.

Therefore, we are not able to provide a similar coverage as elsewhere in this paper. Figures for the USA and Japan are given for comparison.

The financial markets appear to be deepest in the United Kingdom where the financial assets outstanding at the end of 1990 were 8.5 times the value of the GDP. In Finland the corresponding figure was only 3.47, implying that the differences in the relative sizes of the financial systems are quite considerable. Substantial deepening of the financial markets appears to have taken place in all the countries depicted over the 1980s. Hence, financial liberalization and the financial innovation process, which has introduced, for example, a number of new financial instruments has led to a significant volume expansion in financial markets. Goldsmith (1985) presents indicators of the development of the financial systems in certain industrialized countries over a long period of time, starting from the 1910s. With respect to GDP, the dimensions of the financial markets were quite stable until the 1980s in countries that were already significantly industrialised at the beginning of this century, *i.e.* in the USA and the United Kingdom, and possibly also Germany. Against this background, the indicated development during the 1980s is remarkable.

Apart from deepening of the financial markets, other apparent trends can not be observed based on our structural indicators. We can not observe an universal increase in the degree of disintermediation or a fall in the stance of banks during the 1980s. However, significant shifts in this direction have taken place in France, Italy and the USA. Fairly stable internationalization ratios, apart from Japan, indicate that international assets have generally increased in step with overall financial assets.

The development stage of a financial system is usually defined to depend on the depth of the financial markets, but also on its structural features (see Mooslechner 1994). A financial system can be regarded as more developed if it has, in addition to sheer size, a large share of direct finance from capital markets, indicated by a low value of the financial intermediation ratio, and high degree of international openness. Taking into account all these measures, the United Kingdom has the most developed financial system. The importance of the capital markets and the degree of internationalization are the greatest in the United Kingdom among the European countries depicted. The USA and Japan have deep financial markets, but their financial systems have remained relatively closed. The financial systems of Germany and Finland are characterized by strongly bank-based intermediation and relatively thin financial markets as well as a small relative amount of direct finance. France has traditionally had also bank-centred intermediation and a large share of institutionalized intermediation, but in contrast, a high ranking with respect to the size of the financial system. Hence, a clear connection between bank dominance and slow expansion of the financial markets, as sometimes argued, cannot be observed.

Bank dominance has traditionally been one of the central features that distinguishes, in broad terms, countries in continental Europe from the United Kingdom and USA, (which is apparent also in table 1). Large amount of government ownership and close bank-corporate relationships have been additional significant distinguishing features. A wave of privatisations has, however, been taking place in continental Europe, most distinctly in France. In the Anglo-Saxon model of corporate relationships the control over corporate clients is exercised by default of old loans or extension of new credit. Otherwise the relationships between the banks and the corporate clients are quite distant. In the so-called German-Japanese model banks have close relations with their corporate clients, often an equity stake and ability to directly influence managerial decisions. Bank ownership and participation in non-financial firms has been widespread, especially in Germany, and also in the Netherlands, France, and Spain. Government ownership, privatisation trends and the nature of corporate relations have important implications for competition and efficiency considerations in the banking industry as well as in the overall functioning of the financial intermediation process. These issues are, however, beyond the scope of this paper (see *e.g.* Mayer 1990, Bisigano 1992 and Benston 1993 for thorough discussions).

1.2 Banks and the economy

The importance of the banking sector in an economy is usually measured by its contribution to the GDP. Measuring the social value of the banking services in this way is somewhat ambiguous, since the GDP share of the banking services does not characterize the true importance of financial intermediation and production of the payment services for the other economic sectors (see *e.g.* Baltensberger and Dermine 1987 and Santomero 1984). Moreover, banking services do not generate direct consumer satisfaction like consumption goods. Hence, a growing share of the banking services in the GDP does not necessarily reflect increasing welfare, but possibly the contrary. A high share may be due to extensive services provided to domestic and foreign customers or to high prices and inefficient production of banking services.

We calculated the contribution of banking services to the GDP by using the imputed bank service charges obtained from the national accounts collected by the OECD as the measure of the net value added in the banking sector (see table 2). The imputed bank service charge equals the excess interest and property income accruing to banks, and similar credit institutions, over the interest accruing to depositors. Direct service charges are excluded. Hence, the measure concerns the production of traditional financial intermediation services[3] that generate net interest income and that of payment and ancillary services that are paid indirectly in the interest margin. Nevertheless, payment and ancillary services are traditionally priced to a large extent within banks' intermediation margins. This cross-subsidization issue is discussed more in detail in section 3.1.1.

To correct the bias caused by the inclusion of Central Banks among the banking (monetary) institutions in the OECD statistics, we deducted the amount of seigniorage revenues from the banking sectors' GDP share. Seigniorage revenues have traditionally been significant in the Mediterranean countries, Italy, Portugal and Spain, and also in Germany, as compared with the other European countries. We used the *opportunity cost or stock measure of seigniorage*, which measures the savings in interest payments obtained by the monetary authority by being able to issue a zero interest rate bond, money[4] (see *e.g.* Gros 1993).

We see that the banking output has a high share in the GDP in the United Kingdom, and especially Luxembourg, which both represent important international financial centres. The ranking of the United Kingdom would, however, be substantially higher if the whole financial sector was considered (see *e.g.* Steinherr and Gilibert 1989). The rapid increase in the banking and other similar credit institutions sectors' GDP share in the Mediterranean countries, especially Spain and Portugal, to well above the average European level suggests that these countries have turned "overbanked" with low efficiency and banking services have become "overpriced". In these countries banks intermediation margins are high by European standards which supports the "overpricing" hypothesis (see next chapter).

In the case of Italy and Portugal the rise in banks' GDP share reflects in part a significant decrease in seigniorage revenues. A clear increase in the GDP share has also taken place in Finland and Sweden, but it has still remained below the European average in both countries. In Northern EC states, Belgium, Netherlands, and Germany as well as in Ireland, the contribution of banking services in the GDP has decreased since the mid 1980s. However, the relative stability of the GDP share of banking output, apart from the Mediterranean countries (and Luxembourg), implies that the technological improvements have significantly lifted productivity in banking as the volumes of the services produced increased very rapidly during the 1980s. Especially payment transaction volumes have grown very fast[5]. This indicates that the effective prices of the banking services have fallen quite substantially, thereby producing significant welfare gains.

Is banking in Europe a growth industry or is it in decline? This is a fundamental question in regard to the future outlook for the industry. In order to try to partially answer this question, we estimated cross-sectional demand equations for the banking services that generate net interest income for the years 1981, 1985 and 1991, using European cross-country data. The primary aim was to investigate the changes in the income elasticity of demand, and contemplate whether banks are expected to face relatively increasing or decreasing demand for financial intermediation services as economic growth proceeds. The estimation technique and results are presented in Box 1.

In our sample, the estimate of the income elasticity of demand displays a remarkable change over the three periods studied. It decreased from a value clearly over one in 1981 down to a value significantly below one in 1991. In 1985 income levels did not have a significant effect on the GDP shares of the banking services, and hence the estimated income elasticity was close to unity. This represents a trend-like deterioration of the demand for net interest income generating services with respect to economic growth. The below one estimate for 1991 indicates that these services are no longer "luxury goods", and hence have a decreasing share of gross expenditures, which is in sharp contrast to the situation in the early 1980s. In this sense traditional banking no longer seems to represent a growth industry (see attached figure 1).

The prediction is then that banks will have to adjust to smaller demand growth in their traditional operations than that in the other sectors of the economy. This would put pressure on their performance, tighten the competitive situation, and accentuate the importance of efficient operations. Furthermore, the adverse trend in demand is likely to foster the structural change from the production of traditional financial intermediation services toward off-balance sheet activities, securities trading and other areas that offer better growth prospects.

In general, the observed negative trend in the share of banking services in GDP as income levels grow implies growing efficiency in the production of banking services, potentially enhanced by increasing competitive pressures, and thus socially desirable development. As the sample size is small, individual observations may affect the results strongly, *e.g.* the significant rise in the GDP share in Portugal and Spain. Careful interpretation of the results is thus in place.

The price elasticity estimates vary around unity, and hence correspond the similar low values typically obtained in industry-level studies. Low price elasticity implies that banks may have opportunities to exercise collusive conduct and restrict price competition in response to squeezing profitability as the demand for banking services is relatively immobile. Banks' strategic response to the more intense competition is discussed in more detail in section 3.1.4.

Box 1. Demand for banking services: a cross-country analysis

The equation given below was estimated for the years 1981, 1985 and 1991 using data from the 13 European countries depicted in table 2. The obvious outlier, Luxembourg, was deleted from the sample.

$$\ln(\frac{B}{GDP})_i = \alpha_0 + \alpha_1\ln(\frac{GDP}{POP})_i + \alpha_2\ln(\frac{NI}{ATA})_i + \varepsilon_i, \quad i = 1,...,13,$$

where B is our measure of net value added in the banking sector (imputed service charge minus seigniorage), POP population, NI the net interest income of banks, and ATA the average total of banks' balance sheets. The income elasticity, e_1, is defined as $d\ln(B/POP) / d\ln(GDP/POP)$, and thus equals $1+a_1$. $a_2 = d\ln(B) / d\ln(NI/ATA)$ equals 1 minus the absolute value of the price elasticity of demand, e_n, since B can be written as (NI/ATA * Q), where Q represents the volume of banking services. The estimates of the demand intercept and the income and price elasticities are the following: (t-values are given in parentheses)

	1981	1985	1991
a_0	-4.36	-2.48	-1.24
	(-4.23)	(-1.38)	(-2.27)
e_1	1.24	1.08	0.58
	(1.94)	(0.37)	(2.19)
e_n	0.97	1.34	0.60
	(0.11)	(0.70)	(1.89)
R^2	0.33	0.06	0.72

Number of observations

	13	13	13

Data sources: OECD National Accounts 1979-1991; OECD Bank Profitability Statistics

2. Banking industry performance 1980-1992

In this chapter we assess recent trends in margins, costs and profits in European banking industries from 1980 to 1992, and examine the regulatory and macroeconomic aspects as causative factors behind the developments. Banks' aggregate income statement and balance sheet data are obtained from the OECD Bank Profitability Statistics. The aim is to incorporate all deposit taking credit institutions operating in a country into the analyses in order to characterize the performance of the entire industries. This is accomplished to a satisfactory extent in all cases except the United Kingdom as building societies are excluded. The figures for the country groups EC-6 and Scandinavia, presented in comparative tables 3 - 6, are obtained by summing together the respective country-specific accounting information, after conversion into ECUs. In order to highlight the long term trends only average values for the years 1980-1984, 1985-1989, and 1990-1992 are reported.

For purposes of comparison, banks' income, costs and profits must be expressed as ratios to a certain indicator of the volume of banks' business, or in economic terms, service production. The most commonly employed volume indicator is the Balance Sheet Total (BST), but its use causes systematic bias in international comparisons, as banks' business mixes vary significantly across countries. These differences are apparent in the diverging asset structures of banks in different European countries (see table 3). For example the share of interbank assets varies from around 40 per cent in France and Belgium down to 6 per cent in Finland and Norway. Interbank assets generate little revenue compared to other higher-yield asset categories and do not represent financial intermediation carried out by banks. To correct this bias we constructed an alternative volume indicator, Funds Committed to Non-Financial Entities (FCNFE) by subtracting from the BST the amount of outstanding interbank assets and assets held with Central Banks (see de Boissieu 1993)[6]. Although the ratios to the FCNFE are preferable from the analytical standpoint, all ratios are also given in terms of the BST to facilitate comparisons with other studies and data sources. However, various additional country and industry-specific factors affect the composition of banks assets and liabilities, as well as income and cost structure. Therefore, caution should be exercised when making international comparisons.

2.1 Narrowing margins after deregulation

Comparing banks' *intermediation margins*, defined as the ratio of banks net interest income to FCNFE or BST, reveals considerable variation across countries (see tables 4a and b). The use of FCNFE produces somewhat different results than that of the traditional BST, most notably by elevating the ranking of the French banking industry with respect to the width of the intermediation margin. Banks' intermediation margins have been very wide by European standards in the Mediterranean countries, while in Finland and Switzerland they have been atypically narrow.

In most European countries banks were subject to extensive regulations on their lending and borrowing rates and direct service charges, in some cases until the late 1980s (see Box 2). Only in Germany have all banks, and in the United Kingdom commercial (authorized) banks, been traditionally free of these regulations. In the Netherlands, the restrictions on banks' competitive behaviour were largely confined to fees and commissions. According to Gual and Neven (1992), however, in Germany and the Netherlands regulators had a fairly relaxed attitude towards agreements and informal cooperation between banks.

The regulations on rates and fees forced banks to suspend explicit pricing of payment and ancillary services, and push competition into various forms of implicit interest payments. Banks' overall balance was achieved by covering the cost of the payment and ancillary service production from the ample intermediation margin. This denoted extensive cross-subsidization between various types of operations which is reflected in a typically low ratio of banks' net non-interest income to their net interest income.

Abolition of the interest rate and service charge regulations in most countries during the 1980s seems to have significantly narrowed banks' intermediation margins. The most important reduction has taken place in France. Only in Italy, Portugal and Denmark were the average intermediation margins wider in 1990-1992 than in the earlier periods. Cutbacks in intermediation margins constitute evidence in favour of so-called *regulatory capture* (see Neven 1993) whereby regulation shields banks' margins above the level that would prevail in effective price competition. On the other hand, persistence of old margins in the liberalized environment would suggest that banks' have been able to replace public protection by private collusive arrangements limiting the degree of price competition. The reduction in intermediation margins in most countries indicates that the degree of price competition has actually increased. Nevertheless, after the significant wave of deregulation in the 1980s, sizable interest margins on demand and savings deposits continue to exist as compared to money market rates[7] and demand deposit rates are typically very low. Furthermore, while banks have commonly started to raise direct service charges, their share in net banking income has usually not become dominant. These imply that significant degree of cross-subsidization still prevails.

However, considerable differences in banks' income composition characterize the whole period of study. Most distinctly, banks in Finland and Switzerland have generated a substantial share of their income from non-interest sources. In Denmark banks have made relatively large investments in securities, and must have reported their capital gains as non-interest income, which has therefore become highly variable over time. In order to correct the distortions induced by varying degrees of cross-subsidization and diverging income structures, tables 4a and b present the *overall gross margins* specified as the ratio of the net banking income to either of the volume indicators. In fact, one should pay more attention to the changes in banks' income side in general which take into account the country-specific differences and changes in income composition.

While banks' net non-interest income has risen relative to net interest income in most countries during the period of study, most significantly in France and Sweden, the rise has not generally been strong enough with respect to asset growth to offset the fall in intermediation margins. A downward trend therefore tends to characterize the evolution of banks' overall gross margins. In France, banks have had to face the most substantial narrowing. The Mediterranean countries are notable exceptions to this trend. As a result, the overall margins have been considerably wider in the Mediterranean countries than elsewhere during the late 1980s and early 1990s. Sweden and Switzerland represent another exceptions due to significant growth in relative non-interest income. Although showing a downward trend, banks' overall margins have been relatively large also in the United Kingdom. At the beginning of the 1990s banks' overall margins were quite narrow by European standards in Belgium, Germany and the Netherlands, and in Finland relative to the other Scandinavian countries.

Box 2.   An overview of the banking deregulation in Europe during the 1980s

Banking deregulation in the EC area began in the late 1970s. EC legislation, primarily since the White Paper of 1985 "Completing the Internal Market", has significantly contributed to this process by triggering changes in national regulations, also in the EFTA states. Firstly, regulations on banks' competitive conduct have been relaxed and largely eliminated; this has had significant behaviourial effects on the respective banking industries by enhancing price

---

competition. These *conduct regulations* include controls on banks' deposit and lending rates, fees and commissions, as well as direct credit quotas and branching limitations. Secondly, deregulation of the *structural rules* imposing functional separation of financial institutions has generally led to the adoption of the universal banking model as set up by the Second Banking Directive. Structural regulations also encompass discriminatory rules against foreign institutions and prohibitive entry restrictions toward non-bank institutions. When banking deregulation is referred to it has generally meant the abolition of the above restrictions on structure and conduct. Correspondingly, the review below pertains to these regulations. In contrast, international harmonization of the *prudential regulations*, most importantly the BIS and EC capital standards, represents strengthening of the prudential banking regulation. The review below summarises the information presented in Vesala (1993a, chapter 2). The most important primary sources of information are Gual and Neven (1992, Annex 2); BIS, Payment Systems in Eleven Developed Countries (various issues); Committee of Governors of the Central Banks of the member States of the EC, Payment Systems in EC Member States (September 1992); and various publications of European Central Banks and country-specific surveys.

Banking deregulation in the 1980s has significantly affected all countries except Germany, the Netherlands, Switzerland, and the United Kingdom where the banking industry has traditionally been only slightly regulated compared with other European countries. Furthermore, the abolition of all capital movement and exchange controls has advanced banks international businesses, increased foreign currency denominated intermediation and promoted integration of financial markets in Europe.

Spain, France and Italy had strongly regulated banking markets at the beginning of the 1980s with stringent structural and conduct regulations. Rates and service fees were regulated and there were direct regulations on banks' assets and liabilities. Spain and Italy adhered to functional separations and stringent entry requirements, while France had somewhat less restrictive structural rules. Of the three countries Spain experienced the swiftest deregulatory process, principally in the late 1980s. It demolished most conduct rules, *e.g.* rate regulations and credit quotas, and market entry as well as the introduction of new banking products were rapidly eased. France relaxed all structural rules and also significantly conduct regulations, most importantly, all existing controls on credit volumes and time deposit rates in 1986. However, explicit controls on demand deposit rates still remain. Italy has been slowest to deregulate; some structural regulations are still in force and conduct rules, for example quantitative ceilings on bank loans, albeit principally cancelled, have been temporarily restored. Restrictive branching regulations have been in force in Spain and Italy; they were lifted in both countries during the latter half of the 1980s, and ultimately in 1990. (See Gual and Neven 1992 for more details).

Major structural and conduct restrictions that were mainly imposed on the activities of the building societies were lifted in the United Kingdom during the latter half of the 1980s, for example restrictions on societies' product range in 1986 and on wholesale borrowing in 1988. The operations of the commercial (authorized) banks have been largely unregulated. However, a major change, the "Big Bang", took place in 1986 when all authorized banks, both domestic and foreign were allowed to participate freely in the securities business. The Netherlands and Germany were already significantly unregulated at the beginning of the 1980s. Belgium has lifted almost all structural restrictions, but slightly strengthened the conduct rules, for example a maximum interest is set for savings accounts and legal provisions for imposing credit ceilings are still in place. (See Gual and Neven 1992).

In Denmark most of the financial markets' controls, for example credit quotas, were lifted at the beginning of the 1980s; somewhat earlier than in other Scandinavian countries. Denmark did not have much explicit rate regulations even prior to the 1980s. In Finland, Norway and Sweden a large number of restrictive measures were rapidly removed in a few years around 1985, with Sweden being a few steps ahead of the other two countries. Stringent controls on bank lending were exercised via both rate regulations and quantitative controls in Norway and Sweden, while in Finland the former regulations were dominant. As a result, banks were allowed to price their new credits freely, and the use of money market based reference rates was extended. Deregulation has also involved controls on deposit rates, which have taken different forms in the three countries. In Finland implicit controls still pertain to deposit rates through taxation. At the onset of the 1990s all major structural regulations, particularly on the establishment of foreign institutions in the domestic market, have been eliminated in the three countries.

The growth in the share of non-interest income reflects also a general propensity to convert balance sheet assets into off-balance sheet items, and hence a trend toward fee-oriented banking. Judging by the income structures this process, called *off-balance sheet securitization*, has advanced at quite dissimilar speeds in various countries. The more general *disintermediation-type securitization* is apparent as an increase in the share of securities in banks assets in a number of countries. This is because when banks underwrite securities, *e.g.* commercial paper programmes, they may have to purchase some of these securities in their own portfolios.

In order to facilitate credit expansion banks have generally been forced to seek supplementary sources of funds in addition to the traditional deposit funding. The share of non-bank deposits in banks' liabilities has decreased in all countries during the observation period, except in Belgium (see table 3). The most substantial shifts have taken place in Finland, Norway and Sweden, where the growth of banks' assets has also been greatest. The shift from deposits toward purchased funds has had the additional effect of narrowing banks' intermediation margins.

Finally, the level and structure of interest rates has a significant influence on banks' intermediation margins and profitability. In the 1980s the interest rates declined gradually in most countries until 1988 in association with a disinflation process (see table 7). This seems to have, together with increasing price competition, imposed a squeeze on banks' intermediation margins in most countries. Hence, *a positive repricing gap* between banks' assets and liabilities, whereby the average yield on loans rises more than the average cost on deposits increases (because of interest rate ceilings on deposits) when the market interest rates rise, appears to have been prevalent in European banking. In the early 1980s intermediation margins were wider in most European countries than in Germany, the Netherlands and Switzerland, where inflation and market interest rates were significantly lower than elsewhere. Hence, an *inflation rent* was accruing to banks in these other countries, possibly excluding Finland and Sweden, in addition to the rent resulting from direct regulatory protection in the early 1980s. (See also Neven 1993 and de Boissieu 1993)

In the late 1980s and early 1990s market rates started to climb, and in some countries banks' interest margins indeed increased to some extent, suggesting the persistence of a positive repricing gap, although the margins remained in general at a significantly lower level than in the early 1980s. In Finland, Norway, and Sweden banks have faced a massive rise in credit losses and in the amount of non-performing loans in the early 1990s, which has affected their intermediation margins. In these countries, by contrast, a fall in interest rates as experienced since the end of 1992 will probably enhance banks interest income through reductions in credit losses and non-performing loans, which would result in a widening of banks' intermediation margin.

2.2 *Relative share of staff expenses in decline*

Technological change and reorganization of the production and delivery of banking services by *e.g.* ATMs and payment system developments is reflected in the notable fall in the ratio of staff expenses[8] to total operating expenses in all countries (see tables 5a. and b.). In the EC-6 countries combined, their share has dropped by roughly 10 per cent since 1980. In Scandinavia the respective fall has been nearly 20 per cent, and moreover, the relative importance of staff expenses has been significantly lower, indicating more substantial substitution of new banking technology for labour. In this regard, however, Denmark more closely resembles the EC-6 than the other Scandinavian countries. The smallest reduction has taken place in Italy, where the share of the staff expenses has also been highest.

The instalment of new banking technology has in most countries led to an increase in the non-staff operating expenses, but a simultaneous reduction in the staff expenses has typically produced a fall in the total operating expenses when expressed in relative terms. France and Finland display the most significant improvement. Nevertheless, in Germany, Italy and Switzerland the ratio of total operating costs to FCNFE has remained quite stagnant, and risen quite substantially in Portugal. As regards the levels, Belgium, Germany, the Netherlands and Switzerland have had very low relative operating expenses compared with the other European countries, while the Mediterranean countries and the United Kingdom have occupied the upmost end of the spectrum.

The ratio of operating expenses to the volume of business, *i.e.* the average operating cost, represents in fact a measure of banks *productive* (or operating) *efficiency*[9] by relating the costs of service production to a proxy of the production volume. The degree of productive efficiency is related to competitive pressures in the banking industry, as well as to banks' delivery capacity strategies and the use of other productive resources. These issues, and the problems with any such simple inter-country efficiency measurement, are addressed more thoroughly in the following chapter. It is interesting to note here that in countries where conduct regulations have been least stringent, *i.e.* Germany and the Netherlands, banks' productive efficiency is high by international comparison. Thus, regulation seems to protect inefficient operation, and affect banks' competitive strategies in a way that has an impact on their efficiency.

2.3 Squeezing underlying profitability

Operating margin defined as the net banking income minus total operating expenses including depreciation allowances is used here to characterize banks' underlying profitability (see table 6). Credit losses and net provisions are excluded from this measure, since "normal" or "expected" credit losses should be accounted for by appropriate risk premiums, and hence, included within banks' intermediation margins. Abnormally high loan losses, which depress banks' profits, would distort the inter-country comparisons and measurement of the profitability of banks' "regular" operations. We see that banks' operating margins have been declining in most North-European countries implying weakening underlying profitability. Comparing tables 4a - 6 reveals that the squeeze is primarily due to reductions in banks' intermediation margins. The Mediterranean countries, and Sweden and Switzerland, represent exceptions as a widening in both intermediation and operating margins is observed during the period of study.

As the total banking income of the Finnish banks has been low by inter-country comparison, the relatively high operating costs have resulted in weak underlying profitability. In Belgium and the Netherlands operating margins are depressed by the relatively low net banking income. In the case of Switzerland, the lowest relative operating costs generate a reasonable operating margin although banks' overall gross margins have been modest.

2.4 Write-offs and provisions for risk

By deducting from the operating margin the net amount of provisions made by banks we arrive at our final profitability measure, pre-tax profits. Provisions are taken to include all value adjustments with respect to loans and securities, including loan losses and transfers to and from reserves for possible losses on such assets. Even on this after loss basis, the Mediterranean countries again display the highest relative profitability (see table 6).

Among the EC countries, the recent recession in the early 1990s seems to have resulted in higher aggregate write-offs and provisions only in case of the United Kingdom and Portugal. The United Kingdom experienced the most severe recession in the early 1990s in the EC area (see table 7). The stable aggregate provisions reflect the fact that the familiar problems of certain large banks in the EC countries do not show up, apart from the above exceptions, at the industry level. Aggregate write-offs might increase in the short term if the improvement in economic conditions is not strong enough.

In contrast, in Scandinavian countries banks have experienced a vast increase in credit losses in the early 1990s, which has resulted in substantial pre-tax losses. The most dramatic increase in credit losses has taken place in Sweden, where banks aggregate write-offs amounted to nearly five per cent of the BST in 1992. The respective figure for Finland was approximately three per cent. Banks' loan losses increased distinctly in Norway in 1990 while they were still fairly moderate in Sweden and Finland, which have since overtaken Norway. In Denmark banks' write-offs have been relatively large throughout the 1980s and early 1990s. However, as they have not reached an intolerable high level with respect to the solvency of the Danish banks, an acute banking crisis as in the other three Scandinavian countries, where the Governments have been forced to grant banks substantial financial support, has not developed in Denmark.

The recession has hit Sweden, and especially Finland, much more severely than the other European countries (see table 7), but also other important factors that are by and large common to Finland, Norway and Sweden, have contributed to the growth in credit losses. Firstly, an extremely rapid credit extension took place after deregulation in the 1980s, especially into cyclically sensitive domestic service industries, facilitated by a boom in asset values in the real estate and stock market and domestic demand, and loose economic policies. Secondly, banks maintained inadequate risk premiums and collateral requirements in tight loan market share competition. Thirdly, excessive risk taking on part of banks arose due to a moral hazard -like situation when banks expected full Government back-up in bad states of the world as the financial systems in these countries are highly concentrated and bank dominated. Fourthly, rapid expansion in private-sector borrowing resulted in high debt equity ratios. Finally, a rapid fall in real estate and stock prices took place once the economic conditions started to deteriorate; they resulted in negative value adjustments at banks and caused financial difficulties for banks' customers.

2.5 Competitive pressures according to accounting information

An overall depiction, based on banks' intermediation and gross margins, is that competitive pressures vary significantly across national banking markets[10]. Profits are not a good measure of the degree of competition, since large margins due to market (monopoly) power in rate setting do not necessarily imply high profitability if they are accompanied with low productive efficiency resulting, for example, in excess staff or wages.

The overall banking rivalry appears low in the Mediterranean countries as banks' margins and also profits in spite of large relative operating costs, have been very high by European standards[11]. Moreover, banks in the Mediterranean countries seem to have been able to exercise market power and widen margins after deregulation. The most significant tightening of price competition appears to have taken place in France. Overall, competition seems to be the most intense in Germany, the Netherlands. Relatively keen competition is also indicated for Switzerland, Belgium and Finland, where banks margins have been quite narrow. In Germany, the Netherlands and Switzerland banking markets have been longest deregulated and capital controls absent, which seem to have fostered competition[12].

The degree of competition in a market is usually inferred from structural measures of concentration, for example concentration ratios or Herfindahl indices. An increase in market concentration would increase the collusive opportunities between firms and the use of market power and hence lead to higher prices and increased profitability. Although a theoretical basis for this *Structure-Conduct-Performance (SCP)* relationship exists in the multi-firm Cournot oligopoly model, or newer game theoretic oligopoly models (see *e.g.* Slade 1990 for a review), alternative theoretical considerations can undermine it. For example, the theory of contestable markets (see Baumol *et. al.* 1982) states that even monopoly can produce a socially optimal result if its behaviour is constrained by effective potential competition. Moreover, we know that price competition can be fully effective even in a duopoly, *i.e.* the Bertrand outcome.

We see from table 8 that the small banking markets of the Scandinavian countries and the Netherlands are especially concentrated. However, it turns out by relating the margins and profit figures to the concentration data that there is no apparent correlation between market concentration and any of the accounting indicators of market power in the banking markets under study. This, however, represents only casual observation. The validity of the SCP relationship has been widely tested in banking with econometric techniques. Most studies have been conducted, however, in the USA (where states have been taken to represent separate banking markets), and there are only a few European studies[13]. Still, the results from these studies are rather mixed. A positive relationship between market concentration and banks' accounting profitability or intermediation margins is not consistently detected, and in the event a positive correlation is found to exist, the estimated positive impact is usually very small. These studies are, nevertheless subject to serious empirical specification and measurement problems that weaken their results[14]. One could therefore conclude that the empirical studies have not been able to establish reliably the existence of the SCP relationship in banking.

3.   Banks' competitive strategies under change

This chapter takes a more in-depth view of changes in banks' competitive strategies in the European banking industries, making reference to studies in the field of industrial economics. This type of analysis of banking issues has been introduced by Vives (1991) and Neven (1993). They represent very clarifying analyses of the potential structural consequences on the banking industry of the deregulation and financial integration in Europe. The competitive strategies examined here include pricing of services, in particular cross-subsidization, product range choices, strategic cooperation motivated by the downward trend in underlying profitability, and finally delivery capacity adjustments. These strategies are examined in light of the three major trends affecting them, namely tightening price competition, external competitive pressures, and finally, technological development. We try to characterize the effect of these trends on banking industry performance, and ultimately offer some future prospects.

3.1 Tightening price competition

3.1.1 Diminishing degree of cross-subsidization

As discussed in the previous chapter, cross-subsidization still appears prevalent in banking, and banks have not imposed direct service charges to cover the full product-specific costs of their payment and ancillary (*e.g.* account keeping) services, although a trend toward a more extensive use of explicit charges can be observed (see also The Banker, July 1993). Banks' service charge revenues from payment services continue to be typically small compared with the large costs of these services, including branch networks and computer systems, which are estimated to account typically for roughly 50 per cent of banks' all operating expenses[15]. The exact degree of cross-subsidization of these services from the intermediation margin is hard to measure, since many banking services are jointly produced, and banks' sell their services in "product packages". It is thus very difficult to allocate (even for banks themselves) for example the cost of branches to the individual loan and deposit services produced (see Neven 1993).

Banks typically face strong customer resistance toward any direct service charges, which thwarts banks from imposing them unilaterally in the short run, but there are good economic reasons why cross-subsidization could remain to some extent as a long-run industry-wide phenomenon even in unregulated markets. Prior to the wave of deregulation some authors believed that cross-subsidies would disappear when deposit pricing was liberalized (see *e.g.* Fischer 1983, and Tarkka 1994 for a review of the literature). Two lines of explanation have been offered for the observed persistence of cross-subsidization. Firstly, in many fiscal systems, interest income is taxable, but the benefit of free or underpriced services is not taxed, and the direct service charges are not deductible in taxation. In such cases, banks would be encouraged to compete in tax free implicit interest instead of taxable explicit interest accompanied by direct service charges (see Walsh 1983 and Tarkka 1992 for an exposition of this *tax arbitrage explanation*). Secondly, and more generally, cross-subsidization, as also the commonly observed price discrimination across banks' customers[16], are symptoms of imperfectly competitive markets for financial intermediation services, and imperfect substitutability of banks' services, since neither phenomenon would exist in frictionless perfectly competitive markets[17]. Hence, intensifying price competition indicated by the narrowing intermediation margins in most countries would have the effect of reducing the scope for cross-subsidization as well as price discrimination.

The crucial question regarding the substitutability of banks' services by those of non-bank rivals, and consequently the feasibility of cross-subsidization is whether there are significant *economies of scope*, *i.e.* unit cost savings when a particular service is produced jointly with other banking services. The existence of significant economies of scope would favour the universal banking model against the specialized one, and in principle allow a pricing structure that contains cross-subsidies.

Evidence of economies of scope in banking is somewhat inconclusive as *e.g.* variation in obtained estimates is significant depending on the functional form used in econometric modelling. Pulley and Humphrey (1993) show that the translog functional forms or their variants traditionally used in empirical analyses are inherently unable to estimate economies of scope accurately, given the data available[18]. They claim that some considerably large estimates of scope economies that appear in the literature[19] probably result from the shortcomings of the translog form. By using a composite functional form that overcomes most of the limitations of the translog, Pulley and Humphrey arrive at overall 4%-5% cost savings from joint production of five different types of deposits and loans as compared with specialized production. The cost savings from the use of more specialized labour and technology in the specialized production of banking services may well offset the scope economies of this magnitude. The data used by Pulley and Humphrey (1993) cover 205 large US banks in the period from 1978-1990.

In fact, the emergence of specialized banking institutions and increased provision of banking services by non-financial firms, *e.g.* retailers, in most countries suggests that the economies of scope are fairly unimportant. The possibility of competing in price has provided competitive opportunities to offer specialized services such as consumer loans and payment services apparently without incurring a significant cost disadvantage. The specialized institutions should reveal the true costs of producing these services and force banks to price their services accordingly (see Neven 1993 for a more thorough discussion). Hence, increasing competitive pressure on the part of specialized institutions and non-bank rivals is reducing the degree of cross-subsidization at universal banks, *i.e.* squeezing financial intermediation margins and boosting the use of direct service charges. The process also seems to lead to a restructuring of the production of services at universal banks. We have already seen, for example, an increase in phone-based banking services such as marketing of high yield time deposits and non-mortgage credits; this indicates dissociation of these services

116

from joint production with other branch-based services. Moreover, specialized, *niche banks*, have emerged in these markets in many countries. (See Neven 1993, and Geroski and Szymanski 1993).

3.1.2 Toward more specialized banking

Intensifying price competition has underscored banks' ability to operate cost efficiently as it has become decisive for profitability under narrowing margins. In fact, *cost consciousness*, and *customer targeting* and *orientation* appear to be the current buzz words in banking. The general trend towards universal banking until the late 1980s, following deregulation of structural rules (see Revell 1991), has typically led to uniformity of large banking organizations within each country, and also internationally[20]. The aspirations to cover most of the markets for different financial services has typically resulted in a fall in margins as financial liberalization has simultaneously increased competition in various markets. Shaw (1990) finds striking the similarity in banks' responses to strengthened competition, which has amplified the negative effects on banks' profitability. Banks have typically offered the same product innovations and targeted the same market niches. A recent survey by the Lyon-based ADEGE consultants of 13 large banks in Belgium, France, Luxembourg, Spain and Switzerland discovered that banks depend on only a small fraction of their customers for the bulk of their deposits and income, that more than half of banks' deposit-related products, which are practically the same in all banks, are largely unused as one-third of banks' customers typically use only one product, and finally, that over 80 per cent of all computerization investments are devoted to less than 10 per cent of banks' customers (see The Banker, July 1993, p. 68-69). Therefore, banks' production costs are excessive, and specialized skills and technology are not developed in a situation where all banks offer the same universal services. More specialized production concentrating on selected consumer groups would therefore constitute a more cost efficient and competitive strategy.

The competitive advantages of large universal banks are the large and fairly stable customer base and therefore access to comprehensive customer information. Additionally, extensive networks, dominance of payment systems and pure economic power are according to Löhneysen *et. al.* (1990) further significant advantages of the large universal banks. Moreover, long history and familiarity give rise to reputational benefits. However, several authors argue[21] that in the long run traditional universal banks must imitate specialized institutions in respective markets in order to survive in competition. This is obtained only by a change in the overall business strategies and organizational structures. Nevertheless, we will probably see the coexistence of both types of institutions in the future owing to the current dominant market position of the leading universal banks in many countries, but more cost-oriented pricing and careful customer targeting are definitely emerging at the universal banks.

The specialized rivals to universal banks currently comprise the following: (1) Specialized entrants in fund-gathering offering substitutes to bank deposits, chiefly mutual funds, money market funds and cash management systems, and increasingly insurance companies as well. (2) Specialized entrants in credit extension, including other credit institutions and financial firms, insurance companies, and non-financial firms (primarily retailers). (3) Specialized entrants in transaction processing: credit and entertainment cards, and retailer cards. And finally, (4) specialized firms in securities business and investment banking.

Hence, the specialized financial institutions and non-financial rivals are engaged in all major universal banking operations. The competitive impact of the specialized financial institutions on universal banks is, however, often weakened by the fact that they are subsidiaries of the large universal banking groups, and their competitive position varies significantly across the countries under study. The market position of these institutions seems strongest in the United Kingdom, France and Germany. For example, in the United Kingdom the share of specialized institutions in the market for mortgage loans rose over the second half of the 1980s from 1 per cent to 11 per cent, and in France and Germany specialized distributors have grown very rapidly, e.g. UFF France and Deutsche Vermögensberatung that specialize in the distribution of mutual funds' shares and other asset accumulation products using direct sales force (see Löhneysen et. al. 1990). Non-financial firms, chiefly retailers, seem to have entered the market for financial services in most countries. For example, the use of retailer cards is currently significant in many countries, especially in France and Sweden (see BIS Payment Systems in the Group of Ten Countries, 1994).

3.1.3   Banks' strategic response to increasing price competition

Banks clearly have an incentive to soften increasing price competition in order to sustain intermediation margins and profitability by collusive conduct, by trying to cement their current customer base, or by attempting to strategically block entry into the industry. Actual foreign rivalry is still fairly limited in many countries as the market shares of foreign-owned banks are quite small in all countries except the United Kingdom and Belgium[22] (see table 9). However, the pro-competitive effect of the foreign-owned banks has been clearly more important in the wholesale and corporate banking markets, where they have typically positioned themselves, than that implied by their small market shares.

By contrast, retail banking has in general remained national business. In this market, domestic banks may strive to replace the prevailed legal and administrative barriers to foreign entry by strategic conduct now that foreign competition is freed from any legal obstacles in the Single Financial Market. Pure strategic expansion to block entry, especially via branch proliferation, seems to be implausible as light capacity constitutes a competitive advantage in conditions of intensifying price competition. (Although in Italy, by exception, banks seem to be enlarging their networks to reinforce their home territories (see next section). In contrast, domestic mergers or acquisitions may be effective in reducing competitive pressures by diminishing the possibilities of entry by acquisition, a strategy that seems to be employed most distinctly in Italy[23]. The increase in the number of banking mergers (see Abraham and Lierman 1991, Gual and Neven 1992, and Vesala 1993a) and market concentration in many European countries at the end of 1980s and early 1990s may, hence, reflect the desire to limit competition. Based on the rather uncontroversial empirical evidence that scale economies in banking are very small[24], except at very small output levels, the most important goal of the mergers between banks seems to be to enhance market power and profitability. In addition, empirical investigations of bank mergers tend to indicate that they do not on average lead to significant cost savings (see *e.g.* Rose 1989 for a US survey, and Berg 1992 a Norwegian study). However, in certain cases, such as in Finland and Norway in recent years, mergers have been used as means to speed up capacity reductions in order to obtain operating cost savings.

High margins or low productive efficiency of the domestic banks would make entry attractive to foreign institutions. The Mediterranean countries appear to be such countries in particular. Indeed, most of the recent non-domestic acquisitions of financial institutions in Europe have taken place in Spain and Italy, while the buyers have mostly come from the northern EC states and to some extent from the non-European countries. (See Abraham and Lierman 1991, and Gual and Neven 1992 for surveys of cross-country mergers and acquisitions of financial institutions)[25].

Prospects for sustainable collusion without attracting entry are highest in "mass" retail markets of low contestability for transaction (demand, cheque and savings) accounts, payment services, and loans to households and small businesses, where entry barriers, especially, due to demand side "rigidities", and social and cultural factors appear to be the most effective (see Vives 1991, and Vesala 1993a for detailed discussions). Informational obstacles can be important in the granting of loans. Risky commercial loans to small enterprises requires in many cases local familiarity which is not possessed by the potential entrants. By contrast, standardized loans containing low risk like mortgages backed by full security are subject to more effective potential competition. Furthermore, the danger of collusion is greatest in bank dominated financial systems where large universal (core) banks have strong market positions and capital markets are less developed (cf. tables 1 and 8). These factors increase the probability of restrictive strategies especially in the smallest European banking markets. Collusion would naturally not be feasible if potential outside competition is strong enough, or if non-bank institutions are able to pose a significant competitive threat. It can be even argued that European financial integration, in contrast to its objectives, actually widens the scope for collusion as it makes entry less attractive, since integration is expected to have a general price-reducing effect (see Mercenier and Schmitt 1993).

It can thus be concluded that in the long run explicit private cooperation agreements or tacit collusion constitute a potentially serious threat to the attainment of the welfare objectives of European financial integration. Explicit cooperation among banks ranges from marketing and pooling agreements to network cooperation and formal alliances which are strengthened by reciprocal cross-participation or unilateral acquisition of minority holdings in partners' share capital (see *e.g.* Vesala 1993a and Canals 1993). The number of such agreements has recently increased, also between banks from different countries (see Gual and Neven 1992). Thus, an active competitive policy to detect and prevent detrimental strategic conduct is required to ensure efficient operation of the Single Financial Market. We will continue the policy discussion in the concluding chapter four.

3.2 *Technological change and reorganization of the delivery of banking services*

The rapid expansion of banks' ATM networks over the second half of the 1980s constitutes a major change in the delivery of deposit services defined to comprise payment, safekeeping and accounting services associated with demand deposits held with banks. This is since ATMs (including cash dispensers) provide many of the most often demanded deposit services, namely cash withdrawals, and increasingly transfers and payments between deposit accounts as well as cash deposits. Phone-based systems, and computerized services, especially on the corporate banking side, represent analogous displacement of services traditionally provided at branches. Computerized services are also expected to enter the retail banking market to a more significant extent, and banking services will be purchased more extensively at home rather than at branch offices (and perhaps also at ATMs) in the future.

In this section we will first examine the degree of substitution of ATMs for branches in the European banking industries under study, and then analyze the effects of this process on banks' service production costs. We argue that the density of ATMs should be regarded as part of banks' competitive strategy. Therefore, ATM expansion cannot be understood merely by its *presumed* cost effects which may well differ from the realized outcomes.

3.2.1   Substitution of ATMs for branches

Tables 10 and 11 depict banks' ATM and branch capacities in the selected European countries. The population served by ATMs and branches provides a proxy for the proximity of banks' services and customer convenience. The statistics are confined to include all deposit-taking institutions, excluding the postal banking institutions, since services provided by them differ importantly across countries. BIS "red books" are used as a primary data source augmented by data obtained from the Bank of Finland and Finnish Bankers' Association (Payment System Statistics of the Nordic Countries). Spain and Portugal are excluded here as sufficient and comparable data have not been available to the author.

The persisting intercountry differences in banks' ATM and branch capacities indicated by tables 10 - 11 are due to numerous economic, institutional and regulatory reasons, which are commented on in more detail later this chapter. Here we want to point out that regardless of these differences and the varying delivery strategies significant substitution of ATMs for branch offices seems to have taken place in all banking systems under study, except in Belgium, as displayed by the rapid increase. in the relative use of ATMs measured by the ratio of the number of ATMs to branches. In Germany, as in Belgium, the role of branches has remained strong. In Germany, however, there was a substantial jump in the number of ATMs during 1992.

Overall, in the EC-6 countries the ATM network density almost doubled between 1987 and 1992 and still shows an upward trend, while the branch network remained practically unchanged (see attached figure 2 for the growth rates of the ATM and branch network densities). Only in Italy did banks increase their branch network density significantly during the late 1980s and early 1990s, but the number of ATMs grew even faster, supporting the "substitution hypothesis". In Italy regulations effectively curtailed the establishment of branches in the 1980s. The lifting of these regulations, partially in 1987 and fully in 1990, prompted a rapid expansion in the number of branches.

Among the EC-6 countries the degree of substitution of ATMs for branches seems most far-reaching in the United Kingdom, where the branch population ratio fell by about 15 per cent between 1987 and 1992 and the ATM branch ratio approached unity. After a slow start, the setting up of ATMs has been swiftest in the Netherlands, where the number of ATMs was roughly seven times higher in 1992 than in 1987.

In Scandinavia banks have replaced branches by ATMs with a more visible extent than in the EC-6 countries as a smooth downward trend in branch capacity is common for all Scandinavian countries during the period from 1987 to 1992. The population served by branches has fallen by approximately 25 per cent between 1987 and 1992. In 1987 the ratio of branches to population was 18 per cent higher in Scandinavia than in EC-6, whereas in 1992 already 10 per cent lower. Only in Finland is the branch density still above the EC-6 level. At the same time the number of ATMs and the population served by them rose by over 60 per cent. The ATM network seems to have matured, however, quite rapidly as no major changes have taken place after 1989.

In Finland banks have made by far the largest investments in ATMs in Europe. The ATM network is in Norway also very dense relative to the EC-6 countries, while in Denmark and Sweden the ATM capacities correspond fairly well to the EC-6 level. The fall in the number of branches in the Scandinavian countries reflects in part the difficult financial problems of banks - resembling a crisis in Finland, Norway and Sweden - in the early 1990s, which have put heavy pressure on banks to reduce operating costs and capacity.

3.2.2 ATM scale economies and presumed savings in operating costs

If the installation of ATMs has a significant effect on the cost of deposit service production, the impact on banks' profits would be substantial, since - as noted - the deposit services, especially payment services, consume a considerable part of banks' total labour and physical capital input expenditures. I was induced to look into the cost effects of the ATM instalment for Europe by David Humphrey's (1994) recent econometric results of the cost and profit effects of substituting ATMs for branches in the USA. The investigations in this and the following section have greatly benefited from his analyses.

The potential savings in operating costs from the substitution of ATMs for branches follow from the apparent scale economies associated with the ATMs, which result from the fact that the fixed costs of setting up an ATM network make up a considerable share of the total cost of operating it. This makes the marginal cost of a transaction volume increase small. Then, other things equal, the cost of an ATM transaction at large transaction volumes would be substantially lower than the cost of producing the same service at a branch office. Moreover, as large transaction volumes are required for the exploitation of the ATM scale economies, instalment of ATMs is more advantageous for big banks with a large customer base.

Unfortunately, there are only a few empirical studies attempting to measure the degree of the ATM scale economies, and we are only aware of studies made in the USA (see Humphrey 1994 for a review). By relating total ATM costs to ATM transactions, Walker (1978) arrives at a scale elasticity measure of 0.5. More indirectly, Berger (1985) estimates that the fully allocated cost of an ATM transaction is about 50 per cent of the respective cost at a branch office. These figures should have improved over time, since the set-up and operating costs of the machines have decreased. Accordingly, Humphrey (1994) derives from a detailed cost survey a scale elasticity of 0.32 of total ATM costs with respect to a unit increase in the transaction volume. Hence, ATM scale economies appear to be of a substantial magnitude, which justifies the presumption of the cost savings achieved by substituting ATMs for branch delivery methods.

One expects that the substitution of ATMs for branches, and hence human tellers, is more extensive in countries where the relative labour costs are high. High ATM densities in Finland, Norway and Switzerland may be in part explained by high labour costs. Unfortunately, the lack of reliable data on banks' relative input costs hinders verification of this hypothesis. Indirectly, the relative labour costs should be positively correlated with income levels, since the price for and access to technology should not differ significantly across countries due to international competition in the field. However, one can not detect a clear relationship between GDP per capita and the ATM / branch ratio across the countries under study. In fact, both ATM and branch densities seem to be positively correlated with income, meaning that the ATM / branch ratio is largely unaffected by the income levels[26].

3.2.3   ATMs and transaction volumes

Humphrey (1994) argues that the operating cost savings of ATM extension may, nevertheless, be eroded to a significant extent if *(1)* transaction volumes rise considerably relative to the volumes prevailing when branches represent the only delivery method and the lower cost per transaction is offset by higher usage. Or, if *(2)* ATMs are "oversupplied" to extend market shares above the level where operating costs are minimized. The first effect is related to the demand for cash balances by banks' customers, and the second to banks' overall profit maximisation and use of the ATM network density as a competitive strategy discussed in the following section. Let us first consider the impact of ATMs on the demand for currency.

In the literature, ATMs are considered to have a twofold effect on the demand for currency (see *e.g.* Boeschoten 1992, Lempinen and Lilja 1989, and Paroush and Ruthenberg 1986). Firstly, ATMs make withdrawals of cash easier, which would have the effect of increasing cash balances per se. Secondly, ATMs lower the transaction cost of cash withdrawals since they increase the proximity of services by being open 24 hours a day and by increasing the number of points of service. Furthermore, the time required for one transaction is usually smaller at an ATM than at a branch office. According to the Baumol-Tobin model[27] of transactions demand for money, a fall in the transaction cost would lower transaction balances. ATMs would therefore increase the number of withdrawals, but the amount of money withdrawn at each time would fall leading to a negative effect on transaction currency demand[28].

The first effect is expected to dominate in the early phase of ATM instalment, while the second in the long term once people have become accustomed to make full use of the ATMs to economise on their cash holdings. The international evidence from the 1980s indicates that ATMs indeed had an initial positive effect on currency demand[29]. However, attached figure 3. indicates that the predicted long term shift in withdrawal patterns has taken place. The relationship between the demand for currency outside banks and ATM density is clearly negative in 1991 across European countries[30] suggesting that after a period of adjustment to ATMs people have reduced their average cash holdings. Attached figure 4. implies that this has actually resulted in a significant increase in the number of cash withdrawals as the ATM transactions per one ATM have increased, by and large, in step with ATM expansion (see also table 12). Interestingly, the number of ATM transactions per one ATM has been a level higher in the Scandinavian countries, where the ATM network was earlier expanded, than in the EC-6 countries, which supports the existence of a certain period of adjustment to the new delivery technology. The overuse of ATMs is naturally recognized by bankers. In Finland, where ATM establishment has been most extensive, the managing director of the Finnish Bankers' Association Matti Sipilä recently stated: "As long as the use of ATMs is free people overuse the machines in a way which is unbearable for banks" (a quote from Talouselämä (Finnish Business Magazine), 1994).

In contrast to the effect on cash balances held by banks' customers, ATMs clearly increase banks' need for cash if not compensated for by a sufficient reduction in the number of branches. Additional cash is needed for inventories in machines and additional inventories at branches to fill up the machines. This represents an additional cost to banks in terms of the interest foregone on idle cash balances[31].

In order to get some grasp of the postulated effects of ATM use on banks' operating costs we plotted the industry-level relationship between average (or unit) operating cost, defined as total operating expenses per FCNFE, and the ATM / branch ratio representing the degree of substitution of ATMs for branches (as in Humphrey 1994). Taken at face value, attached figure 5 indicates that a high level of ATM utilisation is associated with a higher, not lower, unit operating cost implying a heavy cost burden on banks that have invested most in the new technology. This suggests that the cost-raising effect of an increase in transaction volumes brought about by ATM expansion is quantitatively significant. This might also imply that banks have not yet fully adjusted their production patterns to exploit the possibilities of the new technology. Careful interpretation is, however, warranted, since ATMs account directly for only a part of banks' operating costs and other variables and country-specific factors affecting banks' costs are not controlled for.

As noted, average operating cost also represents a measure of banks' productive efficiency. FCNFE (or BST) is not, however, a fully satisfactory measure of banking output, since off-balance sheet activities and all services whose production does not affect the balance sheet are excluded. Payment services represent the most important category of the latter services whose exclusion causes bias in the efficiency measurement. This bias is likely to be the larger the more banks have invested in technology making the true relationship between ATM usage and efficiency flatter than that presented in figure 5[32].

3.2.4   ATMs as a competitive strategy

ATM density may be used as a competitive strategy, since it is a positively valued part of banks' service quality. Since ATM transactions are generally provided free of charge[33], the customer benefits resulting from increased convenience, reduced transaction costs (including the opportunity cost of time) and increased interest earnings are quite substantial. Customers gain in interest as average demand deposit balances rise and a part of the reduction in average cash balances are likely to be transferred into time and savings deposits or other assets earning higher interest. In fact, the depicted adverse effect of the use of the new delivery technology on banks' operating costs implies that the strategic aspect of the ATM expansion has most likely been more important than the desire to attain cost savings. If ATM expansion brings new depositors, which lowers banks' funding costs and generates additional revenue from other services, it can be optimal for a bank to "oversupply" ATMs in the sense that total operating costs are not minimized (see Humphrey 1994). Then a part of the customer value is recaptured in higher deposit market share or revenues. Figure 6 gives support to the use of ATMs as a means to increase deposit balances. An increase in the ATM usage appears to lead, in our sample of countries, to a rise in the average deposit balances banks can maintain at a given branch capacity [a similar result is obtained by Humphrey (1994) for the USA].

The above discussion leads one to expect banks' average interest costs to be lower when banks have a large number of ATMs relative to branches. We can not, however, establish this relationship in our sample. As in the case of our analysis of average operating costs, a more rigorous analysis holding other influences on costs constant is clearly needed to determine the true relationship between total banking costs and the intensity of ATM usage[34].

The competitive use of ATMs was probably more pronounced in the early phase of ATM establishment when network cooperation between banks was minor, and the establishment of ATMs was apparently not subject to collusive agreements. For example France, United Kingdom and Finland experienced strong competition between isolated networks. However, after a competitive start linkages between networks have been extensively established in most European countries (see Vesala 1993a ch. 4.4 for details), and banks now maintain a single joint network in many countries[35].

In what follows we consider network competition in terms of a spatial locational choice model presented in Box 3. in order to analyze more thoroughly the competition aspect of setting up delivery capacity, and hence increasing service proximity. We conclude this chapter by examining how the shift to joint networks is likely to affect banks strategies.

3.2.5   ATM / branch establishment in a location-choice model

Result (i) presented in Box 3 indicates that an increase in the deposit margin has a positive effect on the deposit service proximity provided, *i.e.* the

ATM and/or branch network densities. This has indeed been observed in international comparisons (see *e.g.* Neven 1993 and Vesala 1993a). Banks will have an incentive to expand proximity to attract more deposits until the marginal cost of deposits, *i.e.* deposit rate plus marginal cost of additional capacity, equals the interbank rate, *i.e.* banks' marginal revenue from the investment of funds generated from deposits. Moreover, if regulation or collusion imposes an effective ceiling on deposit rates, banks' delivery capacity would be larger than under unrestricted price competition. (Neven (1993) presents this conclusion without reference to an explicit model).

In general, the model implies that the degree of price competition has an important effect on banks' capacity choices, and thus illustrates the importance of product market competition for productive efficiency. When price competition is suppressed by regulation or collusion, banks tend to compete in service quality leading to higher ATM and branch network density. In previously heavily regulated banking markets, especially France and Finland, far-reaching quality competition seems to have resulted in extensive delivery capacity, often regarded as excessive in the liberalized environment, and ample use of the new banking technology. This also seems to pertain to the instalment of the EFT-POS systems (see table 13). In the traditionally unregulated banking markets of Germany and the Netherlands such quality competition has not taken place.

Result (ii) predicts that ATM technology would increase the total number of points of service by lowering the fixed cost of setting up additional delivery capacity. The model also predicts that the lower fixed cost ATM delivery technology will be used instead of branches, as has been the case, provided that ATMs are, as they appear to be, as effective as branches in reducing customers' transaction costs. The use of ATMs instead of branches has been further enhanced by their positive impact on demand deposit balances.

Finally, result (iii) predicts that ATM and branch network densities increase with income as income is positively correlated with customers' transaction costs through the opportunity cost of time. This is in accordance for example with international observations by Steinherr and Gilibert (1989).

However, we see that the closer banks are together following quality competition in regulated markets the more they are exposed to price competition. If banks have service points in the same neighbourhood, customers of the rival banks can be attracted by price reductions as banks are undifferentiated in geographical proximity. Thus, when rate setting is freed by deregulation, banks are induced to locate further apart to soften emerging price competition[36]. By doing so banks are able to charge higher prices, and by means of isolation obtain local market power. A halt in the rise of the number of branches, and even a fall in certain countries after the period of deregulation, might reflect this to a certain extent.

Box 3.   Location-choice model of ATM / branch establishment

The following model is an application of Salop's (1979) "circular city" model of monopolistic competition to the analysis of banks' delivery capacity choices. Schmid (1993) presents an extension of the Salop model considering the social desirability of branching restrictions. A summary and a discussion on the basic Salop model can be found in Tirole 1988, ch. 7.1.2.

A two-stage game in which banks decide on their locations in the first stage, and compete in prices in the second stage is considered. There are no barriers to free establishment of delivery capacity other than a fixed set-up cost. Banks' potential customers are assumed equally distributed over a unit circle, where also banks' points of service, n in total, are symmetrically located so that the distance between any two of them is equal to 1/n. The transaction costs of a representative customer are measured by a unit transport cost, t (assumed identical across all customers), times her distance to a service point of a bank i, x_i. Hence, transaction costs are assumed to be linear with respect to customers' distance to the points of service. The rate on deposits offered by bank i is r_{di}. Therefore, the net utility of the consumer from the use of deposit services provided by bank i is equal to $r_{di} - tx_i$.

If it is assumed that customers have perfect knowledge of the rates offered by banks, no two adjacent points of service belong to the same bank, and the above net utility is negative if customers have to travel a distance that is higher than 1/n, bank i has only two real competitors, namely the two banks having neighbouring locations surrounding its own location. A customer located at the distance $x_i \in$ (0,1/n) is indifferent in terms of her net utility between bank i and that of its neighbours offering a deposit rate r_d that is closer to the customer if:

$$r_{di} - t x_i = r_d - t(\frac{1}{n} - x_i)$$

From which:

$$x_i = \frac{r_{di} - r_d + t/n}{2t},$$

where x_i is the distance of a marginal customer, indifferent between the two

---

banks, to bank i. Anyone located closer to the bank i will choose to be its customer. The market share (or demand) captured by bank i is equal to:

$$D(r_{di}, r_d) = 2 x_i = \frac{r_{di} - r_d + t/n}{t},$$

and the profits that bank i seeks to maximise are given by:

$$(i - r_{di} - c)\frac{(r_{di} - r_d + t/n)}{t} - f,$$

where i represents the interbank rate, the rate at which each bank faces a perfectly elastic demand for funds generated from deposits, c the constant marginal cost of providing deposit services, and f the fixed cost of setting up points of service. $(i-r_{di})$ represents the price for the deposit service in terms of the interest foregone on deposit balances.

Free competition (free entry)

In free competition, when there are no barriers to setting up additional ATMs or branches, the total number of points of service is determined by the following zero-profit condition:

$$(i - r_d - c) \frac{1}{n} - f = 0$$

(Since a symmetric Nash equilibrium on deposit rates, when information is symmetric, implies $r_{di} = r_d$ for all i.).

Thus, we can conclude that in free competition:

(i) The number of points of service, n, increases with an increase in the profit margin in the deposit market, $(i-r_d-c)$. Hence, the number of outlets is an increasing function of the price for banks' deposit service, or deposit margin, $(i-r_d)$, and decreasing function of the marginal cost of service production.

(ii) The number of points of service decreases with the amount of fixed investments required to set up outlets, and

(iii) The number of outlets increases with unit transport cost, which reflects the degree of banks customers' transaction costs, which is an increasing function of customers' opportunity cost of time. We obtain this result by solving r_d from the first-order-condition for profit maximization (not shown here) and noting that r_d is a decreasing function of t.

We see that deposit rate regulation by imposing a ceiling rate has an effect on the locational choices of banks by affecting their profit margin on deposit services.

Note: socially (Pareto-) efficient solution

Socially efficient solution would require maximization of the net utility of a representative consumer subject to a given level of profits. It can be shown that under these conditions free competition generates more points of service as compared to the socially desirable level (see *e.g.* Tirole 1988). Thus, free competition would result in higher levels of accessibility than would be socially desirable. This argument can be used in favour of branching restrictions.

3.2.6   Increasing network cooperation

The establishment of jointly supported ATM networks by merging the networks of individual banks or groups of banks reflects attempts to cut costs by deleting overlapping functions (computer systems and networks) and services, but also to enhance customer satisfaction by extending the availability of the deposit services as customers would prefer the services that are most widely available. Thus, network cooperation has been partly competition- driven as banks belonging to narrow networks have been put at a competitive disadvantage. There is a *free-rider problem* in network cooperation (see Katz and Shapiro 1986 for a general treatment of the problem) in the sense that small banks may be able to obtain greater benefits from participating in a joint network than large banks that are themselves able to provide widely available services (and exploit the ATM scale economies). This aspect now seems, however, to be outweighed by the benefits of operating joint ATM networks.

In countries where the ATM network is maturing, network cooperation may lead to a decrease in network density if in the competitive phase several banks installed machines in places where a single machine would suffice. The extra machines can naturally be transferred to locations where no ATMs have been installed. Moreover, the "network cartel" may now effectively limit the availability of services, as discussed above, in order to locate banks apart and reduce competition. In countries where ATM density is growing, network cooperation might slow down the growth rate, since a high ATM density would not constitute a competitive advantage to any individual bank in the event a single network is supported in the country in question.

Customer resistance toward all direct service charges will make it hard for banks to impose fees on ATM transactions although reducing possibilities for cross-subsidization and the apparent cost disadvantages through "excessive" use of the ATMs increase pressures for direct charging. Network cooperation is likely to facilitate the introduction of these fees, although the pricing of services remain in principle uncoordinated, *i.e.* outside the explicit "network cartel". In Finland there are already signs of this development. As banks' customers have become accustomed to using ATMs extensively, even a "network cartel" may find it difficult to reduce ATM capacity. But if explicit charges are introduced reversed development in withdrawal patterns, and reductions in banks' distribution capacity may take place, even quite quickly.

3.3 Extending EFT-POS instalment

The introduction of the EFT-POS systems has taken place at very dissimilar speeds in the countries under observation. Their instalment and use have been especially moderate in Germany and Italy. Finland, France, and Denmark are the most advanced countries in these respects (see table 13).

The introduction of EFT-POS systems resembles that of ATMs in the sense that banks' customers receive an increasing part of their banking services away from the branches. EFT-POS systems also reduce customers' need to hold cash balances and facilitate payment transactions; thereby yielding important customer benefits (see attached figure 7. See also Boeschten 1992). An accurate record of transactions is another benefit to customers, as well as time savings compared with the manual handling of cards (see Whitehead 1990b). Hence, EFT-POS development, as that of the ATM networks, can be regarded as an attempt to maintain position in the retail banking market by increasing service quality (customer value). However, as the EFT-POS systems are generally not bank-specific, they have not provided an individual bank with a competitive advantage, but instead have enhanced competitive position of the banking industry toward non-bank rivals in the payment area.

A reduction in paper-based transactions in favour of electronic payments has in general resulted in significant reductions in banking costs. EFT-POS systems have the effect of decreasing the amount of paper based cheque and card transactions. The introduction of the EFT-POS systems also enhances banks' control over customers' accounts. In fact, Whitehead (1990b) has estimated that in the UK approximately 90 per cent of the cost savings due to the introduction of the EFT-POS have gone to banks[37]. Full realization of the cost savings requires, however, that banks adjust their branch capacity downward to correspond to the reduction in services demanded at branches.

4.   Policy issues

Governments have always followed the operation of banking industries very keenly, since intermediation and payment services are very important for the economic performance of other industries, and bank failures would cause severe negative externalities on all other sectors of the economy. Productive and allocative efficiency, under which waste in the use of productive resources is avoided and banks' customers may purchase the services they desire at fair prices corresponding to the marginal cost of their production, respectively, should be among the primary government objectives for the banking industry as well as for most other industries. Both types of efficiency are obtained in perfectly competitive or contestable markets involving a situation of unrestricted takeovers imposing effective control on banks' management (see. *e.g.* Scherer and Ross 1990). Therefore, competitive policy has a pivotal role in the attainment of efficiency and optimal allocation of resources also in the banking sector.

In banking, price competition has been stimulated by the abolition of the regulations on the pricing of banking services, and of the formal obstacles to foreign entry. For foreign banks taking over an existing domestic bank, instead of setting up extensive delivery capacity, represents the most feasible way to profitably enter a foreign (retail) banking market. Moreover, by acquiring a domestic bank a foreign bank gets a direct access to a customer base and local information. Making cross-border acquisitions and mergers free of all remaining obstacles would therefore be most consequential in raising effective potential foreign competition. The still significant state ownership in the banking industry in many countries, in spite of the recent wave of privatisation, provides opportunities for Governments to introduce new competitors into national markets. However, although no overt legal restrictions on foreign ownership exist in the Single European Financial Market, the objective of many Governments appears to be preserving national ownership of the largest domestic banks, which seems to be related the fear that significant foreign ownership would reduce the availability of services (see *e.g.* Bisigano 1992)[38].

As discussed in section 3.1.4 an active competitive policy may be required to attain efficient operation of the banking markets, and detect and prevent harmful bank strategies aiming at limiting price competition. Muldur (1993) notes that in most European countries active policy of banking competition has been either non-existent or passive, which is worrying regarding the above objective, especially in bank dominated financial systems. This is due to the fact that Governments have also many other policy objectives than efficiency regarding the banking industries. Two major additional objectives are ensuring the availability of basic financial intermediation and payment services, and most importantly maintaining stability in the financial market and payment system. Both of these goals, discussed in turn below, may conflict with the efficiency objective.

The concern about the availability of services has two major repercussions. Firstly, in small banking markets Governments may tolerate a high level of industrial concentration, which may increase the probability of collusion and thus have the effect of restricting price competition although historically the level of industrial concentration does not seem to be related to the use of market power in banking (revert to section 2.5). Relatively large bank size is often required in small countries with less developed capital markets to ensure the provision of the loans and other services demanded by large corporations, since small and dispersed institutions would not have adequate capital bases. Secondly, the Government may wish to extend the provision of the intermediation and payment services beyond the point banks' find profitable, for example in small remote communities, and at prices not significantly higher than those charged in large communities, where customers can be reached at a lower cost (see Berg 1994). Charging universal prices would denote cross-subsidies from customers located in densely populated areas to those living in remote locations. We argued in section 3.2.6 that the trends toward less cross-subsidization and direct cost-based pricing have developed due to increasing price competition and declining bank profitability. Furthermore, under these conditions, banks were found to have incentives to reduce the scope of their distribution networks, a trend which is likely to be enhanced by the recently developed "network cartels". Therefore, the question about the availability of the banking services could become more pronounced in the future, and public intervention may take place if the nationwide availability of the essential services is threatened. Either these services are provided through publicly owned institutions, such as post offices, or private banks are directly subsidized. The Government could restrict price competition by regulatory measures that allow the use of the cross-subsidies, but this seems unlikely under the current conditions of harmonized regulations. Under the home country control-regime adopted in the EC banking legislation, restrictive controls would put domestic banks at a disadvantage in international competition. (See also Berg 1994)

There is a policy conflict between striving to enhance competition, and level-playing-field in banking and preserving stability in the financial system, since stability is enhanced by banks' financial strength, *i.e.* high margins and profitability. Banks' solvency can be jeopardised if they fail to maintain appropriate risk premiums in lending in a cut-throat competition. In Finland, Norway, and Sweden, in the near future after the banking crises, the priorities will be most probably on achieving stability even if it means restricting competition (cf. Berg 1994). For example, authorities have allowed mergers among large banks and other financial institutions in order to have stronger units.

Financially stronger institutions are better able to absorb negative external shocks, but, perhaps more importantly, excessive risk taking is less attractive for well-off institutions whose so-called *charter values* are positive, since they have more at stake in the event of an adverse outcome (see *e.g.* Chan *et al.* 1992). Keeley (1990) argues that positive charter values necessarily reflect imperfect competition, and hence, banks' market power. If it is true that banks must have positive charter values to limit their risk taking effectively (see *e.g.* Furlong and Keeley 1987, and Chan *et al.* 1992), achieving stability and full efficiency would be in fundamental conflict. Concessions are likely to be made on the latter objective.

Table 1. Financial structure

	Size indicator		Financial interme-diation ratio		Bank intermediation ratio		Internationalization ratio	
	1980	1990	1980	1990	1980	1990	1980	1990
Finland	1.78	3.47	0.60	0.60	0.61	0.66	0.11	0.12
France	4.19	6.26	0.50	0.47	0.88	0.74	0.12	0.12
Germany	3.17	3.98	0.53	0.53	0.82	0.77	0.11	0.15
Italy	3.12	3.92	0.50	0.39	0.65	0.58	0.11	0.09
Spain	4.08	5.12	0.38	0.37	0.62	0.71	0.04	0.05
Sweden	3.24	5.06	0.50	0.55	0.49	0.41	0.06	0.07
United Kingdom	na	8.50	na	0.37	na	0.59	na	0.19
United States	4.61	7.50	0.36	0.32	0.52	0.37	0.04	0.03
Japan	4.84	7.56	0.45	0.47	0.35	0.38	0.03	0.09

Data source: OECD, Financial Accounts of OECD Countries (various issues)

Table 2. GDP share of banking services excluding seigniorage, per cent

	1981	1985	1991
Belgium	2.41	3.06	2.53
France	3.07	3.34	3.47
Germany	3.25	3.97	3.45
Ireland	2.82	3.79	3.26
Italy	2.21	2.76	3.91
Luxembourg	13.96	24.81	13.18
Netherlands	2.90	3.45	3.02
Portugal	1.34	1.58	5.45
Spain	2.68	5.10	5.69
United Kingdom	3.07	3.50	4.35
Denmark	1.72	1.76	2.22
Finland	2.18	2.22	2.93
Norway	2.64	2.27	3.00
Sweden	2.06	2.73	3.76

Source: OECD National Accounts 1979-1991; IMF, International Financial Statistics (seigniorage calculations)

Table 3.

Balance sheet structure: average ratios, per cent

	Total loans/BST			Securities held as current and investment assets/BST			Interbank and central bank assets/BST			Non-bank deposits/BST			Annual asset growth		
	80–84	85–89	90–92	80–84	85–89	90–92	80–84	85–89	90–92	80–84	85–89	90–92	80–84	85–89	90–92
Belgium	34.18	27.35	30.02	22.73	28.26	26.66	39.00	40.00	39.00	31.60	30.86	35.43	18.72	7.90	4.61
France	42.95	36.94	37.61	2.62	6.97	10.85	44.00	46.00	40.00	36.10	32.87	35.23	17.29	10.84	7.28
Germany	60.16	56.34	55.87	13.57	15.47	16.22	24.00	25.00	25.00	53.59	53.62	51.95	6.99	7.54	9.42
Italy	26.61	29.62	37.47	23.51	19.35	12.78	15.00	19.00	17.00	54.60	50.52	49.17	17.53	10.14	8.50
Netherlands	56.95	55.10	62.19	7.04	10.15	10.73	31.00	28.00	24.00	46.61	49.68	45.87	7.79	12.57	12.68
United Kingdom	56.81	59.87	60.06	5.48	7.06	8.89	28.00	21.00	17.00	na	na	na	21.45	13.98	6.20
EC-6	48.04	45.67	47.84	11.54	13.27	13.56	29.00	30.00	28.00	46.70*	45.02*	44.78*	13.14	9.82	8.00
Spain	51.76	42.58	46.38	14.86	23.24	19.18	18.00	22.00	22.00	71.94	66.48	67.07	19.56	11.97	11.04
Portugal	61.84	46.00	39.56	5.59	12.26	22.93	14.00	22.00	29.00	76.74	75.67	67.24	28.16	18.24	18.92
Denmark	39.42	41.38	48.59	23.76	22.96	22.49	18.00	18.00	19.00	54.28	48.34	50.02	19.76	12.90	-3.79
Finland	66.72	62.84	63.50	7.12	12.35	15.50	8.00	8.00	6.00	69.03	57.63	51.33	20.19	20.57	3.75
Norway	61.47	71.65	77.36	29.88	18.25	12.06	7.00	6.00	6.00	76.41	58.13	63.94	18.16	14.67	0.45
Sweden	51.70	55.29	57.62	26.96	17.98	19.78	15.00	18.00	15.00	60.54	51.77	45.97	13.80	13.80	5.03
SCANDINAVIA	53.08	56.05	59.70	23.13	18.16	18.23	13.00	14.00	12.00	63.22	53.16	50.82	16.43	13.26	-1.60
Switzerland	55.49	57.21	65.51	10.62	10.60	10.49	27.00	26.00	19.00	53.33	51.00	49.78	10.28	7.26	4.37

Notes: BST = Balance Sheet Total
* excluding the United Kingdom
Data source: OECD Bank Profitability Statistics

136

Table 4a.   Income structure: average ratios, per cent of FCNFE

	Net interest income (Intermediation margin)			Net non-interest income			Net banking income (Overall gross margin)			Net non-interest income/net interest income (%)		
	80–84	85–89	90–92	80–84	85–89	90–92	80–84	85–89	90–92	80–84	85–89	90–92
Belgium	2.82	2.66	2.38	0.64	0.82	0.70	3.46	3.48	3.08	22.79	30.93	29.25
France	4.49	4.16	2.84	0.82	0.76	1.00	5.30	4.92	3.84	18.18	18.42	36.09
Germany	2.94	2.85	2.57	0.66	0.76	0.85	3.61	3.61	3.42	22.61	26.81	33.22
Italy	3.43	3.74	3.98	1.29	1.44	1.28	4.71	5.18	5.26	37.66	38.52	32.25
Netherlands	3.16	3.00	2.27	1.03	1.08	0.92	4.20	4.08	3.18	32.68	36.00	40.43
United Kingdom	4.30	3.83	3.41	1.97	2.19	2.32	6.27	6.02	5.72	46.51	57.44	68.13
EC-6	3.52	3.42	2.94	1.00	1.11	1.15	4.52	4.53	4.09	28.39	32.68	39.21
Spain	4.79	4.92	4.64	0.82	0.99	1.09	5.60	5.92	5.74	17.04	20.11	23.59
Portugal	2.38	3.86	6.03	1.25	0.88	1.56	3.63	4.73	7.59	54.70	23.52	26.26
Denmark	3.80	3.05	3.96	2.67	1.36	0.21	6.46	4.41	4.17	72.09	44.44	6.42
Finland	2.36	1.89	1.66	2.15	2.19	1.82	4.51	4.08	3.48	94.14	115.98	114.52
Norway	3.89	3.36	3.29	0.99	1.13	1.09	4.89	4.49	4.38	25.54	33.58	34.04
Sweden	2.64	3.28	3.01	0.92	1.28	1.66	3.56	4.56	4.67	35.07	38.84	56.52
SCANDINAVIA	3.05	2.89	2.88	1.57	1.49	1.31	4.62	4.37	4.19	51.23	51.60	45.41
Switzerland	1.71	1.80	1.85	1.47	1.75	1.84	3.18	3.55	3.69	86.73	97.32	99.71

Note: FCNFE = Funds Committed to Non-Financial Entities
Data source: OECD Bank Profitability Statistics

137

Table 4b. Income structure: average ratios, per cent of BST

	Net interest income (Intermediation margin)			Net non-interest income			Net banking income (Overall gross margin)		
	80–84	85–89	90–92	80–84	85–89	90–92	80–84	85–89	90–92
Belgium	1.73	1.59	1.46	0.39	0.49	0.43	2.12	2.08	1.89
France	2.50	2.25	1.69	0.46	0.41	0.60	2.96	2.66	2.29
Germany	2.25	2.13	1.92	0.51	0.57	0.64	2.76	2.69	2.55
Italy	2.91	3.02	3.31	1.09	1.16	1.07	4.00	4.18	4.38
Netherlands	2.17	2.16	1.71	0.71	0.77	0.69	2.88	2.93	2.41
United Kingdom	3.10	3.03	2.84	1.42	1.74	1.93	4.53	4.76	4.78
EC-6	2.49	2.38	2.12	0.71	0.78	0.83	3.20	3.16	2.96
Spain	3.90	3.85	3.63	0.67	0.78	0.85	4.57	4.63	4.49
Portugal	2.04	3.01	4.30	1.07	0.69	1.11	3.12	3.70	5.42
Denmark	3.13	2.49	3.20	2.20	1.09	0.17	5.33	3.58	3.37
Finland	2.18	1.74	1.55	1.98	2.01	1.71	4.16	3.75	3.26
Norway	3.63	3.16	3.09	0.93	1.07	1.03	4.56	4.23	4.12
Sweden	2.24	2.68	2.55	0.78	1.04	1.44	3.02	3.73	3.99
SCANDINAVIA	2.65	2.49	2.52	1.36	1.28	1.15	4.02	3.77	3.67
Switzerland	1.25	1.32	1.49	1.08	1.29	1.49	2.33	2.61	2.98

Note: BST = Balance Sheet Total
Data source: OECD Bank Profitability Statistics

138

Table 5a. **Cost structure: average ratios, per cent of FCNFE**

	Staff expenses			Non-staff operating expenses			Total operating expenses			Staff expenses/Total operating expenses		
	80–84	85–89	90–92	80–84	85–89	90–92	80–84	85–89	90–92	80–84	85–89	90–92
Belgium	1.74	1.50	1.38	0.78	0.82	0.75	2.52	2.33	2.13	69.13	64.62	64.92
France	2.40	2.09	1.52	1.20	1.24	1.03	3.59	3.33	2.55	66.63	62.56	59.51
Germany	1.47	1.49	1.41	0.74	0.83	0.81	2.21	2.32	2.22	66.64	64.15	63.48
Italy	2.21	2.39	2.29	0.82	0.95	0.97	3.03	3.34	3.25	72.97	71.52	70.28
Netherlands	1.75	1.64	1.25	0.93	1.06	0.91	2.69	2.70	2.17	65.31	60.83	57.85
United Kingdom	2.81	2.31	2.09	1.59	1.61	1.65	4.40	3.91	3.73	63.71	58.87	55.92
EC-6	2.00	1.90	1.66	0.97	1.06	1.00	2.97	2.96	2.66	67.42	64.12	62.26
Spain	2.52	2.54	2.11	1.23	1.23	1.33	3.75	3.78	3.44	67.10	67.24	61.22
Portugal	1.58	1.81	2.08	0.60	0.85	1.45	2.17	2.65	3.53	72.62	68.18	59.09
Denmark	2.24	1.58	1.79	1.16	0.93	1.14	3.39	2.51	2.93	65.85	62.90	61.22
Finland*	2.00	1.51	1.15	1.71	1.59	1.70	3.70	3.11	2.85	53.86	48.54	40.52
Norway	1.89	1.50	1.46	1.51	1.59	1.71	3.40	3.09	3.17	55.57	48.39	46.43
Sweden*	1.06	1.17	1.12	0.99	1.35	1.34	2.05	2.52	2.46	51.72	46.50	45.68
SCANDINAVIA	1.64	1.42	1.33	1.25	1.34	1.45	2.90	2.76	2.77	56.73	51.31	47.89
Switzerland	1.23	1.30	1.30	0.58	0.66	0.69	1.81	1.96	1.98	68.16	66.25	65.43

Notes: FCNFE = Funds Committed to Non-Financial Entities
* OECD statistics corrected in line with the other countries
Data sources: OECD Bank Profitability Statistics, Bank of Finland (Finland and Sweden)

Table 5b. **Cost structure: average ratios, per cent of BST**

	Staff expenses			Non-staff operating expenses			Total operating expenses		
	80–84	85–89	90–92	80–84	85–89	90–92	80–84	85–89	90–92
Belgium	1.07	0.90	0.85	0.48	0.49	0.46	1.55	1.39	1.30
France	1.34	1.13	0.90	0.67	0.67	0.62	2.01	1.80	1.52
Germany	1.13	1.11	1.05	0.56	0.62	0.60	1.69	1.73	1.65
Italy	1.87	1.93	1.90	0.69	0.77	0.80	2.57	2.69	2.71
Netherlands	1.20	1.18	0.95	0.64	0.76	0.69	1.84	1.94	1.64
United Kingdom	2.03	1.82	1.74	1.15	1.27	1.37	3.18	3.10	3.12
EC-6	1.41	1.33	1.20	0.68	0.74	0.72	2.10	2.07	1.92
Spain	2.06	1.99	1.65	1.01	0.97	1.04	3.06	2.95	2.69
Portugal	1.35	1.41	1.49	0.51	0.66	1.03	1.87	2.08	2.52
Denmark	1.85	1.29	1.45	0.95	0.76	0.92	2.80	2.05	2.37
Finland*	1.84	1.39	1.08	1.57	1.46	1.59	3.42	2.85	2.67
Norway	1.76	1.41	1.38	1.41	1.50	1.62	3.17	2.90	2.99
Sweden*	0.90	0.96	0.96	0.84	1.10	1.14	1.74	2.06	2.09
SCANDINAVIA	1.43	1.22	1.16	1.09	1.16	1.27	2.52	2.38	2.43
Switzerland	0.90	0.95	1.05	0.42	0.49	0.55	1.33	1.44	1.60

Notes: BST = Balance Sheet Total
* OECD statistics corrected in line with the other countries
Data sources: OECD Bank Profitability Statistics, Bank of Finland (Finland and Sweden)

Table 6.

Profitability: average ratios, per cent

	Operating margin/FCNFE			Operating margin/BST			Provisions (net)/FCNFE			Provisions (net)/BST			Pre-tax profit/FCNFE			Pre-tax profit/BST		
	80–84	85–89	90–92	80–84	85–89	90–92	80–84	85–89	90–92	80–84	85–89	90–92	80–84	85–89	90–91	80–84	85–89	90–92
Belgium	0.94	1.15	0.95	0.57	0.69	0.59	0.42	0.56	0.46	0.25	0.34	0.28	0.52	0.59	0.49	0.32	0.35	0.30
France	1.71	1.59	1.29	0.95	0.86	0.77	1.05	0.99	0.91	0.59	0.53	0.54	0.66	0.60	0.38	0.37	0.32	0.23
Germany	1.39	1.29	1.20	1.07	0.96	0.90	0.57	0.50	0.51	0.44	0.37	0.38	0.82	0.79	0.69	0.63	0.59	0.52
Italy	1.69	1.84	2.00	1.43	1.49	1.67	0.95	0.70	0.64	0.81	0.56	0.53	0.74	1.15	1.36	0.62	0.93	1.13
Netherlands	1.51	1.38	1.02	1.04	0.99	0.77	0.94	0.44	0.37	0.65	0.32	0.28	0.57	0.65	0.65	0.39	0.67	0.49
United Kingdom	1.87	2.11	1.99	1.35	1.67	1.66	0.65	1.08	1.44	0.47	0.86	1.20	1.22	1.03	0.55	0.88	0.81	0.46
EC-6	1.56	1.57	1.43	1.10	1.09	1.04	0.77	0.71	0.73	0.54	0.50	0.53	0.79	0.85	0.70	0.55	0.60	0.51
Spain	1.85	2.14	2.30	1.51	1.67	1.80	1.00	0.86	0.78	0.81	0.67	0.61	0.85	1.28	1.52	0.69	1.00	1.19
Portugal	1.46	2.08	4.06	1.25	1.62	2.90	0.91	1.38	2.36	0.79	1.08	1.68	0.55	0.70	1.70	0.47	0.55	1.22
Denmark	3.07	1.91	1.24	2.54	1.53	1.00	1.29	0.88	1.86	1.06	0.72	1.51	1.78	1.02	-0.62	1.48	0.81	-0.51
Finland*	0.81	0.98	0.63	0.75	0.90	0.59	0.49	0.57	1.79	0.45	0.53	1.68	0.32	0.40	-1.16	0.30	0.37	-1.09
Norway	1.48	1.41	1.20	1.38	1.33	1.13	0.60	1.15	2.49	0.56	1.09	2.35	0.89	0.25	-1.29	0.83	0.23	-1.22
Sweden*	1.51	2.04	2.25	1.28	1.67	1.93	1.17	0.92	2.94	0.99	0.76	2.55	0.34	1.12	-0.69	0.29	0.91	-0.62
SCANDINAVIA	1.72	1.61	1.41	1.50	1.39	1.24	0.96	0.86	2.31	0.83	0.74	2.03	0.76	0.75	-0.89	0.66	0.65	-0.79
Switzerland	1.37	1.59	1.70	1.01	1.17	1.38	0.52	0.67	1.03	0.38	0.49	0.84	0.85	0.92	0.67	0.62	0.68	0.54

Notes: FCNFE = Funds Committed to Non-Financial Entities, BST = Balance Sheet Total
* OECD statistics corrected in line with the other countries
Operating margin = Net interest income + net non-interest income – operating expenses (incl. depreciation)
Pre-tax profit = Operating margin – provisions (net)
Data sources: OECD Bank Profitability Statistics, Bank of Finland (Finland and Sweden)

Table 7.   **Macroeconomic indicators, per cent**

	1981	1982	1983	1984	1985	1986	1987	1988	1989	1990	1991	1992
Real GDP growth												
Belgium	-0.98	1.50	0.44	2.17	0.82	1.45	2.05	4.98	3.79	3.42	1.89	0.82
France	1.20	2.30	0.79	1.48	1.81	2.41	2.17	4.25	3.76	2.41	0.71	1.43
Germany	0.10	-0.94	1.76	2.81	2.03	2.35	1.48	3.72	3.62	5.70	4.55	1.56
Italy	0.55	0.22	0.97	2.69	2.60	2.92	3.14	4.07	2.94	2.14	1.25	0.93
Netherlands	-0.71	-1.41	1.40	3.16	2.64	2.75	1.19	2.61	4.68	4.11	2.10	1.40
United Kingdom	-1.29	1.72	3.78	2.47	3.50	4.32	4.76	4.98	2.18	0.39	-2.28	-0.46
EC-6	0.08	0.63	1.71	2.40	2.38	2.87	2.64	4.16	3.28	2.96	1.39	0.97
Spain	-0.18	1.57	2.22	1.46	2.61	3.20	5.64	5.16	4.74	3.62	2.22	0.80
Portugal	1.62	2.14	-0.19	-1.85	2.78	4.16	5.25	3.93	5.14	4.40	2.13	1.10
Denmark	-0.90	3.03	2.52	4.39	4.29	3.63	0.30	1.16	0.56	2.05	1.23	1.23
Finland	1.57	3.58	2.97	3.06	3.34	2.39	4.10	4.96	5.67	0.00	-7.06	-4.03
Norway	0.87	0.34	4.62	5.76	5.27	4.18	2.00	-0.50	0.59	1.66	1.59	3.29
Sweden	-0.01	1.01	1.75	4.05	1.92	2.29	3.14	2.25	2.38	1.36	-1.12	-1.91
SCANDINAVIA	0.29	1.80	2.74	4.28	3.41	3.01	2.47	1.96	2.30	1.28	-1.31	-0.54
Switzerland	1.44	-0.93	1.01	1.76	3.71	2.87	2.03	2.90	3.86	2.30	-0.03	-0.06

Money market interest rate

	1981	1982	1983	1984	1985	1986	1987	1988	1989	1990	1991	1992
Belgium	11.47	11.44	8.18	9.47	8.27	6.64	5.66	5.04	7.00	8.29	9.38	9.38
France	15.3	14.87	12.53	11.74	9.93	7.74	7.98	7.52	9.07	9.85	9.49	10.35
Germany	11.26	8.67	5.36	5.54	5.19	4.57	3.72	4.01	6.59	7.92	8.84	9.42
Italy	19.6	20.16	18.44	17.27	15.25	13.41	11.51	11.29	12.69	12.38	12.18	13.97
Netherlands	11.01	8.06	5.28	5.78	6.30	5.83	5.16	4.48	6.99	8.29	9.01	9.27
United Kingdom	13.12	11.36	9.09	7.62	10.78	10.68	9.66	10.31	13.88	14.68	11.74	9.55
Spain	16.56	17.21	19.4	12.59	11.60	11.50	16.07	11.30	14.39	14.76	13.20	13.01
Portugal	9.24	12.42	18.24	21.27	20.17	14.52	13.69	12.34	12.84	13.73	15.81	17.48
Denmark	14.84	16.92	12.81	11.77	10.33	9.22	10.20	8.52	9.66	10.97	9.78	11.35
Finland	11.46	11.66	14.67	16.50	13.46	11.90	10.03	9.97	12.56	14.00	13.08	13.25
Norway	12.35	13.91	12.27	12.67	12.29	14.15	14.66	13.29	11.31	11.45	10.58	13.70
Sweden	14.35	13.29	10.85	11.77	13.85	10.15	9.16	10.08	11.52	13.45	11.81	18.42
Switzerland	2.93	1.32	1.84	3.34	3.75	3.17	2.51	2.22	6.5	8.33	17.73	7.47

Inflation rate (CPI)

	1981	1982	1983	1984	1985	1986	1987	1988	1989	1990	1991	1992
Belgium	7.58	8.75	7.68	6.35	4.82	1.30	1.58	1.17	3.07	3.45	3.24	2.36
France	13.43	11.84	9.59	7.50	5.71	2.50	3.32	2.74	3.49	3.37	3.18	2.41
Germany	6.29	5.23	3.35	2.41	2.15	-0.10	0.20	1.30	2.76	2.69	3.46	4.07
Italy	19.50	16.48	14.56	10.90	9.17	5.80	4.73	5.14	6.27	6.38	6.38	5.21
Netherlands	6.75	5.86	2.82	3.27	2.25	0.10	-0.70	0.70	1.10	2.47	3.86	3.71
United Kingdom	11.88	8.60	4.54	5.01	6.04	3.40	4.16	4.92	7.79	9.52	5.85	3.68
Spain	14.41	14.46	12.23	11.26	8.81	8.80	5.24	4.80	6.83	6.71	5.92	5.94
Portugal	19.89	22.75	25.10	29.32	19.33	11.70	9.40	9.57	12.62	13.33	11.35	8.93
Denmark	11.71	10.22	6.90	6.23	4.71	3.70	3.95	4.55	4.79	2.62	2.39	2.10
Finland	12.09	9.56	8.35	7.14	5.82	2.90	4.08	5.14	6.57	6.08	4.16	2.56
Norway	13.71	11.25	8.40	6.29	5.71	7.20	8.68	6.70	4.59	4.15	3.40	2.36
Sweden	12.51	8.64	8.84	8.00	7.41	4.20	4.22	5.80	6.44	10.47	9.40	2.23
Switzerland	6.41	5.68	2.96	2.98	3.41	0.80	1.39	1.86	3.17	5.40	5.83	4.09

Data sources: OECD, National Accounts; IMF, International Financial Statistics

Table 8.   **Market shares absorbed by the five largest individual banks in terms of total assets (CR5), per cent**

	CR 5	
	1987	1990
Belgium	58.2	54.9
France	41.4	48.8
Germany	22.0	26.0
Italy	35.0	37.8
Netherlands	86.8	84.1
Spain	28.5	35.4
United Kingdom	33.5	31.4
Denmark	74.3	77.1
Finland	68.1	65.4
Norway[1]	na	66.1
Sweden	57.2	72.1

Data sources: The Bankers' Almanac; OECD, Bank Profitability Statistics (own calculations)
Note [1]: In terms of total bank lending (source: Bank of Norway)

Table 9.   **Market shares absorbed by foreign-owned banks in terms of total assets, per cent**

	1987	1990
Belgium	47.0	47.0
France	11.4	na
Germany	4.2	3.9
Italy	2.9	2.9
Netherlands	10.0	na
Spain	9.7	10.0
United Kingdom	61.6	57.2
Denmark	1.0	na
Finland	1.1	0.9
Norway[1]	na	1.6
Sweden	2.3	1.6

Sources: Gual and Neven (1992), Bank of Finland
Note [1]: In terms of total bank lending (source: Bank of Norway)

Table 10.

Branch network, excluding post offices and postal giros

	Number of branches						Number of branches per 10 000 inhabitants					
	1983	1987	1989	1990	1991	1992	1983	1987	1989	1990	1991	1992
Belgium	7572	9084	11373	10244	10178	10343	7.68	9.21	11.53	10.30	10.19	10.32
France	21491	25492	25212	25569	25589	25489	3.93	4.62	4.53	4.58	4.51	4.47
Germany	28532	44207	44073	48133	49169	49685	4.65	7.25	7.03	6.03	6.12	6.13
Italy	12913	15365	15577	17721	19078	20789	2.27	2.69	2.72	3.08	3.31	3.66
Netherlands	4373	5718	5545	5446	5520	5168	3.04	3.95	3.78	3.67	3.69	3.43
United Kingdom	22044	21961	21443	20560	19475	19024	3.91	3.88	3.77	3.59	3.39	3.30
EC-6	96924	121827	123223	127673	129009	130498	3.82	4.79	4.77	4.62	4.66	4.69
Denmark	3625	3534	3175	3002	2652	2467	7.09	6.92	6.19	5.85	5.16	4.79
Finland	3520	3535	3528	3302	3087	2817	7.24	7.21	7.16	6.66	6.19	5.60
Norway	1969	2166	1880	1796	1774	1614	4.77	5.22	4.49	4.25	4.18	3.79
Sweden	3581	3498	3290	3202	3064	2910	4.30	4.19	3.92	3.77	3.58	3.38
SCANDINAVIA	12695	12733	11873	11302	10577	9808	5.66	5.66	5.24	4.95	4.61	4.25
Switzerland	na	na	4130	4191	4190	4111	na	na	6.35	6.30	6.24	6.05

Data source: BIS, Payment systems in eleven developed countries (various issues). Bank of Finland and Finnish Bankers' Association (Finland, Norway and Denmark).

145

Table 11. **ATM network**

	Number of ATMs						Number of ATMs per 10 000 inhabitants						ATM/Branch ratio					
	1983	1987	1989	1990	1991	1992	1983	1987	1989	1990	1991	1992	1983	1987	1989	1990	1991	1992
Belgium	560	802	913	939	1052	1096	0.57	0.81	0.93	0.94	1.05	1.09	0.07	0.09	0.08	0.09	0.10	0.11
France	5100	11500	13031	14428	16134	17432	0.93	2.08	2.34	2.58	2.84	3.06	0.24	0.45	0.52	0.56	0.63	0.68
Germany	1600	7500	9300	11300	13750	19000	0.26	1.23	1.48	1.42	1.71	2.35	0.06	0.17	0.21	0.23	0.28	0.38
Italy	1500	4367	7791	9770	11571	13917	0.26	0.76	1.36	1.70	2.01	2.45	0.12	0.28	0.50	0.55	0.61	0.67
Netherlands	32	450	1839	2700	3354	3964	0.02	0.31	1.25	1.82	2.24	2.63	0.01	0.08	0.33	0.50	0.61	0.77
United Kingdom	5653	12500	15740	17000	17780	18280	1.00	2.21	2.76	2.97	3.10	3.17	0.26	0.57	0.73	0.83	0.91	0.96
EC-6	14445	37119	48614	56137	63641	73689	0.57	1.46	1.88	2.03	2.30	2.65	0.15	0.30	0.39	0.44	0.49	0.56
Denmark	250	570	1004	1016	1086	1234	0.49	1.12	1.96	1.98	2.11	2.40	0.07	0.16	0.32	0.34	0.41	0.50
Finland	391	1577	2719	2838	2908	2914	0.80	3.22	5.52	5.72	5.83	5.79	0.11	0.45	0.77	0.86	0.94	1.03
Norway	345	1150	1757	1767	1753	1709	0.84	2.77	4.19	4.18	4.13	4.01	0.18	0.53	0.93	0.98	0.99	1.06
Sweden	1126	1650	1928	2102	2221	2203	1.35	1.98	2.30	2.48	2.59	2.56	0.31	0.47	0.59	0.66	0.72	0.76
SCANDINAVIA	2112	4947	7408	7723	7968	8060	0.94	2.20	3.27	3.39	3.47	3.50	0.17	0.39	0.62	0.68	0.75	0.82
Switzerland	na	na	1962	2262	2371	2669	na	na	3.02	3.40	3.53	3.93	na	na	0.48	0.54	0.57	0.65

Data source: BIS, Payment systems in eleven developed countries (various issues). Bank of Finland and Finnish Bankers' Association (Finland, Norway and Denmark).

146

Table 12. **ATM transactions**

	ATM transactions (Millions)					ATM transactions per capita					ATM transactions/ATMs (thousands per year)				
	1983	1989	1990	1991	1992	1983	1989	1990	1991	1992	1983	1989	1990	1991	1992
Belgium	23.84	67.89	70.86	80.79	88.33	2.42	6.89	7.19	8.12	8.84	42.57	74.36	75.46	76.80	80.59
France	107.91	495.29	547.72	614.05	607.15	1.97	8.98	9.85	10.99	10.70	21.16	38.01	37.96	38.06	34.83
Germany	na	na	na	na	na	na	na	na	na	na	na	na	na	na	na
Italy	9.00	80.07	100.66	131.28	162.58	0.16	1.40	1.76	2.28	2.82	6.00	10.28	10.30	11.35	11.68
Netherlands	na	42.00	168.00	355.00	487.00	na	2.90	11.46	23.91	32.58	0.00	22.84	62.22	105.84	122.86
United Kingdom	233.70	912.64	992.00	1066.00	1147.00	4.15	16.12	17.42	18.62	19.98	41.34	57.98	58.35	59.96	62.75
EC-5*	374.45	1597.89	1879.24	2247.12	2492.06	1.48	6.28	7.35	8.70	9.01	29.15	40.64	41.91	45.04	45.57
Denmark	na	15.50	15.50	15.00	13.40	na	3.03	3.02	2.92	2.61	na	15.44	15.26	13.81	10.86
Finland	8.37	101.90	121.00	157.20	182.40	1.72	20.80	24.54	31.69	36.55	21.41	37.48	42.64	54.06	62.59
Norway	10.00	54.70	60.30	66.10	70.10	2.42	13.18	14.39	15.63	16.53	28.99	31.13	34.13	37.71	41.02
Sweden	70.00	174.00	170.00	208.00	218.00	8.40	20.84	20.24	24.50	25.47	62.17	90.25	80.88	93.65	98.96
SCANDINAVIA	88.37	346.1	366.8	446.3	483.9	3.94	15.38	16.19	19.57	21.10	41.84	46.72	47.49	56.01	60.04
Switzerland	11.00	33.30	39.40	45.50	51.50	1.72	5.15	6.06	6.84	7.68	na	16.97	17.42	19.19	19.30

Note: * excluding Germany
Data source: BIS, Payment systems in eleven developed countries (various issues). Bank of Finland and Finnish Bankers' Association (Finland, Norway and Denmark)

147

Table 13.　　　**EFT-POS systems**

	EFT-POS terminals				Number of EFT-POS transactions (Millions)				EFT-POS terminals per 10 000 inhabitants				EFT-POS transactions per capita			
	1989	1990	1991	1992	1989	1990	1991	1992	1989	1990	1991	1992	1989	1990	1991	1992
Belgium	24644	28253	32199	40627	66.50	79.04	98.76	120.74	24.77	28.28	32.13	40.34	6.68	7.91	9.86	11.99
France	160000	180000	203000	320000	618.0	933.0	1051.00	1300.00	28.63	31.73	35.58	55.94	11.06	16.45	18.42	22.73
Germany	10928	23152	34673	51806	0.80	3.50	20.20	28.00	1.74	2.90	4.32	6.40	0.01	0.04	0.25	0.35
Italy	10240	22185	45711	62251	2.40	5.40	8.50	12.68	1.78	3.84	8.05	10.94	0.04	0.09	0.15	0.22
Netherlands	2047	2223	4038	11440	17.00	27.00	32.00	47.00	1.38	1.49	2.68	7.56	1.14	1.81	2.12	3.11
United Kingdom	75000	110000	190000	220000	64.00	192.00	359.00	na	13.10	19.16	32.99	38.06	1.12	3.34	6.23	na
EC-6	282859	365813	509621	706124	768.7	1239.94	1569.46	1508.42	10.95	13.23	18.41	25.39	2.98	4.48	5.67	5.42
Denmark	12602	15804	19289	33411	41.40	61.50	85.30	110.10	24.57	30.75	37.45	64.62	8.07	11.96	16.56	21.30
Finland	16500	26500	33500	39000	53.60	82.70	110.30	119.80	33.27	53.11	66.60	77.08	10.81	16.57	21.93	23.68
Norway	7125	10050	13556	18103	35.60	44.74	58.90	76.60	16.84	23.70	31.82	42.20	8.42	10.55	13.83	17.86
Sweden	3420	6090	8916	14276	5.00	14.00	30.00	41.00	4.03	7.11	10.34	16.45	0.59	1.64	3.48	4.72
SCANDINAVIA	39647	58444	75261	104790	135.60	202.94	284.50	347.50	17.38	25.49	32.64	45.17	5.94	8.85	12.34	14.98
Switzerland	2165	2590	5183	11327	6.20	9.60	13.60	19.40	3.26	3.86	7.63	16.42	0.93	1.43	2.00	2.81

Data source: BIS, Payment systems in the group of ten countries (December 1993). Bank of Finland and Finnish Bankers' Association (Finland, Norway and Denmark).

Figure 1.

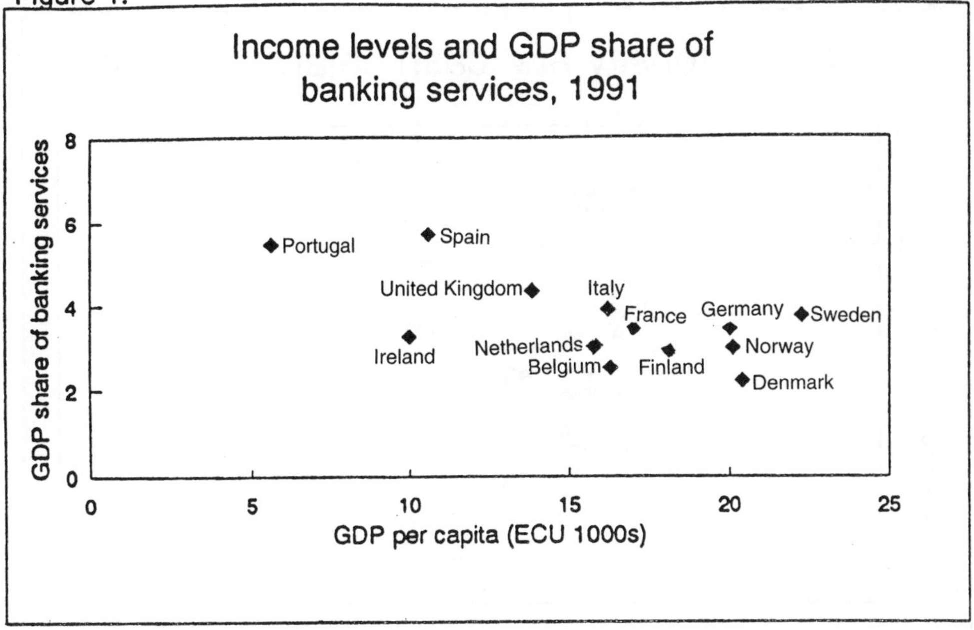
Income levels and GDP share of banking services, 1991
GDP share of banking services
0
2
4
6
8
Portugal
Spain
United Kingdom
Italy
France
Germany
Sweden
Ireland
Netherlands
Norway
Belgium
Finland
Denmark
0
5
10
15
20
25
GDP per capita (ECU 1000s)

Figure 2.

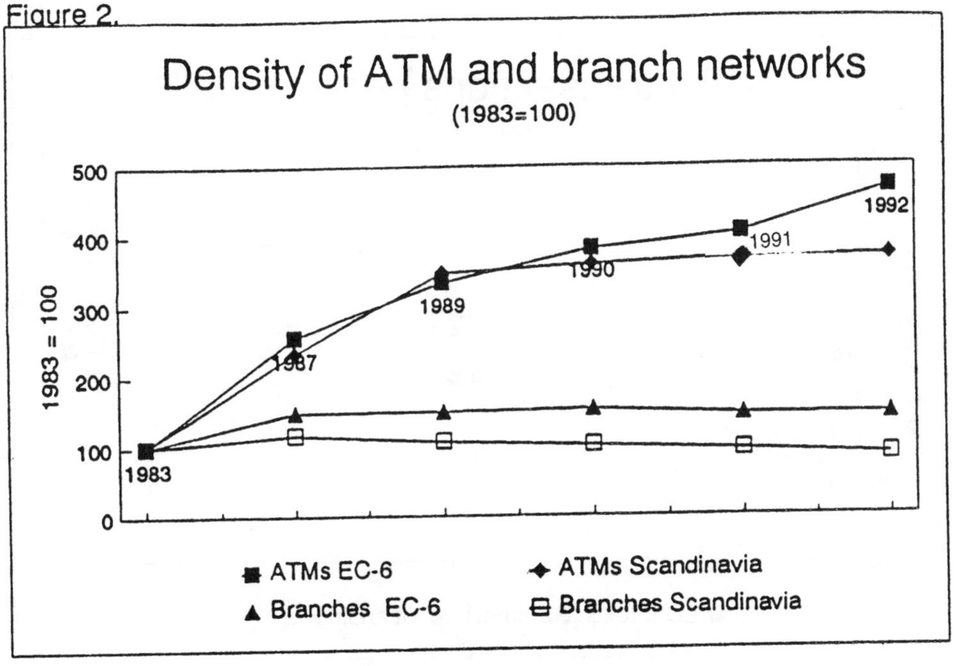
Density of ATM and branch networks
(1983=100)
1983 = 100
0
100
200
300
400
500
1983
1987
1989
1990
1991
1992
ATMs EC-6
ATMs Scandinavia
Branches EC-6
Branches Scandinavia

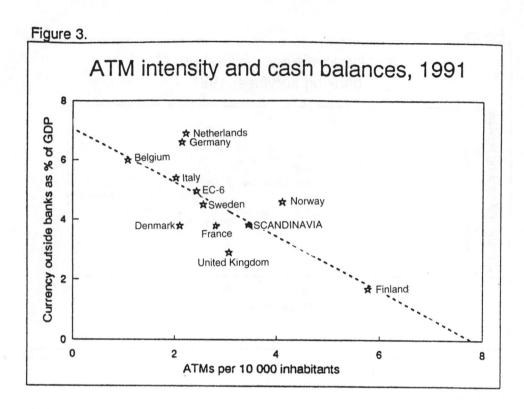

Figure 3.

ATM intensity and cash balances, 1991

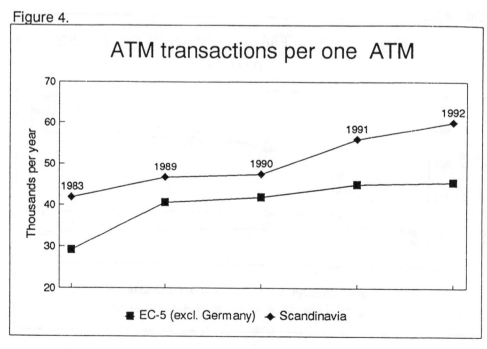

Figure 4.

ATM transactions per one ATM

Figure 5.

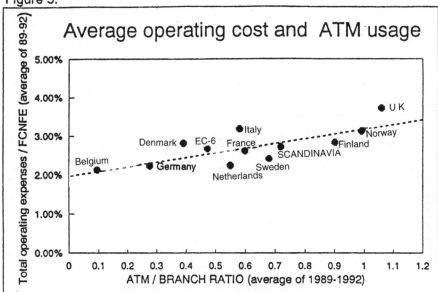

Notes: The UK, excluding building societies
Slope of the fitted line 0.012 (t-stat. 3.60)

Figure 6.

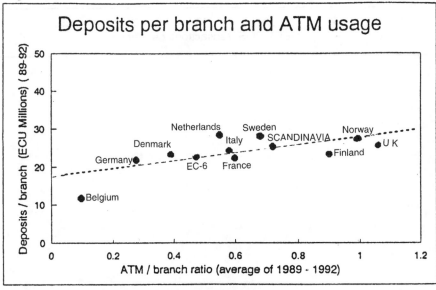

Notes: The UK, excluding building societies
Slope of the fitted line 10.58 (t-stat. 2.99)

Figure 7.

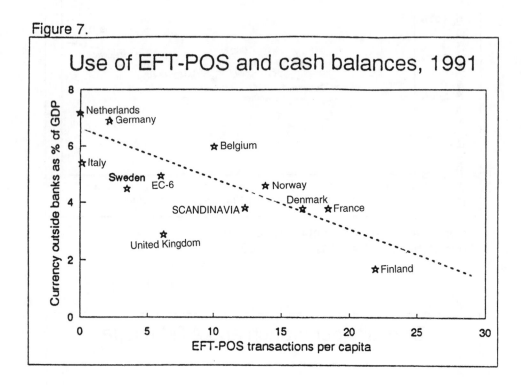

Notes

1   Instead of stocks, accumulated flows of funds could alternatively be used in calculation of the indicators. Using flows might result in somewhat different results. See *e.g.* Mooslechner (1994) for discussion on the measurement issues, and characterization of financial systems with similar flow-based measures as our indicators (1) - (4). See also Mayer (1990) for a presentation of certain indicators based on deflated data.

2   The value of the total financial assets outstanding is the current value of the claims held by the various sectors of the economy, including claims on the agents within the sector, at a given time. The OECD National Accounts has the following sectoring: (i) financial institutions, (ii) central and local government, (iii) non-financial enterprises, and (iv) households.

3   Financial intermediation services of banks include: (1) Transformation of large-denominated financial assets into smaller denomination ones, asset diversification (portfolio management), and asset (credit risk) evaluation and signalling. (2) Intermediation of funds involving the transformation of deposits into loans, and arbitrage across markets offering uncertain rates of return (see *e.g.* Diamond and Dybvig 1986 and Vives 1991).

4   According to the opportunity cost approach the share of the seigniorage revenues in the GDP equals:

$$S = i * \frac{C}{GDP} + (i - i_r) * \frac{R}{GDP} ,$$

where i is the interest rate on government bonds, C currency in circulation, R total required reserves held by banks with the central banks, and ir the interest rate paid on these reserves. The other commonly used measure of seigniorage, the cash flow measure, which captures the marginal impact of a change in currency in circulation and reserves, is not suitable to our needs as we need to measure the effect of the entire stock of cash and reserves outstanding. Furthermore, the opportunity cost measure is much more stable, and thus more apt for comparisons over time.

5   Suominen and Tarkka (1991) report that in Finland the same amount of labour could produce 4-5 times more banking services in 1990 than in 1981, indicating substantial growth in labour productivity. The growth in capital productivity in Finnish banking was, according to Suominen and Tarkka's findings, slower than labour productivity growth, but still quite significant. Substantial growth in total factor productivity was the result. The technological development in the banking sector has been very swift in Finland, which is reflected in these findings. However, comparable productivity growth seems to have taken place in many other European countries as well.

6   Christian de Boissieu (1993) used this correction when examining the profitability of French banks in international comparison in the early 1980s. The term Funds Committed to Non-Financial Entities (FCNFE) is due to him.

7   See Vesala (1993a) Appendix 5 for the evolution of spreads between deposit interest rates and money market rates in certain European countries 1985-1992 based on typical demand deposit rates collected from the OECD Monthly Financial Statistics.

8   Staff expenses include salaries and other employee benefits plus transfers to pension reserves. Non-staff operating expenses consist of all other non-interest expenses related regular banking business including expenses for property and equipment and related depreciation expenses. In the case of Finland and Sweden banks' credit losses are counted among operating expenses in the OECD Statistics. This inconsistency is corrected in tables 5a and b and every subsequent instance where this information is used.

9   Productive efficiency requires that what is produced is produced at least possible cost (see *e.g.* Scherer and Ross 1990). To be precise, average operating costs can degrease either by exploiting economies of scale in production or increasing productive efficiency. However, since the econometric evidence implies insignificant scale economies in banking, reductions in average operating costs would indicate improved efficiency.

10   Measuring competition based on accounting information does not represent rigorous economic analysis as the degree of price competition and the use of market power should be measured by the price-marginal cost margin (the Lerner index). Furthermore, several specification and measurement problems affect the use of accounting information to infer market power (see. *e.g.* Fisher 1987).

11   Banks' profits have been high in Italy and Spain in spite of indicated low productive efficiency (see table 5a). Moreover, Neven (1993) reports that the per employee remuneration in banking relative to that in the other sectors of the economy has been especially high in Italy, and significantly above the European average in Spain.

12   The pro-competitive effect of free capital markets comes from two primary sources. Firstly, banks have access to international financial markets to obtain funds at competitive prices, which places an upper limit that is feasible to pay for domestic funds. This fosters efficiency in the domestic operations. Secondly, large corporate customers have equal access to international finance, thereby restricting the interest rate that could be charged on these clients (see Neven 1993).

13   See Gilbert (1984) for a survey of the early US studies. Later US studies include Berger and Hannan (1989), Calem and Carlino (1991), and Hannan and Liang (1993). Studies using European data include Bourke (1989), Molyneux and Thornton (1992) and Molyneux (1993).

14   These include problems with the use of accounting profits and margins as a measure of banks' market power, specification of the concentration measure (see *e.g.* Fisher 1989), blurred relationships with exogenous and endogenous variables (cf. Demsetz's efficient structure postulate), and problems in making data from various countries compatible with each other. (See Vesala 1993b for a more detailed analysis)

15   de Boissieu (1993) estimates by using analytical accounting data published by the Banking Commission that payment and ancillary services amounted to 48.8 per cent of banks' all overheads and depreciation in France in 1983. Berger and Humphrey (1992) report that in the USA the deposit service production defined to comprise payment, safekeeping and accounting services has used up around 50 per cent of banks' total labour and physical capital input expenditures. See also Vittas et. al. (1988).

16   Customers with higher account balances are often favoured with higher interest rates and lower service charges or both. (See *e.g.* Vittas 1988 and Bryan and Allen 1988 for evidence from Europe and the United States, respectively)

17   The imperfect competition models explaining deposit pricing include *e.g.* Baxter *et al.* (1977), Mitchell (1988) and Tarkka (1994).

18   MacAllister and MacManus (1993) point out further shortcomings of the translog form due to a lack of sufficient flexibility.

19   In general, the empirical studies do not provide consistent evidence of the economies of scope in banking, although some studies using the translog form report very large scope economies ranging from 17% to 42% in Gilligan and Smirlock (1984) to over 100% in Mester (1987). More often, however, pair-wise scope economies, so-called cost complementarities, rather than global scope economies in the production of financial services are evaluated. For example, Berger et. al.(1987) report economies of scope between total deposits and loans, and Lawrence and Shay (1986) between off-balance sheet activities and total deposits, both by using translog functional forms.

20 Revell (1991) explains this development by the observation that overall competition among large organizations tends to create a single model in each market. "All supermarkets have much the same range of goods in their shelves, and all motorcars in the lower price ranges look much like each other apart from the cosmetic differences."

21 See *e.g.* Löhneysen et. al. 1990, Shaw 1990, Whitehead 1990a, Abraham and Lierman 1991, Revell 1991, and Conti and Maccarinelli 1992. Arthur Andersen consultants: "The new challenge is to get the right service to the right customer at the right price, rather than trying to provide all services to all customers" (a quote from The Banker, February 1994).

22 Large penetration of foreign banks into the UK banking market is naturally due to London's stance as an international financial centre. The large market share of foreign, primarily French banks, in Belgium compared with the other northern EC states is somewhat puzzling, since the Belgian banking market does not seem to have offered exceptional profit opportunities. On the contrary, banks' margins have been quite narrow in Belgium. Conceivably, cultural similarities and shared language have facilitated establishment of French banks in Belgium.

23 Italian banks have been considered too small and numerous to cope in international competition. "The need for a higher degree of concentration has been felt and appears to enjoy general consensus" (a quote from Bisoni 1990). See also Landi (1990).

24 A partial list of the studies includes Gilligan et. al. (1984), Berger et. al. (1987), Buono and Eakin (1990), Ferrier and Lovell (1990), Berger and Humphrey (1991), and Berg *et al.* (1992).

25 This also reflects the intention of foreign institutions to take advantage of deficiencies in the Spanish and Italian financial markets by, for example, supplying services these markets were lacking.

26 This is in accordance with result (iii) derived from the location-choice model of ATM / branch establishment presented in Box 3.

27 See e.g Niehans (1978) for a review of the properties of the model.

28 Note that this reasoning pertains only to the transactions demand for currency, and mainly to that by households. However, the currency demand by enterprises and money hoarding should be independent of the number of ATMs, and the effect of ATMs on the transactions demand for currency would translate to the total demand for currency.

29 See Boeschoten (1992) for estimates from cross-country samples and a survey of the literature.

30 We found using the 1991 data of the countries depicted in figure 2. that the coefficient of the ATM population ratio remains significantly negative once the

income levels (GDP per capita), and the use of EFT-POS terminals are controlled for. The elasticity of the demand for the currency outside banks with respect to ATM density was found to be -0.54 (t-stat. -2.85). Careful interpretation is, however, warranted, since this does not represent a rigorous estimation of currency demand.

31 The amount of cash held by banks differs markedly across the countries under study: from 0.37% of GDP in Norway to 1.14 % in Finland at the end of 1991 (see Virén 1993). Factors influencing the level of banks' cash balances include, in addition to branch and ATM networks, the currency distribution system (central bank network) and the amount of interest foregone on balances, which is affected by the institutional details of banks' cash and reserve managements, and monetary authorities' requirements. Thus, a detailed study is needed to measure the net impact of ATMs on banks' cash balances. Boeschoten (1992) reports a significant and positive effect for a group of industrialized countries over the late 1980s.

32 It should be noted here that productive efficiency is found to vary substantially across banks within national industries. Thus, individual banks may well receive good efficiency ratings in international comparisons even though the efficiency of the particular industry appears low. (See *e.g.* Berger and Humphrey 1991 and Ferrier and Lovell for evidence from the USA, and Berg et.al. 1992 from Finland, Norway and Sweden).

33 Based on the information obtained from the Central Banks of Belgium, Germany, the United Kingdom, Finland and Sweden for a study in progress, cash withdrawals in all of these countries are free of charge at the ATMs of the card-issuing institution. In some cases fees are introduced for withdrawals made from ATMs which, even when part of an inter-bank network, are not the bank's own machines. In Norway and the Netherlands banks have set small ATM fees.

34 Using data from 161 US banks in 1991 and 1992, Humphrey (1994) arrives at a slight total cost increase (interest plus operating costs) when ATMs are employed as an alternative delivery method to branches. He does not impose full substitution of ATMs for branches, which would be unrealistic, but instead estimates ATM and branch scope economies from a composite cost function controlling for changes in service production, input prices and the number of branches and ATMs banks maintain. The scope economy measure then indicates the amount of cost savings (found negative but marginal) from the use of ATMs.

35 A single ATM-network in which all domestic banks participate is now in operation for example in Denmark, Finland and Norway. In Italy almost 90% of ATMs are linked through nationwide Bancomat network, in France an extensive Bank Card Consortium has been established. In the Netherlands the BGC network covers practically all banks except Postbank. In Belgium two competing networks (MISTER CASH and BANCONTACT) were merged in 1989 forming an entity called BANKSYS. The UK represents an exception, as there are no bridges

between three principal ATM networks (LINK, MINT and FOUR BANKS). However, some bilateral arrangements between institutions belonging to different networks exist. (See BIS, Payment Systems in the Group of Ten Countries, December 1993 for further details).

36 This conclusion is due to Neven (1993). He arrives at it by making reference to a standard Hotelling-type model of monopolistic competition presented by Eaton and Lipsey (1975).

37 According to Whitehead (1990b), retailers have been willing to install EFT-POS terminals largely at their own expense, since they have regarded it as necessary in order to retain their competitive position.

38 According to Stiglitz and Weiss (1981) optimal behaviour on the part of banks may result in charging higher prices from and allocate less credit to unknown and distant customers. This fear, then, might rationalize the observed hesitation of Governments to allow foreign acquisitions especially of large domestic banks. This concern would not be warranted if foreign banks' local management could run local operations independently, which, however, would not most likely be the case as global optimization for the whole bank can affect the portfolio decisions in individual local markets. (See also Berg 1994).

References

ABRAHAM, J. and LIERMAN, F. (1991) European Banking in the Nineties: A Supply Side Approach, IEF Reserarch Papers, 91/ 8.

BALTENSBERGER, E. and DERMINE, J. (1987) Banking Deregulation, Economic Policy, April, 65-109.

BAUMOL, W., PANZAR, J. and WILLIG, R. (1982) Contestable Markets and the Theory of Industry Structure, HBJ, New York.

BAXTER, W, COOTNER, P. and SCOTT, K. (1977) Retail Banking in the Electronic Age.

ALLANHELD, OSMUN & Co., Montclair, NJ.

BENSTON, G. (1993) Universal Banking: An Analysis of Disadvantages and Advantages, Emory Business School (July).

BERG, S. (1992) Mergers, Efficiency, and Productivity Growth in Banking: The Norwegian Experience 1984-90, Norges Bank, Oslo.

BERG, S., FØRSUND, F. HJALMARSSON, L. and SUOMINEN, M. (1992): Intrascandinavian Differences in Banking Productivity after a Period of Deregulation, Norges Bank, Working Paper.

BERG , S. (1994) Governments' Strategies: The Nordic Banking Industries after the Crises, Paper Presented at SUERF-meeting, Dublin, May.

BERGER, A. (1985) The Economics of Electronic Funds Transfers, Working Paper, Board of Governors of the Federal Reserve System, Washington D.C. (October).

BERGER, A., HANWECK, G. and HUMPHREY, D. (1987) Competitive Viability in Banking: A Restructuration and Reassessment, Journal of Money Credit and Banking, 14, 435-56.

BERGER, A. and HANNAN, T. (1989) The Price-Concentration Relationship in Banking, The Review of Economics and Statistics, 71, 2, 291-99.

BERGER, A. and HUMPHREY, D. (1991) The Dominance of Inefficiencies over Scale and Product Mix Economies in Banking, Finance and Economics Discussion Series, 107, Federal Reserve Board, Washington D.C.

BERGER, A. and HUPHREY, D. (1992) Measurement and Efficiency Issues in Banking, in Grilliches, Z. ed. Output Measurement in the Service Sectors, NBER, Chicago.

BISIGANO, J. (1992) Banking in the European Community: Structure, Competition and Public Policy, in Kaufman, G. ed. Banking Structures in Major Countries, Kluwer Academic Publishers, London.

BISONI, C. (1990) Growth Policies in Italian Credit Institutions: Size and Diversification, IEF Research Papers, 90/1.

BOESCHOTEN, W. (1992) Currency Use and Payment Patterns. Financial and Monetary Policy Studies, 23, Kluwer Academic Publishers, Dordrecht, the Netherlands.

BOURKE, P. (1989) Concentration and Other Determinants of Bank Profitability in Europe, North America and Australia, Journal of Banking and Finance, 13, 65-78.

BRYAN, L. and ALLEN, P. (1988) The Changing World of Banking: Geographic Strategies for the 1990's, McKinsey Quarterly, 52-71.

BUONO, M. and EAKIN, B. (1990) Branching Restrictions and Banking Costs, Journal of Banking and Finance, 14, 1151-62.

CALEM, P. and CARLINO, G. (1991) The Concentration / Conduct Relationship in Bank Deposit Markets, The Review of Economics and Statistics, 73, 2, 268-76.

CANALS, J. (1993) Competitive Strategies in European Banking, Calarendon Press, Oxford.

CHAN, Y., GREENBAUM, S., and THAKOR, A. (1992) Is fairly Priced Deposit Insurance Possible? Journal of Finance 47, 227-45.

CONTI, V. and MACCARINELLI, M. (1992) Bank Profitability, Capital Adequacy and Optimal Size in Modern Banking: Three Studies, IEF Research Papers, 92/20.

de BOISSIEU, C. (1993) The French Banking Sector in Light of European Financial Integration, in Dermine, J. ed. European Banking in 1990's, Basil Blackwell, Oxford.

DIAMOND, D. and DYBVIG, P. (1986) Banking Theory, Deposit Insurance and Banking Regulation, Journal of Business, 59, 1, 55-68.

EATON, B. and LIPSEY, R. (1975) The Principle of Minimum Differentiation Reconsidered: Some New Developments in the Theory of Spatial Markets, Review of Economic Studies, 42, 27-50.

FERRIER, G. and LOVELL, K. (1990) Measuring Cost Efficiency in Banking: Econometric and Linear Programming Evidence, Journal of Econometrics, 46, 229-45.

FISCHER, S. (1983) A Framework for Monetary and Banking Analysis. Economic Journal, 1-16.

FISHER, F. (1987) On the Missuse of the Profits-Sales Ratio to Infer Monopoly Power, Rand Journal of Economics 18, 384-96.

FISHER, F. (1989) Games Economists Play: A Non-Cooperative View, Rand Journal of Economics 20, 113-24.

FURLONG, F. and KEELEY, M. (1987) Bank Capital Regulation and Asset Risk, Economic Review, Federal Reserve Bank of San Francisco, Spring, 20-40.

GEROSKI, P. and SZYMANSKI, S. (1993) Comment on Neven (1993) in Dermine, J. ed. European Banking in 1990's, Basil Blackwell, Oxford.

GILBERT, R. (1984) Bank Market Structure and Competition: A Survey, Journal of Money Credit and Banking 16, 617-45.

GILLIGAN, T. and SMIRLOCK, M. (1984) Scale and Scope Economies in the Multiproduct Banking Firm, Journal of Monetary Economics, 13, 393-405.

GROS, D. (1993) Seigniorage and EMU, European Journal of Political Economy, 9, 581-601.

GOLDSMITH, R. (1985) Comparative National Balance Sheets, University of Chicago Press, Chicago.

GUAL, J. and NEVEN, D. (1992) Deregulation of the European Banking Industry (1980-1991), CEPR Discussion Paper No. 703.

HANNAN, T. and LIANG, N. (1993) Inferring Market Power from Time-Series Data, The Case of the Banking Firm, International Journal of Industrial Economics, 11, 205-18.

HUMPHREY, D. (1994) Delivering Deposit Services: ATMs Versus Branches, Federal Reserve Bank of Richmond Economic Quarterly, 80, 1, 59-81, (Spring 1994).

KATZ, M. and SHAPIRO, C. (1986) Technology Adoption in the Presence of Network Externalities, Journal of Political Economy, 94, 4, 822-41.

KEELEY, M. (1990) Deposit Insurance, Risk, and Market Power in Banking, American Economic Review 80, 1183-1200.

LANDI, A. (1990) Some Prospects on Concentration in the Italian Banking System, IEF Research Papers, 90/3.

LAWRENCE, C. and SHAY, R. (1986) Technology and Financial Intermediation in a Multi Product Banking Firm, in Lawrence, C. and Shay, R. eds. Technological Innovation, Regulation, and the Monetary Economy, Cambridge.

LEMPINEN, U. and LILJA, R. (1989) Payment Systems and the Central Bank, Bank of Finland, D:70.

LÖHNEYSEN, E., BAPTISTA, A. and WALTON, A. (1990) Emerging Roles in European Retail Banking, McKinsey Quarterly, 4 (Winter), 142-50.

MAYER, C. (1990) Financial Systems, Corporate Finance, and Economic Development, in Hubbard, G. ed. Asymmetric Information, Corporate Finance and Investment, Chicago.

MCALLISTER, P. and MCMANUS, D. (1993) Resolving the Scale Efficiency Puzzle in Banking, Journal of Banking and Finance, 17, 389-405.

MERCENIER, J. and SCHMITT, N. (1992) Free-Entry Equilibrium, Sunk Costs and Trade Liberalization in Applied General Equilibrium: Implications for "Europe 1992", University of Montreal (September).

MESTER, L. (1987) A Multiproduct Cost Study of Savings and Loans, Journal of Finance, 42, 423-45.

MITCHELL, D. (1988) Explicit Interest and Demand Deposit Service Charges. Journal of Money Credit and Banking, 20, 270-74.

MOLYNEUX, P. and THORNTON, J. (1992) Determinants of European Bank Profitability: A Note, Journal of Banking and Finance, 16, 1173-78.

MOLYNEUX, P. (1993) Concentration and Rivalry in European Banking, IEF Research Papers, 93/14.

MOOSLECHNER, P. (1994) Institutional Patterns of Financial Systems: Do They Make a Difference, Paper Presented at CEEA Conference, Gerzensee, April 27-29, 1994.

MULDUR, U. (1993) Foreign Competition in the French Banking System, IEF Research papers, 93/1.

NEVEN, D. (1993) Structural Adjustment in European Retail Banking: Some Views from Industrial Organization, in Dermine, J. ed. European Banking in 1990's, Basil Blackwell, Oxford.

NIEHANS, J. (1975) The Theory of Money. The John Hopkins University Press.

PAROUSH, J. and RUTHENBERG D. (1986) Automated Teller Machines and the Share of Demand Deposits in the Money Supply, European Economic Review, 30, 1207-15.

PULLEY, L. and HUMPHREY, D. (1993) The Role of Fixed Costs and Cost Complementarities in Determining Scope Economies and the Cost of Narrow Banking Proposals, Journal of Business, 66, 3, 437-62.

REVELL, J. (1991) Changes in Universal Banks and the Effect of Bank Mergers, IEF Research Papers, 91/15.

ROSE, P. (1989) Profiles of US Merging Banks and the Performance, Outcomes and Motivations for Recent Mergers, In Gup, B. ed. Bank Mergers: Current Issues and Perspectives, Kluwer Academic Publishers, London.

SALOP, S. (1979) Monopolistic Competition with Outside Goods, Bell Journal of Economics, 10, 141-56.

SANTOMERO, A. (1984) Modelling the Banking Firm, Journal of Money Credit and Banking, 16, 577-602.

SCHMID, F. (1993) Should Bank Branching Be Regulated ? Theory and Empirical Evidence from Four European Countries, Warwick Economic Research Papers, 401.

SCHERER, F. and ROSS, D. (1990) Industrial Market Structure and Economic Performance, Houghton Mifflin Company, Boston.

SHAW, E. (1990) Changes in Organizational Structures in Banking, IEF Research Papers, 90/21.

SLADE, M. (1990 Strategic Pricing Models and Interpretation of Price-War Data, European Economic Review, 34, 524-37.

STEINHERR, A. and GILIBERT, P. (1989) The Impact of Freeing Trade in Financial Services and Capital Movements on the European Banking Industry, European Investment Bank.

STIGLITZ, J. and WEISS, A. (1985) Credit Rationing in Markets with Imperfect Information, American Economic Review, 71, 393-410.

SUOMINEN, M. and TARKKA, J. (1991): Trends in the Demand for and Pricing of Banking Services in Finland, Bank of Finland Bulletin, 65, 10, (October).

TARKKA, J. (1992) Tax on Interest and the Pricing of Personal Demand Deposits, Bank of Finland Discussion Papers, 11/92.

TARKKA, J. (1994) Implicit Interest as Price Discrimination in the Bank Deposit Market, Bank of Finland Discussion Papers, 1/94.

TIROLE, J. (1988) The Theory of Industrial Organization, Cambridge MA, MIT Press.

WALKER, D. (1978) Economies of Scale in Electronic Funds Transfer Systems, Journal of Banking and Finance, 2, 65-78.

WALSH, C. (1983) Taxation of Interest Income, Deregulation and the Banking Industry, Journal of Finance, 28, 5, 1529-42.

WHITEHEAD, M. (1990a) The UK Credit Market: Competitive Threats and Opportunities, IEF Research Papers, 90/2.

WHITEHEAD, M. (1990b) Electronic Funds Transfer at Point of Sale: An Appraisal of Developments, IEF Research Papers, 90/10.

VESALA, J. (1993a) Retail Banking in European Financial Integration, Bank of Finland, D:77.

VESALA, J. (1993b) Competition in the Finnish Banking Industry: A Test Based on Reduced Form Revenue Equations, Bank of Finland Research Department Working Paper, 21/93.

VIRÉN, M. (1993) Maksuvälineiden käyttö ja käteisrahan kysyntä Suomessa, Bank of Finland, A:87 (in Finnish).

VITTAS, D., FRAZER, P. and Metaxas-VITTAS (1988) The Retail Banking Revolution: An International Perspective, Lafferty Publications, London.

VIVES, X. (1991): Banking Competition and European Integration, in Giovanni, A. and Mayer, C. eds European Financial Integration, Cambridge University Press.

for large and well-known companies. At the same time, German banks are very important issuers of bonds in both the domestic and the international bond and note markets.

In addition to the legal framework, other structural features of the real economy also favour banking intermediation in Germany. These structural characteristics may have a more important and longer-term impact than the legal differences on the balance between bank intermediation and capital market intermediation. The bulk of the demand for external funds needed by the corporate sector comes from small and medium-size companies, for which the banks continue to be the most efficient intermediaries, and not from the large enterprises. The concentration in German industry is relatively less advanced than is often thought. This decentralised structure also has an influence on the question of where and in what form the liquid financial assets of the corporate sector are being invested.

The assessment of the structural factors which influence the traditional financial intermediation function of banks has led to the tentative conclusion that banks in Germany are likely to stay in a strong position. Considering the needs of the corporate and household sectors, banks seem to be well placed to intermediate funds involving the transformation of deposits into loans, the transformation of large-denomination financial assets into smaller-denomination, and to diversify assets. In relation to the needs of the public sector, there is additional specific phenomenon of on-balance-sheet securitisation, which strengthens the traditional intermediation function of German banks. I will [...] to this development later on.

[...] shift towards more transaction-oriented or fee-oriented banking does [...] to have impaired the principle of relationship banking between banks [...] customers ("Hausbankenprinzip"). This leaves the banks in a strong [...] find counterparties and to evaluate directly the credit risk exposure [...] with such traditional lending, which may nevertheless include the [...] of securities and the purchase of securitised assets for trading and [...] purposes, and finally, and more recently, to engage in off-balance-[...] tives transactions on the basis of underlying cash transactions. Risk [...] involves the continuous monitoring of counterparty risk, which is [...] relegated to secondary importance vis-à-vis market risks, nor is it [...] - in the case of security issues - by the activities of credit rating [...] other important aspect is the cost of such monitoring, i.e. of [...] uate information quickly. What counts in case of repayme[...] [...] ability of banks to defend their creditor position, as comp[...] [...] n of (potential) owners of securities. Finally, the on-ba[...]

Chapter 4

THE CHANGING ROLE OF BANKS IN EUROPE
A GERMAN VIEWPOINT

Dietmar K.R. Klein, Deutsche Bundesbank

I. Background and introduction

When we met at OECD Headquarters in September 1990 to review the general issue of banking structure and regulation and to exchange views on emerging patterns of financial systems, one of the main conclusions was [1]:

"Financial systems will continue to differ from country to country, even within the unified EC market. It has, indeed, been assumed that historically national systems and related traditions, practices and cultures are so different from country to country that it is highly unlikely for national systems to become very similar, even if it were possible to harmonize to a very large extent the basic regulatory frameworks within which financial institutions and markets operate ... Nevertheless, it may be possible to identify a number of structural features which the national financial systems of the future are likely to have in common."

A different, and at any rate a more one-sided position, was adopted by a staff team of the International Monetary Fund in its 1992 report on "International Financial Markets" [2]. In a chapter on "Structural Changes and Related Policy Issues in Financial Markets", the staff team raised the question "which structure is most likely to prevail over the medium term", thereby juxtaposing the United States and Germany. The staff team came to the following conclusion:

"... the evidence indicates that the trend is toward a disintermediated, liquid, securitized structure, although some role for traditional relationship banking will remain ... An alternative to bank intermediation is likely to be within reach. For this reason, say, five years from now, the continental European markets will probably look more like New York and London markets than they do today." Another key statement of the staff team is that "a key feature of the new financial environment is the competition-driven disintermediation from banking systems - particularly from wholesale banking - into securitized money and capital markets".

I would like to argue that thinking in terms of alternatives can be quite fruitful for our discussion, but that in the end we will not have gained very much insight if we insist on clinging to a simple "either-or" approach: a distinction between "bank-based and market-based financial systems" seems ultimately not very meaningful.

II.   Convergence of financial systems?

Instead, I foresee the emergence of "internationalized, market-oriented financial system(s)"[3], where bank intermediation and capital market intermediation operate side by side, with increasingly stronger links between these two kinds of financial intermediation.   The trend towards more convergence of the two systems will continue; no financial system will be left completely unaffected by developments in other open markets, such as the introduction of financial innovations. However, there are a number of different country-specific factors which may continue to exert an influence on the working of the different financial systems for a long time to come; they support the expectation that in Germany and other continental European countries bank intermediation, under competitive market conditions, will continue to play the dominant role.

There is neither an "ideal financial system" for all countries, nor is it possible to construct in the abstract the most suitable, *i.e.* the most efficient, financial system for a particular country. However, a high degree of efficiency in the intermediation process of funds from savers and financial investors to end-users of these funds - that is the "real economy" - can be expected if market forces dominate. This is the justification of a high degree of financial deregulation and cross-border liberalisation. It is a sign of inefficiency if banking systems which are protected from domestic and international competition enjoy relatively high net interest income margins, one of the traditional intermediation indicators. In Germany, which abolished all lending and deposit regulations in the late 60s, they are relatively narrow by European standards.

To the extent that public authorities continue to intervene in the market process for reasons of financial stability, the protection of depositors/investors

168

and so on, there is now a broad and growing consensus regarding the need to establish a level playing field: not only among domestic market participants but also internationally, by adopting international rules (mostly in the form of recommendations).

III. Limits to convergence

Yet, there are limits to this convergence trend. In Germany, for example, the promotion of "Finanzplatz Deutschland", in particular by a step-by-step lowering of minimum reserve ratios in order to reduce the competitive disadvantage faced by German banks vis-à-vis those banking centres abroad where banking liabilities are not subjected to this burden, was not allowed to endanger the effectiveness of minimum reserves as a monetary policy instrument. This is one of the major reasons why non-resident banks, including foreign subsidiaries and branches of German banks, will continue to perform important part of their intermediary function in DM funds outside German Monetary policy considerations were also responsible for the fact that issuance of DM commercial paper by non-financial entities was authorised a few years ago (equally remarkable has been the fact that market succe very limited). Likewise, the Bundesbank, although it continues to harbor objections to pure money market funds on the basis of central considerations, has now given up its opposition to this short-term instrument. At the same time, it has asked the Federal Government to abstain from any financing by issuing Treasury bills.

There are other features of the German legal framework wh favour corporate borrowing from the domestic banking system, a direct recourse to the capital markets. This applies not only to but to a large extent also to medium-sized enterprises. Bar successfully for a significant share of external finance for corporations.

The number of undertakings which are public limit Aktiengesellschaft) is quite small in relation to those w companies (G.m.b.H = Gesellschaft mit beschränkter required by law to adhere to high public disclosure st and transparent rules of corporate governance. marketability of credit contracts. Furthermore, re orate bonds is relatively expensive because the af taxable capital by the local authorities e of issuing corporate bonds in the inte

169

Chapter 4

THE CHANGING ROLE OF BANKS IN EUROPE
A GERMAN VIEWPOINT

Dietmar K.R. Klein, Deutsche Bundesbank

I.   Background and introduction

When we met at OECD Headquarters in September 1990 to review the general issue of banking structure and regulation and to exchange views on emerging patterns of financial systems, one of the main conclusions was [1]:

"Financial systems will continue to differ from country to country, even within the unified EC market. It has, indeed, been assumed that historically national systems and related traditions, practices and cultures are so different from country to country that it is highly unlikely for national systems to become very similar, even if it were possible to harmonize to a very large extent the basic regulatory frameworks within which financial institutions and markets operate ... Nevertheless, it may be possible to identify a number of structural features which the national financial systems of the future are likely to have in common."

A different, and at any rate a more one-sided position, was adopted by a staff team of the International Monetary Fund in its 1992 report on "International Financial Markets" [2]. In a chapter on "Structural Changes and Related Policy Issues in Financial Markets", the staff team raised the question "which structure is most likely to prevail over the medium term", thereby juxtaposing the United States and Germany. The staff team came to the following conclusion:

"... the evidence indicates that the trend is toward a disintermediated, liquid, securitized structure, although some role for traditional relationship banking will remain ... An alternative to bank intermediation is likely to be within reach. For this reason, say, five years from now, the continental European markets will probably look more like New York and London markets than they

167

do today." Another key statement of the staff team is that "a key feature of the new financial environment is the competition-driven disintermediation from banking systems - particularly from wholesale banking - into securitized money and capital markets".

I would like to argue that thinking in terms of alternatives can be quite fruitful for our discussion, but that in the end we will not have gained very much insight if we insist on clinging to a simple "either-or" approach: a distinction between "bank-based and market-based financial systems" seems ultimately not very meaningful.

II. Convergence of financial systems?

Instead, I foresee the emergence of "internationalized, market-oriented financial system(s)"[3], where bank intermediation and capital market intermediation operate side by side, with increasingly stronger links between these two kinds of financial intermediation. The trend towards more convergence of the two systems will continue; no financial system will be left completely unaffected by developments in other open markets, such as the introduction of financial innovations. However, there are a number of different country-specific factors which may continue to exert an influence on the working of the different financial systems for a long time to come; they support the expectation that in Germany and other continental European countries bank intermediation, under competitive market conditions, will continue to play the dominant role.

There is neither an "ideal financial system" for all countries, nor is it possible to construct in the abstract the most suitable, *i.e.* the most efficient, financial system for a particular country. However, a high degree of efficiency in the intermediation process of funds from savers and financial investors to end-users of these funds - that is the "real economy" - can be expected if market forces dominate. This is the justification of a high degree of financial deregulation and cross-border liberalisation. It is a sign of inefficiency if banking systems which are protected from domestic and international competition enjoy relatively high net interest income margins, one of the traditional intermediation indicators. In Germany, which abolished all lending and deposit regulations in the late 60s, they are relatively narrow by European standards.

To the extent that public authorities continue to intervene in the market process for reasons of financial stability, the protection of depositors/investors

168

and so on, there is now a broad and growing consensus regarding the need to establish a level playing field: not only among domestic market participants but also internationally, by adopting international rules (mostly in the form of recommendations).

III. Limits to convergence

Yet, there are limits to this convergence trend. In Germany, for example, the promotion of "Finanzplatz Deutschland", in particular by a step-by-step lowering of minimum reserve ratios in order to reduce the competitive disadvantage faced by German banks vis-à-vis those banking centres abroad where banking liabilities are not subjected to this burden, was not allowed to endanger the effectiveness of minimum reserves as a monetary policy instrument. This is one of the major reasons why non-resident banks, including foreign subsidiaries and branches of German banks, will continue to perform an important part of their intermediary function in DM funds outside Germany. Monetary policy considerations were also responsible for the fact that the issuance of DM commercial paper by non-financial entities was authorised only a few years ago (equally remarkable has been the fact that market success was very limited). Likewise, the Bundesbank, although it continues to harbour some objections to pure money market funds on the basis of central banking considerations, has now given up its opposition to this short-term financial instrument. At the same time, it has asked the Federal Government to continue to abstain from any financing by issuing Treasury bills.

There are other features of the German legal framework which implicitly favour corporate borrowing from the domestic banking system, at the expense of direct recourse to the capital markets. This applies not only to small companies, but to a large extent also to medium-sized enterprises. Banks even compete successfully for a significant share of external finance for large, "blue-chip" corporations.

The number of undertakings which are public limited companies (A.G. = Aktiengesellschaft) is quite small in relation to those which are private limited companies (G.m.b.H = Gesellschaft mit beschränkter Haftung). Only A.G's are required by law to adhere to high public disclosure standards regarding detailed and transparent rules of corporate governance, a precondition for the marketability of credit contracts. Furthermore, refinancing through domestic corporate bonds is relatively expensive because these bonds are considered to be part of taxable capital by the local authorities ("Gewerbekapitalsteuer"). The alternative of issuing corporate bonds in the international market is only feasible for large and well-known companies. At the same time, German banks are very important issuers of bonds in both the domestic and the international bond and note markets.

In addition to the legal framework, other structural features of the real economy also favour banking intermediation in Germany. These structural characteristics may have a more important and longer-term impact than the legal differences on the balance between bank intermediation and capital market intermediation. The bulk of the demand for external funds needed by the corporate sector comes from small and medium-size companies, for which the banks continue to be the most efficient intermediaries, and not from the large enterprises. The concentration in German industry is relatively less advanced than is often thought. This decentralised structure also has an influence on the question of where and in what form the liquid financial assets of the corporate sector are being invested.

The assessment of the structural factors which influence the traditional financial intermediation function of banks has led to the tentative conclusion that banks in Germany are likely to stay in a strong position. Considering the needs of the corporate and household sectors, banks seem to be well placed to intermediate funds involving the transformation of deposits into loans, the transformation of large-denomination financial assets into smaller-denomination ones, and to diversify assets. In relation to the needs of the public sector, there is the additional specific phenomenon of on-balance-sheet securitisation, which strengthens the traditional intermediation function of German banks. I will return to this development later on.

The shift towards more transaction-oriented or fee-oriented banking does not seem to have impaired the principle of relationship banking between banks and their customers ("Hausbankenprinzip"). This leaves the banks in a strong position to find counterparties and to evaluate directly the credit risk exposure associated with such traditional lending, which may nevertheless include the underwriting of securities and the purchase of securitised assets for trading and investment purposes, and finally, and more recently, to engage in off-balance-sheet derivatives transactions on the basis of underlying cash transactions. Risk management involves the continuous monitoring of counterparty risk, which is therefore not relegated to secondary importance vis-à-vis market risks, nor is it fully replaced - in the case of security issues - by the activities of credit rating agencies. Another important aspect is the cost of such monitoring, *i.e.* of gathering adequate information quickly. What counts in case of repayment difficulties is the ability of banks to defend their creditor position, as compared with the position of (potential) owners of securities. Finally, the on-balance-sheet intermediation of funds involves the management of all credit, market, and liquidity risks connected to that function.

IV. Specific structural issues

I am turning now to a number of specific structural issues.

1. The evolving nature of universal banking under competitive conditions

The first structural issue to be taken up is the evolving nature of universal banking under competitive conditions. The changes in competitive conditions since the early sixties have been the subject of many studies in the past, including those made under the auspices of the OECD Committee on Financial Markets and its Experts' Group on Banking.

In terms of relative importance I would mention first the internationalisation of banking and financial markets. The opening-up of financial markets, the supply of cross-border financial services and the impact from the entry of foreign commercial and investment banks have become the most important factors behind changes in competitive conditions. Other factors are the continuous process of deregulation, partly as a consequence of the internationalization of markets, partly as a muddle-through process, but partly also as a result of an endogenous and well-planned political design.

The issue addressed here is what kind of financial intermediaries are most likely to survive in an environment of increasing domestic and cross-border competition. Will it be the universal banks, which may enjoy important economies of scope, and possibly also of scale, or in a small number of cases large financial conglomerates, if the group includes insurance companies? Or will it be instead the more specialised financial institutions with possible economies of scale, such as investment banks and securities houses, excelling in their fields of comparative advantage? Without interference, there will be a natural tendency for large institutions to take on additional functions, but these may not necessarily be performed in-house.

In countries with universal banking systems - today more or less all European countries - banking business can be conducted in a very flexible manner. This means that a bank can largely decide whether:

 i) it does everything it is authorised to do, or whether;

ii) it specializes in certain lines of business on the basis of comparative advantage, or whether;

iii) it concludes that certain financial functions will be performed better via a subsidiary or some other type of affiliate.

But even in these countries public policy may stipulate that - for reasons other than efficiency - certain functions can be performed only in separate entities under strict legal conditions: a case in point in Germany is the issue of mortgage bonds ("Pfandbriefe") and communal bonds ("Kommunalobligationen", most of which are denominated as "Öffentliche Pfandbriefe") by German mortgage banks and public-law banks. left The same applies to the provision of housing loans by German savings and loan associations (Bausparkassen), or the writing of life insurance and other insurance contracts by legally independent companies.

The ownership structure can be very diverse, ranging from truly independent financial institutions - which have no significant capital and management linkages with another bank - to those which are predominantly or even wholly owned by a universal bank. In the latter case, which has increasingly become a characteristic feature of European banking systems, the objective is to generate major synergy effects for the benefit of the whole group. At the same time, it is intended to spread risks, much like in a universal bank, where all banking functions in the broadest sense would be performed in-house. It is therefore logical to stipulate that accounting and reporting should also be placed on a consolidated basis, notwithstanding the fact that, legally, reporting requirements may still differ in certain ways, and that insurance companies in most European countries are still supervised by a separate national authority.

My main thesis, then, is that the segmentation of banking in terms of scope (financial instruments), geography and market participants (customers), which was originally designed in some countries to protect the banks against excessive risks, has proven to be a weakening factor in the longer run. The universal bank, in contrasts, has shown itself to be more adaptable to temporary or permanent shifts in the refinancing and lending pattern. The decentralisation of decision-making in large financial conglomerates seems to be the best response to the challenge to compete in highly diversified financial markets. Retail markets, which by definition remain very important, are most likely to remain local or at most regional. Financial markets in the wholesale sector have usually a national scope, and some have even become truly global in character.

Clearly, the bank has to serve its different types of customers, and to offer those financial products, which are in demand on the part of the type of customers served. Universal banks are in a good position to respond to these rapidly changing needs. Losses suffered in one area may be better balanced by profits in other areas, while growth opportunities can be seized earlier than by competitors in segmented systems. The concept of universal banking has, furthermore, never been identical to that of the traditional lending and deposit business of commercial banks. And there is no requirement stipulating that it should. Investment banking has always played an important role for banks with a proven record of high growth, though that does not mean that every bank must be predominantly an investment bank.

The principle of decentralised decision-making has to be combined with the principle of integrated and centralised risk management. Irrespective of whether financial transactions are executed in-house or elsewhere within a financial group, the overall responsibility cannot be limited or subdivided. At times of impending crisis, limitation of responsibility through some "fire-wall system" could easily reduce the confidence of markets and customers not only in the stability of a particular financial affiliate but also in the stability of the parent bank at the core of a financial group.

An extension of this idea is the deposit-insurance system run by the industry itself. The responsibility assumed in this way goes beyond the provision of any required liquidity; it also includes the collective carrying of eventual losses incurred through the insolvency of a member bank. This lowers the probability of a systemic financial collapse and therefore it also reduces the chance that authorities have to intervene (that is by acting as "lender-of-last-resort" or possibly even by bailing-out banks).

In sum, the typical institutional set-up of a larger financial group in Europe in the future seems to be that of a universal bank at the core of a financial conglomerate, called "Allfinanz" or "Bank assurance", which may encompass a number of subsidiaries, irrespective of whether they have been created in response to legal requirements or for reasons of efficiency.

2. Longer term financing demand and the difference between on-balance-sheet and off-balance-sheet securitisation

There is another important feature of the banking systems in Germany and - to a much lesser degree - in some other European countries which is strengthening the traditional intermediation role of banks. This is the instrument of on-balance-sheet securitisation in order to satisfy longer-term financing needs.

This is a form of financing which plays a rather important role in the financing of residential (and commercial) real estate as well as in public sector deficits. In particular, it should be remembered that public expenditure has been rising in recent years to more than 50 per cent of GDP in Germany - not least in connection with temporary, but presently huge, public transfers from western to eastern Germany, to the tune of DM 170 billion gross per annum or about 5 per cent of GDP. However, in other European countries the public expenditure ratio is also fairly high. The ensuing large public sector deficits have been financed not only directly on the domestic and international capital markets but also indirectly through bank intermediaries.

On-balance-sheet securitisation may work in several different ways. One well-known channel is to buy government paper, especially in recessionary times when the demand for additional funds from the private corporate sector is relatively small or even negative. Much less well-known outside Germany is the large-scale issue of bonds by mortgage banks and public-law banks. If they meet a number of relatively stringent legal criteria, then these bank bonds can be denominated either mortgage bonds ("Hypothekenpfandbriefe"), or when residential or communal real estate mortgages serve as collateral for commercial bonds ("Kommunalobligationen"); the latter collateral is of high quality and consists of counterparty claims on public sector entities, predominantly at the local and regional levels.

In recent years the importance of "Hypothekenpfandbriefe" has been dwarfed by the growing issue of communal bonds, the bulk of which are "Öffentliche Pfandbriefe". At the same time, these special mortgage bonds and communal bonds are issued under the full responsibility of the issuing bank. In addition, universal and specialised banks also issue a huge amount of other types of bank bonds under less stringent conditions.

All these bond types can be considered important forms of asset-related or on-balance-sheet securitisation. In Germany they are by no means new. Actually they have a very long tradition[4]. The intermediation of public debt through on-balance-sheet securitisation started in the late twenties. Today it is very seldom that regional and local authorities offer bonds directly to investors in the markets.

Finally, on-balance-sheet securitisation not only means the securitisation of certain bank assets through the indirect creation of certain securitised bank liabilities but can also mean the purchase of those liabilities by other banks. Indeed, a sizeable share of all bank bonds is being purchased by other banks as an integral part of their own asset and liability management.

Largely the opposite effect results from asset-backed securitization in the form of selling certain types of private sector bank assets to a subsidiary which then issues securities on the basis of that collateral. They are called mortgage-backed securities (MBS) or other asset-backed securities (ABS). This type of off-balance-sheet securitization, which has become very popular in the United States, leads to a shortening, and not to a lengthening, of the bank balance sheet.

In legal terms the creditor has a claim only on the bank subsidiary and the collateral, but not on the bank, even though the bank may continue to be charged with replenishing the collateral where it has a maturity shorter than the securities issued.

The idea of asset-backed securities, and in particular mortgage-backed securities, did not become very popular in Germany, although ABS issues are not legally prohibited. However, the supervisory authorities continue to look upon this construction with some disfavour. This is based on the reasoning that in the case of severe solvency problems, which would first manifest themselves in the form of pronounced price declines, the originating bank might feel itself morally bound to buy those bonds. Furthermore, the danger cannot be excluded that the market might infer from any relatively low level of the bond prices that the bank would not be able to buy the paper in circulation, and this might cast an unfavourable light on the bank's market standing.

In any case, the quality of the ABS depends very much on the quality and size of the collateral relative to the volume of bonds issued. Also of great importance is the entire set of legal arrangements, which are not uniform and therefore not transparent for the average investor. Finally, banks in Germany generally see no advantage in this type of disintermediation.

V.   Bank disintermediation and on-balance-sheet transactions

Another issue is the alleged process of "bank disintermediation", which is often, but mistakenly, seen as being synonymous with "securitisation".

As far as the statistical evidence in Germany is concerned, there is no clear sign of any bank disintermediation in terms of a decline of on-balance-sheet intermediation. Admittedly, it is difficult to come to any definite conclusion about the trend in the nineties. For more than four years the financial system has been coping with the tremendous task of the economic and financial integration of the eastern and western parts of Germany. It is not impossible that the net effect arising from the financing of German integration is a slightly higher intermediation ratio than would otherwise have been the case.

In any case, whether one takes the growth of the balance sheet total, or the growth of the total credit volume extended to the domestic public and private sectors, or the growth of M3 (the relatively liquid part of total bank liabilities) in all cases the growth rate continues to be somewhat higher than that of GDP.

If one would look instead at the changing distribution pattern of financial assets held by the household sector, one observes a certain declining trend in short and longer-term investments held with banks, including non-tradable bank savings bonds, even if allowance is made for a substantial volume of mostly Euro-DM funds held with banks abroad. A growing part of household sector assets is, moreover, held in the form of Pfandbriefe and other bonds issued by banks of all sorts (directly or via investment funds), yet in quantitative terms the overall trend in market shares would still be somewhat negative. This constitutes one of the main reasons why banks are increasingly seeking to respond to households growing preference for insurance products and to develop the off-balance-sheet business.

The picture does not change very much if we calculate all domestic non-financial sectors' financial investment with banks as a percentage share of all financial assets. In the seventies and early eighties this share was slightly above 50 per cent. In the late eighties and the early nineties, the share was just a shade below the 50 per cent mark.

Bank lending to domestic producing enterprises as a percentage of funds borrowed in the market has been quite stable, namely somewhat above the 80 per cent mark through the seventies and eighties up to the end of 1993. The recent introduction of commercial paper issued by a limited number of large companies has so far had a small overall impact only. It is still to early to make a forecast on the net impact arising from the introduction of money market funds in 1994.

VI. Banking intermediation and off-balance-sheet transactions

However, the picture scetched above is still incomplete for evaluating the changing role of banks in the financial intermediation process.

The question arises as to whether the rapid development of the banks' off-balance-sheet business in recent years has a significant impact on the definition of banking intermediation. As the name implies, business activity in this field is not normally reflected on the balance sheet of a bank. However, the financial results of off-balance-sheet activities are entered in the profit and loss account of a bank, though with varying degrees of transparency from bank to bank and country to country.

Certain types of off-balance-sheet transactions have been around for a long time, such as the provision of guarantees, forward transactions, the underwriting of shares and bonds, the provision of credit before the actual drawing-down period has started, the provision of back-up lines of credit to capital market participants, and so on. In more recent years, banks have taken up the business of derivatives transactions in a very big way, though it has to be recognized that the degree of concentration is considerably higher than in the case of on-balance-sheet transactions. Hence they have assumed credit, market, and liquidity risks separately from fund flows, which continue to be recorded on balance sheet.

As long as there was still no systematic unbundling of the usual credit, market, and liquidity risks as separate financial instruments from the underlying cash transactions, these risks were part and parcel of the traditional on-balance-sheet intermediation function. The assumption of credit and market risks has always started at the time when the credit was provided and not when the first tranche of the credit was drawn down and an actual flow of intermediated funds ensued. Why should the situation be different now, when these financial risks are being used as separate off-balance-sheet financial instruments, but which have a direct impact on the assets and liabilities intermediated on balance sheet?

It is therefore fully justified to advocate an integrated approach to the measurement and management of both market and credit risks, as a recent G-30 report on derivatives has done, irrespective of whether they appear on- or off-balance-sheet. Also, the Basle Committee on Banking Supervision stated that a comprehensive risk measurement approach would be needed whereby the risks from derivatives and non-derivatives activities should be integrated into the financial institution's overall risk management system[5]. In this way one can usefully distinguish between[6]:

i) balance sheet risks (*i.e.* mismatches between the currency, maturity and interest rate structure of assets and the liabilities funding those assets resulting in interest rate mismatch risk, liquidity risk and foreign exchange risk), and

ii) transaction risks (*i.e.* credit risks, price risks and operating and liquidity risks).

In this sense, banks act as financial intermediaries, *i.e.* they perform the intermediation function, as long as they assume calculated financial risks in a proprietary function against fee-income, in contrast to merely providing a brokerage service or some other services, thereby also earning some fees.

In terms of the risk-taking and risk-managing function of banks in the process of financial intermediation, there is no obvious difference between on-balance and off-balance operations. However, there may be changes in the composition and weighting of the various functions which banks perform as financial intermediaries.

In assessing the scope of banking intermediation, we should therefore bear in mind all kinds of off-balance-sheet transactions ranging from traditional ones to innovative derivatives market transactions. We should not refrain from doing so by difficult measurement problems.

In any case, the rising share of net fees earned - reflecting by and large a bank's off-balance-sheet activities - in relation to its net interest income - reflecting the relative profitability of the on-balance-sheet business before special provisions and taxes - may be a good indicator of the changing nature of banking intermediation, even though this indicator includes fee income which should not have been included. Fees earned from underwriting business, from the buying and selling of securities, and from any arbitrage business, should be left in.

In terms of additional credit risk incurred through derivatives transactions, the credit equivalent (of maybe 2 per cent of the total nominal value of derivatives) may be another useful yardstick, making a comparison with on-balance-sheet credit business possible.

In conclusion, the widening scope of business opportunities, *i.e.* beyond the traditional lending and depositing functions, in particular in the innovative off-balance-sheet area, has strengthened the risk intermediation role of banks; it has thereby compensated the banks as a whole for possible moderate losses of market shares in financial intermediation, as traditionally defined.

Notes

1   OECD, Banks Under Stress, Paris, 1992, p. 139.

2   International Monetary Fund (M. Goldstein, D. Folkerts-Landau, *et al.*) "International Capital Markets - Developments, Prospects, and Policy Issues", Washington D.C., 1992, p.2 f.

3   See Chapter I in this volume.

4   See country note on Germany in the OECD publication on "Securitisation", OECD, Paris, to be published in 1995.

5   Basle Committee on Banking Supervision, Risk Management Guidelines for Derivatives, July 1994, p. 7.

6   See Chapter I in this volume.

Chapter 5

THE EVOLUTION OF THE NORTH AMERICAN BANKING SYSTEM*

Edward C. Ettin
Board of Governors of the Federal Reserve System, Washington

Introduction

My assignment is to discuss the evolution of the banking system in North America: the United States, Canada, and Mexico. However, most of what I have to say will be about the United States because of my own lack of knowledge about the financial systems of Canada and Mexico.

The paper is divided into two major sections. In the first, I attempt briefly to summarize the institutional structure of the North American banking system and, in the United States case, its trend to fewer and larger depository institutions while still maintaining a large number of organizations. The longer second section addresses the decline in the measured share of financial markets by North American banks and attempts to support the case that, in the United States, the decline is more apparent than real. Improvements in technology, new financial instruments, more active markets, and financial globalization may have reduced the economic need for intermediation. Nonetheless, banks - at least in the United States - have maintained - and perhaps increased - their role as measurers, managers, and acceptors of risk.

---

*   The opinions expressed are not necessarily those of the Board of Governors of the Federal Reserve System. The author would particularly like to thank David Longworth and John Kuszczak of the Bank of Canada; Moises Schwartz of the Bank of Mexico; John Boyd of the Federal Reserve Bank of Minneapolis; and Calvin Schnure, Henry Terrell, Allen Frankel, Myron Kwast, Donald Savage, Larry Promisel, John Mingo, Al Teplin, Thomas Brady, John Rea, and Michael Grupe, all at the Board of Governors, for their help and suggestions. Appreciation is also extended to Scott Garner for his patience and research assistance.

A word at the outset about the "banking system". In a world of global financial markets and in nations with open financial markets, drawing theboundary lines of the banking system must, in the last analysis, be an arbitrary exercise. North American banks have offices worldwide and foreign banks from around the world have offices in the United States, to a lesser extent in Canada,and in the future in Mexico. One could, with some justification, say the North American banking system - especially that in the United States - is made up of the sum of all banking systems. While perhaps true, that definition is not helpful. Nor is the other extreme of just looking at banking offices located in North America. Similarly, one could include all loans made from world-wide offices of North American banks to all borrowers; or one could measure simply loans to North American residents.

For different purposes, different measures are useful. I will try to note which definitions I have used at places in the paper. In all cases, I have defined the North American banking system as at least the banks chartered in North America (both domestic and foreign owned) and, in the United States' case, the US branches and agencies of foreign banks. Some measures show the loans of these organizations to all borrowers, regardless of location. Some show loans from North American offices to North American residents. Some show loans to all parties from North American offices plus loans from offshore offices of North American banks to North American residents, provided the decision to lend is - in some sense - made in North America. As will be discussed at a later point, I have chosen this last definition as the "best" for market share purposes. I admit at the beginning that this boundary, while logical, is still arbitrary.

A final introductory observation. Most of this paper slices and dices statistics to get a "better" measure of bank shares. It is necessary, I think, to answer at the outset the questions "Who cares?" and "Why bother?" As long as the public is having its financing demands met efficiently, why should central banks and finance ministries care which particular set of institutions is providing the funds? In my view, monetary policy is not the issue. Central banking works regardless of the size of the banking system, so long as central banks affect interest rates, and that does not necessarily require banks. A method of addressing systemic risk directly, however, does raise questions about which institutions should have access to central bank credit.

My answer to the questions "Who cares?" and "Why bother?" is that there is considerable public policy discussion that rightly or wrongly focuses on bank shares of markets. For purposes of that discussion, we ought to be sure what we are talking about. The discussion may - at some level - be irrelevant, but public policy decisions may be made on policymaker perceptions of the "facts". It seems obvious that we ought to make these "facts" as accurate as we can. Regardless of what the facts may turn out to be, we ought also to determine if government regulation is itself causing either the decline in bank shares or the change in bank behavior, and if that result is intended or unintended. The government regulation issue, while perhaps critical, is beyond the scope of this paper.

I.   Institutional structure

As chart 1 shows (all charts follow page 23), the United States has an unusually large, but declining, number of depository institutions, of which commercial banks account for less than half. The more recent drop-off in the number of nonbank depositories (the hollow part of the bars), which as a group are called "thrifts" in the United States, reflects the large number of failures in the savings and loan industry[1]. Within the commercial bank sector - the lowest three sections (although it looks like two) of the bars - about 3-1/ 3 per cent were foreign owned in 1993, either US chartered banks or US branches and agencies of foreign banks. (I have counted each "family" of branches and agencies only once.) The far right panel shows the predominance of small US chartered banks in the banking structure of the United States, a heritage of American history. In my view, this structure has enhanced the performance of the economy of the United States by providing innovative and creative financing to smaller businesses in local markets, although Canadian and Mexican authorities feel well served by a structure with a small number of large banks. The role of small banks is a hallmark of the banking system in the United States.

Chart 2 displays the worldwide assets of the depository institutions shown in chart 1[2]. The decline in recent years of thrift assets (the hollow portion of the bars) is clear, although even without the high savings and loan failure rate the trend towards securitization of mortgages would have reduced the portfolios of the mortgage-specializing saving and loans and savings banks. The chart also shows the increasing market share of foreign banks (the hatched and dotted part of the bars) - which by 1993 had reached 20.6 per cent of bank assets. In addition, the far right panel indicates that the few large banks, those with assets over $5 billion (the hollow section of the bar), account for most of the dollar volume of United States chartered bank assets.

The third chart compares the structure in the United States, Canada, and Mexico in 1993. This chart emphasizes the larger number and total scale of

United States institutions, and the much higher level of participation in the United States banking market by foreign institutions[3].

What may be more relevant in considering relative structure, however, is the number of institutions and offices per capita. The hollow bars in the upper panel of the fourth chart highlight the unusually large number of banks in the United States relative to Canada and Mexico, but the solid bars in the upper panel indicate that the number of banking offices per capita is fairly similar in Canada and the United States, although relatively quite low in Mexico. The hollow bars in the lower panel of the chart indicates the number of depository institutions (as opposed to just banks) per capita is also similar in Canada and United States, while the number of depository institution offices per capita (the solid bars) is higher in Canada than in the United States.

To a significant extent, the statistics on US banks overstate the number and importance of individual banks because of the dominance of bank holding companies (BHCs). Chart 5 displays the number of banking organizations, which combines banks in the same holding company into one unit. Fewer than 3 000 of the almost 11 000 banks are "independent", i.e. , not subsidiaries of BHCs. Most of the others are in BHCs that own just one bank (the black section of the bars). Nonetheless, as the dotted section of the bars in chart 6 display, three-quarters of the banking assets are in the far fewer BHCs that own more than one bank - the multi-bank BHCs.

Table 1, following chart 6, shows the assets held by the parent and nonbank subsidiaries of BHCs. In 1993, the total of such assets - about $270 billion - was a small part of the consolidated bank and nonbank assets of BHCs - a little over 7 per cent. The single largest nonbank asset was the securities holdings of securities affiliates (line 1). While not indicated in the table, nonbank asset holdings are very concentrated: two-thirds are held by 10 MBHCs; 80 per cent by the top 20; 88 per cent by the top 100. Only about 1 000 BHCs own any nondepository assets at all.

These data suggest that the banking system of the United States is becoming more concentrated in terms of national market shares of the largest banks. Indeed, last year, the largest 100 banking organizations - represented by the total length of the bars in chart 7 - accounted for 70 per cent of domestic banking assets in the United States, up from a little over half in 1980[4]. As the black and hatched part of the bars indicate, most of this growth occurred outside of the largest 5 or 10 wholesale, money center, banks, reflecting the expansion of the so-called super-regionals in the United States. However, it is important to observe that, despite the larger national market share of the largest banks, local market concentration has not changed dramatically (see table 2) because, in large part, United States antitrust laws prohibit banks from reducing competition beyond a certain point in local markets.

The dominant factor behind the trend toward greater national concentration is mergers. These have largely been between banks with modest market overlap or, for approval, have required divestiture of offices in which local concentration would increase markedly as a result of the merger. Chart 8, which excludes mergers that simply reflect internal restructuring, such as the merger of banks in the same MBHCs, clearly indicates the increasingly large size of banks acquired in recent years (the solid line). Even with the national consolidation trend, most observers do not expect that the number of banking organizations in the United States will decline much below about 5 000, even if interstate branching is authorized, reflecting ease of de novo entry, the lack of clear scale economies, and the revealed customer preference for locally managed banks.

Despite the consolidation among US banks, national concentration is much lower in the United States than in Canada or Mexico. As shown in the upper panel of chart 9, the five largest banks in Canada and Mexico dominate their banking markets, while in the United States they account for less than a fifth of domestic bank assets. The lower panel shows again that the participation by foreign banks is significantly greater in the United States than in the other two NAFTA countries. It also indicates that foreign banks can enter Canada and Mexico only as bank subsidiaries.

II. The nature of banking and market shares

With this institutional background behind us, we can now move on to discuss the changing role of banks in North America. The focus of the discussion will be on the degree to which banks are facing a declining role in financial markets, how they have responded, and the implications that might be drawn - especially with regard to the measurement of bank shares.

A. *United States bank shares*

A technical issue has to be faced before beginning any discussion of market shares for banks. As can be seen in the upper panel of chart 10, issuance of debt by all levels of government in the United States has increased dramatically since the late 1970s[5]. Commercial banks - whose raison d'être is to finance private sector credit demands, not to act as mutual funds for securities with no or minimal credit risk - have not maintained their 1950-70s share of public securities outstanding[6]. (See lower panel of chart 10.) As a result, any measure of bank shares that include public debt will have a significant downward bias.

This is shown in chart 11, which displays how shares of all debt, public and private, held by financial institutions in the United States have changed over the post-World War II period. This chart is "layered": each industry's share is placed on top of the one below it so that the "other" measure at the top of the chart brings the cumulative share up to 100 per cent. An entity type's share is the area between the upper and lower line that the caption describes. The lower two lines (the grey shaded areas) encompass "banks" in the United States - defined to include not only US owned banks but foreign banks as well: both US bank subsidiaries of foreign banks included in the lowest "US Chartered Commercial Banks" area and US branches and agencies of foreign banks shown separately in the area just above it. The banks included in this definition have, since the mid-1970s, seen their share of total credit market lending decline quite sharply. But, as in chart 12, if one excludes all government debt from the portfolios of financial institutions - and from the aggregate measures of credit market lending (the denominator of the share calculation) - one gets an entirely different indication. In private credit markets, banks in the United States have maintained and even increased their share of credit market lending by all financial institutions to all non-financial borrowing sectors.

In my view, the scaling of market shares by private, rather than total, credit market lending (*i.e.*, chart 12 instead of chart 11) is the more reasonable standard. The test for a private lender ought to be their ability to service private borrowers. The economic franchise of banks - as will be discussed more fully in section C below - is to measure, manage, and accept risk. To be sure, there is interest rate risk in public debt, and I do not mean to downplay it. But, the fundamental risk that banks - and other financial institutions - are designed to evaluate is credit risk, of which there is little to none in most public debt.

Thus, in most of the analysis that follows, the focus will be on private credit flows, on lending rather than on securities purchases by banks. And - as indicated above - chart 12 suggests that banks have been able to maintain private credit market shares among financial institutions since the 1970s. Over this period, foreign banks have increased market share quite dramatically, but, even so, the decline of national market share by United States owned banks of the aggregate lending by financial institutions seems modest[7]. It is important to emphasize that these credit statistics for banks - including loans to all borrowers all over the world - measure only loans booked in the United States by both United States and foreign banks.

The declining thrift share (the cross hatched area in chart 12) from S&L failures is clear. By 1993, the proportion of financial institutions' lending by all depository institutions (the sum of the lower gray and cross hatched areas) had declined to about 54 per cent from its 67 per cent high in 1978, owing entirely to the decline in the thrift share. Mutual funds expanded their share notably, as households shifted their portfolios from deposits to higher yielding bond funds (equity funds are excluded since all charts measure only debt). While smaller than in the 1950s and early 1960s, insurance companies and pension fund shares have increased since the mid-1980s, as has that of finance companies.

Chart 13 focuses on domestic and foreign banks in the United States - the two dark shaded areas at the bottom of chart 12 - but scales their activity not to lending by all financial institutions (as in chart 12) but rather to borrowing from all sources by non-financial bank customers. For reference, the upper panel includes US government and agency, as well as State and local bonds, in both the bank numerator and the total debt denominator, while in the lower panel the numerator includes only loans to all sectors except governments and excludes banks' modest holdings of corporate bonds and the denominator excludes the debt of all levels of government. But, while, as I have noted, I prefer the private measure in the lower panel of chart 13, by either measure it is clear that something has happened, with measured bank shares having declined sharply in the last 20 years or so[8].

Chart 14 provides some additional insight by comparing bank loans to the total of borrowing from all sources by each of the private domestic nonfinancial sectors. That is, bank loans to a sector are scaled to total borrowing from all sources by that same sector.

As shown in the lower line in the upper panel, "regular" bank loans have been declining as a source of total nonfinancial business credit, largely a reflection of funding by larger borrowers directly in money and capital markets and others turning to specialists that I will discuss shortly. It is this decline to which many observers point when noting the relative decline of banking - or at least traditional banking. But, that downtrend is far less pronounced if one adds the amount of commercial mortgages held by those banks to the business sector borrowing[9]. (Such loans are included in both panels of chart 13.)

Bank loans (including home mortgages and consumer credit) to households and nonprofit institutions as a share of their total borrowing - indicated by the top solid line in the middle panel - have shown some downtrend. These borrowers have increasingly turned to finance companies - especially those owned by the manufacturers of the product being financed ("captives") - for auto loans, and to a wide spectrum of lenders for mortgages, many of which are subsequently securitized and resold. Indeed, banks purchase and hold a significant volume of securitized mortgages, a large part of which are originated by other banks; these purchases are not included in the loan line in our chart because they are classified as securities. (They are included in the top panel of chart 13 but excluded from the lower panel of that chart.) More important for our purposes, banks originate and sell for securitization a large volume of residential mortgages. The first dashed line of the middle panel of chart 14 raises the loan share to account for an estimate of the still outstanding amount of such bank originations of residential mortgages that have been sold, mainly for purposes of securitization[10]. While not held as loans, these originations are a measure of value added and risk evaluation of credits by banks[11]. Measures of bank loan shares that ignore these originations understate, in my view, the role of banks. Banks also securitize and sell to other lenders a significant volume of consumer loans (credit cards and automobile paper). The upper dashed line adds back an estimate of the still outstanding amount of those sales - sales which are not included elsewhere on the bank balance sheet[12] - since their origination, like those for residential mortgages sold, reflects significant bank participation in the consumer credit market. Note that the securities created are held mostly by some other financial institutions, but these holdings are not included in their loans. In reflection of the banks' role in creating the underlying credits, these adjustments soften - and, if data were available for a longer period, might even eliminate - the apparent decline in the banks' share of the consumer credit market.

The sharp drop-off in the bank share of loans to foreigners booked in the United States - shown in the lowest panel - reflects foreign borrowers' increasing shift to commercial paper finance-most often with bank guarantees - and to the US bond markets.

Chart 15, which is a layered chart like chart 12, provides more detail on borrowing by the business sector, which most observers believe to be so critical to the future of banking. The chart distributes all debt of nonfinancial businesses to its source; the panels thus sum to 100 per cent. The bottom two grey areas replicate the upper panel of chart 14 - the bank share of credit flows to nonfinancial businesses (including through commercial mortgages). The increasing reliance of businesses on finance companies, offshore credit, and commercial paper is clear in this chart. Please also note in the highest dotted area of the chart the almost decade long, and accelerating trend, of increased nonfinancial business issuance of bonds. In the 1990s, a significant part of the proceeds of such issues has been used to repay bank loans and, until recently, bank loan demand itself has been quite modest, reflecting a weak economic recovery. A significant decline in measured bank loans - the lowest area - is thus in large part a reflection of a cyclical phenomenon of credit demands and of corporate refunding of short-term debt in capital markets.

B. *Canadian and Mexican bank shares*

Chart 16 indicates that, in contrast to the United States, Canadian nonbank depositories (the counterpart of US "thrifts") have increased market share among financial institutions at the expense of banks, while finance company market shares have, also in contrast to the United States, declined. In the 1990s, however, Canadian banks - the lower shaded area - have regained some of their lost share of lending by financial institutions, but this has reflected their acquisition of some of the larger trust and mortgage loan companies that had run into some financial difficulties. Bank loans as a proportion of all private sector nonfinancial borrowing (the lower line in chart 17) have declined since 1982 in Canada, but not as dramatically as in the United States (compare to lower panel of chart 13), falling back only to the 1980 share[13]. Moreover, again in part reflecting acquisition of trust and mortgage loan companies, banks have regained share in the 1990s. The second line of chart 17 adds bankers acceptances sold by the banks into the market. Bankers acceptances create a direct, on-balance sheet liability of the bank and require the bank to use its credit evaluation expertise to evaluate the riskiness of the borrower. The borrower makes its decisions on a bank loan vs. a bankers acceptance totally on the basis of interest cost and fixed vs. floating rates. The bankers acceptance initially goes into bank portfolio and the decision to sell or keep the acceptance depends on banks' liquidity position and funding costs. Thus, the bankers acceptances sold should be thought of as part of bank loans. The resultant "adjusted" bank loans as a share of private domestic nonfinancial debt - the dashed line - declines by less than unadjusted loans.

In the important nonfinancial business sector (chart 18), Canadian banks have seen their share of corporate funding decline by more than in the United States, but still retain a much larger share of the total than their American counterparts (compare chart 15). Canadian bank loan data are biased downward by bank sales of their bankers acceptance in the money market. Consequently, I have shaded bankers acceptance outstanding the same as bank loans to suggest that the area under the two lower lines in chart 18 measure adjusted bank loans to business. But, even these adjusted loans relative to total business funds raised declined quite sharply in the 1980s and early 1990s. Businesses in Canada have turned increasingly to the commercial paper market, to finance

189

companies, to trust and mortgage companies, and to mortgage financing from life insurance companies, while relying less on bond markets.

In Mexico, the commercial banks' share of credit market lending by financial institutions has declined since the early 1980s, mainly in reflection of the rising share of development banks and development funds. (See chart 19). It should be noted that for the decade or so ending in 1991-92 the Mexican commercial banks were nationalized. As shown by their small shares, non-development nonbank financial institutions play a quite modest role in the Mexican financial system.

C. The changing nature of banking

Each of the NAFTA countries thus appears to have at least some indications that their banking sectors are accounting for a smaller share of credit flows. Some observers, particularly in the United States, have argued that commercial banking may in fact be a dying industry, unable to compete. These United States commentators have argued that banks face excessive regulatory costs and restrictions - especially the prohibition or limitation on securities underwriting - and face increasingly sophisticated borrowers with direct access to money and capital markets that no longer need the credit intermediation that banks offer. Banks' ability to profit from their special expertise in collecting information on, and evaluating, borrowers has been diminished because information can be collected and transmitted to many lenders more cheaply due to the information revolution accompanying the computer. In short, less and less information asymmetry exists from which banks have traditionally made their basic core profits. Banks, the argument concludes, have been left with the higher-cost and higher-risk borrowers and have not yet developed the skills to price such credits appropriately.

Put another way, banks' traditional role has been (1) to intermediate between depositors seeking liquid claims and borrowers wishing to borrow at intermediate-term using illiquid instruments and (2) to use their expertise to collect and evaluate information not available broadly to others. This role has meant that banks have evaluated and pooled risk for their own diversification and have provided safety and liquidity to their customers. In addition, they have taken considerable credit and market risk by providing a variety of payment services. In sum, traditional banking, as Federal Reserve Chairman Greenspan has observed, "...can be viewed, at an elemental level, as simply the measurement, management, and acceptance of risk"[14].

Has the economic need for this "...measurement, management and acceptance of risk" by banks declined, and is this the reason for the falling share of banks in the credit process highlighted in the charts? Have other institutions become more adept at providing this function, displacing banks? Or have the methods by which banks "measure, manage, and accept risk," and as a result the way we should measure banks' role, changed?[15] I believe the third alternative is closer to reality.

Chairman Greenspan, in a recent speech[16], noted:

> "Banks still perform... traditional functions. But today we are increasingly recognizing that banking also involves understanding, processing, and using massive amounts of information regarding the credit risks, market risks, and other risks inherent in a vast array of products and services, many of which do not involve traditional lending, deposit taking, or payments services. Today, banks can be said to be part of a technological revolution in risk information processing. Moreover, risk information processing - defined broadly to include the measurement, management, and taking of risk - can be said to have remained the basic business of banking. A crucial difference between the banks of today and those of our traditions, however, is that risk information processing now lies more visibly closer to the core of the banking business because of the blossoming of new financial products and services that rely so critically on fast and high quality risk information and risk analysis.
>
> It is easy to become awed by the incredible variety of new financial instruments that this risk management revolution has helped to bring about. It is even easier to become convinced that banking has been transformed into a completely new creature. But at root I believe that the basic functions of banks remain unchanged.
>
> Let me give a few examples. As I just indicated, the traditional bank provides risk reduction benefits associated with asset pool diversification, with the asset pool remaining on the bank's books. More recently, banks have continued to combine assets into pools, but now these pools are often sold rather than kept on the balance sheet. Often, a bank guarantee, such as a standby letter of credit or a limited recourse agreement, is attached to these pools. The resulting products are "new," but has the fundamental banking function really changed? Banks perform the same functions for the economy through overall risk reduction and bring the same skills to bear whether they are selling a liability backed by a diversified asset pool plus bank equity -

which we call traditional intermediation - or selling a share in a diversified asset pool backed by limited recourse - which we call securitization. Similarly, bank functions remain essentially the same if banks are selling shares in a diversified, but unbacked asset pool managed by, but not owned by, a bank - a product we call a mutual fund. While in the case of mutual funds banks may not assume explicit credit risk, they are performing identical tasks for the economy. Moreover, bank guarantees are a natural outgrowth of the bank's value added in collecting, processing, and understanding the information needed to assess the riskiness of the pool. Similar arguments can be made regarding the basic functions being performed by banks in assessing and managing the credit and other risks associated with, for example, underwriting many other types of securities, or creating and dealing in swaps and other derivative products."

Let me quickly note that Chairman Greenspan was not arguing that banking was becoming solely a financial management, advisory, and communications industry with small balance sheets. Rather, he was simply noting that a part of banking was changing and that these significant changes had to be recognized, even though banks would still be involved in significant traditional intermediation. Indeed, he noted, "...the information revolution...[that has]...deprived banks of some of the traditional lending business with their best customers, has also benefitted banks by making it less costly for them to assess the credit and other risks of customers they previously would have shunned."

For present purposes, what needs to be emphasized is that the changing nature of activities as the result of the increasing volume of nontraditional banking has distorted banking statistics, making any appearance of a decline in bank shares of credit flows more apparent than real. A recent important paper by John Boyd at the Federal Reserve Bank of Minneapolis and Mark Gertler of New York University addresses this measurement issue[17]. Their paper raises critical questions about US measures, challenging scholars in other countries, and at organizations such as our OECD hosts, to do similar analysis for other banking systems. I should nevertheless emphasize that their work is preliminary and part of ongoing research by them and others in the Federal Reserve System.

I would like to spend some time going through their arguments and statistical adjustments. Indeed, I have asked the OECD to make copies of their preliminary paper available to you today. It should be emphasized that I have used some slightly different statistics, with perhaps a slightly different focus,

192

but the balance of this paper is really reporting the creative and original work of these scholars.

D. Adjusting market shares for banks in the United States

Boyd and Gertler note at the outset - as shown in the upper panel of chart 20 - that noninterest revenue (fees and trading) as a share of total revenue has risen sharply at US banks and BHCs in the last 15 years, just as on-balance sheet activities and measured bank shares of credit flows have been showing some decline[18]. These results, of course, reflect the unbundling of bank services such as asset transformation through derivatives rather than loans, payments services, sales of asset pools, guarantees of commercial paper borrowers, security trading, etc. Moreover, as the lower panel of the chart shows, the growth of noninterest revenue, while greater at the ten largest banks - which account for virtually all the industry's derivatives activities - has occurred at banks in all size categories[19].

The first step in the statistical adjustment by Boyd and Gertler is to convert off-balance sheet activity to on-balance sheet equivalents. Boyd and Gertler do that in two ways. One is to use Basle Accord procedures to convert off-balance sheet positions to credit equivalents, *i.e.* , to estimate "...on-balance sheet asset holdings that would result in the same amount of risk exposure for the bank..." under Basle rules. As Boyd and Gertler note, this approach understates the on-balance sheet equivalent because only activities with significant risk exposure are measured under the Basle Accord. Be that as it may, the lower two lines in the lower right corner of chart 21 show these estimates as a per centage of the total bank loans, estimated prior to 1990 with a 1990-91 overlap of estimated and actual data, suggesting those prior year estimates were too low[20].

The second approach used to convert off-balance sheet to on-balance sheet positions is to capitalize the noninterest income from off-balance sheet activity, *i.e.* , to estimate the quantity of balance sheet assets that would be required to generate the observed level of noninterest income. The rate of return of on-balance sheet activities before deduction of operating costs is used to capitalize noninterest income in two ways. The first is to capitalize all noninterest income. The second capitalizes estimates of only "risky" activities by assuming that all pre-1970 activities were non-risky and using those to estimate the amount of deductions post-1970 to obtain new ("risky") activities. The results for banks are shown in the top two lines on chart 21, again as per centages of on-balance sheet loans of banks.

Both of the non-Basle credit equivalent measures are quite large, representing by 1993 an amount between 85 and 105 per cent of on-balance sheet loans. I have no doubt that, for various reasons, these measures overstate the on-balance sheet equivalent of off-balance sheet activities. The issue, however, is not how large any one of these measures may be. The more basic issue is that all measures increase sharply just when the other measures of bank activity weaken. Readers may choose to use different or lower estimates, but off-balance sheet activity cannot be ignored.

The second basic adjustment Boyd and Gertler make is to adjust for certain offshore loans by United States banks[21]. Recall that the loans by banks in the United States in the charts so far are only those booked onshore, although made to residents all over the world. A true measure of bank activity in any nation should also include at least some measure of loans in fact made by banks in that country but booked abroad. To make such an adjustment, Boyd and Gertler use the measure of offshore loans by United States banks estimated by Rama Seth, of the Federal Reserve Bank of New York. This time series shows all loans to nonbank United States residents from all offshore offices of domestic and foreign banks with United States offices. In my judgment, these data overstate the measure we are looking for: the role of the United States banking sector in United States credit markets. As the reader will recall, I have defined the United States banking system to be United States chartered banks (regardless of ownership) plus United States agencies and branches of foreign banks. This implies that the desired adjustment measure is offshore credit to United States nonbank residents by all United States banks' offshore offices plus that amount of offshore credit to United States nonbank residents made by those foreign banks that are under the management and control of United States branches and agencies of foreign banks. Fortunately, data on the latter loans exist, but, unfortunately, only for 1993 and partially for 1982.

These data (shown in table 3) are reported to the Federal Reserve and are defined as loans to United States nonbank residents booked at offshore branches of non-US banks that are managed and controlled by the United States offices[22]. These loans by United States branches and agencies of foreign banks are booked offshore for tax, reserve requirements, and pricing reasons, i.e. , are really United States bank loans booked offshore for technical, regulatory, and administrative purposes. The total of such loans in 1993 - loans to United States nonbank residents by United States branches and agencies of foreign banks that are controlled and managed by United States offices and all loans to United States nonbank residents by United States chartered banks - was $115 billion[23]. These loans were 5 per cent of total loans booked in the United States[24].

Still another set of loans not included earlier in our measures of bank credit - or by Boyd and Gertler - are loans made by the parent holding company and nonbank affiliates of banks that are subsidiaries of BHCs - shown in table 4. Virtually all of these loans are included in some nonbank category in chart 12 - such as loans by thrifts, finance companies, and mortgage bankers. But the entities in table 4 are owned by banking organizations and are booked outside of the bank itself mainly because United States banking organizations have used their nonbanking units to avoid geographical restrictions. Indeed, the growth of interstate banking - as well as overall weak loan demands - explains the decline in such loans since the late 1980s. Nonetheless, the United States statistics continue to carry these loans categorized by the legal subentity rather than as made by banking organizations.

Each of these adjustments - on-balance sheet equivalents of off-balance sheet activity, offshore loans, loans by BHCs and their nonbank affiliates, and the previously noted still outstanding amounts both of securitized consumer credit sold to nonbanks and bank sales of residential mortgages that they originated - are ways of estimating the perhaps ultimately unmeasurable on-balance sheet loan equivalent of the recent changes in banking. They are designed roughly to correct the statistical distortion that results from using traditional data sources that do not capture the changing nature of banking. These imperfect measures are not precise reflections, and are not always additive. With these caveats, charts 22 and 23 do try to summarize.

The left panel of chart 22 repeats the highest estimate of the off-balance sheet equivalent - the capitalization of all noninterest income at banks. This measure of off-balance sheet activity is probably an overstatement, which is why Boyd and Gertler use the Basle capital equivalent in their summary charts, although that measure is an understatement. Even if there were less biased measures, these on-balance sheet equivalent statistics are difficult to use for share purposes because other lenders' data would also have to be similarly adjusted, a complex statistical problem.

The on-balance sheet adjustments - shown in the right panel of chart 22 - simply reallocate credit flows from others to the banking sector; they clearly raise measured bank shares at the expense of other lenders. Combined in 1993, they increase measured bank loans by about 25 per cent[25]. In chart 23, I have added the on-balance sheet adjustments to three measures of bank credit shares. Owing to limited data, the additions can only be made in total for one year - 1993 - and partially back only to 1988. It is thus difficult to show the effect of the adjustments over time. However, there is reason to think that the adjustments have been rising over time.

As shown in the far left panel of chart 23, it is clear that the on-balance sheet adjustments raise the bank share of lending by all financial institutions - which had shown no downtrend in chart 12 - almost to 50 per cent. In the far right panel, the adjustments offset virtually all of the decline in the ratio of bank loans-to-private nonfinancial borrowing from the early 1970s peak - a peak which itself was an outlier for the post war period. Only in the middle panel - where the scaling denominator includes all US Treasury, agency, and state and local debt - does the adjusted bank share still remain far below the unadjusted highs. This latter series is - as noted earlier - a poor measure since banks' true economic role is to make loans, not buy government securities.

The data in chart 23 are, I submit, impressive indicators of the distortion in measured bank share and strongly suggest that banks' share is, in fact, quite strong. And, such measures exclude the off-balance sheet equivalent, at least some part of which should be added to get a "truer" adjustment measure.

E. *Other ways of viewing bank shares*

Some may feel that the slicing and dicing of statistical data to adjust bank shares is simply too arbitrary. Boyd and Gertler suggest two other ways of evaluating whether or not banks positions are deteriorating.

The first is to compare bank assets and loans to nominal Gross Domestic Produce (GDP) - measures of bank activity relative to the macroeconomy. Such ratios are plotted in the final chart, chart 24. The early decline in the ratio of bank assets to GDP in the upper panel reflects the working off of the liquid assets built up by banks in World War II; it does not show up in the loan-to-GDP ratio in the lower panel. Both ratios show a rising trend - for assets, after the excess liquid asset holdings were used up by the late 1950s and for loans, throughout the post war period. The most recent decline in the loan-to-GDP ratio has, as I noted earlier, significant macroeconomic and corporate capital structure restructuring elements, both of a temporary measure.

Without any adjustments, these ratios are inconsistent with a banking system of declining importance; quite the contrary[26]. Simply as reference points, the plus signs indicate the separate and independent effects on the 1993 ratios of adding either the on-or the off-balance sheet adjustments.

Finally, while not reproduced here, Boyd and Gertler use labor and capital measures to establish the US GDP value-added by the financial services and banking industries. These estimates use none of the adjustments made in earlier sections of this paper, but imply such strong activity as to cause Boyd and Gertler to conclude that the "...financial intermediary sector [in the US] including banks has been a growth industry, relative to the overall economy"[27].

III. Concluding comments

I think Boyd and Gertler are right, and I believe that US bank shares of credit flows - when properly visualized and measured - are not declining. Banks are changing dramatically how they do - and how they account for- their business; US statistical measures are not. Drawing on the work of Boyd and Gertler, I have suggested several adjustments to the standard banking statistics that attempt to capture the numerical counterpart of the changes in banking in the United States. Other approaches are consistent with the implications of these adjustments.

I hope that experts will use the Boyd and Gertler approach - which I have simply repeated or modestly changed - to explore adjustments for Canada, Mexico, and other nations. For the United States, it seems clear that banks are still not only in the business of measuring, managing, and accepting risk, but also that they are doing quite well at capturing business. The more basic and important question may really be: are they measuring, managing, and pricing risk correctly? But that is another question!

Table 1
Nonbank Assets Held by Bank Holding Companies
by Type of Activity, 1987–1993
(Billions of Dollars)

Activity	1987	1988	1989	1990	1991	1992	1993
Securities brokerage & underwriting	21.0	32.3	44.4	52.2	62.1	76.6	115.9
Other depository institutions	17.9	19.7	18.4	27.7	25.2	33.9	34.3
Mortgage banking	29.6	27.5	30.3	22.1	20.8	19.2	19.4
Commercial finance	33.9	37.1	26.7	23.9	18.0	16.2	20.1
Consumer finance	25.2	24.0	23.6	18.8	15.7	11.8	14.5
Leasing	9.0	9.2	11.5	9.4	6.7	5.6	5.2
Small business investment company	0.6	0.7	0.7	2.8	4.3	4.0	6.3
Data processing	2.0	2.3	2.0	2.2	1.7	1.8	1.9
Insurance underwriting	1.8	1.7	2.3	2.6	2.5	1.8	1.8
Insurance agency	0.5	0.3	0.6	0.3	0.4	0.4	0.7
Other nonbank assets	56.9	55.5	65.3	53.7	51.8	40.7	47.7
Aggregated nonbank assets	198.4	210.3	225.8	215.7	209.2	212.0	267.8

Source: Federal Reserve Board

Table 2
Average three firm concentration ratio
1976-1992

Year	Metropolitan statistical area	Non-metropolitan countries
1976	68.5	90.0
1977	67.9	89.4
1978	67.4	89.9
1979	66.8	89.7
1980	66.4	89.6
1981	66.1	89.4
1982	65.9	89.4
1983	66.0	89.4
1984	66.4	89.4
1985	66.7	89.5
1986	67.5	89.5
1987	67.7	89.5
1988	67.8	89.7
1989	67.5	89.7
1990	67.3	89.7
1991	66.7	89.3
1992	67.5	89.2

Source: Summary of Deposits, 1976–1992, Federal Deposit Insurance Corporation.

Table 3
Bank Lending to U.S. Nonbank Residents
from Offshore Offices that are
Under the Management and Control
of U.S. Banks
and
U.S. Branches and Agencies of Foreign Banks
(billions of dollars)

	December 1982	December 1993
From offshore offices of U.S. banks		
in the Caribbean	16.0^e	19.5
elsewhere	5.0^e	7.0
From Caribbean offices of U.S. branches and agencies of foreign banks	18.0	88.1
TOTAL	39.0	114.6

^{e}—estimated

Source: Federal Reserve Board

Table 4
Loans and Lease Financing Receivables
Held by Nonbank Subsidiaries of Bank Holding Companies
(Billions of Dollars)

Activity	1987	1988	1989	1990	1991	1992	1993
Securities brokerage & underwriting	1.1	1.1	0.4	0.4	0.4	0.6	1.2
Other depository institutions	14.2	15.8	15.3	19.6	19.2	22.9	22.9
Mortgage banking	16.3	16.3	17.1	12.3	12.7	10.8	10.9
Commercial finance	28.9	32.7	22.1	19.1	14.5	12.2	14.3
Consumer finance	23.6	21.4	21.7	16.7	13.0	9.3	12.1
Leasing	7.3	7.9	9.1	6.7	5.4	4.3	4.1
Small business investment company	0.0	0.0	0.1	0.2	0.3	0.1	0.1
Data processing	0.0	0.0	0.1	0.1	0.1	0.1	0.0
Insurance underwriting	0.0	0.1	0.1	0.2	0.2	0.0	0.0
Insurance agency	0.0	0.0	0.0	0.0	0.1	0.1	0.1
Other nonbank assets	4.1	5.3	4.9	4.1	6.6	5.1	4.8
Total loans	95.5	100.6	90.9	79.4	72.5	65.5	70.5

NOTE: Loan data are net of unearned income and loan loss allowances.

Source: Federal Reserve Board

201

Chart 1

Number Of Depository Institutions In The U.S.

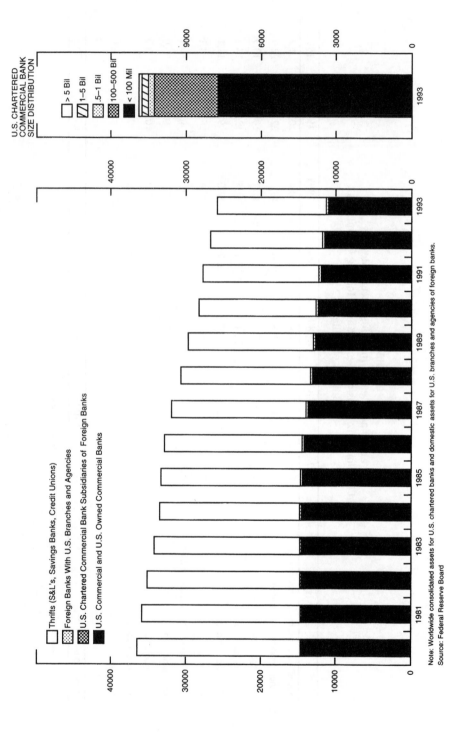

Thrifts (S&L's, Savings Banks, Credit Unions)

Foreign Banks With U.S. Branches and Agencies

U.S. Chartered Commercial Bank Subsidiaries of Foreign Banks

U.S. Commercial and U.S. Owned Commercial Banks

U.S. CHARTERED
COMMERCIAL BANK
SIZE DISTRIBUTION

> 5 Bil
1–5 Bil
.5–1 Bil
100–500 Bil
< 100 Mil

Note: Worldwide consolidated assets for U.S. chartered banks and domestic assets for U.S. branches and agencies of foreign banks.
Source: Federal Reserve Board

Chart 2

Assets Of Individual Depository Institutions In The U.S.
(Billions of dollars)

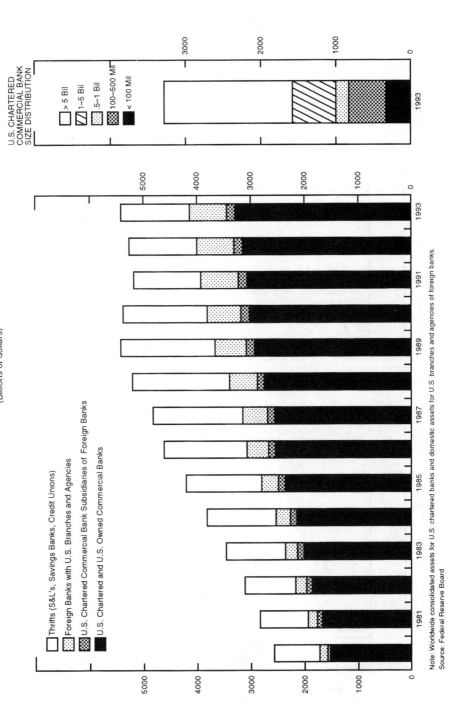

U.S. CHARTERED
COMMERCIAL BANK
SIZE DISTRIBUTION

☐ > 5 Bil
▨ 1–5 Bil
▒ .5–1 Bil
▦ 100–500 Mil
■ < 100 Mil

☐ Thrifts (S&L's, Savings Banks, Credit Unions)
▒ Foreign Banks with U.S. Branches and Agencies
▦ U.S. Chartered Commercial Bank Subsidiaries of Foreign Banks
■ U.S. Chartered and U.S. Owned Commercial Banks

Note: Worldwide consolidated assets for U.S. chartered banks and domestic assets for U.S. branches and agencies of foreign banks.
Source: Federal Reserve Board

203

Chart 3

North American Banking Structure In 1993

NUMBER

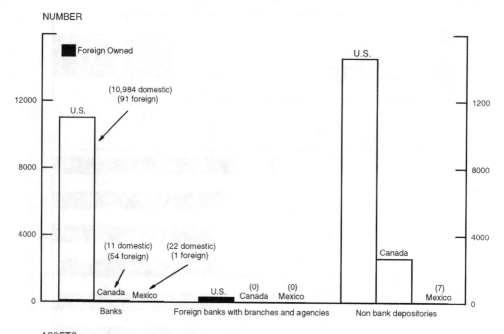

ASSETS

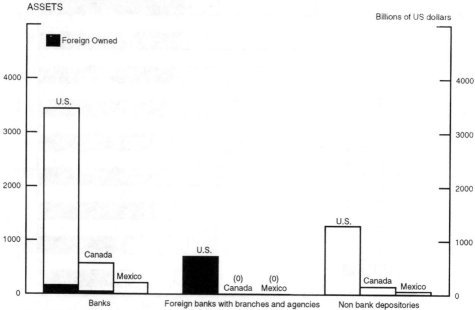

Note: Worldwide consolidated assets for U.S. chartered banks and domestic assets for U.S. branches and agencies of foreign banks.
Source: Federal Reserve Board, Bank of Canada, Bank of Mexico

Chart 4

Depository Institutions Per 100,000 Inhabitants in North America
(As of end of 1992)

COMMERCIAL BANKS

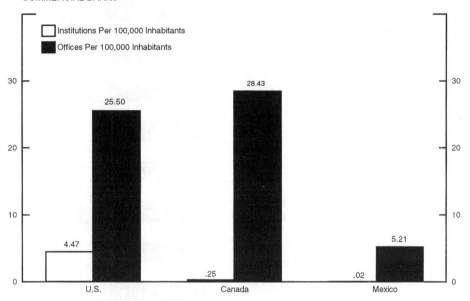

ALL DEPOSITORY INSTITUTIONS

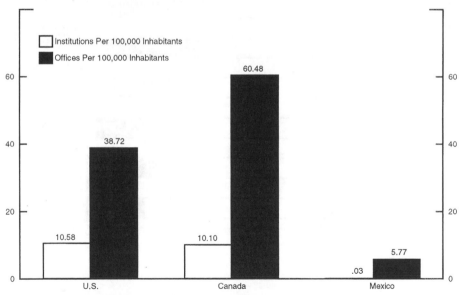

Source: Bank for International Settlements: Payment Systems in the Group of Ten
Bank of Mexico

205

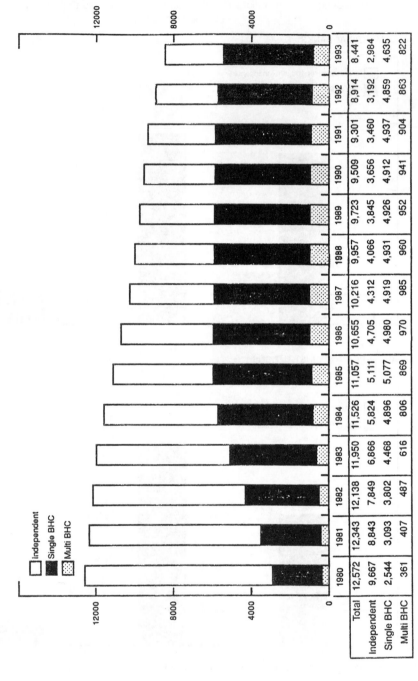

Chart 5

Number of US Banking Organizations
Bank Holding Companies and Independent Banks

	1980	1981	1982	1983	1984	1985	1986	1987	1988	1989	1990	1991	1992	1993
Total	12,572	12,343	12,138	11,950	11,526	11,057	10,655	10,216	9,957	9,723	9,509	9,301	8,914	8,441
Independent	9,667	8,843	7,849	6,866	5,824	5,111	4,705	4,312	4,066	3,845	3,656	3,460	3,192	2,984
Single BHC	2,544	3,093	3,802	4,468	4,896	5,077	4,980	4,919	4,931	4,926	4,912	4,937	4,859	4,635
Multi BHC	361	407	487	616	806	869	970	985	960	952	941	904	863	822

Source: Federal Reserve Board

Chart 6

Distribution of US Banking Assets
by Organization Type

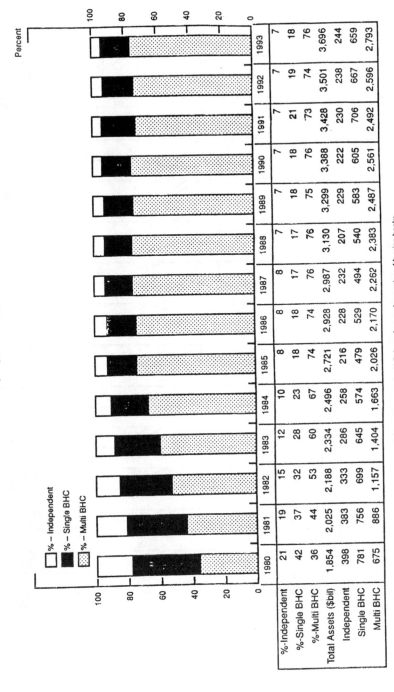

	1980	1981	1982	1983	1984	1985	1986	1987	1988	1989	1990	1991	1992	1993
%-Independent	21	19	15	12	10	8	8	8	7	7	7	7	7	7
%-Single BHC	42	37	32	28	23	18	18	17	17	18	18	21	19	18
%-Multi BHC	36	44	53	60	67	74	74	76	76	75	76	73	74	76
Total Assets ($bil)	1,854	2,025	2,188	2,334	2,496	2,721	2,928	2,987	3,130	3,299	3,388	3,428	3,501	3,696
Independent	398	383	333	286	258	216	228	232	207	229	222	230	238	244
Single BHC	781	756	699	645	574	479	529	494	540	583	605	706	667	659
Multi BHC	675	886	1,157	1,404	1,663	2,026	2,170	2,262	2,383	2,487	2,561	2,492	2,596	2,793

Note: Worldwide consolidated assets for U.S. chartered banks and domestic assets for U.S. branches and agencies of foreign banks.
Source: Federal Reserve Board

207

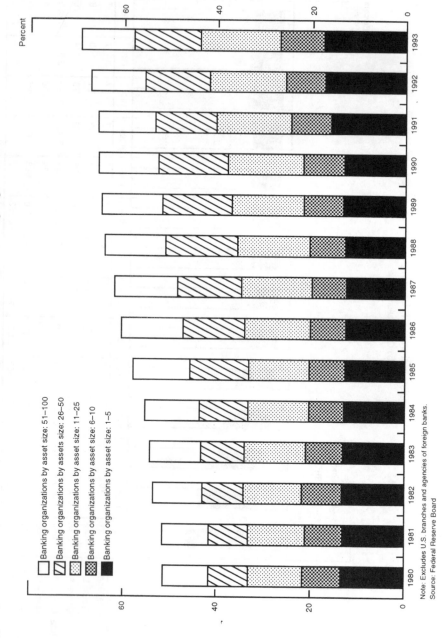

Chart 7

Shares of Domestic Commercial Banking Assets Held
By One Hundred Largest U.S. Commercial Banking Organizations

Percent

Banking organizations by asset size: 51–100
Banking organizations by assets size: 26–50
Banking organizations by asset size: 11–25
Banking organizations by asset size: 6–10
Banking organizations by asset size: 1–5

60

40

20

0

1980 1981 1982 1983 1984 1985 1986 1987 1988 1989 1990 1991 1992 1993

Note: Excludes U.S. branches and agencies of foreign banks.
Source: Federal Reserve Board

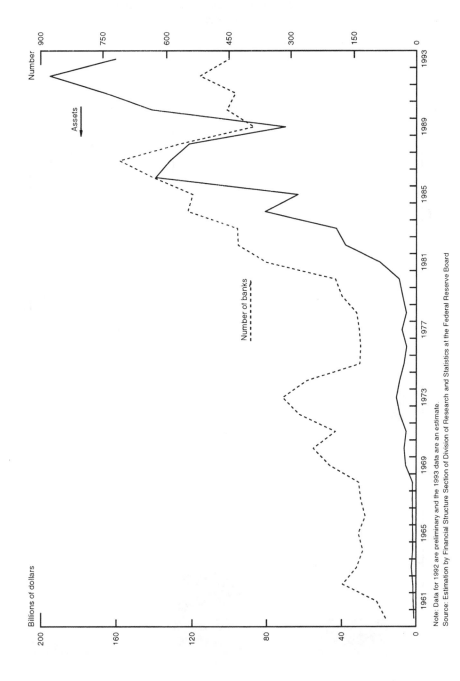

Chart 8

Acquistions Through Mergers In The U.S.

Number of banks

Assets

Number

Billions of dollars

Note: Data for 1992 are preliminary and the 1993 data are an estimate.

Source: Estimation by Financial Structure Section of Division of Research and Statistics at the Federal Reserve Board

Chart 9

Share of Domestic Commercial Banking Assets
(As of end of 1993)

LARGEST 5 BANKING ORGANIZATIONS

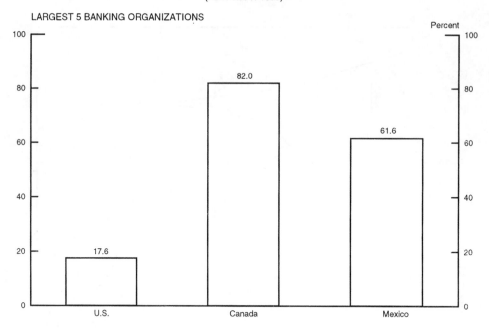

FOREIGN BANKS

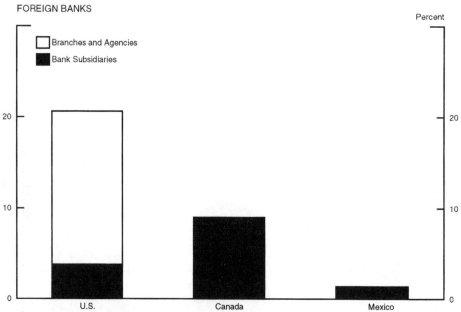

Note: Includes U.S. branches and agencies of foreign banks.
Source: Federal Reserve Board, Bank of Canada, Bank of Mexico

Chart 10

Public Debt

OUTSTANDINGS

Billions of dollars

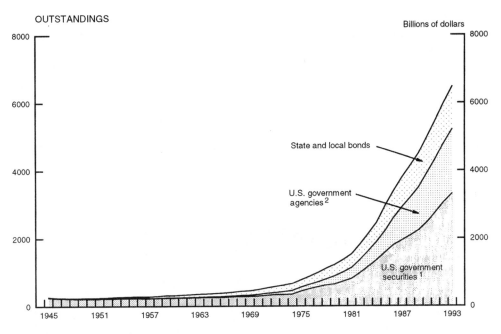

State and local bonds

U.S. government agencies[2]

U.S. government securities[1]

COMMERCIAL BANK[3] PURCHASES AS A PROPORTION OF OUTSTANDING PUBLIC DEBT

Percent

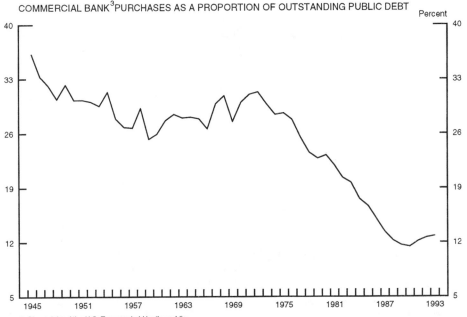

1. Direct debt of the U.S. Treasury held by the public.
2. Mortgage pools, debt issued by Government Sponsored Enterprises, and debt issued by on–budget agencies — all held by the public.
3. U.S. chartered banks and U.S. branches and agencies of foreign banks.

Chart 11

U.S. Shares of Total Credit Market Lending
By U.S. Financial Institutions[1]

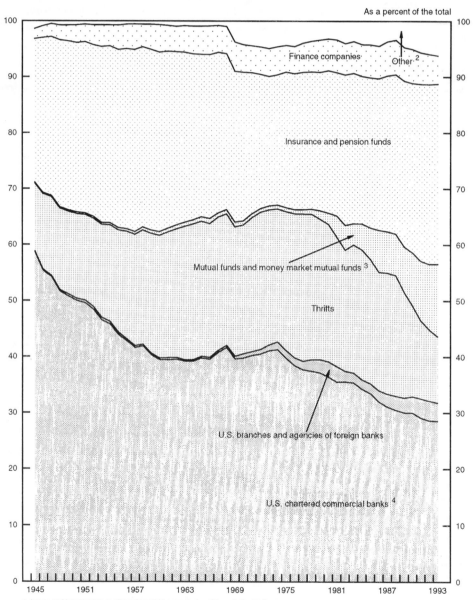

As a percent of the total

Finance companies   Other [2]

Insurance and pension funds

Mutual funds and money market mutual funds [3]

Thrifts

U.S. branches and agencies of foreign banks

U.S. chartered commercial banks [4]

1945   1951   1957   1963   1969   1975   1981   1987   1993

1. Loans and investments to all nonfinancial borrowers by all financial institutions.
2. Includes mortgage companies, REITS, brokers and dealers, and bank personal trusts.
3. Excludes holdings of equities.
4. Includes foreign owned U.S. commercial bank subsidiaries.

Source: Federal Reserve Board

Chart 12

U.S. Shares Of Private Credit Market Lending
By U.S. Financial Institutions[1]

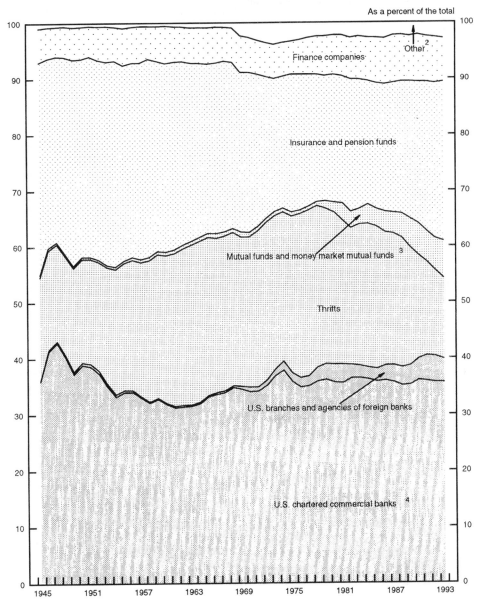

As a percent of the total

'Other'[2]

Finance companies

Insurance and pension funds

Mutual funds and money market mutual funds [3]

Thrifts

U.S. branches and agencies of foreign banks

U.S. chartered commercial banks [4]

1. Loans to all nongovernment, nonfinancial borrowers by all financial institutions. (Excludes U.S. government
   and agency securities and state and local bonds in the portfolio of all lenders.)
2. Includes mortgage companies, REITS, brokers and dealers, and bank personal trusts.
3. Excludes holdings of equities.
4. Includes foreign owned U.S. commercial bank subsidiaries.

Source: Federal Reserve Board

Chart 13

U.S. Bank[1] Shares Of Nonfinancial Debt Outstanding

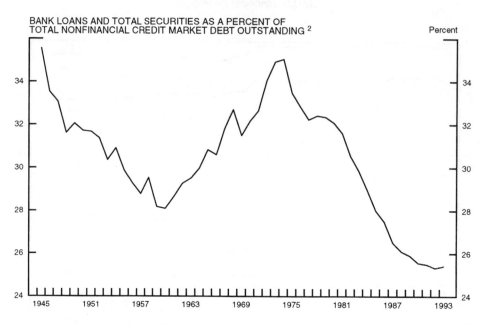

BANK LOANS AND TOTAL SECURITIES AS A PERCENT OF
TOTAL NONFINANCIAL CREDIT MARKET DEBT OUTSTANDING [2]

Percent

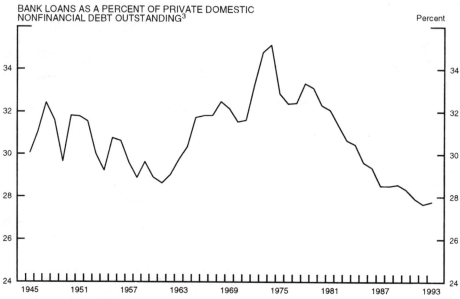

BANK LOANS AS A PERCENT OF PRIVATE DOMESTIC
NONFINANCIAL DEBT OUTSTANDING[3]

Percent

1. Includes branches and agencies of foreign banks in U.S.
2. Total nonfinancial credit market debt excludes equities, but includes all debt obligations of all U.S. nonfinancial business,
   households and nonprofit institutions, U.S. and state and local government bonds, and all foreign borrowing in the U.S.
3. Private domestic nonfinancial debt excludes borrowing by the U.S. and state and local governments. Bank loans exclude
   all securities holdings.

Source: Federal Reserve Board

Chart 14

U.S. Bank Loan Shares[1] By Sector Borrowing
(Private Domestic Nonfinancial Borrowing)

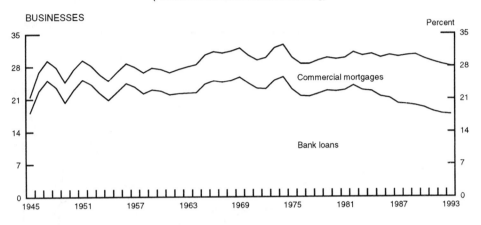

BUSINESSES

Percent

Commercial mortgages

Bank loans

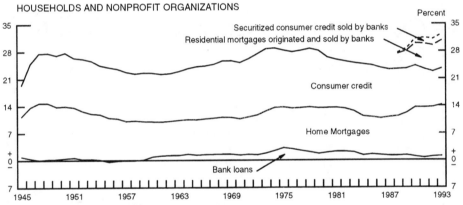

HOUSEHOLDS AND NONPROFIT ORGANIZATIONS

Percent

Securitized consumer credit sold by banks
Residential mortgages originated and sold by banks

Consumer credit

Home Mortgages

Bank loans

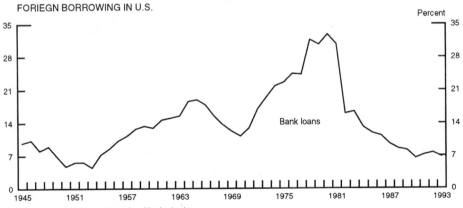

FORIEGN BORROWING IN U.S.

Percent

Bank loans

1. Includes U.S. branch and agencies of foreign banks.
Source: Federal Reserve Board, Department of Housing and Urban Development

Chart 15

Components Of Nonfinancial Business Funds Raised In the U.S.

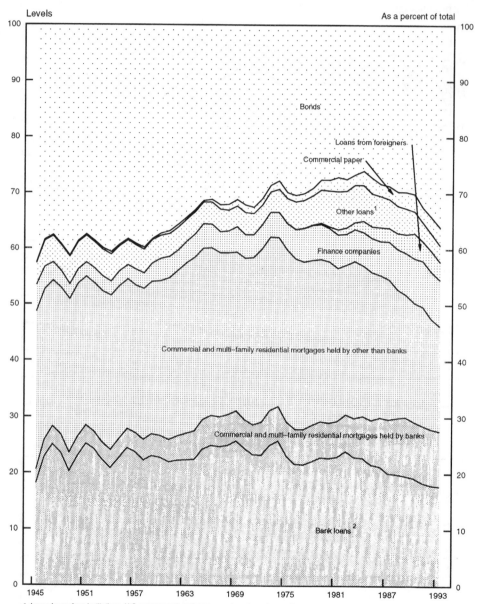

Levels   As a percent of total

Bonds

Loans from foreigners

Commercial paper

Other loans[1]

Finance companies

Commercial and multi-family residential mortgages held by other than banks

Commercial and multi-family residential mortgages held by banks

Bank loans[2]

1. Loans by savings institutions, U.S. government, and government sponsored agencies.
2. Includes loans made by U.S. branches and agencies of foreign banks and U.S. chartered commercial banks (including
   those foreign owned).

Source: Federal Reserve Board

Chart 16

Canadian Bank And Non Bank Shares Of Credit Market Lending
By Financial Institutions [1]

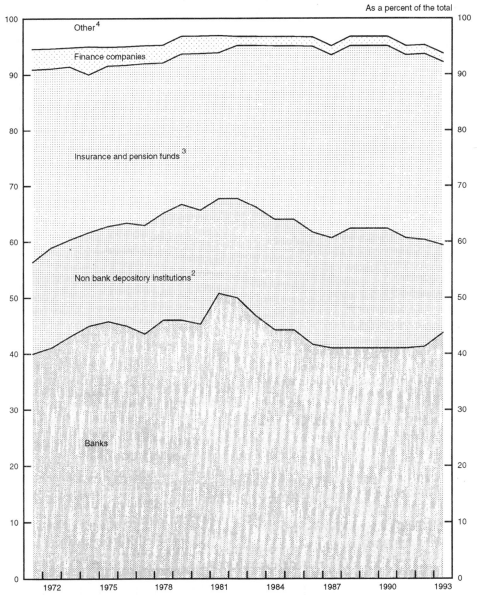

As a percent of the total

1. Canadian and foreign currency debt.
2. Trust and Mortgage Loan Companies, Credit Unions, and Caisse Populaires and provincial government savings banks.
3. Includes life and property and casualty insurance companies.
4. Department store credit card balances, mortgage held by mutual funds, mortgage of Central Credit Unions,
   mortgages held by Canadian Mortgage and Housing Corporation, and mutual fund holdings of marketable debt securities.

Source: Bank of Canada

Chart 17

Canadian Bank Share Of Lending In Credit Markets

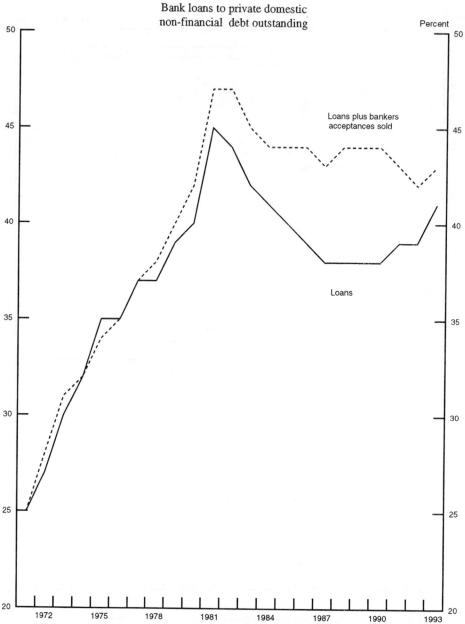

Bank loans to private domestic
non-financial debt outstanding

Note: Includes Canadian and foreign currency debt. Borrowings by government of Canada nonfinancial enterprise included, but borrowing by provincial government nonfinancial enterprise is excluded. Includes non–residential public sector foreign currency loans. Excludes all other loans to all governments.

Source: Bank of Canada

218

Chart 18

Components Of Domestic Nonfinancial Business Funds[1]
Raised In Canada

As a percent of total

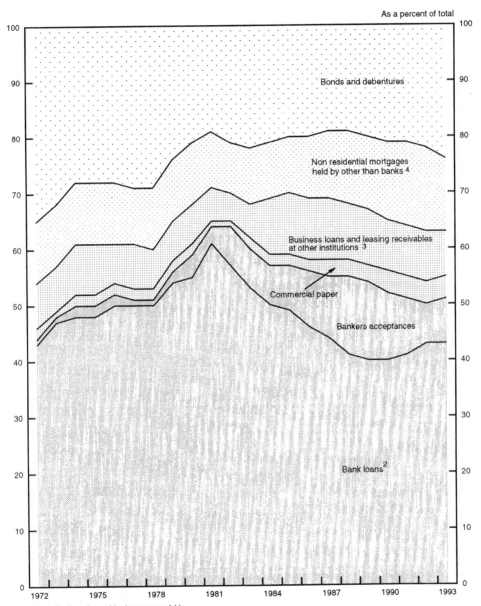

1. Includes Canadian and foreign currency debt.
2. Includes leasing and receivables, estimated prior to 1977, and non residential mortgages.
3. Includes business loans made by sales finance companies, trust and mortgage loan companies, Alberta Treasury Branches, and
   estimates for credit unions and caisses populatires as well as leasing receivables at sales finance companies and trust
   and mortgage loan companies.
4. Estimated for 1972.

Source: Bank of Canada

Chart 19

Mexican Bank And Nonbank Shares Of Credit Market Lending
By Financial Institution

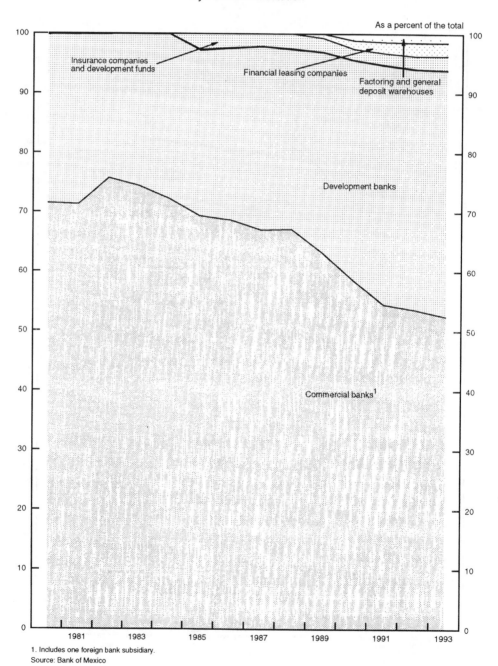

As a percent of the total

1. Includes one foreign bank subsidiary.

Source: Bank of Mexico

Chart 20

Fees And Non–Interest Income At U.S. Banks

AS A SHARE OF REVENUE [1]

Percent

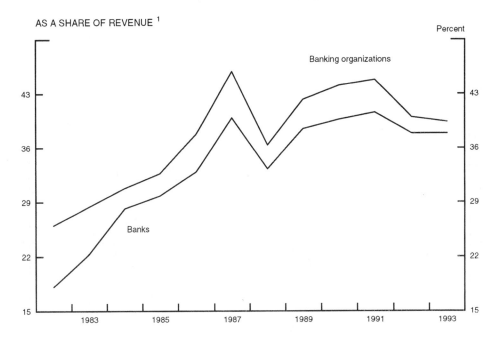

Banking organizations

Banks

AS A PERCENT OF BANK ASSETS

Percent

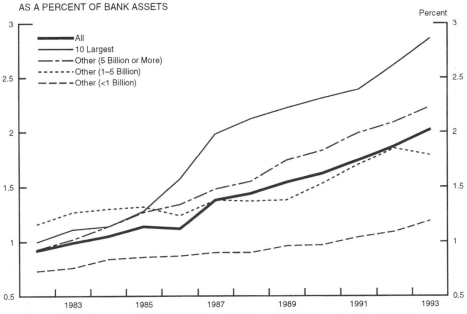

All
10 Largest
Other (5 Billion or More)
Other (1–5 Billion)
Other (<1 Billion)

1. Calculated as non–interest income divided by the total of non–interest income plus interest income less interest expense less loan loss provision.

Source: Federal Reserve Board

Chart 21

Estimate Of On–Balance Sheet Equivalents Of Off–Balance Sheet Activities As A Percentage Of U.S. Bank Loans

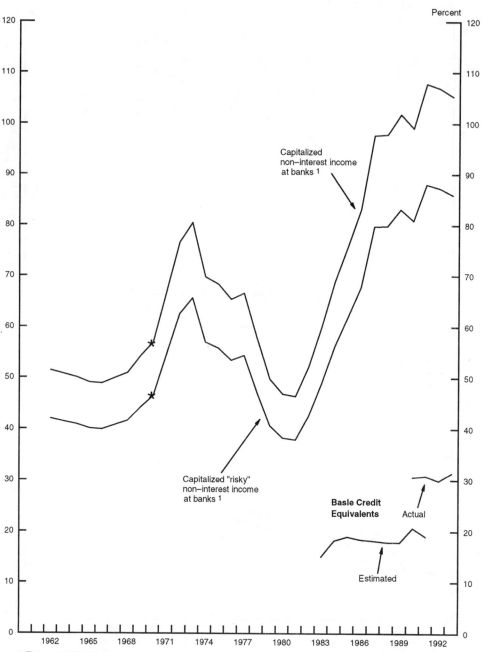

Percent

Capitalized
non–interest income
at banks [1]

Capitalized "risky"
non–interest income
at banks [1]

**Basle Credit
Equivalents**   Actual

Estimated

1. Three–year trailing average.
* Break in the series.

Source: Boyd and Gertler: "Are Banks Dead? Or, Are The Reports Greatly Exaggerated?", Chart 4.
        Federal Reserve Board

Chart 22

Adjustments To Bank Loans
As A Percentage Of Bank Loans

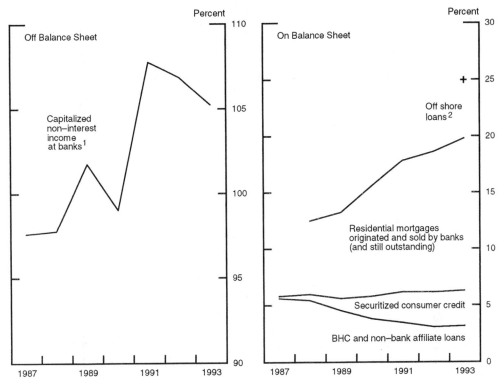

Percent   Percent

Off Balance Sheet   On Balance Sheet

Capitalized
non–interest
income
at banks[1]

Off shore
loans[2]

Residential mortgages
originated and sold by banks
(and still outstanding)

Securitized consumer credit

BHC and non–bank affiliate loans

1987   1989   1991   1993   1987   1989   1991   1993

1. Three–year trailing average.
2. Under U.S. bank management and control.

Source: Federal Reserve Board

Chart 23

On-Balance Sheet Adjustments To Bank Shares

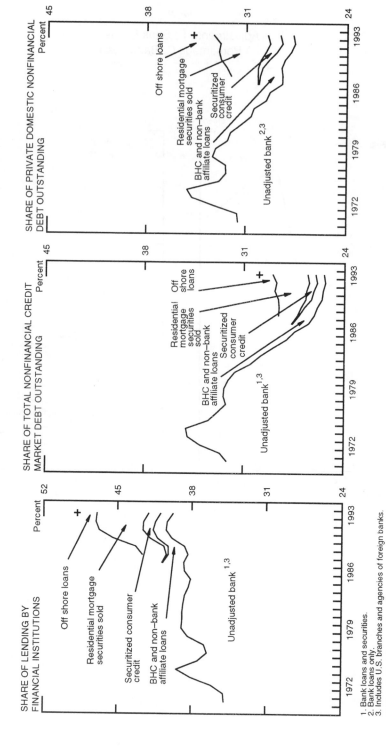

Chart 24

U.S. Bank Measures Relative to Nominal GDP

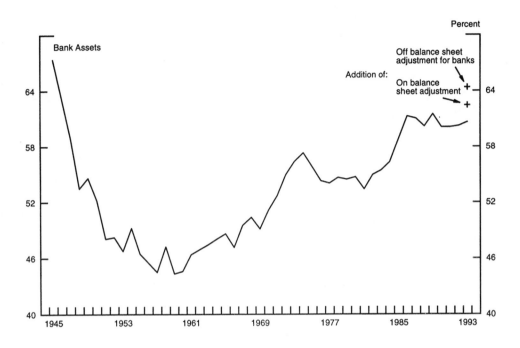

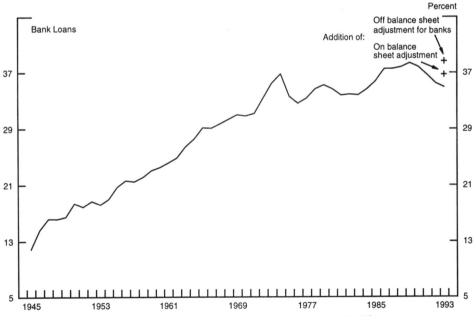

Note: Includes U.S. branches and agencies of foreign banks. All assets and loan data are booked in the U.S.
Source: Federal Reserve Board

Notes

1   Savings and loans specialize in mortgages; savings banks also tend to be significant holders of mortgages; the third thrift - credit unions - specialize in consumer credit.

2   Except for US branches and agencies of foreign banks, for which only US booked assets are shown.

3   Although US banks are exempt, other foreign bank subsidiaries in Canada cannot collectively exceed 12 per cent of total bank assets. As in other countries, foreign banks in Canada tend to focus their activities on commercial lending, where they play a significant role - although less than in the United States.

4   Twelve of these 100 are subsidiaries of foreign banks that accounted for 5.5 per cent of 1993 domestic bank assets in the United States.

5   Most of the increase in outstanding US government agency debt is accounted for by mortgage pools guaranteed by the Government National Mortgage Corporation (Ginnie Mae), Federal National Mortgage Association (Fannie Mae), Federal Home Loan Mortgage Corporation (Freddie Mac), and Farmers Home Administration (Farmer Mac).

6   To do so would have required them to purchase almost $1 trillion more of such debt by 1993 than in fact they did.

7   This apparent contradiction may reflect the fact that in the United States, as in most countries, offices of foreign banks are making loans to their home countries' firms that have operations in the host country, loans that would have been booked in the home country if the bank had not followed its national customers for convenience, local currency funding, etc.

8   Both chart 11 and the upper panel of chart 13 are consistent: if all public debt is included, bank shares decline. But, chart 12 and the lower panel of chart 13 seem inconsistent. In the former, if public debt is excluded bank shares are constant, while in the latter, bank shares decline when public debt is excluded. There are two explanations: (1) direct finance has increased, at the expense of both banks and all financial intermediaries (the only values measured in chart 12), and (2) the denominator of chart 13 measures borrowing from the borrowers' side while the numerator is from the lender's side. From the borrower side mortgages are a private debt, but when such debt is securitized and guaranteed by the government its holdings by a bank (or any other financial institution) are excluded from the "loan" category. Pooling and government guarantees of mortgage loans turns a "loan" with risk into a "security" with little or no credit risk. In chart 12 we

removed that "security" from the numerator and denominator; in the lower panel of chart 13 we included it as a "private debt" in the denominator but excluded it as a "guaranteed debt" from the numerator. It is not clear to me which is biased, but one shows a declines in bank share and one does not.

9   The addition of commercial mortgages is a (hopefully small) overstatement of nonfinancial business borrowing from banks. United States data do not permit a breakdown of the mortgage assets of the lender by borrower sector. Most commercial mortgages are surely to nonfinancial businesses, but small shares also go to financial businesses, households, and nonprofit institutions.

10 The estimates include some purchases - thought mainly to be from bank affiliates - in the originations that are later resold.

11 In 1993, banks held about $330 billion of residential mortgage securities, some of the underlying mortgages of which were no doubt originated by banks.

12 Except for what are thought to be a small amount of purchases by other banks, who hold them as securities, not as loans.

13 In 1981-82, Canadian banks had participated actively in the boom in mergers and acquisitions, a large part of which was in response to a government program related to the ownership of the energy sector.

14 Remarks before the 30th Annual Conference on Bank Structure and Competition, Chicago: May 12, 1994.

15 These changes, as noted earlier, could be induced by economics, government regulation, or both.

16 Ibid.

17 Are Banks Dead? Or, Are the Reports Greatly Exaggerated?, Working Paper 531, Research Department, Federal Reserve Bank of Minneapolis, June 1994.

18 The 1987-89 variation is due to sharp changes in loan loss provisioning, which influences the denominator of the fees-to-revenue ratio. A fall off in provisioning and a pickup in interest margins affected the last two observations.

19 Other researchers in the United States have noted that the increase in noninterest income was caused by an overall shift from lending activities to nonlending activities rather than an increase in the relative profitability of one or two nonlending activities. Profit margins on these activities are smaller and they use greater leverage because of their relatively lower credit risk and less cyclical cash flows. See Robert DeYoung, Fee Based Services and Cost Efficiency in Commercial Banks, Office of the Comptroller of the Currency, Economic and Policy Analysis Working Paper 94-3, April 1994.

20 While not shown on the chart, Boyd and Gertler note that the credit equivalents for derivatives are only about one-third of the total estimate.

21   Chart 15 shows offshore loans from all sources to non-financial businesses.

22   Such loans by United States branches and agencies of foreign banks are predominantly from their affiliates in the Bahamas and Caymans.

23   Such loans exclude another $109 billion of loans by US banks' offshore offices to nonbank non-US residents, $13 billion of loans to nonbank non-US residents by US branches and agencies of foreign banks that are under US office control and management, and an unknown volume of loans to US nonbank residents by foreign bank' head offices and offshore offices not under US office management and control.

24   These data also suggest that most of the nonfinancial business loans from abroad takes the form of loans from offshore offices under US management and control.

25   If one combined the off- and on-balance sheet adjustments, the still outstanding amount of securitized consumer credit and residential mortgages would have to be removed to avoid double counting since its servicing and/or sale by the bank creates noninterest income.

26   Banks, of course, could still be losing share to other lenders, while still growing relative to GDP.

27   Boyd and Gertler, *op. cit.* , p. 17.

Chapter 6

STRUCTURAL CHANGES IN JAPANESE FINANCIAL MARKETS: TRENDS AND PROSPECTS IN BANKING

Yasuhiro Hayasaki, Bank of Japan

Introduction

Recent years have witnessed dramatic changes in the Japanese financial system. In the first half of the 1980's, financial institutions were faced with an acceleration of the financial liberalisation and internationalisation process. In the last half of the decade, which was characterised by the emergence of the "bubble" economy, financial institutions, encouraged by the ongoing process of liberalisation, expanded lending. This led to an excessive risk exposure, and as asset values declined in the 1990's, the asset quality of financial institutions deteriorated significantly.

This paper is an attempt to assess trends in and prospects for the Japanese financial system. First, it will, examine changes in the flow of funds during the last ten years and the response of financial institutions to these changes, in particular that of banks. Next, the future of the banking industry will be assessed. Finally, the role of the central bank in a changing environment will be discussed. Changes in the relations between banks and their customers will be dealt with in an appendix.

1. Trends in the Japanese financial system

This chapter examines features of the Japanese financial system in the last decade from two angles. First, it is assessed how the share of bank lending and deposit taking changed in the overall flow of funds. Second, the reactions of banks to such changes is studied.

Changes in the flow of funds

The share of the banking sector in the overall financial system seems to have been declining for the last ten years. Tables 1 to 4 show some recent changes in fund-raising by the corporate business sector and the personal sector. Several points can be observed from these tables.

i) The share of borrowing from private financial institutions declined 6 per cent from 1983 to 1993, while fund-raising in the form of securities increased (Table 1);

ii) Table 2 indicates that, among private lenders, the share of insurance companies and trust banks (which manage pension funds) has increased. The table also shows that the share of smaller financial institutions has been eroded by larger institutions;

iii) Table 3 shows that borrowing from private financial institutions remains significant for small and medium sized firms. On the other hand, for large firms, borrowing has been substituted by funding from the bond and capital markets;

iv) Table 4 not only shows the magnitude of the bubble economy and subsequent fall in financial activities after its burst, but it also illustrate some features of the bubble. First, during the bubble period, the corporate sector increased funding by utilising the capital and other markets: the share of borrowing from private financial institutions declined (although an increase was seen in absolute terms). Second, the personal sector expanded borrowing during that period. Third, the period after 1991 can be characterised by an increased share of borrowing from public financial institutions and funding by issuing bonds.

Financial investment in the last decade is shown in Tables 1 to 4. Two features can be distinguished:

a) The share of trust accounts and insurance institutions for investment purposes increased by 11 per cent while that of deposits with private institutions and investment in securities declined;

b) The share of postal savings remains at almost the same level. However, after the bursting of the bubble, the rate of their increase exceeded the growth of private deposits.

Trends in the Japanese financial system can be summarised as follows. Since 1980, the banking sector has faced competition from two sides -- securities markets and non-bank and public financial institutions. As deregulation progressed, the corporate sector, especially large firms, began to utilise the capital and bond markets. In the bubble period, stock issuance was preferred to issuing bonds, since it was widely believed that stock issuing costs were almost negligible. In the 1990's, the corporate sector has relied more on bonds when it became clear that the costs of issuing stock was much larger than anticipated.

With regard to the competition from non-banks and public financial institutions against the backdrop of an ageing Japanese society, life insurance institutions and pension funds tend to attract demand of the personal sector for savings in preparation for the future, by providing more flexible and longer-term products than banks. Meanwhile, postal savings attract funds in cases where their interest rates, not perfectly reflecting market rates, are higher than the level acceptable to private banks.

In the banking sector, city banks have increased their share of loans to small and medium sized corporations, which used to be the customers of regional banks and even smaller financial institutions. City banks also moved into the consumer and housing loan markets. Consequently, the operations of small financial institutions have been eroded (Table 5).

Banks' response to changes

During the last decade, banks also changed in parallel with the progress of financial liberalisation (Tables 6 to 8). For instance, with respect to securities operations, banks were permitted in 1984 to deal in securities. In 1993 they were allowed to have subsidiary securities companies -- five have been set up and others established by major city banks will follow soon. Discussions on the expansion of the range of business which these securities subsidiaries can engage in as well as the entry of banks to the insurance field, may commence in the future.

Overseas business expanded in the 1980's: Japanese banks gained substantial shares in the world market not only in lending but also in market transactions. In addition, Japanese banks have tried to establish fee businesses as a major profit source, including mergers and acquisitions and payment services. Finally, Japanese banks have increasingly made use of derivatives not only for trading purposes but also for the risk management of customers and themselves.

In this way, the range of services which banks and/or banking groups offer has been widened. This will help banks meet a great variety of customer demand and diversify business risks, although Table 8 shows that income from such new businesses has fluctuated.

2. Future of the banking industry

In this section, prospects are to be presented with regard to the future of the traditional banking -- bank lending and deposit taking -- and of the banking business *per se.*

Future of traditional banking

As has been noted, the share of services offered by banks in fund raising and financial investment of the non-financial sector is declining. This tendency may continue, but it is unlikely that the traditional banking, business of lending and deposit taking will become completely irrelevant.

With regard to fund raising, large corporations have already made intensive use of capital markets, such as the bond market and the market for commercial paper (CP). Taking into account that some of these corporations have higher credit rating than banks, this development is understandable. Even when corporations with lower ratings borrow money from banks, the fact that they can access markets directly works as an advantage. However, for some firms, access to capital markets is difficult because the cost of convincing investors of their profitability is high, especially when these firms are too small to attract investor attention or when firms are starting new businesses. Therefore, demand for bank lending will continue.

On the financial investment side, it is plausible that some degree of risk aversion will continue. For risk averse investors, bank deposits would be a primary choice because the banking sector is endowed with the ability to assess information on borrowers' creditworthiness and to absorb risks arising from intermediation between borrowers and depositors. Of course, products other than bank deposits could also offer safety and soundness. For example, funds invested only in the highest rated CPs and TBs would attract very risk averse investors, although, in Japan, the present market for CPs and TBs is not large

234

enough for this type of product to be provided on a sufficient scale. In addition, the degree of safety and soundness of bank deposits depends on how safe and sound banks are. However, it is unlikely that the attractiveness of bank deposits will be lost in the foreseeable future.

Future of the banking sector

Functions performed by the banking sector can be divided into four categories:

i) the examination of borrowers' creditworthiness (issuers of securities, etc.);

ii) the intermediation between borrowers and depositors (investors) and absorbing the associated risks;

iii) the provision of products to meet customer needs, including risk management and information services; and

iv) the provision and improvement of payment services.

Not only has the banking sector been the only player which deals with all these functions simultaneously but it is also the most important and influential player in each of them. However, recent years have witnessed some changes.

For example, rating agencies play a substantial role in judging the creditworthiness of corporations. Securities houses provide more attractive services involving securitisation technology to customers. Non-bank financial companies work as intermediaries between borrowers and investors. In the field of payment, non-bank institutions (securities companies and even retail stores), assisted by technological developments, have started to invade the territory of banks. For instance, investors in money market funds (MMFs) are now able to withdraw funds on the same day they cancel all or part of the contract. This opens the possibility that MMF accounts, offered by securities houses, can be used for payment purposes. In addition, it is now possible to pay public utility charges at some convenience stores, although usage remains low. In this way, the traditional functions of banks are being eroded or unbundled.

These examples indicate that specialisation could be more efficient rather than to engage in a wide range of businesses. On the other hand, as mentioned, the scope of business which banks are engaged in has widened -- these banks are operating on the assumption that economies of scale are important. As financial liberalisation and technological development progress, there will be greater freedom for institutions in choosing the sort of business they want to engage in. Universal and specialised financial institutions will co-exist and the concept of banks will become vaguer. However, it is very likely that banks as we know them at present will continue to play a significant role in the financial system. The expertise and equipment accumulated by banks will work as a great advantage in their competition with other financial sectors (for spending on technology, see table 9).

3. Problems to be tackled by banks

Although it is likely that banks will play a significant role in the future financial system, problems remain and have to be overcome for them to meet domestic and international competition.

Establishing better risk management

In the first place, improvement of risk management is necessary. To contain risks, it is not only important to analyse the risks of individual loans, but also to consider how the emergence of one type of risk affects other risks faced by the lender. Meanwhile, as financial instruments are becoming highly complex, skills of management of risks other than credit risks need to be improved. All this means that banks must assign even greater importance to the establishment of appropriate risk management systems.

Meanwhile, some of the reasons behind the aggressive lending stance of banks during the bubble period could be linked to their inability to adjust adequately to the ongoing process of financial liberalisation. Until financial liberalisation started, banks were assured of a considerable margin between deposit and lending rates. As a result, the larger the bank, the more profits it could earn. Banks could not forget this mode of thinking even after financial liberalisation began. When banks were faced with narrower margins due to a rise in deposit rates relative to lending rates (the liberalisation of lending rates lagged) and tougher competition from other financial sectors, they responded by increasing their size.

236

Generating innovations

As mentioned before, Japanese banks are increasingly engaged in new businesses, such as derivatives. However, most of these new products are imported. The reason behind this seems to be the lack of understanding that competitive market mechanisms should be applied to the development of financial activities. In addition, Japanese banks always compare themselves to other banks and seek to stay in line with competitors rather than to beat them by being innovative.

Recently, however, the situation has begun to change. The government is regarding deregulation as one of the most significant policy goals and has already taken some measures in this direction. The newly released report of the Committee for Financial System Research states that self-discipline and the more active utilisation of market mechanisms are imperative for the maintenance of the sound banking system and that regulation should be supplementary. Together with the changes in the financial infrastructure such as changes in the payment system, disclosure rules, accounting, and the legal framework, further deregulation will lead to an environment where Japanese banks are expected to generate innovative activities more vigorously.

Enlarging capital position

Since the introduction of the capital adequacy regulation, Japanese banks have tried to raise capital ratios by controlling asset growth on the one hand, and by strengthening their capital position through stock issuance and subordinated borrowing on the other. As a result, Japanese money centre banks have succeeded in raising their ratios to the 9-10 per cent level despite the reduction in unrealised capital gains on securities due to falling stock prices. However, their European and US counterparts maintain even higher ratios, which could work as a disadvantage to Japanese banks when they compete in the world market. In addition, an acceleration of the disposal of bad assets requires additional capital. Therefore, it is desirable for banks to utilise the capital market more effectively.

4. The role of the Central Bank

This paper has assessed past trends in the Japanese financial system since financial liberalisation and internationalisation started a decade ago and analysed prospects for the future of the financial system, focusing on the banking sector.

The essence of the previous sections can be summarised as follows. The role of the banking sector in the financial system has changed during the last decade; there is even evidence of a decline in the role of banks. This trend may continue and the concept of banks may change. Nevertheless, banks will undoubtedly continue to function as important players in the financial system.

In this context, the Bank of Japan understands that financial liberalisation and internationalisation have already passed the point of no return: it continues to emphasise their importance for more effective monetary policy and a more vigorous financial system. A key issue is how such changes (will) affect the role of the central bank. There are several points to be considered.

Firstly, as the border between banks and other financial institutions becomes vaguer, the question arises whether the scope of services provided by the central bank should be changed. At present, banks are "special" in the sense that they dominate payment services. For this reason, the central bank allows commercial bank to have accounts with the central bank. When financial institutions other than banks enter the realm of settlement services, the question whether they should be allowed to have accounts with the central bank will need careful consideration.

Secondly, as financial institutions other than banks play more important roles in the financial system, it will become difficult to limit the function of the lender of last resort only to banks. Indeed, there has already been a case about thirty years ago when the Bank of Japan extended loans to some securities companies (through banks) with the objective of maintaining the stability of the credit system. Consequently, the problem of how to prevent moral hazard problems, while maintaining stability of the financial system, has become more complex.

Bearing these points in mind, the Bank of Japan will do its best to strengthen the financial system in a changing environment.

Appendix

FUTURE RELATIONS BETWEEN BANKS AND THEIR CUSTOMERS

One of the characteristics of the financial system and the corporate governance structure in Japan is the so-called "main bank" system. The term "main bank" usually refers to a bank (or sometimes a couple of banks) with special relations with borrowers: it has the largest lending share, it holds a substantial portion of borrowers' stocks, it provides all kinds of financial services other than lending and deposit taking, and it is involved in the management of the borrower (sometimes dispatching executives). When a borrower is in trouble, its main bank is expected to help. In this sense, the role of a main bank is fraught with risks, but in normal situations a main bank can profit from borrowers' operations.

However, these are indications that the relations between a main bank and a borrower has been changed in the past decade:

i) its main bank citing the rhetoric of lender's liability. In some other Corporations tend to reduce the number of lenders as access to the bond and other markets becomes easier. In the process, the lending share of a main bank sometimes increases. However, this does not necessarily mean that the position of a main bank has been strengthened. Among the companies listed on the Tokyo Stock Exchange 27 per cent changed their largest long-term lenders and 19 per cent changed their short-term lenders in the period 1985-90. In the years 1981-85, the comparable figures had been 18 per cent and 16 per cent, respectively. During the bubble economy period, banks competed in expanding assets and thus offered better conditions to borrowers to win main bank status. The figures indicate that the position of a main bank became fragile in that period.

ii) Although no exact evidence is available, it is often said that financial institutions and corporations have begun to reduce mutual cross stock holdings to improve profitability. Meanwhile, it has become easier for shareholders to file law suits against corporations; this could lead to a

239

decline in the influence of a main bank on the management of borrowers.

iii) Since the bursting of the bubble, disagreements between main banks and borrowers have sometimes surfaced. For instance, a main bank withdrew executives seconded to a borrower and ceased supporting it when it was in trouble. Also there was a case where a borrower filed a suit against cases, there was serious debates on how to share losses stemming from the default of a borrower between the main bank and other lenders.

These phenomena are indicative of a change in, and possible weakening of, the relations between a main bank and borrowers and the role of a main bank in terms of corporate governance. It is difficult to tell whether this is a trend or a temporary phenomenon and, if it is a trend, how fast the change will occur. However, there are three points to note.

Firstly, traditional roles of main banks have been to help troubled borrowers and to absorb disproportionate losses in case rescue operations fail. Whether these roles should and could be maintained in the future needs careful consideration.

Secondly, there is a possibility that the role of main banks in terms of corporate governance will be less important. In this case, how to encourage general stockholders to become interested in supervising management will be an important consideration. In this regard, the development of a better disclosure system is a key issue.

Finally, the role of main banks will not completely disappear although the form may differ. In the first place, borrowers, even with direct access to financial markets, may face a liquidity problem. Corporations consider ties with banks, especially in the realm of short-term borrowing, as a facility to reduce the difficulties arising from liquidity risks. Secondly, banks can offer other kinds of services. In particular, corporations appreciate accurate information on financial markets and the high level of know-how on risk management provided by banks. In this way, there are incentives for corporations to maintain stable relations with a bank or a number of banks.

Table 1. Financial assets and liabilities accounts, End of calendar year (Corporate business sector + personal sector)

(share to total, per cent)

		1983	1986	1990	1993
Fund raising	Borrowing from private fin.insts	76.2	75.7	70.9	70.3
	Borrowing from public fin.insts.	13.1	11.8	12.6	13.7
	Securities Except Stocks	3.6	5.2	7.7	8.3
	CP	0.0	0.0	1.7	1.1
	Stocks	7.1	7.3	7.1	6.7
	Total	100.0	100.0	100.0	100.0
Financial Investment	Deposits	48.5	43.2	43.1	42.4
	Postal savings	13.3	12.0	10.3	12.9
	Securities	21.6	26.8	23.5	17.4
	Trusts	6.0	6.5	8.0	9.0
	Insurance	10.6	11.5	15.0	18.3
	Total	100.0	100.0	100.0	100.0

Source: Bank of Japan (Flow of Funds Accounts in Japan)

Table 2. Share of each financial sector in loans + securities

(percentage)

	March 1983	March 1988	March 1993
All banks	49.6	51.7	56.2
Financial institutions for small business	21.7	17.8	12.3
Financial institutions for agriculture, forestry and fishery	8.8	6.2	6.1
Foreign banks	1.5	0.9	1.0
Trust accounts	9.2	13.0	10.8
Insurance institutions	9.2	10.4	13.6
Total	100.0	100.0	100.0

1. These figures include both domestic and international assets.

Source: Bank of Japan (Flow of Funds Accounts in Japan)

Table 3. Fund raising and financial investment, by size of corporations

(annual average, trillion yen)

			1984-1986	1987-1990	1991-1993
Large Firms	Investment to Deposits and Securities		5.1	13.1	Δ 4.4
(capital > 1 billion yen)	Fund Raising	Short term borrowing	3.2	5.0	Δ 1.0
		Long term borrowing	0.5	5.5	3.5
		Bonds	2.4	5.2	2.5
		Capital	1.3	3.7	1.1
Medium and Small Firms	Investment to Deposits and Securities		5.5	7.6	Δ 1.6
(capital < 1 billion yen)	Fund Raising	Short term borrowing	6.7	8.4	2.9
		Long term borrowing	5.9	16.5	9.5
		Bonds	0.1	0.1	0.5
		Capital	Δ 0.1	Δ 0.2	Δ 0.5

1. Due to yearly changes in sampling of data in regard to medium and small firms, the figures involve some irregularity.

Source: Ministry of Finance.

Table 4. Fund raising and financial investment

(annual average, trillion yen)

(1) Corporate business sector + personal sector

		1984-86	87-90	91-93	84-93
Fund raising	Borrowing from private fin. insts.	31.5	55.8	20.3	37.8
	Borrowing from public fin. insts.	3.1	8.6	12.0	8.0
	Securities except stocks	2.8	7.5	5.5	5.5
	CP	0.0	3.9	Δ1.6	1.1
	Stocks	2.2	6.0	0.9	3.3
Financial investment	Deposits	27.7	42.5	12.3	29.0
	Postal savings	8.0	6.2	15.7	9.6
	Securities	6.4	8.9	Δ3.4	4.5
	Trusts	6.8	11.8	6.1	8.6
	Insurance	12.2	22.3	21.2	18.9

(2) Personal sector

		1984-86	87-90	91-93	84-93
Fund raising	Borrowing from private fin. insts.	8.5	22.6	5.2	13.1
	Borrowing from public fin. insts.	2.2	3.8	3.7	3.3
Financial investment	Deposit	15.4	27.8	15.7	20.4
	Postal savings	8.0	6.2	15.7	9.6
	Securities	4.6	6.3	Δ3.4	2.9
	Trusts	3.3	5.6	3.6	4.3
	Insurance	12.2	22.3	21.2	18.9

(3) Corporate business sector

		1984-86	87-90	91-93	84-93
Fund raising	Borrowing from private fin. insts.	23.1	33.2	15.1	24.7
	Borrowing from public fin. insts.	1.0	4.8	8.3	4.7
	Securities except stocks	2.8	7.5	5.5	5.5
	CP	0.0	3.9	Δ1.6	1.1
	Stocks	2.2	6.0	0.9	3.3
Financial investment	Deposits	12.3	14.7	Δ3.4	8.5
	Securities	1.8	2.6	Δ0.0	1.6
	Trusts	3.5	6.2	2.5	4.3

Source: Bank of Japan (Flow of Funds Accounts in Japan)

Table 5. Number of financial institutions and branches

		March 1983	March 1988	March 1993
City banks	number	13	13	11
	branches	3 026	3 437	3 829
Long-term credit banks	number	3	3	3
	branches	86	115	153
Trust banks	number	7	7	7
	branches	373	436	500
Regional banks	number	63	64	64
	branches	6 099	7 164	7 913
Regional banks II	number	71	68	65
	branches	4 096	4 417	4 843
Credit unions	number	456	455	435
	branches	6 460	7 730	8 371
Credit corporatives	number	468	439	393
	branches	2 681	2 899	3 912
Total	number	1 081	1 049	978
	branches	22 821	26 198	28 621

Number of mergers

FY81	82	83	84	85	86	87	88	89	90	91	92
6	4	2	4	3	4	4	13	4	10	20	10

Table 6. Ratio of loans to total assets and ratio of securities to total assets

(end of fiscal year, in per cent)

	Ratio of loans to total assets	Ratio of securities to total assets
1981	58.60	15.48
1982	58.37	15.03
1983	59.16	14.76
1984	58.30	14.20
1985	59.55	15.26
1986	58.92	15.80
1987	58.76	15.60
1988	58.29	15.41
1989	55.81	15.92
1990	57.08	16.26
1991	59.99	16.04
1992	62.33	15.90
1993	64.28	16.35

1. City banks, Long-term credit banks, trust banks and regional banks

Table 7. Ratio of cross-border activity to total activity

(FY, %)

	Income from international operations to total income	International assets to total assets
1982	10.27	26.69
1983	10.59	27.66
1984	12.25	31.67
1985	12.50	30.62
1986	12.60	32.13
1987	12.32	33.19
1988	12.21	33.91
1989	11.92	36.39
1990	16.17	35.96
1991	18.41	34.04
1992	17.31	30.09
1993	16.52	27.29

1. City Banks, long-term credit banks, trust banks and regional banks

Table 8. Changes in bank profitability and its components

	1982	1983	1984	1985	1986	1987
Change of net income before tax from a year earlier and percentage contribution						(FY, %)
Net income before tax	43.8	5.6	-4.0	6.4	49.8	12.6
Gross income	60.4	13.4	6.1	15.9	59.8	21.8
Domestic	n.a.	12.5	0.4	13.1	51.9	19.8
International	n.a.	2.4	5.7	2.8	7.8	2.0
Net interest income	63.2	10.3	-1.2	-0.1	41.5	15.9
Income from forex	-10.9	0.4	0.3	4.8	1.9	2.9
Income from securities dealing	0.0	0.0	0.0	9.2	4.9	0.9
Securities gains (losses)	1.0	5.8	7.9	0.3	0.2	10.8
Other non-interest income	8.1	2.7	5.0	4.0	11.4	3.0
Non-interest expense	-16.0	-9.0	-9.8	-9.5	-8.9	-9.0
Share to gross income						(FY, %)
Gross income	100.0	100.0	100.0	100.0	100.0	100.0
Domestic	89.2	89.4	87.7	87.5	87.4	87.7
International	10.3	10.6	12.3	12.5	12.6	12.3
Net interest income	85.2	84.9	82.8	78.7	77.2	76.6
Income from forex	1.4	1.5	1.6	3.0	3.0	3.8
Income from securities dealing	0.0	0.0	0.0	2.8	3.7	3.7
Securities gains (losses)	2.9	4.6	7.1	6.9	5.8	9.4
Other non-interest income	13.3	13.6	15.0	15.5	16.1	15.9

1. Accounting method changed in FY 1989.

Table 8. Changes in bank profitability and its components (cont'd)

	1988	1989	1990	1991	1992	1993
Change of net income before tax from a year earlier and percentage contribution						(FY, %)
Net income before tax	7.9	-24.5	-15.2	28.1	26.1	-5.2
Gross income	17.4	-12.0	-4.5	39.8	30.8	-5.3
Domestic	15.6	-9.9	-16.4	24.8	28.8	-2.4
International	1.9.	-2.1	12.0	15.1	2.0	-3.0
Net interest income	17.8	-11.4	-8.1	55.9	21.2	-11.7
Income from forex	0.3	5.4	4.4	-10.4	-2.6	-1.6
Income from securities dealing	-5.6	-1.2	2.9	-0.2	0.6	-1.5
Securities gains (losses)	18.7	44.1	0.6	0.9	10.0	7.5
Other non-interest income	4.9	0.7	-4.4	-6.3	1.6	2.0
Non-interest expense	-8.7	-10.7	-13.4	-12.4	-5.2	-0.5
Share to gross income						(FY, %)
Gross income	100.0	100.0	100.0	100.0	100.0	100.0
Domestic	87.8	88.1	83.8	81.6	82.7	83.5
International	12.2	11.9	16.2	18.4	17.3	16.5
Net interest income	78.3	77.4	75.8	82.5	81.2	78.3
Income from forex	3.7	6.3	7.9	4.4	3.2	2.6
Income from securities dealing	1.3	0.8	1.8	1.6	1.6	1.1
Securities gains (losses)	16.1	-2.7	-2.5	-2.0	1.2	4.1
Other non-interest income	16.7	18.0	16.7	13.4	12.6	13.6

Table 9. Spending of banks[1] on information technology[2]

	Yen billion	increase from a year earlier per cent
1982	371	-1.49
1983	391	5.36
1984	426	8.92
1985	457	7.27
1986	481	5.36
1987	534	10.88
1988	606	13.54
1989	697	14.96
1990	789	13.25
1991	860	8.94
1992	901	4.78
1993	888	-1.36

1. City Banks, long-term credit banks, trust banks and regional banks
2. Depreciation and rental for machines

Chapter 7

RISK MANAGEMENT IN NATIONAL PAYMENT SYSTEMS*

Bruce Summers

1. Introduction

The monetary sectors of developed financial economies, including the interbank and other financial markets, have become significantly larger and more diversified in the last decade. Developments in these markets, including widespread use of new instruments and products, have led to tremendous increases in the value and velocity of transactions and to new types of risks borne by market participants, including settlement risk. Efforts to control and manage risk in this environment have naturally included improvements to the infrastructure that is relied upon to clear and settle transactions efficiently and safely. In fact, growth in the interbank and other financial markets has increased the attention given to needed changes in payment practices and in national payment systems. The purpose of this paper is to provide a broad overview of recent operational responses in national payment systems, particularly interbank payment systems, stimulated by developments in financial markets. It uses actual developments in a variety of payment systems around the world to illustrate key initiatives and trends.

---

*   The author has benefitted greatly from conversations with and comments made by a number of central bankers, commercial bankers, and others, and would like to acknowledge their help without implicating them in any errors or controversial views contained in the paper. Within the Federal Reserve System, thanks to Ed Ettin, Jeff Lacker, Jeff Marquardt, Heidi Richards, and Jeff Stehm. Thanks as well to Peter Allsopp, Jim Dingle, Patrizio Ferradini, Chuck Freedman, Clyde Goodlet, Yumiko Horii, Yvon Lucas, Hermann-Josef Persé, Patrick Poncelet, John Veale, Clay Simpson, Dirk Schoenmaker, Noriyuki Tomioka, Christian Vital, and Tsutomu Watanabe.

The paper has four main sections. First, I describe the principal design alternatives for interbank payment systems and highlight the importance of "central bank money" as a settlement medium in these systems. Second, I illustrate how payment flows have changed in recent years and examine some of the consequences of these changes for payment-related credit and risk management practices. Third, I review some recent developments in national payment systems in response to new demands for timely and safe settlement of very large aggregate values arising in connection with growth in the financial markets. Fourth, I present some general conclusions regarding the development of national payment systems.

2. Interbank settlement design alternatives

Understanding the interbank settlement process requires an understanding of correspondent banking. In this regard, the feature that distinguishes commercial banks as financial inter-mediaries is their unique role as issuers of liabilities -- demand or call money deposits -- that are widely accepted as payment. As described by Blommestein and Summers (1994), economic actors in a modern financial economy essentially rely on deposit money held in banks to satisfy their payment obligations. In the process, commercial banks become parties to the payment transactions.

Interbank settlement obligations arising from customer payments, and from direct dealings between banks, can be settled in three basic ways. First, a creditor bank can, but certainly does not in the modern world, accept transfers of currency from another bank wishing to discharge its interbank obligation. Second, creditor banks can agree to accept increases in the balances they hold in nostro accounts with debtor banks, which is essentially the substitution of one form of indebtedness, a contractual payment obligation, for another, an equivalent increase in the "due from" deposits held with the other bank. Third, creditor banks can agree to accept increases in balances they maintain with a third bank, either another commercial bank or the central bank. Reliance on correspondent banking arrangements for settlement can involve a chain of commercial banks, in which case the number of reciprocal accounts and amount of balances that must be held by any one institution may be lower than what would be necessary if bilateral account relationships were established with each potential counterparty. Settlement through a chain of accounts, however, can introduce operational inefficiencies and additional settlement risk considerations.

The banking and payment systems in a mature, market-oriented economy will be characterized by many participants, large interbank obligations, and a desire to achieve final settlement on a timely basis within the same day. In such a system, incentives are created to use balances held in accounts with the central bank to discharge interbank obligations. The reason is twofold. First, as suggested above, it is inefficient for commercial banks to maintain large numbers of bilateral nostro account relationships, which would also require holding sufficient funds on deposit in a multitude of nostro accounts to meet settlement obligations. Alternatively, relying on a lengthy chain of intermediaries, while perhaps permitting a reduction in the total amount of settlement balances that would need to be held in numerous bilateral relationships, can increase the number of steps and time needed to settle a payment. The central bank contributes significantly to the efficiency of the interbank settlement process by serving as a common nostro bank to all deposit taking institutions. Second, an important method used by banks to control their interbank credit risk is to require payment for interbank obligations through final transfers of central bank money[1]. The deposit liabilities of the central bank, referred to here as "central bank money," are attractive as a settlement medium because of the unique attributes of central banks and the money they issue. Central bank money is free of credit risk -- the central bank cannot fail. Further, central banks do not pose liquidity risks -- the central bank has the power to create high-powered money. Central bank money is therefore ideally suited to serve as a risk-free (but not costless) settlement medium.

Central banks provide support for interbank settlement by offering accounts and facilities, or services, to transfer funds between these accounts. Moreover, central banks may also act as providers of payment-related credit. Such credit is especially important to settlement efficiency in developed financial markets with active trading that gives rise to high aggregate values of payment obligations each day. Examples would include obligations to settle cash, futures, and forward trades, as well as obligations arising in connection with daily market-to-market margin requirements. Participants in markets giving rise to such obligations may find it difficult to synchronize the timing of incoming and outgoing payments and therefore have a special need for intraday bank credit.

As will be discussed below, the aggregate value of financial markets transactions can exceed the stock of central bank money used to settle the interbank obligations that result -- in some cases, by a wide margin. This gap results in high daily turnover in accounts held with central banks, which is an indication of monetary efficiency as a given stock of reserves supports a larger flow of transactions. High turnover can be accompanied by asynchronous payment flows through these accounts, thereby resulting in situations where funds on deposit are insufficient to meet settlement requirements or payments that the account holder desires to make at a particular point in time, even though there is an identified source of covering funds which may be received within a short period of time. Thus, in a modern financial system, intraday credit, that is, credit with a dura-tion of less than 24 hours that is not overnight credit, is especially important as a source of intraday working capital to banks. In turn, commercial banks provide payment-related credit services to their clients.

Intraday credit poses risk management concerns because, if they are not extinguished, intraday loans become overnight loans. Thus, there is a potential connection between intraday credit, which does not appear on bank balance sheets, and over-night or interday credit, which appears on balance sheets as loans. The developments in national payment systems described in this paper, in large part, involve responses to increased demands for, and management of the risks associated with, intraday credit provided by the banking system. Different institutional responses in national payment systems therefore represent approaches to distributing and controlling risk. With respect to interbank credit arising from payment relationships, whether through real-time gross settlement or multilateral netting systems, the main choice involves the extent to which credit risk is shouldered, either implicitly or explicitly, by the central bank or internalized by commercial banks.

Central banks support interbank settlement in two principal ways. First, they may provide interbank settlement services to multilateral netting systems that rely on central bank money for settlement. In this case, individual interbank transactions are cleared using facilities that may or may not be operated by the central bank, and only net obligations and entitlements are processed through central bank accounts at the end of a defined clearing cycle. As discussed below, large-value transfer systems based on multilateral netting either presently conform to or are being modified to conform to international standards which establish minimum requirements for risk control. These standards are designed to ensure that the commercial banks participating in such systems have incentives to manage risk and set aside financial reserves to assure settlement in the event of a failure to settle by the largest net debtor in a multilateral netting arrangement. An open question is the appropriate distri-bution of burden between the central bank and the commercial banking system in managing the risks and bearing the costs of even greater settlement failures, such as the risk that the largest net debtor **and** one or more additional institutions default on their settlement obligations. The second way in which central banks support interbank settlement is to operate funds transfer systems that are specifically designed to provide real-time gross settlement of payments made to satisfy individual interbank obligations. In this case, the central bank is explicitly accountable for managing its credit exposures to users of the system on a bilateral basis. As noted, there may be an operational connection between multilateral netting and a real-time gross settlement system operated by the central bank, if the latter is relied upon to achieve final settlement in central bank money of obligations arising from netting arrangements.

The discussion that follows identifies and describes three general designs of large-value transfer systems used for interbank settlement. Horii and Summers (1994) examine three general types of large-value transfer systems, taking into account *(1)* whether settlement over the system is gross or based on multilateral netting; *(2)* who operates the system, that is, the central bank or a private organization; and *(3)* whether the system provides intraday credit. In a gross settlement system, each transaction is settled individually, and settlement deci-sions are made sequentially. If processing occurs transaction-by-transaction, then payments are handled individually on a flow basis as compared to the batch processing alternative, in which a number of payments are accumulated over time and submitted for processing as a group. In a multilateral netting system, payment values are offset multilaterally within a given clearing cycle. Net settlement for all the transactions processed within the clearing cycle occurs at or sometime after the end of the cycle[2].

The first general design of a large-value transfer system is a gross settlement system operated by the central bank without intraday credit. In this type of design, a payment order will be honored only if funds are on deposit at the time the order is made. Otherwise, the payment order is returned to the originator (rejected) or held until covering funds become available (pended or queued) during the clearing cycle, which is generally the banking day. This type of system implies *(1)* real-time computer processing where each transaction is handled as soon as it is received and *(2)* a direct link to deposit accounts, so that balances can be monitored as part of the decision process. The prototype of such a system is the Swiss Interbank Clearing System (SIC).

The second general design of a large-value transfer system is a gross settlement system operated by the central bank with intraday credit. Again, this type of system is based on real-time computer processing. In this type of design, the central bank will honor payment orders during the day, even if an originating bank's account does not contain sufficient funds to settle the payment. Intraday credit to cover payment orders is provided with the expectation that covering funds will be depo-sited in the account before the end of the business day. The credit extension can be partially or completely collateralized as a risk management measure and limits on the amount of credit used, called caps, can be established. An example of a system that provides intraday credit subject to caps which can be monitored and enforced in real time by computer, and for which collateral is not required for financially healthy institutions, is the Fedwire funds transfer system in the United States.

Each unit of intraday credit, represented by a deficit in a reserve account, is matched by a unit of reserve money held in the account of another institution having a positive balance. Thus, such credit adds liquidity to the financial system during the day. By the end of the day, however, intraday credit is expected to be extinguished, and therefore such loans should not add to the total stock of bank reserves. Measurement of the stock of reserves occurs at a single point during the day for the purpose of creating daily balance sheets and fulfilling legal reserve requirements, assuming there is a binding reserve requirement in place for depository institutions. Adjustment in the interbank market for reserves is geared to the particular point during the day when the official measurement of reserves balances occurs, which is sometime after the close of a nation's large-value transfer system on, say, day t and before the opening of that system on day t + 1. It is at this point that banks target their overnight reserve positions and the need for overnight adjustment credit from the central bank may arise.

The third general design of a large-value transfer system is deferred settlement based on multilateral netting. In such a system, settlement does not occur payment-by-payment, but at designated times during the day. Between, or at, designated settlement times, payments exchanged between banks are multi-laterally netted, resulting in one net obligation for each net debtor bank that is due at the designated settlement time. Netting, of course, acts to reduce the demand for whatever settlement medium is used -- in the case of interbank settlement, central bank money. In a netting system, liquidity needs during the clearing cycle are met by implicit or explicit extensions of credit between the participants in the system. Such intra-cycle credit extensions can be said to be explicit if procedures and systems are in place that allow participants in the netting scheme to measure and keep track of their bilateral exposures. If such procedures and systems are not in place and exposures arise, but are not identified and measured, then the credit extensions are implicit. In the case where explicit extensions of credit are controlled in real time and where strong measures are in place to assure settlement in the event of default, including loss-sharing and full collateralization of exposures, a multilateral netting arrangement can approach the degree of integrity provided by real-time gross settlement.

An example of a deferred net settlement system operated by the central bank is the Bank of Japan Financial System Network (BOJ-NET)[3]. An example of a private net settlement system is the Clearing House Interbank Payments

System (CHIPS) in the United States, which is owned and operated by the New York Clearing House Association. The netting principles that underlie the operation of deferred net settlement systems are the same, regardless of whether the system operator is a central bank or a private entity. The legal basis for multilateral netting may differ, depending on the jurisdiction within which the system operates. Participants in large-value transfer systems that operate as multilateral netting systems often seek to achieve final settlement through the transfer of central bank money, as this form of final settlement is seen as strengthening interbank settlement of netted obligations, thereby adding to the integrity of the underlying payments made through the system during the clearing cycle.

Additional important design considerations in large-value payment systems concern *(1)* the timing of the delivery of payment instructions from the originating bank to the intended receiving bank in relation to the timing of the settlement for these payments and *(2)* the accessibility by intended receiving banks to information on payments that have been ordered but not made. In netting systems that process payment instructions in real time, payments are, by definition, delivered from originating to receiving banks in advance of settlement, because settlement is deferred until the end of the clearing cycle. Indeed, this is, in part, why such systems create potential risks for their users. By acting on payment instructions received before final settlement, for example, by giving third-party customers use of the funds during the clearing cycle but before settlement, receiving banks that are in a bilateral net debit position vis-á-vis the originating bank(s) are entering into commitments and counting on money that is not yet received to meet new obligations[4]. For this reason, it is important that netting systems are designed so as to provide financial assurances that settlement will occur even in the event of default by one or more net debtors. As noted, depending on the strength of the financial assurances employed, multilateral netting systems can approach the integrity of real-time gross settlement systems.

The timing of the delivery of payment instructions (information) in relation to the timing of settlement in real-time gross settlement systems can occur in one of two basic ways. First, some real-time gross settlement systems are designed so that a payment instruction is sent to the receiving bank only when the payment order is accepted and settled by the central bank. This is implemented in the so-called "V," "Y," or "L" designs. In the United States, for example, Fedwire is based on the "V" design. A bank originates a payment order to a Federal Reserve Bank through Fedwire, which will notify the receiving bank of final payment by passing on the payment instruction. If the Federal Reserve Bank does not honor the payment order, the payment is rejected back to the originating bank, or pended, and the receiving bank is not notified of the attempted payment by the Fedwire system. The Swiss Interbank Clearing System is also based on the "V" design, and only settled payments are sent on to the intended receiving banks[5].

The Bank of France contemplates using a "Y" design in the new Transfer Bank of France (TBF) large-value transfer system. In this design, which will be implemented through operating facilities provided by the Society for Worldwide Interbank Financial Telecommunications (SWIFT), a payment order is sent by an originating bank to a central processor located at the joint of the "Y." The SWIFT processor strips settlement information from the payment instruction, sends the settlement information to the central bank, and completes delivery of the instruction to the receiving bank only after receiving confirmation of settlement back from the central bank. In this arrangement, the central bank operates its own internal facilities for settlement processing that connect to the processing system operated by SWIFT, which is used to exchange payment instructions among banks.

Finally, the new Clearing House Automated Payment System (CHAPS) in the United Kingdom, which will be operational before the end of 1995, will be based on the so-called "L" design[6]. Under this design, each payment that is originated will involve sending a settlement request to the Bank of England. Only after the Bank of England honors the settlement request by sending a confirmation to the originating bank will the CHAPS computer allow the payment instruction to be routed on to the receiving bank.

The principal alternative to the "V," "Y," and "L" designs described above is the so-called "T" design, whereby a payment message is sent simultaneously to the receiving bank and to the central bank. If, for any reason, the central bank does not settle the payment when it receives the order, for example, if the originating bank has reached its funding limit, settlement is delayed even though the receiving bank has been notified of an intended payment. The "T" design is attractive to commercial bankers who may view information about a payment as being almost as important as the settlement value, because such information helps cash managers optimize their investment decisions during a given clearing cycle. Yet, at the same time, this approach may pose risk management issues for users of real-time gross settlement systems that are like some of the issues faced by participants in multilateral netting systems, to the extent that banks would choose to act on unsettled large-value payment instructions. Indeed, a question is whether the types of risk management standards that have been adopted for multilateral netting systems, such as bilateral credit limits and system net debit caps, are applicable in the context of real-time gross settlement systems that permit payment instructions to be exchanged during the clearing cycle without settlement having occurred. The "T" design was the basis for a product developed by SWIFT and intended as a turn-key approach to installing a national large-value payment system. In mid-1994, the design basis was changed from the "T" to the "Y" approach[7].

With respect to accessibility to information on pay-ments ordered but not settled, practices again differ by country, even for the same basic design governing information flow. The difference between the United States and Switzerland, for which both Fedwire and SIC are based on the "V" design, is a case in point. In the case of Fedwire, information regarding the account positions of a bank vis-à-vis a Federal Reserve Bank is proprietary to the account-holding bank. This is also true for information on the status of payment orders made by a bank that may not be immediately honored by the Federal Reserve Bank (Federal Reserve Banks may choose to pend or reject payment orders originated over Fedwire). Decisions made by a Federal Reserve Bank whether to honor payment orders and whether to provide intraday credit may constitute important information about a bank's financial condition -- information that neither the Federal Reserve nor the bank originating the payment would want to broadcast or otherwise make available to other banks.

In contrast, SIC, which builds queues of unfunded payments as part of its operational design, allows each participating bank to view the backlog of all payments it is destined to receive. The philosophy under which SIC operates is that payment system efficiency is enhanced if receiving banks are given the ability to access information regarding the payments that have been directed to them but that have not been settled. These payments are held in SIC queues and have not been honored by the Swiss National Bank, which has not delivered them to the intended receiving banks.

The type of large-value transfer system that best meets the needs of a particular economy is a major public policy issue. The economic incentives for using a real-time gross settlement versus a multilateral netting system depend to a large extent on the cost of holding central bank money for use in settling pay-ments. Since multilateral net settlement arrangements defer final settlement until a designated settlement time and rely on private credit and mutual offsetting of obligations, these systems, by definition, make less intensive use of central bank money to settle a given value of payments than do real-time gross settlement systems. Accordingly, the higher the cost of using central bank money to settle payments, the greater the incentive to use multilateral net settlement.

As discussed by Marquardt (1994), some of the key factors influencing the cost of using central bank money for settlement, and therefore the choice of large-value payment system design, include *(1)* the reserves maintenance regime, specifically the level of required reserves and policies regarding payment of interest on reserves, *(2)* the optimal size of the reserve balance needed for operational purposes, and *(3)* interest rates. The marginal cost of holding central bank money is one of the most relevant financial costs to consider for purposes of evaluating real-time gross settlement versus multi-lateral net settlement alternatives.

The standard concept for measuring the incremental or marginal cost of central bank money is the concept of opportunity cost. This concept recognizes that central banks typically do not pay interest on overnight reserve balances and that legal requirements may require that banks hold some level of balances with the central bank. The higher the required reserve ratio, the greater the stock of central bank money that must be held and that is available to meet operational requirements for interbank settlement, assuming that required reserves can be met on an average interday basis. Thus, the opportunity cost of holding central bank money is the risk-adjusted rate of interest foregone by holding balances in excess of required reserves that do not earn interest. Monetary control procedures in many developed financial economies have shifted away from reliance on reserve requirements as a tool of monetary policy. Accordingly, required reserves are declining and have been reduced to zero, or near zero, in several countries. This development can significantly increase the opportunity cost of using real-time gross settlement systems compared to multilateral net settlement systems.

The availability and cost of intraday balances, supplied by intraday credit extensions, can also influence the relative cost of net versus gross settlement. In particular, the greater the supply of intraday credit from the central bank, for example, the higher the net debit cap, and the lower the cost of this credit, the greater the incentives to use real-time gross settlement. Explicit fees and collateral requirements both raise the cost of using real-time gross settlement systems. The Federal Reserve's experience with explicit fees for intraday credit supplied over Fedwire is described below. Full collateralization of intraday exposures is the approach to controlling risk being taken by a number of European central banks.

With respect to collateralization, recent analysis by Schoenmaker (1994) suggests that a real-time gross settlement system that requires full collateralization of peak intraday exposures may be relatively more expensive to use compared to a multilateral netting system for which net exposures must be collateralized. The extent to which collateralization of central banks' intraday exposures raises costs for banks using their real-time gross settlement systems depends, in part, on the banks' portfolio preferences, that is, on the extent to which the banks may not mind encumbering high-quality assets to meet central bank collateral requirements.

Explicit fees for intraday credit and/or collateral requirements raise the comparative cost of using real-time gross settlement versus the alternative of multilateral netting and creates an incentive to shift payments from real-time gross settlement to deferred net settlement arrangements. There are also costs associated with multilateral netting systems, however. The financial controls that have been identified for multilateral netting systems in recent years have increased the costs of using these systems. In particular, the adoption of financial guarantees and liquidity arrangements, such as confirmed letters of credit and dedicated pools of high-quality collateral, raise the costs of using multilateral netting systems. Further, heightened awareness of the unique risks associated with multilateral netting probably also adds to the imputed cost of using such systems. The variety of comparative costs involved makes it clear that the choice between using real-time gross settlement compared to multilateral net settlement systems is a complex matter.

In the end, issues of risk management, legal certainty, and cost will all combine to influence views about the relative attractiveness of real-time gross settlement versus netting systems. The commercial attractiveness, and even the viability, of large-value transfer systems will depend, in part, on the perceived benefits of enhanced risk control traded off against increased costs associated with gaining that control. Further, it may be that the trade-off will be seen somewhat differently by central bankers than by commercial bankers. Clearly, determination of the optimal design of a nation's large-value transfer system must result from an active dialogue between the private and public sectors, and from an official oversight process which respects the need to seek practical and cost-effective solutions to payment system risk management problems.

3.   Payment flows and payment-related credit

This section illustrates the effects of developments in financial markets on payment flows within the economy. Chart 1 shows the ratio of the gross value of payments to GDP for eight countries for the years 1988 and 1992. It should be emphasized at the outset that these figures need to be used with caution, as both intertemporal and cross-country comparisons pose substantial problems in interpretation. With respect to cross-country comparisons, the values captured for the payment systems listed in the BIS "Redbook," the source of the data used to compute these ratios, may not represent a standard set of underlying payment transactions for each country. In particular, money settlement for some securities-related transactions may be included in the measure of payment system value for some coun-tries but not others. Cross-country distortions are probable because of the very large money settlement values associated with securities trading. Further, intertemporal comparisons may be distorted due to the introduction of specialized clearing and settlement systems for certain classes of financial transactions between 1988 and 1992.

With these caveats in mind, the data do suggest that in virtually every country shown, the ratio of payment value to GDP is quite high. For several countries, the figures indicate that the value of payments settled every several days is equivalent to annual GDP. In Japan and Switzerland, for example, which have the highest ratios, payment value totals aggregate GDP approximately every three days. Accordingly, domestic payment systems in these countries must have the operational capacity and financial controls needed to process large values of transactions efficiently and safely.

Chart 2 shows the estimated daily turnover of balances held in accounts at central banks for the years 1988 and 1993. Daily turnover is defined, for these purposes, as the estimated daily average value of payments over major payment systems, divided by the daily average value of balances held on deposit at the central bank. For the same reasons noted above in connection with Chart 1, caution is needed in making intertemporal and cross-country comparisons using these data. In particular, and as mentioned earlier, monetary control procedures in a number of countries have shifted away from reliance on reserve requirements as a tool of monetary policy, and the reserve requirement "tax" on banks has been lowered substantially in a number of cases. This alone would account for a much higher turnover ratio in a number of countries. In any event, the data again indicate a significant increase in the intensity of use of a given stock of central bank money for purposes of settlement during the five-year period. In every case shown, turnover has increased several times during the period. In the United States, for example, the data suggest that a dollar of central bank money is now moved between accounts held by depository institutions with the Federal Reserve Banks approximately fifty times every day[8]. A turnover of fifty times per day is a tremendous velocity that has significant implications for liquidity needs in the financial markets and that creates significant operational and risk management challenges.

Intraday liquidity needs related to high turnover of balances held with central banks may lead to increased demand for intraday credit, depending on the design of the country's large-value transfer system. In the case of Switzerland, where SIC operates as a real-time gross settlement system without credit and incorporates sophisticated operational controls over the flow of payments, intraday credit from the central bank is, by definition, zero. In contrast, in the case of the United States, the Federal Reserve has been a large provider of intraday credit through Fedwire. As described below, before the implementation of fees for the intraday credit that is provided by the Federal Reserve, the amount of intraday credit extended totaled about $70 billion per minute, on average[9].

Calculation of the quantity of intraday credit depends on the accounting rules used. Rules are now in place in the United States to govern the time during the day at which credits and debits associated with a wide array of transactions processed by the Federal Reserve Banks, such as wire transfers, ACH, check, cash, etc., are accounted for on, or "posted to," the books of the Federal Reserve Banks. The accounting rules have been estab-lished to reflect the operational and legal characteristics of each particular type of transaction, and they define when these transactions are settled. These rules are somewhat complex, and this complexity was a serious source of concern to banks. The intraday accounting rules have now been accepted, however, and management of account positions during the day according to these rules is becoming a way of life in the commercial banking system.

Fedwire funds and securities transfers, which account for the largest portion of total payment value, are posted to accounts as they occur during the day, in real time. Non-wire transactions are assigned posting times appropriate to the unique characteristics of the instruments in question, accumulated, and posted at 15-minute intervals during the day. The accounting rules that determine the quantity of intraday credit subject to fees went into effect in October 1993, approximately six months before implementation of the fees. In this way, depository institutions with accounts at Federal Reserve Banks were given an opportunity to anticipate and begin managing their use of intraday credit[10].

Changes in the accounting rules and methods used to calculate intraday overdrafts over time make it difficult to construct a consistent time-series for intraday credit. Nonetheless, it can be said that growth in extensions of intraday credit has continued over the years, notwithstanding implementation of the Federal Reserve's payment system risk reduction program in the mid-1980s. Introduction of the program raised awareness of payment system risk issues, however, and almost surely has resulted in lower utilization of intraday credit than would have been the case had voluntary constraints on credit use not been introduced. But, so long as intraday credit provided by the Federal Reserve was a free good, it was difficult to limit demand. The early response to fees, which became effective on April 14, 1994, is described in the next section.

4. Developments in national payment systems

Several major developments have occurred in national payment systems within just the last few years, with respect to both netting arrangements and real-time gross settlement systems. For netting systems, it is now virtually universally accepted that such systems should conform to the six so-called Lamfalussy standards, which are the **minimum** risk management standards such systems should meet[11]. Perhaps the prototypical application of these standards is on CHIPS, which has, over a number of years, adopted a system of bilateral credit limits and sender net debit caps to limit both individual participant exposures and the entire netting system's vulnerability to credit risk. The bilateral credit limits, whereby each participant establishes the maximum net amount it is willing to receive from, or the amount of net credit it is willing to extend to, another participant, are enforced automatically in real-time by the CHIPS computer. Similarly, the sender net debit cap, which limits the amount that any one participant can owe to the entire CHIPS system, is also enforced by computer. All CHIPS participants agree to partici-pate in a scheme for guaranteeing the daily settlement so that if a participant with a large settlement obligation ever fails to meet its obligation, private resources are immediately available[12] to provide the liquidity necessary to allow settlement to occur on time. Further, a loss-sharing arrangement is in place to allocate any resulting losses in a pre-agreed manner.

The November 1993 report to the Committee of Governors of the central banks of the EU countries, titled "Minimum Common Features for Domestic Payment Systems," establishes the principle that every member state should have a real-time gross settlement system **and** that as many large value payments as possible should be channeled through these systems. Adoption of this principle is an important development indeed. Exactly how the use of real-time gross settlement and multilateral netting systems will evolve in the EU countries in light of this principle and the relative costs of using the two different type systems in the European context is a matter of interest. The offering of real-time gross settlement services by central banks is a reasonably straightforward matter. The interplay of incentives to use such systems for large-value payments, as compared to netting systems, is difficult to predict. It can be said, however, that the integrity and safety of major netting systems are being improved in a number of countries, perhaps motivated in part by the willingness of central banks to offer real-time gross settlement services.

For example, the Ecu Banking Association (EBA) has devoted attention to modifying the Ecu clearing system to conform to the Lamfalussy standards. Binding end-of-day multilateral limits on exposures were adopted in 1993, together with a loss-sharing arrangement based on bilateral limits, and work continues to limit exposures in the system. Changes are being made to operational systems to enforce the multilateral limits during the day, for implementation in 1996. Further, collateral arrange-ments to ensure liquidity and loss-sharing are being investigated in keeping with the principle established by the EU central banks that all large-value net settlement systems meet the Lamfalussy standards in full[13].

Also, the German EAF system, used to settle the DM side of foreign exchange transactions, is being significantly modified[14]. The EAF system is a multilateral netting arrangement. The new system, called EAF-2, will be introduced in 1995 and will incorporate two important changes in DM settlement procedures. First, the Bundesbank will require that the combined collateral and funds that EAF-2 participants have on deposit is adequate to cover their settlement exposures. Second, EAF-2 is being substantially redesigned around a two phase clearing procedure. Under the first phase, lasting approximately the first four and three-quarter hours of the EAF-2 operating day, individual payments exchanged bilaterally between pairs of banks will be accumulated and settled every twenty minutes, based on mutual set off of payments sent and received. Individual payments will be settled with finality at the end of each twenty minute cycle, to the extent that payment flows between pairs of banks support set off.

Further, each bank may establish a "sender ceiling" vis-à-vis each of its counterparties that applies during the first phase. A bank may send payments to a particular counter-party in excess of what it receives from that counterparty during a particular twenty minute cycle, and the payments can be settled by virtue of an extension of credit by that counterparty. This loan is collateralized by the sending bank's balance in its EAF-2 account at the Bundesbank, which is pledged to the receiving bank from the beginning to the completion of the first EAF-2 phase. A bank receiving payments under the "sender ceiling" can use the proceeds during the first phase only to fund its own payments to the particular counterparty to which the collateralized loan is granted.

Subsequent to this first, bilateral settlement phase, an EAF-2 multilateral netting phase begins at 1:00 p.m. and closes at 2:15 p.m. Only payments that cannot be settled during the first phase can be entered into the second, multilateral netting phase[15]. Essentially, therefore, the latest time a payment instruction can be made for same-day settlement through EAF-2 is just prior to 1:00 p.m. If one or more participants have unfunded payments in the system at the end of the multi-lateral netting phase, the settlement will be partially recast. Under the recast procedure envisioned, an algorithm will be used to determine which of a participant's payments must be removed from the netting to bring the participant into a position that can be settled, relying on funded credits due to it in the system. Thus, the EAF-2 settlement design assures that system settlement will occur on the same day, although it does not assure that all payments entered into the system will be settled. Only payments settled with finality will be sent to the receiving bank. Banks may view the EAF-2 queue of payments sent to them which are not settled and therefore face some uncertainty whether all the payments will be settled. The exposure faced by banks intending to receive payments might be termed a random exposure, in light of the recast method followed at the end of the multilateral netting phase.

Reliance on fees to limit use of intraday credit is an approach used to date only by the Federal Reserve. The early experience with fees for intraday credit in the United States is therefore of considerable interest. Chart 3 shows the per-minute average amount of aggregate (that is, funds and securities trans-fer) intraday overdrafts at 15-minute intervals during the first quarter of 1994 compared to the period from April 14 to August 3, 1994. On a per-minute average basis, the amount of intraday credit used has declined by 35.2 percent, from $72.2 billion to $46.8 billion. The steepest decline has been in securities-related overdrafts, shown in Chart 4, which have fallen 42.1 percent, from $45.4 billion to $26.3 billion. Note in Chart 4 as well that the time during the day at which securities overdrafts peak has moved considerably earlier, from around 11:00 a.m. Eastern time to 9:30 a.m. This shift is due to changes in market practices to settle repurchase agreements earlier, stimulated by the desire to avoid overdraft charges. Finally, funds-related overdrafts have declined by 23.5 percent, from $26.8 billion to $20.5 billion.

It has taken nearly a decade for the Federal Reserve to develop a program of charging for intraday credit. Indeed, market concerns about the possible outcomes of charging fees have been great. These concerns have included gridlock, or a drying up of necessary intraday liquidity as a result of delayed originations of payments. The early experience with fees suggests that there may be some, but so far not a significant, shift in the value of payment activity to later in the day. In addition, there have been concerns that payments might shift off Fedwire onto CHIPS to a significant extent, thereby limiting the benefits of real-time gross settlement. In fact, the Federal Reserve's program of charging fees for intraday credit was deliberately timed to follow the adoption by CHIPS of enhanced risk control measures, so as not to create incentives for payment activity to migrate from a real-time gross settlement system to a netting system that did not provide at least minimally acceptable risk controls. It is much too early to tell what effects charging fees for intraday credit over Fedwire will have on the choice of the real-time gross settlement versus netting alternatives. To date, however, there has been no noticeable shift of transaction activity from Fedwire to CHIPS.

While experience with fees is limited, early indications are that the program has succeeded in providing incentives for more careful management and use of intraday credit. To date, the effects of fees on use of intraday credit associated with funds transfers have been largely in line with expectations about market responses[16]. While a formal market for intraday funds has not developed, there is evidence of some informal price tiering in the overnight market. For example, quotes on interbank funds can now be seen to differ depending on the time of day funds are sent or returned, earlier sends and later returns lengthening the duration of overnight loans and thereby adding a few basis points to the value of the deal. Also, there is some evidence that interbank brokers are beginning to make markets in overnight funds transactions of different standard durations.

Conversely, no one predicted the immediate and significant adjustments that would occur in the market for repurchase agreements which have resulted in sharply reduced reliance on Federal Reserve intraday credit. Intraday overdrafts related to Fedwire securities transfers are incurred primarily by two large clearing banks, which have been able to calculate the amount of intraday credit used by their large dealer customers. By announ-cing that they would pass on to dealers the charges assessed to them by the Federal Reserve, the clearing banks created incentives for dealers to modify their practices in ways that would result in less use of intraday credit. As it turns out, the procedural and operational changes by dealers necessary to reduce reliance on intraday credit are fairly straightforward and not so expensive. Predictably, the markets have reacted by implementing changes in trading and settlement procedures whose costs are less than the cost of credit. Accordingly, there is now substantially reduced reliance on intraday credit provided by the Federal Reserve, and as a result, the stock of central bank money is being used more efficiently for purposes of settlement through the Fedwire real-time gross settlement system.

Another significant development in national payment systems which is motivated by the desire to control better the risk associated with international transactions involves the hours of operation for large-value transfer systems.

Coordination of the hours of operation of national payment systems can provide opportunities for the simultaneous settlement of trans-actions involving multiple currencies. To illustrate the importance of multi-currency payments in the case of an actively traded currency, consider the US dollar. It is estimated that 25 to 30 percent of all US dollar clearings are related to settlement of the dollar side of foreign exchange transactions.

Foreign exchange transactions, and other multi-currency transactions, raise special issues in that they involve the operation of two or more national payment systems. For such transactions, risk management is complicated by time zone differences and differences in the hours of operation of national payment systems. In February 1994, the Federal Reserve Board took action to expand the operating hours of the Fedwire funds transfer system to eighteen hours per day, opening at 12:30 a.m. Eastern time and closing at 6:30 p.m. Eastern time. The expanded Fedwire funds transfer operating hours will be implemented in the fourth quarter of 1997. The principal motivation for this change is to provide the markets with greater opportunity to devise enhanced settlement systems for managing Herstatt-type risk[17].

In addition, the Bank of Japan has expanded the opera-ting hours of BOJ-NET until 5:00 p.m. Tokyo time. The immediate motivating factor for extending BOJ-NET hours is to provide an opportunity for the Zengin funds transfer system to settle on the same day through BOJ-NET. The expansion of BOJ-NET operating hours to later in the day, however, is entirely consistent with, and reinforces, expanded Fedwire hours. In combination, the expanded BOJ-NET and Fedwire operating hours will reduce the gap in operating hours of these two countries' payment systems and eventually lead to overlapping operating hours[18].

The developments with respect to expanded operating hours in Japan and the United States are consistent with a similar intention expressed by EU central banks, although the EU intention is motivated more by concern about efficient handling of cross-border payments in a single market, and later in a single European currency[19]. Moreover, the broad background to all of these developments is the cooperative effort of the G-10 central banks, reflected in a recent report on central bank payment and settlement services for cross-border and multi-currency transactions, to offer solutions to multi-currency risk management problems[20].

Lying behind the central bank actions to extend operating hours for real-time gross settlement systems is the knowledge that two consortia of banks are attempting to design and implement multi-currency, multilateral settlement systems for foreign exchange transactions. These systems are the Exchange Clearing House Organization (ECHO) in London and the Multinet system in North America. The reasons which call for banks to rely on central bank money to settle interbank obligations arising in connection with multilateral netting in national payment systems apply equally to banks' participation in these multi-currency netting systems. Extended hours of operation of national payment systems should make it easier for such systems to synchronize their multi-currency settlements and thereby better manage Herstatt risk.

5. Conclusions

Significant increases in financial markets activity have contributed to significant increases in the values handled by national clearing and settlement systems, especially on an interbank basis. Ultimately, in most payment systems, interbank settlement occurs through transfers of balances held in accounts at central banks. Different measures of turnover in these accounts suggest that a given unit of central bank money is being used much more intensively for settlement purposes today than it was five or six years ago, in part because of higher payment value and in some countries because of lower reserve requirements.

Reliance on central bank money for settlement is not costless, and central banks have begun to impose explicit or implicit costs on use of their intraday credit. Multilateral netting has become increasingly attractive as a means of satisfying interbank payment obligations, and the relative use of real-time gross settlement in central bank money versus multilateral net settlement will be determined over time, at least in part, by the relative costs of using the two different types of arrangements. For this reason, it is very important that multilateral netting systems embody robust risk controls that minimize systemic risk.

The national payment systems of a number of countries are evolving so as to permit better management of the risks associated with increased settlement activity. Central banks in a number of major countries now either offer, or are preparing to offer, real-time gross settlement services for transferring funds across their books. Most of these services are designed so that only settled payments are delivered to receiving banks. The G-10 central banks have also published the Lamfalussy standards, which establish minimum risk controls for large-value multilateral netting systems. The application of these minimum standards is becoming widespread, but is uneven, especially the standard addressing capabilities to ensure timely completion of net settlement.

Somewhat different approaches are being taken to imple-ment improved control over use of intraday credit and settlement risks in both real-time gross settlement and multilateral netting systems. With regard to multilateral netting, greater adherence to the Lamfalussy standards involves building into netting systems mechanisms and financial guarantees for controlling risk directly. Limiting application of the standards, especially the standard regarding pre-commitment of liquid resources to ensure settlement, would tend to leave control over systemic risk in the hands of individual system participants, acting individually.

Among the G-10 central banks, only the Federal Reserve System has adopted explicit fees for intraday credit. Early experience indicates that interbank funds and securities markets have adjusted quickly and smoothly to the introduction of fees for intraday credit. Further, the incentive provided by even a relatively small fee of 10 basis points at an annual rate has been enough to induce major behavioral changes in the markets. In this regard, since the imposition of fees on 14 April 1994 through 3 August 1994 use of intraday credit provided by the Federal Reserve has declined about 35 percent, with the steepest decline occurring for securities-related overdrafts. A number of central banks are relying on full collateralization of intraday exposures to control their payment system risk and to provide a financial incentive to use intraday credit wisely.

Central banks are taking other actions to help control Herstatt risk in cross-border payments by extending the hours of operation of their real-time gross settlement systems. Such actions are being taken in the context of a broad policy frame-work for risk reduction crafted by the G-10 and EU central banks.

Recent developments in national payment systems all point to achievement of the same goal -- risk reduction. Many paths are being taken to achieve risk reduction. This is true notwithstanding the adoption by the G-10 and the EU central banks of common standards or principles regarding the development of large-value transfer systems. Therefore, those concerned with risk management worldwide must continue to analyze carefully clearing and settlement policies and practices country-by-country, at least for the foreseeable future. There appears to be room for further coordination among central banks in the implementation of standards and policies to help improve further control over payment system risk.

Chart 1. Ratio of payment value to gross domestic product[1]

Country	1988	1992
Canada	30.0	41.3
France	29.5	35.3
Germany	43.8	59.3
Italy	5.4	21.2
Japan	5.4	21.2
Switzerland	94.2	98.7
United Kingdom	43.7	41.0
United States	69.7	76.3

1. Calculated as the gross value of payments over major payment systems (excluding securities settlement systems) from the "redbook" country tables, divided by gross domestic product.

Source: Bank for International Settlements, *Payment Systems in the Group of Ten countries*, Basle, December 1993.

Chart 2. Estimated daily turnover of balances held in accounts at the central bank[1]

Country	Daily 1988	Turnover 1993
Canada	26	75
France	7	455[2]
Germany	6	12[3]
Italy	8	16[4]
Japan	32	70
Switzerland	23	64
United Kingdom	[5]	[5]
United States	38	51[6]

1. Daily turnover is the estimated daily average value of payments over major payment systems, divided by the daily average value of balances held by banks and other deposit-taking institutions in accounts at the central bank for a representative period at the end of the year.
2. The turnover ratio increased dramatically as a result of a reduction in reserve requirements in August 1992.
3. Required reserves were lowered substantially beginning 1 March 1994. If calculated today, the turnover rate would likely be in the range of from 21 to 24. The daily average value of payments used in the calculation includes only payments made using Bundesbank processing facilities, so the ratio is likely to be understated compared to that for some other countries.
4. The figures used for payments include only payments settled directly with the Bank of Italy, so that the ratio is likely to be understated compared to that for some other countries. The daily average value of central bank balances is that for clearing balances only, which are balances available in settlement accounts at the Bank of Italy at the end of the day.
5. Not included because of unique attributes of the data sets and changes in institutional arrangements for the United Kindom that make intertemporal and cross-country comparisons especially inappropriate.
6. Reflects reductions in reserve requirements in December 1990 and April 1992. Voluntary holdings of clearing balances have increased and totaled about 23 per cent of the stock of required reserve balances at the end of 1992.

Source: Estimates prepared by staffs of the respective central banks.

Chart 3

Aggregrate Daylight Overdrafts Recorded by the Twelve Federal Reserve Banks

Per-Minute Average at 15-Minute Intervals

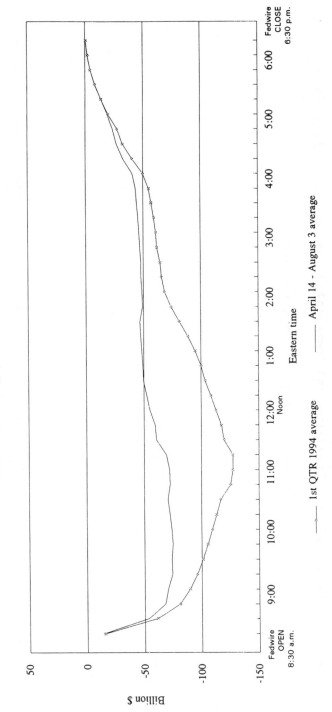

Source: Board of Governors of the Federal Reserve System.

Chart 4

Aggregate Securities-Related Daylight Overdrafts Recorded by the Twelve Federal Reserve Banks

Per-Minute Average at 15-Minute Intervals

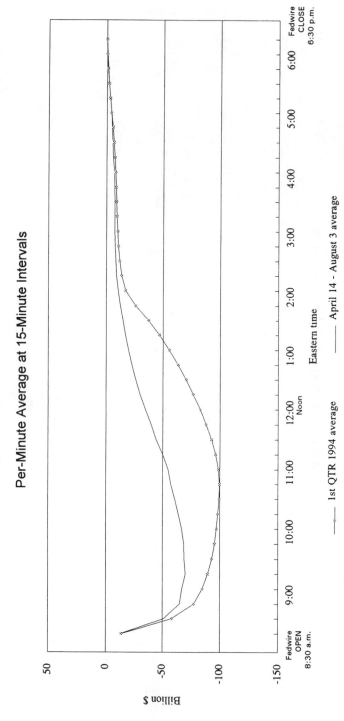

Source: Board of Governors of the Federal Reserve System.

Notes

1   A final transfer is one that is unconditional and irrevocable.

2   Some systems may operate on the basis of bilateral netting, in which case actual exposures are explicitly recognized as being the bilaterally netted amounts. An example is the Clearing House Automated Payment System (CHAPS) in the United Kingdom. See "The Development of a U.K. Real-Time Gross Settlement System" (1994).

3   The Bank of Japan provides both real-time gross settlement and deferred net settlement services through BOJ-NET.

4   Note that netting systems that incorporate real-time risk controls, such as bilateral credit limits and sender net debit caps, also provide the operational means to allow participants to manage extensions of credit bilaterally and/or at the aggregate system level.

5   See Vital (1994).

6   See "The Development of a U.K. Real-Time Gross Settlement System" (1994).

7   The new SWIFT concept that is based on the "Y" design is referred to as SHORE (Strip-Hold-Rebuild functionality).

8   The turnover ratio for the United States is estimated to have been only 0.9 in 1960. See Mengle, *et al.*(1987).

9   The calculation of the volume of Federal Reserve intraday credit used in this paper is based on the same methodology used to determine the amount of credit that is subject to fees. Fees are assessed on the per-minute average of total overdrafts during the Fedwire operating day. Intraday credit extensions cited in this paper are the per-minute average of total overdrafts at 15-minute intervals. This methodology may be different from that used in some other contexts. For example, a significantly higher volume of intraday credit extended is reported in the BIS "Red-book" for the year 1992, but that figure is for the daily average of **peak** intraday overdrafts for the year.

10   Statements estimating the fees that would apply to the amount of intraday credit used, as if fees were in effect, were also provided to depository institutions.

11   See the 1990 Report of the Committee on Interbank Netting Schemes of the Central Banks of the Group of Ten Countries.

12   The CHIPS approach to providing liquidity relies on the contingent obligations of the non-defaulting participants, cal-culated as an "additional settlement obligation" or ASO. The ASOs are secured by a dedicated pool of US government securi-ties collateral. This approach does not strictly meet the fourth Lamfalussy standard dealing with capabilities to ensure timely completion of settlement in that the arrangements do not guaran-tee that the necessary liquidity will be available exactly at the moment needed, even though the ASOs and collateral ensure that the contingent obligations can be met.

13   See principle number 5 in "Minimum Common Features for Domestic Payment Systems" (1993).

14   See Hartmann (1994), Friederich (1994), and "Recent trends in the Deutsche Bundesbank's cashless payments" (1994).

15   Friederich (1994) cites simulations that indicate 70 to 80 percent of payments would normally be settled by 10:30 a.m., about halfway through the bilateral settlement phase.

16   See Mengle, et al. (1987).

17   See the Federal Reserve staff memorandum "Expansion of Fedwire Operating Hours" (1994) and Kelley (1994).

18   See Nambara (1994).

19   See "Minimum Common Features for Domestic Payment Systems" (1993).

20   "Central Bank Payment and Settlement Services with Respect to Cross-border and Multi-currency Transactions" (1993).

References

BLOMMESTEIN, Hans J. and Bruce J. SUMMERS. *Banking and the Payment System,* in Bruce J. SUMMERS (ed), *The Payment System: Design, Management, and Supervision,* International Monetary Fund, 1994.

"Central Bank Payment and Settlement Services With Respect to Cross-Border and Multi-Currency Transactions." Report prepared by the Committee on Payment and Settlement Systems of the central banks of the Group of Ten countries, *Bank for International Settlements,* September 1993.

"Expansion of Fedwire Operating Hours." Staff memorandum to the Board of Governors of the Federal Reserve System, 7 February 1994.

FRIEDERICH, Hans-Jürgen. *The converging of net and gross: The evolution of the German large funds systems.* Paper presented at the EFMA conference Systèmes de Paiement, Brussels, 27 May 1994.

HARTMANN, Wendelin. *Developments in German Money Policy and Payment Systems,* remarks given at the International Symposium on Banking and Payment Systems, Washington, D.C., March 1994.

HORII, AKINARI and Bruce J. SUMMERS. *Large-Value Transfer Systems,* in Bruce J. SUMMERS (ed.), *The Payment System: Design, Management, and Supervision,* International Monetary Fund, 1994.

KELLEY, Edward W., Jr. *Developments in the Dollar Payments System,* remarks given at the international Symposium on Banking and Payment Systems, Washington, D.C., March 1994.

MARQUARDT, Jeffrey C. *Monetary Issues and Payment System Design,* in Bruce J. SUMMERS (ed.), *The Payment System: Design, Management, and Supervision,* International Monetary Fund, 1994.

MENGLE, David L., David B. HUMPHREY, and Bruce J. SUMMERS. *Intraday Credit: Risk, Value, and Pricing,* "Economic Review," Federal Reserve Bank of Richmond, January-February 1987.

"Minimum Common Features for Domestic Payment Systems." Report of the Committee of Governors of the Central Banks of the Member States of the European Economic Community, November 1993.

NAMBARA, Akira. *The Role of Japanese Banking and Payment Systems in the International Economy*, remarks given at the International Symposium on Banking and Payment Systems, Washington, D.C., March 1994.

PADOA-SCHIOPPA, Tommoso. *Central Banking and Payment Systems in the European Community*, remarks given at the International Symposium on Banking and Payment Systems, Washington, D.C., March 1994.

"Recent trends in the Deutsche Bundesbank's cashless payments." *Deutsche Bundesbank Monthly Report*, August 1994.

Report of the Committee on Interbank Netting Schemes of the Central Banks of the Group of Ten Countries. Bank for International Settlements, Basle, November 1990.

SCHOENMAKER, Dirk. *A Comparison of Net and Gross Settlement.* Undated manuscript received by the author in May 1994.

"The Development of a U.K. Real-Time Gross Settlement System." *Bank of England Quarterly Bulletin*, May 1994.

VITAL, Christian. *An Appraisal of the Swiss Interbank Clearing System SIC*, presentation at the EFMA Conference on Payment Systems, Brussels, 27 May 1994.

Chapter 8

CENTRALISED FOREIGN EXCHANGE AND OTC DERIVATIVES CLEARING -- ISSUES TO BE CONSIDERED*

Graham M. Duncan

Introduction

Risk management is, first and foremost, the responsibility of individual market participants. However, there is an important role to be played by co-operative market institutions. Many of the risks faced by financial institutions are the function of the operation of the clearing, settlement and payment systems supporting the markets.

The increased awareness of the need to eliminate unnecessary risks in financial markets has renewed interest in improving the infrastructure of the markets. Some markets have traditionally had sophisticated infrastructure, for example the stock markets with their formalised trading and settlement arrangements. Other areas, however, have lagged far behind. The OTC markets in foreign exchange and derivatives are good examples.

I. Foreign exchange clearing

Recent developments in the FX markets have brought the centralised clearing of foreign exchange to the point of implementation. The Exchange Clearing House (ECHO) is poised to launch a FX clearing house, based in London, serving all the major international financial centres. This development

---

*   The views expressed in this paper are those of the author alone and do not necessarily represent the views of ECHO of its shareholders.

has been backed by 15 international banks from seven countries. The principal motivation for the participants is the strong desire to tackle the twin dangers of settlement (Herstatt) and replacement risk.

The scale of settlement risk, in particular, is staggering when looked at in aggregate. It is not uncommon for two large banks to owe each other USD 2 billion in FX settlements alone on a single day. This is equivalent, in risk terms, to the banks lending each other USD 2 billion overnight at an interest rate of 0 per cent. Each bank has a risk on the other but gets no return for that risk. The risk is an avoidable side effect of FX trading. Given that the FX market is too competitive for banks to raise their return to compensate for this risk, the only way they have of improving the risk/reward ratio is to reduce the risk.

In addition, the cost of processing and settling FX trades is an increasingly significant issue for all banks. Estimates of the cost of each trade vary widely depending on the sophistication of the back office systems and the currencies involved. However, a survey carried out by management consultants, KPMG Peat Marwick, in conjunction with ECHO suggests that USD25 - 30 per trade is a reasonable benchmark range. One major international bank has estimated that using a fully developed clearing house will save it around USD 1 500 000 a year in operating costs.

The clearing house will have a number of functions. It will:

   a) act as the common counterparty to all transactions;
   b) manage the central netting and settlement systems;
   c) monitor and control the settlement payment flows;
   d) ensure the liquidity of the settlement process;
   e) manage the replacement of positions in the event of a member's default.

ECHO will net FX contracts with maturities from spot up to 2 years, in up to 24 currencies. As ECHO is a global clearing house there is no geographic limit to the location of branches which can be participants in the system. However, there will be a requirement that the country of operation as well of incorporation has a legal system which will support multilateral netting. This may mean that some countries are excluded for legal reasons.

Although the clearing house is the party to all transactions, the risk of loss lies ultimately with the participants which chose to deal with the defaulter and not with the clearing house itself. Any loss is recovered through a loss allocation arrangement with the Users. This is the "decentralised" approach described in the Lamfalussy Report. The clearing house only reduces the risk run by participants (albeit significantly), it does not remove it. This contrasts with the "centralised" approach of most futures clearing houses which bear all the risk themselves.

This approach was selected for a variety of reasons. The most important was the scale of the potential losses involved even after the significant risk reductions yielded by multilateral netting. A futures clearing house only has to collateralise the forward or replacement risk, a relatively modest amount. The settlement risk caused by time zones and less than perfect national payment systems means that a clearing house could face losses well in excess of a billion US dollars in the event of a large bank failure. To adopt the "centralised" model of risk management would be uneconomic since it would require all participants to post huge amounts of margin to cover such risks.

In order to ensure that the overall exposures to the system are kept within reasonable bounds, ECHO will have a series of limits which will restrict the amount of exposure which a User can present to the system without having to lodge collateral to cover the excess. Firstly, there is the Direct Exposure Limit which restricts the aggregate of the Clearing House's net settlement exposure to the User and the mark-to-market value of the User's overall book with the Clearing House.

Secondly there is the Direct Exposure Limit which restricts the amount of risk a User is permitted to take on any other participant and hence which it might have to pay under the Loss Allocation. The Clearing House depends upon the Users to pay up under the Loss Allocation and so needs to have confidence that the amount is not excessive for that User. In both instances the limits are based on a formula which takes into account both credit quality (expressed in the credit rating) and size (in terms of Tier 1 capital). Thus the larger and better the bank, the larger the Direct and Indirect Exposure limits.

Research indicates that settlement risk will be reduced by as much as 95 per cent by the use of centralised clearing. The FX market is currently estimated to be in excess of USD 1 000 billion a day, giving rise to settlements of the order of USD 2 000 billion. The potential for achieving material reductions in (unnecessary) risk is clearly enormous.

II.   Derivatives clearing

The debate about the implications of the growth of the OTC derivatives markets raises the question of whether central clearing has a role to play in reducing the associated risks and costs. To begin to come to some conclusions about this possibility it is necessary to consider what an OTC derivatives clearing house might look like and what problems it would face.

Firstly, what are the main issues to be addressed? Briefly they are:

a)   *Operational complexity*

It is part of the attraction of the OTC markets that they are able to offer highly tailored products which exactly match the customer's requirement. This in turn means that there is much less uniformity of products than in the exchange-traded sector. Take, for example, an interest rate swap. The notional principal amount can be constant, increasing, decreasing or a complex combination of all three. The interest rates can be fixed versus floating or floating versus floating (with different bases). There can also be various caps, collars and floors built in as part of the tailoring. The permutations within a single contract may be literally endless. For a clearing house this is a challenge as it must have precise, standardised, electronic contract descriptions to be able to process such contracts efficiently. Anyone who has had to generate swap confirmations will appreciate the difficulty of standardising the process to the point where reliable electronic confirmation matching and processing would be possible. However, the problem could be reduced by concentrating on clearing the more standardised contracts which banks use to hedge their risks in the interbank market.

b)   *Risk management complexity*

Allied to the variety of products is the complexity of risk management. Given that part of the reason for having a clearing house is the concern over risk it is essential that the management of the risk be effective and comprehensive. Many of the techniques are available but the practical difficulties of applying them are not yet clear. This is partly because the wide variety of products adds an additional layer of complexity to the risk management from a clearing house perspective.

c)   *Legal complexity*

Cross-product netting adds an additional degree of complexity to the legal structuring of a clearing house, especially one which seeks to operate internationally as an OTC clearing house would need to do. The recent moves to address the shortcomings in various jurisdictions

284

have made this process easier but there is still a great deal to be done. Specifically, the absence of an EU directive on insolvency, particularly of financial institutions, is a significant hurdle. It is difficult to see how a true single market can exist in the absence of such a basic common structure.

d) *Regulatory complexity*

The derivatives markets are subject to a patchwork of (sometimes competing) regulatory regimes which would make achieving any regulatory consensus difficult. Further complexity may be caused by some regulators being responsible for supervising types of institution whilst others supervise particular markets. Their priorities may differ markedly. This has obvious implications for the establishment and operation of an OTC clearing house.

e) *Competitive pressures*

There are a few key players in the derivatives markets whose support would be essential to make a clearing house a success. it remains to be seen whether they will all agree to back such a venture. Of particular importance would be the impact that they perceive a clearing house would have on their respective competitive positions. This is compounded by the greater diversity of participants in the derivatives markets compared with, say, the foreign exchange markets.

Secondly, what should be the risk structure of the clearing house? Should it, in the terms of the G10's Lamfalussy Report, be a decentralised or a centralised clearing house for risk management purposes? The question turns on the issue of collateralisation (margining) of exposures. Should the clearing house bear the risks of a participant's failure (and hence require collateral for all exposures) or should it allocate the losses to those participants which dealt with the defaulter. The former is the approach adopted by traditional futures clearing houses. The latter is the basis for the ECHO FX clearing house. The answer might be crucial in achieving market acceptance of the clearing house.

The argument for collateralisation is that it eliminates default risk in the market and hence helps minimise systemic risk. The argument against is that strong, well capitalised participants lose their competitive advantage because the clearing house eliminates differences in credit quality between participants. For short-dated contracts this may be less significant but in longer-dated contracts credit quality directly influences pricing and market access.

In addition, collateralisation costs money and there is a balance to be struck between eliminating risk and the costs involved. In this context it is worth bearing in mind that financial institutions, and banks in particular, are risk takers. They are paid to take and manage counterparty risk.

Another important consideration is whether total risk elimination is actually beneficial to the quality of the market. Counterparty risk is one important factor in retaining discipline in the market. If risk is eliminated then there is no incentive for the participants to be concerned about the quality of other participants (or indeed of themselves).

Some of the debate surrounding centralised clearing of derivatives has presumed that the "exchange-traded" model is the only option. This presumption is premature and is something of a distraction from the debate about what any such arrangements would achieve.

III. Conclusion

Although properly structured clearing arrangements would offer much to the OTC derivatives markets they are not a panacea. Much of the current debate on derivatives has been generated by news of losses by users and traders of swaps, options etc. These problems would not be solved by an OTC clearing house.

Chapter 9

TRENDS, STRUCTURAL CHANGES AND PROSPECTS IN OECD CAPITAL MARKETS

H.J Blommestein and K. Biltoft

Introduction and summary

Over the past two decades, OECD capital markets have changed beyond recognition. New securities issues and trading increased exponentially and in all OECD countries financial intermediation through the securities markets gained in importance. Domestic deregulation and external liberalisation resulted in major changes in competitive conditions. Advances in communications and information systems enhanced the capacity of financial market participants to use the opportunities offered by the liberalised environment, including the use of sophisticated and state-of-the-art concepts for the development of new products and financial techniques.

The rapid development of securities-related activity is set to continue in the 1990s. Innovations and structural changes are also likely to continue, although the pace and direction of these developments is inherently much more difficult to predict. In all probability, investment decisions will be increasingly dominated by institutional investors (investment funds, pension funds and insurance companies). This class of professional investors may be expected to take an increasingly sophisticated approach to investing, utilising advanced conceptual and technological tools and testing new market instruments to attain the best possible risk and return combinations.

The demand of investors for a broad range of assets with different risk-return characteristics may well lead to a marked acceleration in the creation of asset-backed and mortgage-backed securities; this trend would be also strengthened by the desire of banks to bring under better control the size of their balance sheets. At present, this technique is widely used in only a handful of

OECD countries and, therefore, there is a vast potential for an expansion of securitisation throughout the OECD area.

The markets in derivative products may be reasonable expected to expand at least as fast as the underlying cash markets. Derivative instruments are major tools for the management of risk by market participants, in particular the larger professional investors. Exchange and over-the-counter (OTC) markets for derivatives markets will continue to be both an indispensable complement and substitute for cash markets.

In both cash and derivative markets, the traditional exchanges are likely to be challenged by alternative systems for trading, including the OTC markets. Competition among trading systems will intensify because of advances in information and communication technology and also due to the aggressive policies of institutional investors to direct orders to the cheapest trading systems. This development has already put pressure on the profitability of the brokerage business. As a result of these trends, the major intermediaries are likely to de-emphasise secondary market brokerage activities. Instead, put greater emphasis on proprietary trading in both cash and derivative markets, by temporarily taking large net positions using the institution's own capital. In pursuing this strategy, the intermediaries are in many cases opting to deal in the lower-cost, less regulated environment of OTC markets rather than trading on the exchanges.

These trends and structural changes present major challenges for the functioning of existing supervisory and regulatory regimes. Investor protection systems have usually been designed to protect investors by requiring adequate disclosure of information and specific rules for market operations. However, there are many indications that some of the beneficiaries of these traditional investor protection schemes, such as institutional investors and major intermediaries, prefer to deal outside the established markets and that they consider existing regulatory schemes to be of declining value. Moreover, the internationalisation of the securities business could render traditional regulatory schemes less effective.

Securities clearance and settlement systems are an essential part of the operational infrastructure of efficient capital markets. Policy makers in OECD countries have played an important role in the development of more efficient security settlement systems. Regulations and supervision to ensure the safety and soundness of securities settlement systems constitute another main public policy issue.

I. Trends and developments in securities markets

In the 1980s, the securities and derivatives markets of OECD countries underwent a period of extremely rapid expansion and structural change. Volumes of new securities issues and secondary market trading soared, equity indices rose, and in all OECD countries securities markets gained in importance as conduit for financial intermediation. What is more, the transformation of capital markets was not only a simple expansion in activity. Structural forces changed radically capital market institutions and activities. There was a basic change in the nature of securities business from a highly regulated, tradition-bound activity somewhat at the margin of most financial systems to one which became a leading force in changing the financial landscape in OECD countries. The intensification of competition in an increasingly deregulated environment, combined with the use of sophisticated financial techniques supported by significant advances in information technology, set into motion a process of innovation in which new financial instruments, techniques and strategies are being developed at an astounding pace. It is expected by most analysts that these developments will continue in the years ahead and that, therefore, the increase in importance of the role of capital market in the emerging financial landscape will continue.

Widespread **deregulation of capital markets** reflects the increasing reliance of OECD countries on market principles as opposed to official guidance in the financial sector. An important feature of the liberalisation of OECD capital markets was the growing impact of international competitive forces on products and activities in national financial markets. Offshore financial centres, including several based in OECD countries, were critical in the development of an internationalised, market-oriented financial system. In the early 1980s, an international process of transmission of financial innovation was set in motion, with the United States usually the leading originator -- and exporter -- of new products and techniques. Through the mid-1980s, financial innovation was frequently undertaken by financial institutions operating in the relatively un-regulated environment of the offshore centres. From the mid-1980s onwards, however, development has been relatively faster in domestic securities markets, reflecting the need to preserve the international competitiveness of domestic markets, particularly in Europe. Wherever it originated, innovation was speedily diffused to all major financial centres. As a result, the average OECD level of financial sophistication has risen with astonishing speed.

By the end of the 1980s, securities markets in OECD countries had been transformed beyond recognition. The securities markets proved to be able to draw business away from traditional banking activities. Markets in derivatives grew at a astounding pace and, by the early 1990s, most OECD countries had established exchanges dealing in futures and options. The authorities of OECD countries played an important role in these developments by taking a broad range of actions to facilitate the modernisation and internationalisation of their capital markets. As mentioned above, governments deregulated domestic markets and abolished exchange controls. In addition, most governments took the following measures:

- reforms of government securities markets in order to deepen money and bond markets and provide for a full yield curve of liquid instruments[1] ;

- the development of money markets by removing restrictions on money market instruments such as money market mutual funds, commercial paper and certificates of deposit;

- modernisation of the brokerage profession, securities trading systems and the organisation of secondary markets;

- introduction of legislation to permit the formation of financial groups which offer both banking and securities services;

- the introduction of legislation for the creation of futures and options markets;

- modernisation of supervisory and regulatory regimes for securities markets;

- agreements among supervisors of securities and derivatives markets to facilitate cross-border trading while co-ordinating supervisory surveillance over trading and intermediaries;

- introduction of new provisions on investor protection.

Bonds

At the end of 1993, the total amount outstanding of publicly traded bonds was some $16 trillion, which represents an spectacular increase compared to the figure at the end of 1980 (Chart 1). The US dollar was the most important currency of denomination, accounting for 46 per cent of the total. The other major currencies were Yen (19 per cent), Deutschemark (10 per cent), Italian lira (5 per cent) and French franc (5 per cent)[2].

The growth of bond markets was spurred in part by the rise in real interest rates that accompanied the sharp reduction in the rate of inflation of the early

1980s. In addition, market-based financing of budget deficits has been a major factor behind the growth of the global bond market. In some countries, another important reason for governments' issuance of bonds was the necessity to secure balance of payment financing when private sector capital inflows proved to be insufficient. Consequently, the share of government bonds increased in five of the G-7 countries during the period from 1980 to 1993 (Table 1). There has also been an important change in the way deficits are financed. In many OECD countries, the government traditionally relied on privileged access to private sector financing, obliging banks and institutional investors to purchase government debt, while the central bank acted as a buyer of last resort. However, since the 1980s, an increasing number of OECD governments have adopted measures to strengthen the role of market principles in government debt management by improving primary and secondary market arrangements[3].

Along with an improved infrastructure -- including advanced clearing and settlement systems and modernisation of the regulatory framework -- as well as deregulation, the flow of government bonds helped to establish more liquid benchmark issues, which facilitated issuance also by other borrowers. Thus, larger corporate borrowers came to issue bonds and shorter dated securities such as commercial paper on a major scale. And in recent years, developing countries have re-emerged as important issuers in the international bond markets. Such capital market operations often replaced traditional credit lines of banks, thereby contributing to the process of disintermediation. During parts of the 1980s, a significant amount of issues by the private sector was the result of mergers and acquisitions, which in the United States were a driving force behind the growth of lower-rated corporate paper, the so-called "junk bonds".

During the 1980s, a phenomenon known as securitisation started to play an increasingly important role in the euro-markets and some domestic markets, notably in the United States. In its initial stages, securitisation meant the replacement of external funds raised in the form of traditional bank loans by the placement of securities directly with investors -- mainly bonds, but in some cases also short-term money market paper. More recently, "securitisation" has been used to describe operations in which cash flows of specific assets are being used to support marketable securities. Also, an important source of new bond offerings is the financing of housing. The size of the mortgage bond market varies across OECD countries but in some countries with a long tradition in this type for financing it is very significant, accounting for more than 50 per cent of all bonds outstanding.

Deregulation, which had already begun in some countries in the later part of the 1970s, accelerated in the 1980s and at the beginning of the 1990s, financial markets had been profoundly transformed. Capital controls had been virtually abolished in the OECD area and domestic markets were extensively deregulated. Of particular importance was the removal of the various regulations which sought to secure the flow of capital to specific sectors or were aimed at keeping long-term interest rates below market-clearing levels. There are, however, still quite a few regulations in place, in particular covering access to bond markets by certain categories of borrowers in several countries and freedom of placement in securities by institutional investors. External and domestic deregulation have been crucial factors behind the increased integration of financial markets. Growing links among bond market compartments meant that major markets, including the euro-market, became increasingly integrated into a global market where arbitrage opportunities are quickly traded away.

Two other developments have played a crucial role in fostering this stronger integration across markets. The revolutionary changes in information technology have facilitated large transactions volumes on and between markets at very low cost. Secondly, the emergence of large and liquid derivatives markets has greatly facilitated the exploitation of arbitrage opportunities across markets. For example, the development of forward exchange markets has been essential in binding national money markets together and the swap market is performing a similar role in linking different bond markets. Thus, bond yields appear increasing to be determined in the context of a "single" world market. The stronger integration of markets is reflected in the fact that, in particular since the removal of most capital controls in the mid-1980s, short-term interest rates have become highly interdependent[4]. There is also evidence that long-term rates have become more interdependent (Table 2). Studies attempting to measure international capital market integration have taken several different approaches, such as the law of one price, off-set coefficients, correlations between savings and investments and international comparisons of consumption behaviour. The general conclusion of these studies appears to be that capital market integration has increased markedly over the last 10 years. However, there is not yet a single, global capital market, where a wide selection of financial assets have the same risk-adjusted expected return[5].

Equities

Since the beginning of the 1980s, capitalisation of equity markets has grown significantly, reflecting both rising share indices and increasing equity offerings. Furthermore, there has been a large expansion in issuance of equity-related products, such as convertible bonds, bonds with warrants attached and equity-based derivatives.

Even though equity markets are lagging behind money and bond markets, the general trend towards more internationalised securities markets is also evident in equities markets[6]. Foreign demand and cross-border portfolio investment in shares have become important elements in the price determination process. It is estimated that total gross cross-border equity holdings in Europe, the United States and Japan increased from $800 billion in 1986 to $1 300 billion in 1991[7]. Also the issuance of new stock has increasingly included an international portion. Thus, placement of new international equities amounted to $44.9 billion in 1994, compared to just $2.7 billion in 1985 and $23.4 billion in 1990 (Chart 2). Finally, an increasing number of large companies are listed on more than one national stock exchange.

The following major determinants of the growth of equities markets can be distinguished:

1. Institutional investors -- a more and more important category of wealth-holders -- have increasingly been seeking to diversify their portfolio through the purchase of foreign shares, which at the same time have become easier and less costly to trade as a consequence of deregulation, in particular the removal of capital controls.

2. The desire of many larger companies to diversify their equity base, in particular through more placements abroad (ADRs, etc.) and listings on foreign stock exchanges, to attract local investors.

3. Large-scale privatisation programmes were undertaken during the 1980s in some OECD countries, most notably the UK and France, and in an increasing number of developing countries. Since 1990, a remarkable acceleration of privatisation has been taking place in many countries inside and outside the OECD area. This process is exerting a strong influence on the growth of capital markets, where planned privatisations will significantly increase market capitalisation[8].

4. Since the early 1980s, markets have undergone profound structural changes following efforts to upgrade trading systems as well as to reform institutional and regulatory structures. Reform in this area is likely to gain further momentum from the announced large-scale privatisation programmes.

Derivative markets

Since the mid 1980s, the volume of trade in derivative products, such as futures, swaps and options, has increased dramatically. Derivative products (*e.g.* futures, options, swaps, forward rate agreements, and related hedging instruments) have evolved from being the basis of a risk management technique used only by the most sophisticated market participants in the most advanced financial markets to one that is now routinely used by a growing range of participants, in particular institutional investors, banks and major corporations, in nearly every significant market in all OECD countries.

The following factors behind this development can be identified:

1. The increased use of derivatives has been greatly facilitated by major advances in the application of information technology.

2. Derivatives markets have benefited from the widespread liberalisation of markets and cross border transactions.

3. The use of derivatives instruments has progressed from being the domain of a limited number of sophisticated market participants to being utilised by a wide range of players, in particular end-users such as institutional investors and major corporations. The expanded use of derivatives must be seen as an integral part of the overall process of financial innovation, which has resulted in an increasing number of complex combinations of existing cash and derivative products.

4. Countries have generally realised that derivative markets are necessary for the modernisation of capital markets, which has led to the establishment of derivative exchanges in nearly all OECD countries.

The main characteristics of the derivatives markets since the mid-1980s are that:

- the number of exchange-traded contracts has continued to grow;

- the over-the-counter (OTC) market in derivatives is now expanding more rapidly than the traditional exchanges;

- financial engineering has made it possible to use derivatives to formulate complex investment strategies.

The notional amounts outstanding at end-year of exchange-traded instruments and instruments traded over-the-counter (OTC) has grown some 800 per cent in the period from 1986 to 1992, far above the growth rate of other financial instruments. At the end of 1993, the outstanding notional amount was around $15 000 billion (Table 3).

The development of off-exchange derivative products has been one of the most striking features of the past few years. In particular, the exchanges that trade financial futures and options have received increasingly competition from the OTC market. The shift from trading on exchanges to over-the-counter trading is driven by several factors, in particular the lack of regulatory constraint gives the OTC market a flexibility that is difficult for the exchanges to match. Moreover, OTC derivative products can be tailored to the specific needs of clients with respect to expiration dates, industry composition of equity indices, etc. On the other hand, the derivatives exchanges argue that trading in recognised exchanges provides significant benefits in terms of transparency, liquidity, and reduced counterparty risk. In addition, the exchanges are seeking to rely increasingly on automation. As a matter of fact, the derivatives exchanges and the OTC markets complement each other as well as compete for business. Thus, much of the net risk that is acquired in the swap market is eventually hedged using exchange-traded derivatives. Also, intermediaries can use a mix of exchange-listed contracts and OTC products in creating tailor-made investment instruments.

Trade in derivatives on the OTC market was originally based on interest rate swaps but is increasingly expanding to other innovative products. Since its inception, this market has developed from being almost exclusively US dollar based and very dependent on bond issuance, into a market encompassing a wide selection of major currencies and being used as a hedge against shorter-term interest rate exposure. The outstanding amount of exchange-traded derivatives at the end of 1993 was around $8 000 billion. The most popular instrument was interest rate futures, accounting for more than 60 per cent of the total.

The derivatives market may be considered as both a complement to, and as a substitute for, the underlying cash market. Thus, an understanding of the linkages between the two markets is important, in particular the direction of this interdependence and its impact on the price discovery process. In many markets, the trading volumes in exchange-traded derivatives exceed the volumes traded on the cash market (Table 4). Price discovery is a feed-back process between the cash and derivatives markets, taking into account both macro-events that affect the entire market as well as asset-specific information.

Some observers have noted that prices in the cash market more often reflect trading in derivative markets, rather than the other way around.

A much debated issue is whether derivatives increase or decrease price volatility on the underlying cash market. Although no firm conclusion can yet be draw, it would appear that under normal market conditions derivatives reduce price volatility as they facilitate arbitrage across markets and enhance market liquidity. However, in periods of significant market uncertainty, it is possible that derivatives contribute to price volatility, as they facilitate a very rapid accumulation of large positions. Also, it appears that the impact on price volatility is more severe on smaller and less liquid markets[9].

Financial engineering enables the creation of so-called synthetic market positions which are either impossible or undesirable to establish directly in the market. This process of financial innovation has resulted in an increasing number of very complex financial products, based on combinations of existing derivatives and cash instruments. Financial engineering has been beneficial in the sense that it has expanded the range of tools available for risk management and has helped reducing transaction costs.

However, financial innovation also carries a number of potential dangers. As a consequence of the increased complexity of financial products, the risks involved with these products may not be always be fully understood by intermediaries or end-users. This is in particular the case for derivatives products which are "customer tailored" in the OTC markets. Improved risk management practices by banks and other financial institutions are the key for addressing these problems. In this context it has been recommended, for example, that the major intermediaries calculate their exposure on at least a daily basis and perform stress simulations to gauge their exposure in case of adverse events with a low probability. However, the assumptions underlying these simulations -- in particular regarding liquidity and volatility -- may be invalidated in situations of fundamental changes in market sentiment. Moreover, there is the systemic risk problem resulting from the possible contagious effects when one or more major financial intermediaries would experience problems. In this context, it has been noted that the size and concentration of derivatives activity, combined with derivatives-related market linkages, could cause a financial disruption to spread faster and to be more difficult to contain[10]. These may require adaptations to the regulatory and supervisory systems (see below).

II. Institutional investors

One of the most striking developments in international capital markets since the beginning of the eighties has been the fast growing importance of institutional investors, *i.e.* pension funds, insurance companies, and collective investment instruments such as investment funds. Institutional investors play an ever-increasing role as: collectors of savings; investors in securities and other financial assets; operators in the securities markets; cross-border portfolio investors; major owners of publicly-held companies. A strong community of institutional investors seems to be a precondition for the development of deep securities markets dealing in sophisticated financial instruments. Many of the trends that have characterised securities markets in the past fifteen years -- such as securitisation, the increasing growth and sophistication of bond markets, the use of derivatives, highly-leveraged corporate restructuring, the growth of equities markets -- developed in large measure in response to the demands of the institutional investor community. In view of the growing influence that institutional investors exert on the structure and modus operandi of financial systems, it is generally recognised that financial policy makers need to take a close look at both the functioning and the regulation of these institutions.

The main structural factors driving the growth of institutional investor activities are the following:

1. Deregulation of the banking and securities industries since the beginning 1980s has heightened competition between and among banks and other financial institutions. New capital standards for banks were introduced in the same period. In response to these pressures, banks have massively expanded, or moved into, the life insurance and investment fund business in search of new activities that generate earnings in the form of commissions and fees, while they do not necessarily absorb additional capital.

2. The increasingly active role of the fund management profession has also contributed in various ways to the transformation and growth of the institutional investor industry. The management of funds by these professionals has of course common features but the exact strategy is adapted to the specific institutional setting. For example, fund managers working under the umbrella of banks with ambitions to increase their market shares in the sale of investment funds have largely concentrated their efforts on the creation and management of new investment funds adapted to the preferences of the banks' investor clientele.

3. The rising needs for retirement benefits of an ageing population in conjunction with more sophisticated and wealthier private investors have had a significant impact on the growth of demand by private households for retirement benefit products of the different types of financial institutions -- banks, life insurance companies, and investment funds.

4. Deregulation of the financial services industry, in particular the opening up of national borders for the sale of life insurance products and investment funds, has been very favourable for the growth of institutional investors.

Investment strategies of institutional investors are influenced by a variety of factors which may differ widely according to the investment objectives of the different types of institutions, the nature of the products they offer and the liabilities which result, the market environment in which they operate, and regulations and other institutional factors governing the structure of portfolios. Considering the nature of the products as an important factor determining investment strategies, a basic difference exists between **investment funds** (unit trusts, investment trusts, mutual funds), on the one hand, and long-term contractual savings institutions such as **life insurance companies and pension funds**, on the other hand. Within the categories of investment funds there is, of course, a wide range of funds with different investment objectives. For example, some hedge funds assemble pools of private savings to engage in highly leveraged position-taking. Investment funds of the open-end type need to stand ready to meet at short notice request for reimbursement of potentially large numbers of investment certificates and, therefore, they need to hold a relatively large proportion of liquid assets[11].

All types of institutional investors are generators of substantial international flows of portfolio capital. The impact of the growing financial muscle of institutional investors on the functioning of financial markets became very clear during the stock market crash of October 1987, the turbulent events in the foreign exchange markets in 1992 and 1993, and the turbulence in the first half of 1994 on bond markets. Policy makers have in this context raised questions as to whether and to what extent institutional investors as holders of large amounts of financial assets have the potential for triggering shocks to securities markets and other financial markets, which may endanger the stability of the financial system as a whole.

In this context, hedge funds have recently attracted a lot of attention. Hedge funds are normally private partnerships of wealthy individuals and are structured in such a way that they do not fall under tight prudential oversight and do not face specific regulatory constraints. The name "hedge funds" is not always an accurate description of their activities as the managers of many of these funds take higher-than-average risks in search of large gains. In doing so, they take aggressive and often highly leveraged positions. It has been noted in a recent G-10 report that this feature may exacerbate financial crises because some hedge funds may assume a role of market leader, especially at times of great uncertainty and volatility[12].

The total assets of institutional investors (excluding hedge funds) in 10 European countries, Japan and the United States at the end of 1991 is estimated to have been around $ 11.6 trillion (Table 5). It should be noted, however, that the statistical coverage of institutional investors is in many cases not fully satisfactory; in particular, the statistical information on hedge funds is scanty. During the period from 1981 to 1991, the growth of life insurance companies, pension funds and investment funds was 17 per cent, well above the growth rate of commercial banks; it is estimated that the assets of the 200 leading funds amounted to around $8 trillion at the end of 1991[13]. Market estimates for the United States indicate that hedge funds -- totalling around 800 -- have some $ 60-75 billion under management[14]. It is assumed that these funds - depending on the type - are leveraged within the range of 2 to 20 times, the average being around 10 times.

As mentioned above, the investment strategy of institutional investors is dependent on a number of factors, including the type of institutional investor. However, there is a common trend -- with institutional investors steadily increasing the share of foreign securities in their portfolios (Table 6). This trend is expected to continue and it is estimated that the share of assets denominated in foreign currency in the portfolios of the world's 300 largest pension funds will reach about 12 per cent in the next couple of years[15].

A number of questions arise from the larger role played by institutional investors on international and national capital markets. A first key issue is the effect of the emergence of institutional investors on market volatility. Some observers have argued that many of these investors are using the same models of the economy, the same sophisticated information technology and are focusing on the same news, while they are employing similar portfolio diversification and hedging strategies[16]. The result could be that, in particular in periods of market tensions, they may find themselves all on the same side of the market. This may lead to intrinsically more volatile markets. Moreover, it might be argued that situations with asymmetric information where institutional investors are more professional and better informed than other, mostly smaller, investors, may lead to increased volatility[17]. An intuitive argument in favour of this conjecture is that relatively uninformed investors tend to mimic -- probably with a short time-lag -- the selling and buying behaviour of institutional investors, thereby contributing to price swings. However, other analysts have pointed out that institutional investors may follow quite different investment strategies, thereby reducing the chances that they may find themselves on the same side of the market. Yet, although no clear trend can be discerned in the longer-run volatility of bond yields, stock prices and exchange rates, short periods of heightened price volatility seem to have become more common, especially in the smaller and less liquid segments of the capital markets.

The relationship between market liquidity and the growing role of institutional investors is the second key issue in considering changes in the functioning of capital markets. A liquid market is one in which an individual transaction does not disrupt the continuity of the market[18]. Liquid capital markets help investors making better decisions. If the market is liquid, then trades are frequent and prices constitute reliable signals for making investment decisions. Market makers, dealers, and securities exchanges are the institutions that provide continuity in the pricing of securities, thereby contributing to market liquidity. The question then is whether institutions with considerable financial strength are willing to act as market makers, and in doing so, enhance market liquidity. Recent periods of market turbulence seem to suggest that even very large institutions are not always willing or able to fulfil this function in situations of massive imbalances between supply and demand in some markets. Moreover, a striking feature of the recent periods with volatility on OECD bond markets, was the number of large institutional investors -- apparently with short-term horizons -- operating on the same side of the market. In these situations, markets may become less liquid and more volatile, in particular the smaller ones. In other words, institutional investors may find themselves exposed to a risk, which seems very difficult to quantify, namely the risk that by their own investment decisions they may affect the direction of markets in which they are operating. It is not yet clear what the implications are (if any) for the process of price formation. However, from a theoretical point of view, the understanding of pricing on capital markets may increasingly have to turn to game theory.

The growing importance of institutional investors is generating an increasing demand for risk-transfer techniques, which enable the investor to choose desired combinations of return and risk. Such techniques include both securitisation, which enable the investor to transfer the credit risk as well as the market risk, and derivatives, whereby market risk is reallocated among market participants. However, a recent development is credit derivatives which enable market participants to transfer credit risk separately.

The emergence of institutional investors as major market players has also raised questions as to how patterns of **corporate control and governance** will be changed. Institutions have the potential to exert more effective control over management than a widely dispersed group of portfolio investors. There is growing evidence that, in several countries, institutional investors have adopted a more activist stance. In any event, there appears to be a trend towards greater shareholder demand for more adequate corporate disclosure, more adequate representation for institutions on boards of directors, and greater capability to apply strict performance criteria to corporate management.

The structure of corporate control varies across OECD countries because the relative importance of factors that determines control over large enterprises differs greatly. Corporate control systems are dependent on a number of interrelated factors including[19]:

- the combination of shareholders versus debt claimants;

- the legal infrastructure, in particular bankruptcy laws;

- the relative importance of the banking system and the capital market in long-term lending to enterprises as well as legal limits on equity stakes by banks;

- the presence and role of large shareholders, including institutional investors;

- the composition and role of enterprise boards.

The emergence of institutional investors will influence the relative importance of these factors, although the precise impact on patterns of corporate control is not yet entirely clear. There are, however, signs that large institutional investors increasingly are taking an active role in corporate governance questions.

III. Exchanges versus over-the-counter markets

Securities exchanges provide a central forum for buyers and sellers to meet, whereas market makers buy and sell securities for their own accounts. Both these two institutional arrangements have evolved to increase liquidity. A securities exchange increases the liquidity of the market because it reduces the need to call on credit lines from banks instead of a securities sale to provide funds. The market maker stands ready to buy at a bid price and sell it at an offer price. The costs of maintaining liquid markets is covered through the market-maker's bid-offer spread.

Advocates of exchanges argue that investors and issuers are better off trading on an exchange -- in which the market maker or specialist is given a monopoly -- because of their preference for liquidity under extreme circumstances. In return, they are prepared to pay a slightly higher bid-offer spread. Critics point out that the growth of off-market dealing has occurred mainly because it provided a more cost-effective channel for arranging large institutional transactions. They are also of the opinion that the rules designed to maintain liquid markets in adverse circumstances are not enforceable, making the main benefit of exchange-based trading illusory.

Traditional exchange-based trading in both cash (especially equities) and derivatives markets is being seriously challenged by off-exchange (or OTC) trading. It is likely that this trend will continue in the future. It is worth emphasising that what is at stake is not simply the old issue of technical differences across traditional exchanges, such as trading on floors versus trading on screens or auction systems versus quote-driven systems. A more fundamental issue at stake is between, on the one hand, all of these systems which are characterised by trading procedures which are externally determined by some combination of self-regulation and official regulation and which requires that orders are exposed to the market; and, on the other hand, a "dealer" market organised by the intermediaries themselves, such as those exist in most bond and foreign exchange markets. Competition among trading systems and the aggressive policies of institutional investors to direct orders to the cheapest trading systems, have put strong pressure on the profitability of the brokerage business.

Some OTC trade is done directly between the dealer and the client whereas other trades take place on alternative systems. An important trend in recent years has been the growth of these alternative **Proprietary Trading Systems** (PTSs). No universally accepted definition of PTSs has emerged, but they are normally considered to be automated trading systems not formally registered or recognised as an exchange. Some of the systems are operated by industry "outsiders" while others are run by "insiders", such as internal networks owned by banks and securities firms. The exact number of of systems in operation is not known but according to some estimates it is within the range of 50 to 70 systems world-wide. The majority of systems are, however, in the United States. The technical features of PTSs vary greatly. For example, some systems rely heavily on the price discovery found on regulated markets while others have more of an independent price formation.

Another important development in recent years has been the proliferation of electronic cross-border linkages between markets. These linkages take different forms, such as electronic quotation systems and export of trading facilities. An example is the link being established between the futures exchanges of Germany (DTB) and France (MATIF). Through the instalment of screens in France, members of MATIF have direct access to selected products of the DTB. Conversely, MATIF products will be listed on the DTB. For the time being, the linkage does not involve a connection of the clearing systems. Potentially, the integration of clearing systems would reduce membership and margin cost for users dealing on several exchanges.

One of the consequences of the development of alternatives to trading on the traditional exchanges is that many instruments are now traded in several market simultaneously. As mentioned previously, a similar development is occurring in derivatives markets. The interpretation of this development is a matter of controversy, although it is likely that the impact of "market fragmentation" per se is negative because of the introduction of impediments to the price discovery process. It is, however, not entirely clear whether the multiplicity of trading systems is in all cases tantamount to "market fragmentation". It has argued by some analysts that there is a serious risk of "market fragmentation" whereby an increasing share of transactions is not exposed to the broad market. In addition, some in the exchanges characterise those who trade off the exchange as "free riders", who benefit from the price discovery process of the exchanges while avoiding the costs of supporting the exchanges.

The role of intermediaries (banks and securities houses) is changing in response to changes in competitive conditions. To the extent that exchanges continue to have dominant positions in secondary trading, intermediaries will need to operate on the exchanges. However, their profit margins are being squeezed by the growing market power of institutions to obtain bids from a number of competing intermediaries and markets. As a result, the profitability of the brokerage business has been sharply eroded and many intermediaries have vastly expanded **proprietary trading** in order to earn profits from market intermediation. Many large intermediaries observe that, even though the bid-offer spreads of exchange-based trading are relatively high, the commissions earned through the exchanges tend to be subdivided among a series of intermediaries. To lower trading costs in a highly competitive environment, both investors and intermediaries will be seeking the cheapest forms of execution. This has resulted in the common situation in which the same product is traded on more than one exchange as well as on the OTC market. Many analysts believe that a multiplicity of trading systems will become the norm; some contend that the exchanges may remain relatively efficient for the execution of relatively small transactions but that the biggest deals -- involving in many cases institutional investors -- will inevitably require highly capitalised intermediaries willing to take large net positions.

IV. The supervision and regulation of securities markets

Many of the trends that are changing the role of capital markets can be expected to exert significant strains on existing supervisory and regulatory systems[20]. Securities market regulation often was founded upon the assumption that investors were mainly individuals and that the balance of market power favoured the issuers and the intermediaries, thus requiring an officially-supervised, formal framework for investor protection. It was necessary to require those who made public securities issues to provide information at the time of issue and throughout the period during which the security was publicly traded. Additionally, securities regulators (frequently in collaboration with self-regulation by exchanges) have usually sought to establish specific rules for secondary market trading, especially of equities, in order to protect investors from market manipulation.

One of the key issues under consideration is the following. Recent experience seems to indicate that, in a market basically focused on professional business, there is a declining demand for the kind of investor protection that has been traditionally offered by securities supervisors. At the same time, individual investors are increasing their holdings of equities either directly or via instruments for collective investment. One of the adjustments that regulators have made to accommodate the ongoing changes in financial markets has been to increase the differentiation between retail and institutional investors.

However, other problems also remain. The fact that large volumes of business are moving away from the traditional exchanges presents the regulators with many dilemmas. The growth of Proprietary Trading Systems has brought forward the questions of whether and how these systems should be regulated. As mentioned above, a particular concern is whether PTSs may be "free riding" on the price discovery found elsewhere and that they may be resulting in "market fragmentation". At the same time, the rise of PTSs has underlined that the definition of a market in national legislation is far from straightforward and that there is no internationally agreed definition. This being said, it should be noted that many countries still have only limited experience with PTSs. Also, a number of the concerns related to PTSs have been analysed by some regulatory authorities, notable in the United States. The United States study did not find support for the claim of "market fragmentation". On the contrary, a system with a wide variety of trading systems was felt to be more competitive as it provides participants with alternatives[21].

Another important development has been the expansion of direct cross-border trading linkages, involving both regulated exchanges and PTS. This development, which is likely to gain further momentum in the near future, has raised some fresh challenges for regulators which must consider which -- if any -- regulatory requirements must be fulfilled in the host country. In theory, several models are possible, including:

- full recognition of home country regulation, *i.e.* regulation is performed by the home country with little or no interference by the authorities of the host country;

- shared regulation between the home and the host country, possibly with primary home country regulation or appointment of a lead regulator;

- global regulation, *i.e.* entities are submitted to both home and host country regulation.

The globalisation of capital markets has also opened new opportunities for large-scale, dishonest and fraudulent behaviour, such as cross-border front running. This raises another fundamental problem for regulators, which must either attempt to enforce national legislation extraterritorially or find effective means of co-operation with other regulators. The response of regulators has increasingly been to expand their co-operation and harmonisation efforts. A number of countries have introduced or amended legislation permitting national securities regulators to co-operate with their counterparts abroad. The recent period has also witnessed a series of agreements, technically known as "memoranda of understanding", on the exchange of information and on co-operation between securities regulators. Normally, these agreements are bilateral.

While the traditional concerns of investor protection may seem less urgent than in the past, there clearly remain needs for official supervision of the markets.

- First, there has been several cases of market manipulation and fraud by major market intermediaries, which seem to indicate that significant potential exists for market manipulation, even in internationalised markets dominated by professionals.

- Second, the large volume of funds being managed by institutional investors also raises issues of prudential supervision, particularly since these institutions are increasingly a major repository for the savings of small savers.

- Third, given the internationalisation of business, the need for greater compatibility of regulations across countries has grown.

- Fourth, as mentioned above, the issue of systemic risk remains serious. In particular, the large-scale trading of OTC derivatives and the potential destabilising impact of certain classes of institutional investors are areas of major concern from a public policy standpoint.

Considerable work on analysing issues in capital market regulation and in international co-operation of supervisors is being undertaken by IOSCO[22]. However, compared to the close co-operation among banking supervisors, multilateral co-operation on regulatory issues in the securities field appear to be somewhat slow and inadequate. More generally, it would seem that additional attention should be paid by supervisors and others to the risks and (potential) problems associated with[23]:

- inadequately supervised financial centres or, more generally, major differences in regulatory regimes;

- the lack of comparability of regulatory standards such as those related to cross-border depositor protection;

- legal and practical problems that can arise in connection with the liquidation of institutions with multiple cross-border offices;

- the supervision of financial conglomerates;

- the legal uncertainties associated with the application of domestic laws to international financial transactions;

- the effects on the stability of financial systems of the use of new financial instruments by financial market participants, including institutional investors such as the (unregulated) hedge funds;

- clearing and settlement systems for payments and securities.

V. Capital markets and securities settlement systems

An important factor behind the rise in the overall value of payments has been the rapid growth of turnover in securities markets, in particular government securities. A significant part of this growth has taken place in international markets and has represented cross-border investments[24]. These developments indicate why well-functioning payment and securities settlement systems are of great importance for the evolution of efficient capital markets.

Governments and financial market participants have made significant progress in improving securities settlement systems over the past five years[25]. These efforts have focused on making the transfer of the securities from the seller to the buyer as well as the transfer of funds from the buyer to the seller more efficient, reliable and safe. A shortening of the time-lags between trading and settlement (settlement lags) and the introduction of delivery versus payment (or DVP) mechanisms have been and continue to be the key elements of reform in this area.

Concerns about risks in securities transactions has been an important driving force shaping the measures to improve the oversight of payment and settlement systems and the prudential regulation of banks and securities firms. Financial transactions generate a range of risks for counterparties that undertake them, their bankers and other intermediaries that process the transactions, and central banks through which final interbank settlement occurs. These risks are greatest in large-value interbank funds and securities transfer systems that support trading in financial markets[26]. A key public policy issue is what the respective roles of the private sector and the public authorities are in managing and containing risks in the payment system, in particular when financial markets are changing rapidly and fundamentally. The clearing and settlement system for payments and securities is one of the first places where financial stress can manifest itself-- *i.e.* through the inability of one or more participants to meet their payment obligations. There is broad agreement that it is the responsibility of the public authorities to lay out clearly the principles and rules governing the safe operation of the payment system (for example, rules for governing settlement and the irrevocability of payment instructions) and that compliance

307

with these rules is also best supervised by the authorities. Within that framework, the payment system generally works best when run by private agents in a competitive environment. The regulatory structure of the payment system should establish the proper incentives for payment system participants to manage their risks.

Of critical importance for the overall stability of the financial system is the supervision and regulation of private clearing and settlement arrangements that support large-value transfers[27]. In many OECD countries large-value funds transfer systems channel the payment leg of securities transactions. The interactions between the payment system and securities settlement systems provide a prima facie case for regulation and supervision of securities markets by the authorities -- in particular the possibility that problems in securities settlements might result in losses and liquidity pressures that cannot be managed and contained with existing private arrangements and that, as a result, the stability of the payment system might be endangered[28]. Thus, the oversight of payment and settlement systems and the prudential regulation and supervision of banks and securities firms share the fundamental concern for the solvency of financial institutions and, ultimately, for the stability of the financial system. However, while the concerns overlap considerably, there are fundamental differences in approach between the two areas of oversight[29]. Prudential regulation and supervision concerns individual institutions, while the oversight of the payment and settlement systems focuses on the relationship between institutions, in particular how settlement risk is being managed.

Chart 1. DEVELOPMENT OF THE WORLD BOND MARKET (1)

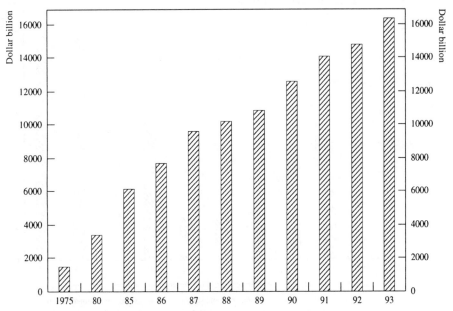

1. Nominal value outstanding of publicly issued bonds converted into US dollars.

Source: Salomon Brothers

Chart 2. NEW INTERNATIONAL EQUITIES (1)

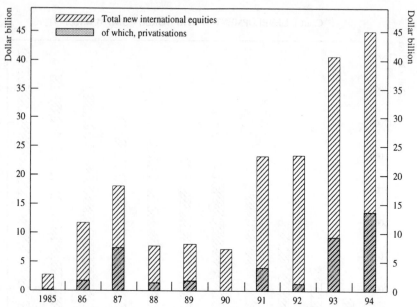

1. New issues and initial public offerings (IPO's) of common and preferred shares, participation
   certificates, 'certificats d'investissements' and similar instruments and international offerings
   taking place in the context of privatisation. Also includes secondary offerings, private placements,
   issues of redeemable convertible preference shares and internationally placed units of closed–end funds.

Source: OECD/DAF

310

Table 1. Share of Government Bonds[1] in total outstanding in selected markets[2]

Per cent

Market	1980	1988	1991	1992	1993
US Dollar	49.7	55.4	54.8	55.2	55.3
Japanese Yen	64.2	64.4	57.8	57.1	56.9
Deutschmark	18.8	30.0	30.6	33.0	35.4
Italian Lira	61.1	80.9	81.6	81.8	81.4
French Franc	72.4	79.3	76.4	75.5	73.1
Canadian Dollar	32.9	38.3	37.8	38.2	38.1
UK Sterling	92.0	72.1	59.3	62.0	64.6

1. Central government and government agency bonds.
2. Percentage of publicly issued debt.

Source: Salomon Brothers

Table 2. Correlations of international bond yields

(correlation coefficients between levels of 10-year bond yields, montly data)

	1970-79	1980-84	1985-89	1990-94
(a) Correlations with United States				
Japan	0.38	0.18	0.67	0.96
Germany	-0.24	0.78	0.65	0.93
United Kingdom	0.63	0.60	0.54	0.96
Canada	0.94	0.93	0.98	0.97
(b) Correlations with Germany				
France	-0.14	0.79	0.47	0.97
Italy	-0.54	0.54	0.69	0.74
United Kingdom	0.12	0.77	0.69	0.94
Belgium	-0.12	0.83	0.74	0.96
Netherlands	0.52	0.90	0.88	0.99
Sweden	-0.61	0.54	0.61	0.88
Switerland	0.86	0.88	0.74	0.91

Source: OECD, Main Economic Indicators

Table 3. Markets for selected derivative instruments

Notional principal amounts outstanding at end-year, in billion of US dollars equivalent

	1988	1989	1990	1991	1992	1993
Exchange-traded instruments	**1306.0**	**1768.3**	**2291.7**	**3523.4**	**4640.5**	**7839.3**
Interest rate futures	895.4	1200.6	1454.1	2157.1	2902.2	4960.4
Interest rate options[1]	279.2	387.9	599.5	1072.6	1385.4	2362.4
Currency futures	11.6	15.6	16.3	17.8	24.5	29.8
Currency options[1]	48.0	50.1	56.1	61.2	80.1	81.1
Stock market index futures	27.8	41.8	69.7	77.3	80.7	119.2
Options on stock market indices[1]	44.0	72.2	96.0	137.4	167.6	286.4
Over-the-counter instruments[2]	-	-	**3450.3**	**4449.4**	**5345.7**	-
Interest rate swaps	1010.2	1502.6	2311.5	3065.1	3850.8	-
Currency swaps[3]	319.6	449.1	577.5	807.2	860.4	-
Other derivative instruments[4]	-	-	561.3	577.2	634.5	-

1. Calls and puts.
2. Data collected by the International Swaps and Derivatives Association (ISDA) only; the two sides of contracts between ISDA members are reported once only; excluding instruments such as forward rate agreements, currency options, forward foreign exchange contracts and equity and commodity-related derivatives.
3. Adjusted for reporting of both currencies; including cross-currency interest rate swaps.
4. Caps. collars, floors and swaptions.

Source: BIS

313

Table 4. Relationship between interest rate futures and cash markets

	1988	1989	1990	1991
Ratio of futures[1] to cash transactions in government securities				
France	2.5	3.4	4.6	5.4
Germany	1.3 [2]	1.5	1.5	3.5
Italy	n.a.	n.a.	n.a.	n.a.
Japan	1.3	1.5	1.5	1.6
Netherlands	0.1	0.4	0.4	0.1
United Kingdom	0.2	0.1	0.1	0.2
United States [3]	0.4	0.4	0.4	0.4
Ratio of open positions [4] in futures to outstanding interbank claims [5] at end-year				
Euro-dollar	0.25	0.25	0.23	0.40
Euro-yen	n.a.	0.16	0.32	0.34
Euro-Deutsche Mark	n.a.	0.03	0.08	0.18
Euro-Swiss franc	n.a.	n.a.	n.a.	0.09
French Franc (PIBOR)	0.35	0.20	0.20	0.33
Three-month sterling	0.32	0.65	0.53	0.81

n.a. = not applicable

1. Transactions in futures cover contracts on government securities traded on exchanges worldwide.
2. Bond futures contract first introduced on LIFFE in September 1988. Ratio calculated for the last three months of 1988.
3. Cash transactions include Treasury bills.
4. Open positions in futures cover contracts traded on exchanges worlwide.
5. Cross-border plus local Euro-claims of BIS reporting banks in the same currency as the futures contract.

Source: BIS.

314

Table 5. The size and growth of institutional investors

OECD Region	Compound average annual rate of growth			Total assets outstanding at end-1991 in billion US dollars
	1981-91	1981-86	1986-91	
Life Insurance Companies				
Europe (10 countries)	15	9	22	1200
North America	12	12	11	1700
Japan	24	25	22	1100
Total	15	14	17	4000
Pension Funds				
Europe (10 countries)	15	17	13	1300
North America	16	18	13	3300
Japan	23	26	19	300
Total	16	18	14	4900
Investment Funds				
Europe (10 countries)	25	31	19	1000
North America	19	24	14	1400
Japan	26	44	10	300
Total	22	28	15	2700
Growth of all Institutional Investors				
Europe (10 countries)	17	17	17	3500
North America	15	17	13	6400
Japan	24	29	19	1800
Total	17	18	15	11700
For comparison: Growth of Commercial Banks				
Europe (10 countries)	13	11	15	9800
North America	5	7	4	3900
Japan	17	18	16	5900
Total	12	11	12	19600

1. The ten European countries taken into account are: Austria, Finland, France, Germany, Italy, Netherlands, Spain, Sweden, Switzerland and the United Kingdom.

Source: Institutional investor data: country submissions received by OECD; some country data for 1981 and 1986 have been estimated. Banking data: OECD annual statistics on financial statements of banks.

Table 6. Institutional investor's holdings of foreign securities

Countries and items	1980	1985	1990	1991	1992	1993
	as a percentage of total securities holdings at year-end					
Austria						
Insurance companies	14.1	11.6	10.1	9.4	10.5	9.9
Investment funds	27.0	13.2	18.7	22.4	22.8	25.1
Australia						
Life ins. and pensions			14.0	16.2	16.8	18.8
Belgium						
Insurance companies	5.5	8.6	5.2	4.2	4.1	-
Canada						
Life ins. companies	2.2	2.3	2.4	2.8	2.7	3.1
Pension funds	6.1	6.6	7.0	8.5	10.2	10.6
Italy						
Insurance companies			13.6	12.2	13.2	12.2
Japan						
Private ins. companies	8.1	23.2	29.9	28.4	27.0	22.3
Postal life insurance	0.0	6.7	11.6	12.1	13.1	12.3
Netherlands						
Insurance companies	6.9	22.9	20.2	20.4	22.6	26.0
Private pension funds	26.6	28.1	36.6	38.2	39.2	36.9
Public pension funds	14.7	9.9	16.6	17.2	18.9	20.2
Sweden						
Insurance companies			10.5	12.1	11.0	12.3
United Kingdom						
Insurance companies[2]	6.3	14.1	14.6	15.8	15.5	-
Pension funds[3]	10.8	17.3	23.2	25.2	23.8	-
United States[4]						
Mutual funds				4.0	5.1	8.0
Private pension funds[5]			4.1	4.6	5.0	7.1

1. Preliminary.
2. Long-term funds.
3. Pension fund exclude the central government sector but include other public sectors.
4. As a percentage of total assets.
5. Tax-exempt funded schemes (excluding IRAs).

Source: BIS.

Notes

1 For a further discussion, see Bröker, G., 1993, "Government Securities And Debt Management In The 1990s", OECD.

2 In addition to the publicly traded bonds, the bond market also encompasses privately placed bonds, which are not accounted for in these figures.

3 Trends in Government Debt Management and Government Securities Markets, in Financial Market Trends no. 57, OECD, February 1994.

4 Biltoft K. and Boersch C., 1990, "A note on International Interest Linkages: the choice of data frequency", unpublished, Danmarks Nationalbank.

5 Goldstein, M. and Mussa, M. (1993) The Integration of World Capital Markets, IMF Working Paper (WP/93/95).

6 Chou R.Y., Ng V.K. and Pi, L.K. (1994) show that cointegration relationships across stock markets have become stronger. IMF Working Paper (WP/94/94).

7 "International Capital Markets", Part I, International Monetary Fund, April 1993.

8 For a further discussion of the impact of privatisation on capital markets, see "Privatisation and Capital Markets in OECD Countries" in Financial Market Trends No. 60, February 1995.

9 See also Deutsche Bundesbank Monthly Report, November 1994.

10 United States General Accounting Office, "Financial Derivatives -- actions needed to protect the financial system", May 1994. For a discussion of guidelines on the management of risks associated with derivatives, see Group of 30, 1993, "Derivatives; Practices and Principles" and in Basle Committee on Banking Supervision (Group of Ten), 1994, "Risk Management Guidelines For Derivatives", Bank for International Settlements (BIS). Also, the BIS has recently published a number of reports discussing various issues related to derivatives, such as "A discussion Paper on Public Disclosure of Market and Credit Risks by Financial Intermediaries" (September 1994), "Macroeconomic and Monetary Policy Issues Raised by the Growth of Derivatives Markets" (November 1994), and "Issues of Measurement Related to Market Size and Macroprudential Risks in Derivatives Markets" (February 1995). An overview of key issues can be found in Crockett, June 1994, "Views on global financial markets and derivative instruments", Remarks by the General Manager of the Bank for International Settlements to the 24th International Management

Symposium in St. Gallen and in Crockett, November 1994, "The challenge of derivatives", Remarks by the General Manager of the Bank for International Settlements at the Frankfurt European Banking Congress. Finally, see also Brockelmann, October 1994, "Do derivatives require special vigilance on the part of supervisors and central banks", Address by the Economic Advisor of the Bank for International Settlements at the International Conference on Derivative Instruments organised by the Institute of Advanced Legal Studies at the University of London.

11   An excellent overview of the mutual funds industry in the United States can be found in: Mack P.R., "Recent Trends in the Mutual Funds Industry", Federal Reserve Bulletin, November 1993.

12   Group of Ten, International Capital Movements and Foreign Exchange Markets, April 1993.

13   International Monetary Fund, ibid.

14   The Economist, A Quantum Dive, 5 March 1994.

15   International Monetary Fund, ibid.

16   See also Deutsche Bundesbank, ibid.

17   For a formal presentation, see Black J. and Tonks I., "Asset Price Variability Under Asymmetric Information", The Economic Journal, supplement 1990 page 67-77. Financial Markets Group, Discussion Paper No. 40, September 1988.

18   A distinction must be made between a liquid security and a liquid market. A liquid security is one that maintains its value in terms of the unit of account. See P. M. Garber, and S. R. Weisbrod, The Economics of Banking, Liquidity, and Money, D. C. Heath and Company, Lexington, 1992.

19   Hans J. Blommestein and Michael G. Spencer, (1993) The role of Financial Institutions in the Transition to a Market Economy, IMF Working Paper, (WP/93/75).

20   See for an overview of measures affecting the functioning of securities markets in OECD Member countries, Organisation and Regulation of Securities Markets, Financial Market Trends No 54, OECD, Paris, 1993.

21   See the "Market 2000" study by the Securities and Exchange Commission (SEC) of the United States, January 1994.

22   The International Organisation of Securities Commissions (IOSCO) was created in 1983. In 1987, IOSCO established the so-called Technical Committee which has the mandate to review regulatory problems related to international securities transactions and to propose practical solutions to these problems. The Technical Committee has five working parties, which investigate issues related to multinational disclosure and accounting; regulation of secondary markets;

regulation of market intermediaries; enforcement and the exchange of information; investment management.

23 G. Corrigan,1992, Challenges facing the International Community of Supervisors, Quarterly Review, Federal Reserve Bank of New York, volume 17 number 3; Systemic Risks in Securities Markets, OECD, 1991; Delivery Versus Payment in Securities Settlement Systems, BIS, September, 1992; Financial Market Trends No 50, OECD, October 1991; Financial Conglomerates, OECD, 1993; Recent Developments in International Interbank Relations, BIS, October, 1992.

24 BIS, 64th Annual Report, 13 June 1994.

25 BIS, 64th Annual Report, 13 June 1994; BIS, Delivery versus payment in securities settlement systems, September 1992; Morgan Guaranty Trust Company, Cross-border clearance, settlement, and custody: beyond the G30 recommendations, June 1993.

26 Paul van den Bergh and John M. Veal, Payment System Risk and Risk Management, in: Bruce J. Summers, ed., The Payment System: Design, Management, and Supervision, IMF, 1994. See also the overview chapter 7 in this publication by Bruce J. Summers.

27 Bruce J. Summers, Clearing and Payment Systems: the Role of the Central Bank, Federal Reserve Bulletin, February 1991.

28 Systemic Risks in Securities Markets, OECD, 1991; Delivery Versus Payment in Securities Settlement Systems, BIS, September, 1992; Financial Market Trends No 50, OECD, October 1991.

29 BIS, 64th Annual Report, June 13th 1994.

Chapter 10

STRUCTURAL CHANGES IN THE NORTH AMERICAN CAPITAL MARKETS

Mary Ann Gadziala

Introduction and summary

The capital markets in North America have undergone fundamental and pervasive structural changes over the last decade. These generally well developed markets have become larger, faster, more dispersed and more diverse. They have also become deeper, more liquid, more globalized, more complex, more tailored to specific needs, and more interconnected. In summary, the North American capital markets have undergone a far-reaching quiet revolution with reverberations felt by everyone in that region and far beyond. These developments likely foreshadow the future direction of change in other developed capital markets. While such changes always involve some measure of risk, these were not haphazard or destabilizing events, but rather significant positive movements responsive to the needs of market participants.

The major phenomena responsible for the structural changes in the North American capital markets may be divided into five general categories. First, there has been a very substantial increase in the need for new capital leading to an expanding and increasingly diverse market to satisfy these needs. Second, more sophisticated and demanding suppliers and users of capital have required

*   Prepared by Mary Ann Gadziala of the Division of Market Regulation, US Securities and Exchange Commission. The Securities and Exchange Commission, as a matter of policy, disclaims responsibility for any private publication or statement by any of its employees. The views expressed herein do not necessarily represent the views of the Commission or the Division of Market Regulation.

and received innovative products and services tailored to their particular needs. Third, there has been a large scale need to bring geographically separated capital and capital users together, thus generating market expansion and globalization. Fourth, there has been a need for increased linkages among markets to accommodate product and geographic diversification as well as operational needs. Finally, some structural changes have resulted from regulatory changes intended to protect market integrity by placing limitations on market developments perceived as having the potential to create unsafe or destabilizing effects. Each of these five areas is discussed in greater detail below. A more thorough data analysis follows the discussion.

These five phenomena have been propelled by three pervasive fundamental forces: first, the rapid improvement in the capacity to process information; second, a broad-based global trend toward deregulation of capital markets and capital flows; and finally, economic and financial volatility driven by underlying, macroeconomic factors. These will be discussed throughout the analysis.

The first impetus to structural changes in the North American capital markets has been an environment suited to economic growth and development. This has precipitated the expansion of all sectors of those capital markets. The amount of Government bonds in the United States has quadrupled since 1981. Thus, the growing scope of the US budget deficit has been a significant factor in capital market developments to accommodate federal financing needs. The growth is the same for corporate and foreign debt. The capitalization of United States equity markets quadrupled since 1980. Initial public offerings increased an astronomical 40-fold, from only $1.4 billion in 1980 to $57.4 billion in 1993. Mortgage-backed securities in the US increased more than 10-fold during that period, from $142.3 billion to $1.55 trillion, securitizing a huge market hitherto dominated by direct portfolio investment by financial institutions. All of these financial instruments have contributed to sustained and increasing economic growth in the United States, supporting Gross Domestic Product (GDP) of approximately $6.4 trillion in 1993. While the US capital markets have grown significantly over the past decade, the world capital markets, particularly emerging markets, have grown at an even more accelerated pace. This translates into a declining per centage of US capitalization with respect to world capitalization.

Market capitalization in Canada rose from $140.6 billion in 1983 to $243 billion in 1992. New equity financing in Canada also showed substantial growth. The most dramatic growth in North America took place in Mexico where equity market capitalization skyrocketed from only $3.4 billion in 1983 to $139.1 billion in 1992. While the Mexican stock market experienced some pulling back in the early part of the second quarter, it has recently resumed its upward climb.

The increased amount of capital instruments has been accompanied by another structural change, substantial increases in trading volume and activity. From 1982 to 1992, annual equity trading volume on the US exchanges and the National Association of Securities Dealers Automated Quotation (NASDAQ) system surged from only 28.6 billion to 111.9 billion shares, a 290 per cent increase. Average daily volume is now 200 million shares per day on each of the New York Stock Exchange (NYSE) and on NASDAQ. In Canada, the Toronto Stock Exchange experienced a record breaking trading year in 1993. This has meant that technology has been put to use to create systems that permit rapid turnover of vast amounts in the capital markets on a sustained basis. This has been further impacted by such market activity as expiration of stock index options and futures and equity options, program trading, and dynamic hedging, all of which may significantly increase order flow. In sum, the past decade has witnessed massive capital increases accompanied by technical and operational improvements to handle the increased volume and sophisticated processing. As the economies in North America continue to expand and technological advancements multiply, it is expected that the North American capital markets will exhibit sustained and accelerated growth.

The second major force behind structural changes in the North American capital markets arises from consumer demands. Both suppliers and users of capital have become more sophisticated and demanding, requiring innovative products and services tailored to specific needs. Much of the driving force behind this structural change is the advanced technology that, in a less regulated competitive financial system, educates customers about choices and encourages the creation of complex financing products. The capital markets can now disaggregate, transform and redistribute risks, and sell risks to those investors most willing and able to bear risk; thus moving from plain vanilla debt and equity to a whole smorgasbord of customized products.

Even the most conservative sector of the capital markets in the United States, the Government securities market, has recognized that it must respond to customer needs in order to maximize investor participation and cost effectiveness. For example, to improve its service to the customer base of individuals, the US Treasury has developed TREASURY DIRECT. This system allows investors to maintain book-entry accounts of Treasury securities directly with Treasury at no cost. There is currently $63 billion par dollar amount outstanding in TREASURY DIRECT. Private issuers have also been considering direct registration systems for their securities. The US Treasury has also made savings bonds rates consistent with those prevailing for marketable Government securities, rather than setting them at low fixed rates that have no relation to competitive rates. To take advantage of investor interest and cost savings associated with zero-coupon securities, the Treasury created STRIPs in 1985. STRIPs are separate interest and principal payments of US Government securities. The amount of US Government securities currently held in STRIP form is now over $220 billion. Treasury derivatives products, including futures, forwards, and options, have also kept this market competitive and vibrant. Despite the ever increasing amounts of Government securities issued, there are always willing buyers for, and traders in, these instruments and their derivatives.

Over the past decade, the non-government bond area has introduced a number of innovative new products in the United States, the most prominent of which is mortgage-backed securities (MBS). Increased standardization and computing efficiency facilitated MBS development. MBS products offer significantly higher yields than Government securities, while at the same time offering a guarantee by a government sponsored enterprise or some other form of credit enhancement. This makes MBS an attractive and relatively safe, higher yielding investment than Government securities. Through the development of MBS, the mortgage business is able to tap the depth and liquidity of the global capital market with its full array of potential investors, rather than being restricted to the confines of direct investment by financial institutions. The mortgage borrower has been among the beneficiaries of this development.

Derivatives are another innovative product specifically tailored to satisfy the diverse needs of particular users. As business operations and investor portfolios have become more complex, their risks have also become more complex. Rather than scaling down activities to make them more riskless or operating in the face of unmanageable risks, businesses and investors have sought financial products specifically designed to alleviate their particular sets of risks. The market has responded with complex, tailor-made derivatives. This permits an investor or a business to enter into contracts or transactions that best suit its particular needs, and then to purchase a customized derivative product tailored to wring out the risks associated with the venture. An intermediary will provide such a derivative and then sell the products, often repackaging the risks and offering enhancements or collateral to back the transaction. Derivatives have grown dramatically so that notional values have been estimated as high as $17 trillion. Of course, it is important to emphasize that the credit equivalent exposure is a small fraction of that notional amount. To satisfy customer needs, derivatives have also become increasingly complex and sensitive to economic and financial volatility, thus requiring constant vigilance. The recent Group of Thirty report on derivatives emphasized the need for sound risk management systems by institutions, enhanced expertise by supervisors, and improvement in legal and financial infrastructures.

It is not only new products that have developed to respond to customers' needs, new and diverse markets for these products have also been developed over the past decade. For example, securities may be traded on the exchanges, on NASDAQ, proprietary trading systems, and in the third and fourth markets. There are auction systems, dealer systems, and negotiated trades. Each of these offers significant diverse benefits to suit particular customer needs. While there are some who have argued that this array of markets has fragmented the equity markets to the detriment of investors, the US Securities and Exchange Commission determined in its recent **Market 2000** study, on the contrary, that the current system is more vigorously competitive and provides investors with a wide range of alternative trading mechanisms from which to choose to do business.

A final example of a market success in responding to customer needs over the past decade is the mutual fund. Mutual funds in the United States exploded from only $135 billion in 1980 to $1.6 trillion today. Canada also has a growing mutual fund industry, with 5.3 million accounts and almost $60 billion in assets as of September 30, 1992. The explosive growth in mutual funds has not been a random accident, nor was it always assured. In fact, some believed that mutual funds were headed for extinction with the bear market of the 1970's. It was at that time that the introduction of the safe, short-term money market fund resurrected the industry. Until the early 1980's, rising interest rates, low stock prices, and a sluggish economy kept the vast majority of funds assets in money market funds. However, with a changed economic environment, in 1992, equity and bond funds had taken the lead role.

The mutual fund industry has continued to develop a variety of new types of funds to satisfy differing investor needs. These range from Government bond funds, to tax-exempt funds, to growth and income funds, to international funds. There are currently 3848 available funds, a dramatic 600 per cent increase from the 564 funds in 1980. In addition, the mutual fund industry has recognized that investors seek choices, not only with their initial investment, but thereafter as well. As a consequence, they developed large complexes offering all varieties of mutual fund products and simple relatively cost-free procedures for moving from one type of fund to another. Therefore, as a customer's investment needs changed, whether in response to economic factors or changed personal circumstances, the customer would have no need to leave the mutual fund complex to achieve desired new investment objectives. Rather, the customer could simply move investments to different mutual funds within the complex. The development of the mutual fund industry allows a wide array of issuers to tap the full range of investors through low cost intermediation. The benefits accrue to both issuers and investors. Again, technological advances in information processing have made such developments feasible and cost effective.

In sum, the capital markets over the past decade have developed complex and diverse products specifically tailored to customer needs. Advanced technology and sophisticated pricing techniques permit the transformation and redistribution of risk through customized contracts. In addition, market developments have made it easier for the customer to move funds or change capital designs to suit changing needs. This allows the customer the maximum amount of choices and flexibility for precise risk management and cash flow needs. All indications are that this customizing process may have just passed its infancy phase and will proliferate in years to come. These developments free the process of capital flows from the rigid confines required by a perfect fit between the needs of the ultimate issuer and investor.

The third major influence on changing market structure in North America over the past decade has been the trend toward bringing geographically dispersed capital users and investors together. Certain areas may have significant capital needs but little or no available capital. Others may be capital rich with little opportunity for investment. This may be true with respect to local communities. It may also be true on a broader basis, such as country to country. For example, well developed, capital rich countries are pursuing investments in developing nations where there is significantly greater opportunity for profitability, accompanied, of course, by greater risk. Capital mobility has become an overriding need in today's market, thus leading to globalization or internationalization of our capital markets. Capital markets are increasingly replacing direct investment by financial institutions in intermediating these capital flows.

One of the challenges to capital mobility over this decade was to transform illiquid financial products into products with depth and liquidity so as to make them freely tradeable in the secondary markets. Securitization has been particularly successful in accomplishing this goal by pooling illiquid loans and creating tradeable securities that represent an interest in that pool. This is a convenient vehicle for providing local borrowers with ready access to the depth and liquidity of the broader capital markets. The mortgaged-backed securities (MBS) market is the most well developed in this area. This market has expanded in the United States to $1.55 trillion in a very short period of time. In addition, there are continuing developments of securitizations in new areas creating increased depth and liquidity for a wide variety of financial products including credit card receivables, auto receivables, commercial real estate loans, and many other products. This has meant an increased role for banks, with and through the capital markets, rather than simply acting as a separate conduit for capital flows largely independent of the broader capital markets.

While securitization has served to make illiquid financial products liquid, it could not create capital mobility without a broad investor base to absorb the securities. One of the fastest growing segments of this base is the mutual fund noted above. There are approximately 140 mutual funds with almost $100 billion in assets invested primarily in MBS in the United States. Mutual funds, with their $1.6 trillion of available capital, are also major investors in corporate debt and equity, and US Government securities. Most recently, they have dramatically increased their foreign and international funds, thus funneling the capital of those seeking the potential for higher returns to developing countries with capital deficiencies. International and global funds skyrocketed to $152.5 billion in 1993, an unparalleled 30-fold increase from $5.2 billion in 1985. Institutional investors, such as mutual funds and pension funds are a dominant investing force that has made our capital markets far more fungible and mobile.

Globalization is also evident from the increased number of foreign companies listed on US markets. As of May 31, 1994, there were 612 foreign issues listed in US markets, an increase of 100 since 1991. US corporate securities have also experienced globalization. Foreign transactions in US corporate securities rose from $40.6 billion in foreign sales and $38.8 billion in foreign purchases in 1981, to $319.4 billion in foreign sales and $297.9 billion in foreign purchases in 1993. Foreign transactions in US corporate bonds followed a similar pattern, with foreign purchases and sales at $17.3 billion and $12.2 billion respectively in 1981, and $283.7 billion and $217.6 billion in 1993. The foreign transactions in 1993 were an alltime record and showed unparalleled increases from the prior year.

Over the past decade, capital markets have become more and more globalized. Capital rich areas find capital poor areas with significant growth potential. Conservative investors in areas with volatile markets can move their capital to areas with less risky investments. Intermediaries serve to bring them together. Technological advancements have facilitated both the rapid dissemination of information among geographically separated markets, as well as the transmission of orders to and from dispersed areas. In general, capital has become mobile and markets have become globalized. With the fall of communism and the movement of developing countries toward market-based economies, this is a trend that is expected to continue and likely intensify.

The fourth determinant over the past decade of changing capital market structure in North America has been the need for linkages among markets. These linkages take two general forms. First, there are linkages among financial industries and products to provide customers to some degree with one-stop shopping. This means a wide array of diverse products offered to customers through one central location. The second type of linkage that has developed over the decade is the system of operational connections of internal workings of intermediaries.

The linkages among industries to offer more choices to customers in the United States have mainly involved increased combined bank and securities activities offered by the same entity or through a networking or contractual arrangements. These combinations had not evolved in an orderly progression paralleling market needs because of a restrictive set of laws in the United States, primarily the Glass Steagall Act, inhibiting joint business endeavors.

While the Glass Steagall Act remains intact, market demands have prevailed to a large extent as a consequence of innovative structuring and more permissive regulatory interpretations. Banking organizations now participate in virtually every type of securities business. The assets of so-called Section 20 affiliates, which can perform all major securities activities, including debt and equity underwriting, have grown dramatically from only $17.2 billion in 1987 to $155.8 billion in 1993. It is remarkable that such growth has taken place under a regime that severely restricts bank securities activities. Banks have also significantly increased their mutual fund activities. As the low interest rate environment threatened their customer base, they expanded their offerings to cover higher yielding mutual funds. About one third of all mutual funds are available through banks and approximately 15 per cent of new sales of long term funds are made through banks. Banks found expanding into mutual funds to be a low risk way to leverage off their retail distribution network and to preserve their customer base. The structure of bank and securities activities in Mexico and Canada show far more combined services than in the United States, as these markets evolved in response to market needs without such constraining restrictions as the Glass Steagall Act.

Internal linkages involve the payments system, clearance and settlement systems, and interconnected financial deals, as well as markets. With the growth and maturation of the derivative markets, there has been increasing recognition of linkages among stock, stock option, stock index option, and stock index futures markets, which as noted in the report of the Brady Commission in 1988, tend to operate as a single market. In addition, the increasing dominance of institutional investors and large market professionals have added to the linkages among the securities, options and futures markets through sophisticated trading strategies. These strategies include index arbitrage, index substitution, dynamic hedging and other sophisticated financial techniques. The operational systems now in use must carry hundreds of trillions of dollars annually, involving unprecedented amounts and intricacies in interconnected transactions. All of these linkages have created a more unified and fungible market. These linkages have also raised concerns of systemic risk based upon the question of whether failures can be localized and controlled in such an interconnected market. Some of the more recent issues in this area involve T+3 settlement in the US stock market, foreign exchange settlement risk (so called Herstatt risk), and concern by central banks with respect to daylight overdrafts. Linkages of both types are expected to continue to develop, with regulators continuing to keep a watchful eye to protect against conflicts of interests and systemic and other risks.

The fifth and final force that has influenced market changes over the past decade is regulation. Regulation can directly determine market structure. This is true, for example, for US banks, which are limited in their geographic and product expansion by statutory prescriptions. Regulated entities, including banks and broker dealers, are also limited by capital requirements that may inhibit risky activities and products. In addition to such direct structural design by regulation, regulation may cause structural developments as a consequence of market participants seeking to avoid regulation. For example, hedge funds, a type of limited partnership consisting of a small number of high net worth and sophisticated investors have begun proliferating in the United States. These entities pool the funds of their investors and engage in complex financial transactions intended to outperform the market and add to the depth and liquidity of the markets. These funds also expect cost savings by avoiding the costs of regulation.

Another series of controls that have had an effect on market structure in the United States are the coordinated circuit breaker mechanisms that were implemented after the October 1987 market break. These are mechanisms which substitute planned, synchronized trading halts for unplanned and destabilizing market closings when markets are experiencing significant turbulence. For example, there is a one-hour trading halt of all securities and related derivative instruments after a 250-point decline on the Dow Jones Industrial Average, and a two-hour trading halt after a 400-point decline.

Parallel trading halts are instituted in the related market for stock index futures. In addition, there is a rule designed to ensure that index arbitrage is exercised only in a market-stabilizing manner during times of significant market volatility. There are also set price limits for stock index futures contracts. These controls are not intended to prevent significant market increases and decreases but to make sure they take place in a more orderly manner.

While there are many regulatory controls in effect that have an impact on market structure, there has been a dramatic worldwide trend towards deregulating capital markets and freeing capital flows. This worldwide deregulatory trend has been a prime force underlying the globalization of capital markets. There is no doubt but that regulation will continue to play a role in structuring the capital markets, not only in North America, but around the world. The challenge is to protect market stability and integrity without inappropriately stifling innovation and competitiveness.

In conclusion, the North American capital markets have undergone major structural changes over the past decade. They have grown dramatically in virtually all segments, contributing to significant economic expansion. Technological advancements have permitted explosive growth in trading volumes and in the complexity of products offered, allowing specific tailoring to customer needs. The capital markets are mobile, fungible, and globalized. They have significant intermarket and international linkages. While there is a general trend towards deregulation, capital markets have sometimes developed in convoluted ways to accommodate regulatory restrictions. The fastest growing products are derivatives and asset-backed securities. The fastest growing type of investor is the institutional investor. There have been many other less dominant structural changes that are not discussed above. A more detailed discussion of analytical data evidencing all of these changes follows.

I. Government securities

The US government securities market is a deep and liquid market with razor thin bid/ask spreads and significant worldwide trading volume. These securities serve as a safe investment with a steady income stream and as an income earning cash substitute to satisfy liquidity needs. Even with steady growth in volume, almost quadrupling in size over the past decade, US Government debt has consistently found market participants willing to commit increasing amounts of capital to trading and investing in them. As is discussed below, the proportion of investments among the investor mix has changed over the years to accommodate market developments and needs.

Total gross US public debt did not reach the $1 trillion mark until 1981. Five years later, it had more than doubled, and as of year-end 1993, outstanding US public debt had escalated to more than $4.5 trillion. The most recent data reported by the Federal Reserve segmenting amounts of US debt held by various categories of private investors is 1992, when gross US public debt outstanding was $4.2 trillion. The top private investor was the category designated "other," which is currently dominated by massive corporate pension funds. This category held more than $700 billion in US public debt in 1992, and has over the past decade consistently held approximately 15 per cent or more of the total outstanding amount. Two categories, "state and local treasuries" and "foreign and international," have been virtually tied over the past decade for second place. Each of these categories has held on average about 12 per cent of US public debt, and in 1992, each held about $550 billion of the $4.2 trillion total. "Individuals" and "commercial banks", which in the early 1980's each had approximately the same level of investment as the former two categories, now both lag substantially behind with only $300 billion each or 7 per cent of the 1992 total. While the proportionate investment of "individuals" has in general steadily declined to the current level, "commercial banks" recently climbed out of an all time low of only 5 per cent of total US public debt in 1990. These shifts resulted from the search for higher yields, diversification, and investment in closely related new products, such as the securities of government sponsored enterprises. There has also been significant movement from direct investment to indirect investment through institutional investors.

The most dramatic increase in the per centage investment of US public debt over the past decade was in the category of "other companies," which would include investment companies. Between 1980 and 1992, their per centage investment increased ten fold. As discussed later in this paper, investment companies have been one of the fastest growing financial markets in the US this decade. Finally, the most volatile investor in US public debt was the category denominated "money market funds." (See Chart A for data on private investors in US Government debt.)

Perhaps in response to the trend by individuals to reduce their proportionate share of US public debt and as a cost saving effort, the US Treasury introduced a number of innovations to stimulate individual investment. For example, Treasury recently established *Treasury Direct*, a book-entry system that allows investors to hold Government securities directly with the US Treasury. There are no custodial or transaction fees for using this system, which was designed primarily for investors wishing to hold their securities to maturity. *Treasury Direct* began operations in 1986. In 1987, $10 billion was reported on the system. Investments grew steadily to $64 billion where they generally leveled off. As of April 1, 1994, *Treasury Direct* had $63 billion par dollar amount outstanding. (Information from US Treasury).

Another innovation aimed at increasing individual investment was keying the interest rate paid on US savings bonds to other marketable Government securities to ensure attractive yields over time. The Treasury also created a new type of savings bond whose funds were dedicated to future use for college tuition, allowing tax exempt status for the earnings on such bonds.

In response to market needs for instruments to hedge interest rate risks, derivatives of US Government securities, including forwards, futures and options have been developed. Over the past decade, the use of these instruments has become widespread. Another sophisticated financial instrument, the Treasury STRIP (Separate Trading of Registered Interest and Principal), was developed to permit Treasury to take advantage of a market innovation, zero-coupon securities. These securities represent individual interest or principal payments of a US Government security. This program was initiated in 1985, and by February 28, 1990, the portion of Treasury securities held in STRIP form had reached $90.4 billion. As of April 30, 1994, that number more than doubled to $221.2 billion, evidencing significant market interest in the more volatile interest rate sensitive Treasury STRIPs. (Information from US Treasury.)

The financing techniques for US Government securities have also undergone significant structural changes in the past several years. These changes were precipitated by the 1991 Salomon Brothers scandal involving unauthorized bids in several Treasury auctions. Following Salomon's admission of several violations of the Treasury auction rules, a comprehensive study of Treasury financing techniques was undertaken by the relevant US government agencies. As a result, major changes were effected. For example, a project to fully automate Treasury auctions was significantly accelerated. Auction participation was broadened by eliminating impediments to bidding by entities other than primary dealers and by increasing opportunities for entities to become primary dealers. In addition, Treasury began experimenting with new auction techniques to replace the multiple-priced sealed bid auction that has the disadvantages of the "winner's curse" and could engender incentives to collude. Another effort to discourage market participants from generating a squeeze was the adoption of a policy of reopening issues whenever an acute, protracted squeeze occurs. These and other changes implemented following the Salomon Brothers scandal have contributed to increased efficiencies through a comprehensive modernization of operational practices in the Treasury market.

They have also served to ensure the maintenance of the highest integrity and confidence in this market.

II. Corporate bonds

Outstanding corporate and foreign bonds in the United States, like US Government securities, quadrupled between 1980 and 1993. Of the separate categories of investors identified by the US Federal Reserve Board, the most significant increases in the proportion of investments were by mutual funds and foreign investors. The former increased five fold and the latter almost doubled. This is evidence of the increasing prominence of mutual funds in the financial markets and the trend toward escalating globalization. The single category experiencing a systematic decrease in the proportion of bonds was municipal pension funds, which were approximately halved over the 1980 to 1993 period. Investments by households had been general stable at about 6 or 7 per cent, but nose dived to 3.6 per cent in 1993. (See Chart B)

As stated above, foreign investment has played a significant role in the market for US corporate bonds. In 1981, foreign purchases totaled $17.3 billion and foreign sales totaled $12.3 billion. By 1993, those numbers had risen steadily to $283.7 billion and $217.6 billion respectively. In addition to the dramatic increase in transactions, net purchases have also increased and stood at $66.0 billion in 1993 compared to $5 billion in 1981. This is a record amount with the previous highest amount of net purchases occurring in 1986, when it exceeded $50 billion. This is evidence of increasing internationalization of financials markets. (Chart C)

Net new issues of corporate and foreign bonds have consistently been in the positive range from 1980 through 1993, with 1986 and 1993 as the peak years. During each of those years there was more than $200 billion in net new issues. (See Chart D) These years had comparatively favorable economic and interest rate environments.

Between 1980 and 1993, gross corporate debt issues grew from $41.6 billion to just under $1 trillion. Almost half of that amount was mortgage-backed securities, which grew from only $500 million in 1980 to $421 billion in 1993. Much of that growth can be attributed to mortgage-backed issues of FNMA (the Federal National Mortgage Association and FHLMC (the Federal Home Loan Mortgage Corporation), which together hold approximately 95 per cent of this exploding market. (Chart E) Such securitization has made

market for such loans far more liquid and deep, thus expanding the range of
market to a national and even global scope.

Another interesting area was high-yield securities, which grew substantially
through most of the 1980's, dropped off in the early 1990's and in 1993 reached
an all time record amount of issuances. (Chart E) While the risks associated
with high yield securities discouraged investment for some years, improvements
in valuation and design, as well as low interest rates, have lured back a
substantial amount of investment capital. Mutual funds, which have grown
significantly in recent years and are a major component of high-yield investors,
have also contributed to this increase in high-yield securities.

III. Equity markets

The US equity markets have experienced dramatic growth, increased
globalization, and significant change through technological innovations.
Outstanding corporate equities, which in 1980 had already exceeded the
$1.5 trillion mark, continued to escalate to more than $6.1 trillion in 1993. This
is approximately twice the amount of capitalization of the second most highly
capitalized market in the world.

In the United States, households own $3.0 trillion of the $6.1 trillion in
corporate equities. While households are by far the largest holder in dollar
volume, their proportionate interest has slipped since 1980 from approximately
two-thirds of all equities to only one half of all equities. This may be in large
part attributable to their indirect investment in equities through institutional
investors, such as mutual funds and pension funds, the next two largest investors
in corporate equities. Private pension funds hold $1 079.4 billion in outstanding
US corporate equities, while mutual funds hold $667.3 billion. The more
remarkable statistic is the meteoric rise in mutual fund holdings from only
$42 billion in 1980, a 16-fold increase, compared with a 5-fold increase by
pension funds. Foreign investors also showed significant gains, rising from
$64.6 billion in 1980 to $320.6 billion in 1993. (Chart F)

Initial public offerings in the US have also shown substantial gains. They
rose from only $1.4 billion in 1980 to $57.4 billion in 1993, an increase of over
40-fold. Thus, capital from the equity market has been a significant contributor
to sustained economic growth in the United States. (Chart G)

In the United States, corporate equities trade in various markets. They may
trade on the NYSE, the American Stock Exchange (AMEX), the NASDAQ, The

regional exchanges, as well as in the third and fourth markets. Looking first at the exchanges and NASDAQ, we find significant increases in share volume and value of shares traded in all, except AMEX, which showed lesser increases. Overall, from 1982 to 1992, annual equity trading volume on the exchanges and NASDAQ increased from 28.6 billion shares to 111.9 billion shares, an increase of more than 290 per cent. Average daily volume at both NYSE and NASDAQ is approximately 200 million shares. However, there have been a number of days, even outside of the market breaks in 1987, 1989, and 1991, where daily volume exceeded 400 million shares. This is evidence of significant technological advancements in the markets. Another indicator of growth in the US equity market is the significant increase in the Dow Jones Industrial Average, which soared from 800 in 1989 to 3900 earlier this year. It is interesting to note that although both share volume and values of aggregate shares traded have increased significantly since 1980, the average stock price on NYSE and the regional exchanges has remained relatively stable. On the AMEX that price actually slipped from $22.01 to $11.75. Comparing share volume among NYSE, NASDAQ, and AMEX in 1983 and 1993, we find NASDAQ increasing its per centage of total shares from 40.2 per cent to 48.2 per cent, and NYSE and AMEX both decreasing. (Chart H)

Transactions in NYSE listed stocks may be executed in several different markets. The NYSE continues to receive the majority of orders in these stocks, accounting for 70 per cent of total transactions and 79 per cent of volume in its stocks in the first six months of 1993. Half of the NYSE volume results from block transactions, which are often negotiated off the floor of an exchange. Looking at the number of transactions during the first 6 months of 1993, the regional exchanges accounted for approximately 20 per cent of orders, the third market (OTC trading of listed stocks) for 9.4 per cent, and proprietary trading systems for .21 per cent. The bulk of regional business comes from small customer orders. Third market trades are primarily block trades off an exchange or small orders in the most active listed stocks from retail firms or discount brokers. Competition for small order flow remains strong because the transaction volume allows market markers to profit by capturing the bid/ask spread and provides revenue for the markets through consolidated tape fees. (Chart I)

One other facet of trading listed stocks is the gradual increasing impact of program trading. Average program trading volume executed on the NYSE as a per cent of NYSE volume has grown from 9.9 per cent in 1989 to 11.9 per cent in 1993. Three per cent of NYSE volume or ten million shares a day are executed as program trades after NYSE close, either on the NYSE's after-hours crossing session or through the foreign desks of US broker-dealers. Additional overseas trading by US firms takes place in London (under one million shares) or through foreign desks of US firms (at most two million shares per day). (Chart J)

NASDAQ, which began operations in 1971, has proven to be strong competition for the exchanges. As of 1992, NASDAQ trading represented 42 per cent of share volume and 29.2 per cent of dollar volume of US equity markets. There are currently 472 active NASDAQ market makers and 52 000 market making positions.

Proprietary trading systems (PTSs), which are screen-based trading systems used by institutions and broker-dealers, now have 13.5 per cent of NASDAQ share volume. In addition to PTS, there is a second type of automated trading systems, internal systems operated by large broker-dealers that cross orders from customers and other broker-dealers. Orders for listed stocks are sent to the exchanges for execution and orders for NASDAQ stocks are sent to NASD for trade reporting.

The US Securities and Exchange Commission recently reviewed this multifaceted equity market structure in its **Market 2000** study. The study concluded that the alternative markets have provided a vigorous and beneficial competitive challenge to the primary markets without jeopardizing the viability of the latter. While some questions were raised concerning market fairness and competitiveness these could be addressed by incremental changes, leaving the current structure intact to develop in accordance with market needs.

There have also been significant developments with respect to foreign entrants into the US capital markets. Some examples are increased foreign listings on US exchanges and foreign stock offerings in the United States. As of May 31, 1994, there were 612 foreign issues listed in US markets. This is over 100 more foreign listings than existed in 1991. Rule 144A encourages cross-border capital flows by reducing certain registration requirements and restrictions in connection with the sale of securities to institutional investors in the United States. It is intended to encourage foreign companies to sell securities directly to institutional purchasers in the United States. Between 1990 and May 1994, the total number of 144A foreign offerings has risen from 24 in the amount of $2.5 billion to 225 in the amount of $23.0 billion. (Data from US Securities and Exchange Commission.)

A United States effort to facilitate cross-border offerings of securities between the US and Canada is the Multijurisdictional Disclosure System. This system permits cross country disclosure for securities offerings. Since this system was implemented, there have been 82 offerings in the amount of $14 billion taking advantage of its procedures. (Data from US Securities and Exchange Commission.)

Globalization is also evidenced through data on foreign transactions in US corporate stocks. In 1981, foreign sales and purchases were $40.6 billion and $38.8 billion respectively. In 1993, those amounts had escalated to $319.4 billion and $297.9 billion. (Chart K)

Another important issue under consideration with respect to the internationalization of the securities markets is the extension of trading hours on the NYSE and NASDAQ to coincide with other major market trading sessions. The current time extensions have been at the fringes - an hour at the back and front end of regular trading hours - but there will no doubt be further developments towards round-the-clock trading hours and a truly global market on our exchanges. Electronic trading alternatives to the traditional exchanges, such as Instinet, Posit and the Wunsch Auction System have already made significant strides toward 24-hour trading services.

Market capitalization rose in Canada from $140.6 billion in 1983 to $243 billion in 1992 (in US dollars). While there are several stock exchanges in Canada, the Toronto Stock Exchange (TSE), a central auction market for equities and equity derivatives, is Canada's leading stock exchange with 78.9 per cent of market share in 1993. That was a record breaking year for TSE during which 14.9 billion shares worth $147 billion (all amounts for Canada in Canadian dollars unless otherwise noted) were traded. While TSE ranked second for a number of years among North American exchanges based upon share value, it moved into second place based upon value traded for the first time in 1993. TSE attributed this record-breaking year in large part to low interest rates and improved earnings of Canadian listed companies. Looking at all North American exchanges, three Canadian exchanges were the top three in per centage change of value traded between 1992 and 1993. The Alberta Stock Exchange (ASE) grew 118.3 per cent, TSE grew 93.1 per cent, and the Vancouver Stock Exchange (VSE) grew 89.9 per cent. Looking at volume over that period, ASE grew 156.7 per cent, TSE grew 103.1 per cent, and VSE grew 47.4 per cent.

TSE has grown steadily over the past 5 years. The number of TSE listed companies grew from 1193 in 1990 to 1209 as of April 1994. During that same time period, total quoted market value grew from $703.3 billion to $867.4 billion, and total outstanding shares grew from 37.8 billion to 44.5 billion. Trading levels have also increased during that period. Daily shares

337

traded grew from 22.5 million to 73.4 million, with daily value growing from $254.5 million to $866.6 million. New equity financing in Canada has also shown substantial growth, rising from $2.3 billion in 1990, to $11.6 billion in 1993. In fact, the $4.8 billion of new financings in the first four months of 1994, have more than doubled the total for all of 1990. TSE also reports that almost 22 per cent of adult Canadians invest directly in the stock market, up from 16 per cent in 1989. (Data from The Toronto Stock Exchange Annual Report, 1993.)

Market capitalization skyrocketed in Mexico from only $3.4 billion in 1983, to an astounding $139.1 billion in 1992. During that period, listed companies grew from 163 to 195, and the local BMV General Index rose from 2.5 to 1759.4. More recent data shows continued dramatic growth with the BMV General Index rising as high as 2822.98 in February 1994, and after dipping to about 2200 in late April, recovering to 2485.05 as of May 27, 1994. Some of the volatility in the Mexican stock market was attributable to reshuffling of foreign speculative investments between stocks and Mexican Government Bonds reacting to fluctuating interest rates, concerns over the passage of NAFTA, and exchange rate fluctuations. The number of Mexican stocks listed in their market rose from 21 in 1983 to 66 in 1992.

The positive developments in the Mexican equity markets parallel economic developments. Increased GDP in Mexico has been particularly noticeable since 1987 when it was $14.4 billion, rising to $282.6 billion in 1991. Mexico has also made significant strides in reducing inflation, having brought down the change in the consumer price index from 131.8 per cent in 1987 to only 15.5 per cent in 1992. (Data from Emerging Stock Markets Factbook, 1993.)

IV. Institutional investors

The investment company market has exploded in the US since 1980, with total net assets growing from $61.8 billion in 1980 to $2.07 trillion in 1993. Since 1980, investment company assets have doubled every four years. In 1991, aggregate investment company assets rose above assets in insurance companies for the first time and continued escalating toward the amount of aggregate bank deposits, which were reported at $2.4 trillion in 1992.

A mutual fund is a type of investment company that pools investors' funds, invests them in securities, and stands ready to redeem shares at net asset value. Mutual funds constitute the major portion of all US investment companies with

338

3,800 funds holding $1.6 trillion in assets as of 1992. Households have been significant escalating purchasers of mutual funds, quadrupling from 6 per cent in 1980 to 27 per cent of all households in 1992. The sustained period of low interest rates has been a major impetus for individuals to move their investment funds to mutual funds to achieve higher yields. While this growth has been significant, mutual funds in 1992 still held only 15.8 per cent of all US households' discretionary assets. The largest proportion is invested in deposits followed by corporate equities and bonds. However, mutual funds are the only component that has shown steady growth. (Data from Mutual Fund Fact Book (1993).)

The success of the mutual fund industry in the US has not always been so pronounced. In fact, during the bear market of 1973-1974, mutual fund assets actually shrank 40 per cent, casting significant doubts on their future prospects. The mutual fund industry recognized that potential investors had become concerned about risks associated with equities and responded with the relatively low risk, short-term money market funds that breathed renewed vigor into the mutual fund industry. Thereafter, significant new product innovations were developed to offer investors diverse choices of fund categories and investment objectives and risks.

The distribution of financial assets at mutual funds has changed considerably between 1980 and 1993. In 1980, almost 70 per cent of mutual fund assets were invested in corporate equities. That number dipped below 39 per cent in 1990 and now has rebounded, but still remains considerably below 50 per cent. Notwithstanding this reduced proportion of investment, corporate equities remains the largest investment of mutual funds at $667.3 billion of the $1,426.8 billion in 1993. US Government securities constitute more than 20 per cent of mutual fund assets ($289 billion), municipal securities over 15 per cent ($218 billion) and corporate and foreign bond, 13 per cent ($186 billion). Thus, mutual funds contribute significant amounts of capital to all the principal capital users. (Chart L)

The most significant increase in mutual funds assets has been in international and global funds, which skyrocketed from $5.2 billion in 1985 to $152.5 billion in 1993, an unparalleled 30-fold increase. (Chart L.) The most recent data for April 1994 from the mutual fund industry's trade association shows strong investor preference for diversified international funds. It has been estimated that over 480 investment companies have a majority of their assets invested in securities of non-US issuers. In addition sixty-two funds with $10 billion in assets concentrate their investments in emerging markets in Latin America, Asia and Eastern Europe.

Over the past decade, US mutual funds have also become significant investors in mortgage-backed securities, including GNMAs, FNMAs, and FHLMCs. Approximately 140 mutual fund portfolios with almost $100 billion in assets invested primarily in mortgage-backed securities. Thus, mutual funds have contributed significant capital from diversified areas to the US housing industry.

Mutual funds have also begun investing in derivatives, including options, futures, swaps and other instruments. Often, these instruments are used to hedge against risks of currency fluctuations, interest rate volatility or declines in stock or bond prices. They may also be used for speculative purposes. A recent survey of derivatives held by long-term (non-money market) funds showed the total market value of the participating funds was $7.5 billion. This amounted to 2.13 per cent of the total net assets of the participating funds reporting derivatives and .78 per cent of total net assets of all funds participating in the survey. The total notional amount of these derivatives was $54.3 billion, representing 15.5 per cent of the total net assets of participating funds reporting derivatives. The survey also found that fixed income funds were the most significant users accounting for 84 per cent of derivatives used by all the funds in the survey with derivatives. While this survey suggests that mutual fund use of derivatives is quite limited, both the Securities and Exchange Commission and the industry in the United States are conducting studies to learn more about the extent of mutual fund activities in these sophisticated financial products.

Another method of analyzing the changing structure of mutual funds is to examine the per cent distribution of total net assets by type of fund. Comparing distributions in 1982 and 1992, one finds a significant realignment between taxable money market funds, decreasing from 69.6 per cent to 28.0 per cent, and bond and income funds, increasing from 8.9 per cent to 36.3 per cent. Equity funds also grew from 17.1 per cent to 29.7 per cent. Net sales of equity, and bond and income funds reached a record high of $197 billion in 1992. These shifts reflected the economic changes from double digit interest rates, low stock prices and a recession in 1982, to record low interest rates, escalating stock prices, and economic growth a decade later. (Data from Mutual Funds Fact Book (1993).)

Diversity in investment opportunities and flexibility to quickly and easily realign investments have been recent requirements of investors. Responding to these needs, the mutual fund industry has dramatically increased the number of funds available. In 1980, there were only 564 funds. In 1992, that number had escalated to 3848, a dramatic 600 per cent increase. The industry also worked to facilitate selection and moving among different types of funds. A major innovation to accomplish this goal was the organization of most mutual funds into large groups of mutual fund portfolios, or "complexes" with a common investment adviser, underwriter, or sponsor. These complexes have used technological advancements to facilitate speedy and easy transfers among the many funds with differing objectives within the complex. There are currently approximately 600 complexes with the largest consisting of over 200 portfolios holding over $200 billion in assets. Taking advantage of the ease of moving funds, investors began leaving bond funds earlier this year as increasing interest rates caused the funds to drop in value. While bond funds had been growing steadily throughout 1993 and into January 1994, investors pulled $8.7 billion out of bond funds in February 1994, $7.7 billion, in March and $4.8 billion in April. This responsiveness to economic conditions is evidence to some degree of increased customer sophistication and awareness, as well as the ease of realigning one's investments.

Further evidence of investor interest in diversification and quick response to changing economic conditions is the fact that between 1991 and 1992, there was a 164 per cent increase in Flexible Portfolio Funds. A Flexible Portfolio Fund may be invested by the portfolio manager in any amount of stocks, bonds or money market instruments depending upon economic and market conditions. (Data from Mutual Fund Fact Book, 1993).

Canada has a growing mutual fund industry with assets totaling $57.9 billion and 5.3 million accounts as of September 30, 1992. Mexico likewise has prospects for development in this area. With the passage of the North American Free Trade Agreement, it is expected that movement of funds among these three nations will become more prevalent.

The mutual fund industry has over the years demonstrated immediate responsiveness to investors. It has broadened product lines, increased flexibility and diversity, and expanded services to accommodate customer needs. This responsiveness has been rewarded as mutual funds have advanced from a fledgling infant industry to a principal financial mainstay in the United States.

Before leaving the discussion of institutional investors, we should take a look at a relatively newly expanding phenomenon, the "hedge fund". Hedge funds are pooled investment vehicles, often organized as limited partnerships, that are not registered under the securities laws as public corporations, investment companies or broker-dealers. Therefore, there are no precise figures of hedge fund activity in the United States.

There has been some recent concern regarding market volatility, systemic risk, and counterparty credit risk associated with hedge fund activity. Some believe that because the activities of these firms account for significant trading volume, added to the fact that they are unregulated, may be highly leveraged, and their trading activity is confidential, they may be able to disproportionately influence market movements.

In addition, some are concerned that the failure of a large, highly leveraged hedge funds might precipitate the failure of creditors or counterparties of a hedge fund. However, there is no actual data substantiating this fear. In fact, the US Securities and Exchange Commission concluded that through the recent period of market volatility in the United States, no major broker dealer had excessive credit exposure to its hedge fund customers. The Commission estimated that the exposure of major US securities firms to large hedge fund customers is less than one per cent of total industry capital of approximately $70 billion.

In general, hedge funds are investment vehicle created in response to the needs of sophisticated investors. These investors have significant funds and are willing to risk those funds on more speculative investments in hope of achieving significantly greater profitability than may be available with more conservative investments. While there are no precise numbers, anecdotal evidence suggests that this is a popular and significantly growing investment alternative.

V. Securitization

Securitization has had a significant impact on market structure in the United States. The most dramatic growth has taken place in the mortgage loan sector. It is not difficult to understand why the mortgage-backed securities (MBS) market grew so phenomenally. This is a convenient vehicle for providing local borrowers with ready access to the depth and liquidity of institutional investors and the broader capital markets. As local portfolio lenders, such as banks and thrifts were pulling back in the late 1980's, the mortgage market benefitted from access to national, and indeed global, markets through securitization. This financing technique permits generally illiquid assets to be pooled and converted into capital market instruments. Sponsors benefit because they can better manage their loan portfolios. They can convert financial assets into cash, increase liquidity, diversify credit risk, strengthen their financial condition, and gain access to alternative sources of funding. Investors benefit from risk diversification and fairly safe investments with good rates of return. Homeowners and other borrowers benefit from reduced costs and increased sources of funding. Intermediaries also benefit from fees and other profits gained in structuring and selling these securitized assets.

Most of the growth in the MBS market has been in agency or Government Sponsored Enterprise (GSE) related MBSs, which clearly dominate with an estimated 95 per cent of the entire MBS market. In 1980, the aggregate amount of MBSs issued or guaranteed by the Government National Mortgage Association, FHLMC, and FNMA was only $142.3 billion. By 1993, the amount grew more than 10-fold, to $1.55 trillion. The $1.55 trillion in MBSs in the US accounted for almost one-third of the total outstanding mortgage debt. Breaking this down to types of loans, we find that 1-4 family residential real estate loans have the highest per centage of securitization, with multifamily MBSs running a distant second, and commercial mortgages remaining virtually untouched. Of the $2.9 trillion in outstanding mortgages on 1-4 family residences in 1992, approximately $1.2 trillion, or 42 per cent, was securitized. Since new originations are being securitized at a substantially higher rate, the overall number is expected to rise. Turning to mortgages on multifamily residences, only $25 billion or eight per cent of the $300 billion in 1992 was securitized. Finally, of the $750 billion of commercial real estate loans, it was estimated that less than five per cent had been securitized in 1992. These two areas are clearly targets for significant future potential growth in securitizations. (Data from Federal Reserve Board Flow of Funds.)

Because of the success of FNMA and FHLMC in developing the secondary market for residential real estate, some have suggested the expansion of their role to cover other real estate areas and even asset-backed securities in other sectors. Others suggest the creation of new similar government sponsored enterprises. While GSEs did contribute substantially to the success of the secondary market in residential real estate, concerns have been raised with respect to expanding their role. It could displace a fully private market, which is under development, and could limit innovation. Moreover, it would add to the more than a trillion dollars of GSE securities, as to which there is at least the perception of an implicit US Government guarantee. It is questionable whether there will be any future expansion of GSEs to cover new markets.

The MBS market in the United States is barely 25 years old and it has already reached the milestone of surpassing the trillion and one-half dollar mark. It has been one of the premier growth areas of the 1980's and it has the potential for substantial future growth. The US mortgage market is no longer dependent upon local conditions and constraints, but through securitization can now access institutional investors in the national and global capital markets. The securitization trend has also spread to other markets, including credit cards, automobile receivables, and other areas. New product development, technological advances, and intensified competition are expected to produce continued innovation and expansion in this fluid market.

VI. Banks and capital markets

Since the 1930's, cross-industry combinations between bank and securities activities in the United States have been inhibited by a Depression-era statutory scheme, principally contained in the Glass-Steagall Act. Notwithstanding the continued existence of the statutory provisions, the requirements of a competitive financial services market place combined with more permissive regulatory interpretations have substantially eroded the barriers of Glass Steagall.

The role of banks and traditional financial institutions has undergone some fundamental changes. These institutions no longer simply represent a separate conduit for capital flows largely independent of the broader capital markets. Rather, they are now more significantly involved in working with and through the capital markets to facilitate the efficient flow of capital. Commercial banks in the United States can now engage either directly or through subsidiaries or affiliates in virtually all securities activities. They are directly and substantially involved in MBS and US Government securities activities. However, there are some remaining restrictions. Underwriting and dealing in corporate debt and equity securities must be performed in separate so-called Section 20 affiliates, subject to credit and funding "firewalls" and revenue limitations. The principal prohibited activity for US banks is sponsoring, organizing, or controlling a mutual fund; however, even that activity may be performed if structured within a subsidiary of a state-chartered bank that is not a member of the Federal Reserve System. Securities firms in the United States are legally prohibited from entering the traditional bank deposit market. However, they now have customer accounts with checking privileges, permit the use of ATM cards, and engage in many activities similar to, and therefore competitive with, bank products.

Since the US Federal Reserve Board has only recently begun permitting banks to engage in virtually the full range of securities activities, the growth in this area has been dramatic. As recently as 1986, the Federal Reserve had not yet authorized bank holding company Section 20 affiliates to engage in securities activities and there were consequently no assets dedicated to these operations.

344

By 1987, eight banking organizations were authorized to operate Section 20 affiliates and these Section 20's had aggregate assets of $17.2 billion. By year-end 1993, that number had risen to 30 organizations with $155.8 billion in assets. Their 1993 underwriting revenues were concentrated in debt underwriting, with $428.5 million of the $437.2 million in reported revenues resulting from that activity. Total revenues were $8.97 billion, primarily in Government securities and other permissible activities, as dictated by regulatory prescription.

The participation of banking organizations in mutual fund activities is another area showing remarkable growth. A decade ago, banks were just beginning to receive authorizations from bank regulators for such operations. Banking organizations are now permitted to perform all the major mutual fund activities except, for the most part, mutual fund distribution and sponsorship. The permissible activities include serving as investment adviser, transfer agent, custodian, registrar, and administrator of a fund, and the brokering of mutual funds.

Customer desires for higher yields and banks' financial ability to venture into new areas have propelled banks into the mutual fund business. Banks found expanding into mutual funds to be a low risk way to earn fees while leveraging off their retail distribution networks, and at the same time preserving their customer base. Bank mutual fund activities proceed in a number of ways. Some banks have developed their own group of proprietary funds and others offer private-label funds created by investment companies. Some banks sell nationally known funds such as Fidelity, Nuveen, or Dreyfus. Finally, a number of banks have entered into networking arrangements whereby a broker-dealer provides securities services to the bank's customers and gives a per centage of the commission to the bank. Banks benefit from fees as well as being able to keep customer relationships.

A recent survey showed that about one-third of all mutual funds are available through bank sales. That is, 1,100 of 3,523 funds in 1991, and 1,253 of 3,657 funds as of June 30, 1992. New sales of long term funds sold through banking organizations amounted to $28.1 billion in 1991 and $23.7 billion for the first half of 1992, representing 13 and 14 per cent of total new sales of long-term funds respectively. Banks are even more dominant in new sales of money market funds, having sold $577.1 billion in 1991, and $385.6 billion in the first half of 1992, accounting for approximately on-third of the new sales in this market over both time periods. The assets of money market and long-term mutual funds attributable to bank sales represent approximately 12 per cent of all industry assets. Assets attributable to bank sales were $158.2 billion of the

$1,360.8 billion total in 1991, and $175.5 billion of the $1,480.5 billion through June 30, 1992. Currently 118 bank subsidiaries advise over 1000 mutual funds and bank mutual funds have $219.4 billion in assets. (See, Testimony of Arthur Levitt, Chairman of the Securities and Exchange Commission, concerning H.R. 3447, April 14, 1994.) A number of analysts have suggested that banking organizations will have up to 50 per cent of the market share by the end of the decade.

As the data demonstrate, banking organizations have made substantial inroads into securities activities in the United States over the past decade. While securities firms are prohibited from taking traditional deposits in the US, they offer customers full service accounts with checking privileges. Securities firms also underwrite and sell commercial paper and have begun to make commercial loans. Thus, each industry has penetrated the market of the other and both industries compete for much of the same customer base.

Even the major inroads made by banks and securities firms into the others' market have not been without costs. Financial firms and their regulators continue to struggle under the restrictions of Glass Steagall, a law framed over a half century ago when the financial world and its problems were much different. All combined bank and securities operations are done within a complex structure created to conform to the restrictions of Glass Steagall, rather than as a result of rational regulatory and market responses. This not only creates operational inefficiencies but may also result in regulatory risks. By eliminating unnecessary constraints, the market will perform more efficiently. This will, in turn, benefit investors, consumers, and the economy.

Legal and regulatory requirements can and do influence market developments. Even a regulatory structure that was perfect at the time of its inception, can over the years become unworkable or at least in need of adjustment. This is especially true in a dynamic market where the proliferation of new products and technological advances create market conditions that were not envisioned at the time the regulatory structure was created. While the linkages between banking and securities activities will no doubt continue to expand, they will not achieve optimal efficiency and productivity until outdated legal restrictions are removed.

The laws of both Mexico and Canada are more flexible than those of the United States in permitting the integration of financial services. Mexico authorizes its banks to engage in securities trading, both on an exchange and over-the-counter. There is a pending proposal to permit options and futures trading, and both brokers and banking institutions are authorized to enter into

346

contracts with their customers to trade forward foreign exchange and options contracts in international markets. In addition, banks may engage in real estate activities through affiliates. Canada restructured its financial services industry in 1992, and now allows its banks to engage in unlimited securities, insurance, trust company and real estate activities through subsidiaries. Banks are also permitted to hold up to 10 per cent of any industrial firm, providing that its aggregate shareholdings do not exceed 70 per cent of its capital. Conversely, industrial firms are permitted to hold up to 10 per cent of any bank. There has already been significant movement towards establishing financial conglomerates that combine these various sectors of the financial services market. Canada also removed many of the financial and administrative burdens that kept foreign entities form establishing a banking presence, thus encouraging increased foreign entry across their borders.

VII. Derivatives markets

A discussion of the changing financial structure of the world's capital markets would not be complete without an analysis of the revolutionary changes in the derivatives market. In general terms, a derivative is a financial product that derives its value from another product. Derivatives include options, futures, swaps, forwards, and a multitude of other exotic and innovative products structured to meet the specific needs of an ultimate user. While certain relatively simple derivatives products have existed and traded for decades, it is only during the 1990's that the explosive growth in volume, complexity and diversity have centered worldwide attention on these products.

There are a number of economic and financial developments that may account for the recent proliferation of derivatives. First, with the internationalization and diversification of business activities, there is a business need for derivatives as risk management tools to protect against foreign currency and interest rate risks, and changes in commodity prices or other products. Investors are likewise seeking more cost effective and liquid means to hedge against portfolio risks, thus achieving their desired exposure and matching portfolio investment strategies. In addition to serving as risk management tools, intermediaries or dealers have created derivatives for arbitrage transactions and many have designed products to bet the market, thus speculating in search of profitability that exceeds usual market profitability. The latter activity may be particularly widespread when interest rates and other returns are low.

The highest notional value recently reported for derivatives contracts was the $17.64 trillion figure for 1992 cited by the US Government Accounting

347

Office (GAO). GAO showed a 145 per cent increase since 1989, when the notional amount was $7.2 trillion. The vast majority of underlyings were interest rates, at about 62 per cent of the 1992 total. Foreign exchange derivatives ranked second at 37 per cent and equity and commodities derivatives combined amounted to a minuscule one per cent.

According to information filed with the US Securities and Exchange Commission, showing more conservative amounts than those of GAO, major US non-bank affiliated broker-dealers and their affiliates showed $5.1 trillion in derivatives in 1993, a 38 per cent increase over the $3.7 trillion at the end of fiscal year 1992.

Looking at derivative product types in 1992, GAO reported forwards with 42 per cent, futures 18 per cent, options 13 per cent and swaps 27 per cent of all contracts. Over the period 1989 to 1992, all types of derivative products increased at similar relatively high rates, approximately 150 per cent. While notional amounts of derivatives are often cited as reflective of the explosive growth in this market, it is important to note that the risks inherent in derivatives are only a fraction of notional values. In fact, a recent study of the Federal Reserve Bank of New York estimated the risk, referred to as replacement risk, at about 3.5 per cent of the notional amount.

A unique characteristic of derivatives activities is that they are currently concentrated in a very small number of sophisticated, global, highly capitalized conglomerates. A recent report sponsored by the international financial policy organization, the Group of Thirty, provided that eight US bank dealers accounted for 56 per cent of worldwide interest rate and currency swaps in notional amounts as of December 1991. Data from US bank regulators indicates that seven US bank derivatives dealers accounted for more than 90 per cent (notional values) of all derivatives activities in US banks in 1992. Data filed with the US Securities and Exchange Commission showed similar concentration in securities firms, with the top five firms accounting for 87 per cent (notional values) of securities firms' derivatives activities.

As earlier stated, the risk exposure associated with derivatives activities is only a small fraction of the notional amount. The GAO analysis indicated that credit exposures of the major US bank dealers with respect to derivatives activities represented less exposure than their lending activities. Aggregate replacement cost or estimated exposure for derivatives activities at securities firms reporting to the SEC surged 70 per cent from fiscal year 1992 to year-end 1993, from $18.2 billion to $30.9 billion. While this increase was significant, it is still an extremely small fraction of notional value, it is primarily confined to investment grade entities, is short-term, and is not concentrated within a particular counterparty.

The 1994 GAO study also surveyed users of derivatives products to determine the amount and reason for use. Among those surveyed, the GAO found private pension plans to be the most active users, with about 75 per cent of the respondents using derivatives. They reportedly used futures, options, and foreign exchange derivatives more than interest rate swaps and forwards. On the other hand, local governments in the survey principally used interest rate swaps. The GAO survey also found that hedging was the most popular reason for using derivatives, although maximizing investment returns was also of significance.

The development and expansion of the derivatives markets have led to increased market linkages among stock, stock option, stock index option, and stock index futures markets. Recent reports, including *The Report of the Presidential Task Force on Market Mechanisms* (January 1988), *and The October 1987 Market Break, A Report by the Division of Market Regulation of the United States Securities and Exchange Commission* (February 1988), provide data and analyses to substantiate this phenomenon.

The derivatives market in the United States has over recent years, developed new foreign-based products. For example, the American Stock Exchange has introduced the Hong Kong Option Index and a number of the exchanges have listed securities issued by registered closed-end management investment companies that invest in foreign securities. A number of new foreign currency options have also been listed. Internationalization is clearly an expanding feature of the derivatives market.

While some concern has been raised about the risks associated with derivatives, a variety of studies, such as the Group of Thirty report on derivatives, have explored the developments necessary to address derivatives risk. All agree that institutions engaged in derivatives activities need to establish sound risk management systems. Supervisors of financial institutions need the expertise to assess such sophisticated risk management systems. Finally, improvements need to be made in legal and financial infrastructures supporting derivatives. For example, netting must be established on a sound legal basis in relevant jurisdictions and clearance and settlement systems for derivatives and related products need to be improved. These efforts continue.

Based upon current data, derivatives appear to be the fastest developing financial product of the 1990's. They have demonstrated dramatic growth, increasing complexity, and significant linkages of global markets. While they are revolutionizing today's markets with sophisticated risk management techniques, they are also raising some systemic concerns among regulators. With intense customer demands, and technological advancements that permit innovations, these complex products will no doubt continue to proliferate despite the intense scrutiny.

The forces underlying structural changes in the capital markets are not likely to abate in the future. These changes will continue within already highly developed markets and likely spread to developing capital markets, as well. While there is always some measure of risk in rapid change, increased efficiencies in capital flows are likely to benefit global economic activity in the years ahead.

Private Investors In U.S. Government Debt
($ Billions)

	Total Gross Public Debt	Commercial Banks	Insurance Companies	Other Companies	State & Local Treasuries	Individuals	Foreign and International	Other	Money Market Funds
80	930.2	112.1	24.0	19.3	84.4	117.1	129.7	126.3	3.5
81	1028.7	111.4	29.0	19.9	85.6	110.8	136.6	167.8	21.5
82	1197.1	131.4	39.1	24.5	127.8	116.5	149.4	217.8	42.6
83	1410.7	188.8	56.7	39.7	155.1	133.4	166.3	259.8	22.8
84	1663.0	183.4	76.4	50.1	179.4	143.8	192.9	360.6	25.9
85	1945.9	192.2	93.2	59.0	224.0	154.8	214.6	434.2	25.1
86	2214.8	203.5	105.6	68.8	262.8	162.7	263.4	506.6	28.0
87	2431.7	201.5	104.9	84.6	284.6	171.3	299.7	584.0	14.6
88	2684.4	193.8	111.2	86.5	313.6	186.6	362.1	587.2	11.8
89	2953.0	164.9	125.1	93.4	487.5	216.4	392.9	520.7	14.9
90	3364.8	171.5	142.0	108.9	490.4	233.8	458.4	637.7	45.4
91	3801.7	233.4	168.7	150.8	520.3	263.9	491.8	651.3	80.0
92	4177.0	294.0	197.5	192.5	534.8	289.2	549.7	702.4	79.4
93	4535.7								

Source: Flow of Funds, Board of Governors of the Federal Reserve System. The remainder of gross public debt is held by U.S. agency trust funds and Federal Reserve Banks.

Distribution of Outstanding Corporate Equities

($ Billions)

Chart B

Period	Total	House— holds	Life Insurance Companies	Other Insurance Companies	Private Pension Funds	Municipal Pension Funds	Mutual Funds	Other Domestic	Foreign
1980	1,568.9	975.4	46.3	32.3	223.5	44.3	42.4	140.1	64.6
1981	1,456.1	879.5	46.2	32.4	218.5	47.8	37.4	129.9	644.4
1982	1,642.0	941.8	52.9	38.5	282.9	60.2	49.4	140.0	76.3
1983	1,956.2	1,071.0	62.2	48.1	350.3	89.6	74.4	164.2	96.4
1984	1,887.2	994.1	60.3	44.7	359.0	96.5	80.6	155.9	96.1
1985	2,404.1	1,261.1	74.0	57.0	464.4	120.1	113.7	188.2	125.6
1986	2,794.2	1,436.5	76.4	61.2	550.9	150.2	161.2	188.9	168.9
1987	2,792.4	1,402.7	80.5	65.1	538.9	169.6	181.7	178.3	175.6
1988	3,105.5	1,528.5	89.3	71.4	609.5	219.7	187.6	198.5	201.0
1989	3,812.9	1,831.2	106.5	84.0	734.7	300.1	250.5	245.3	260.6
1990	3,543.7	1,738.7	97.9	79.9	657.6	296.1	233.2	218.6	221.7
1991	4,869.4	2,482.8	117.9	94.1	888.5	386.6	351.1	276.5	271.9
1992	5,540.6	2,884.3	134.6	97.3	962.1	448.9	451.7	261.5	300.2
1993	6,120.7	3,009.4	167.7	111.8	1,079.4	506.7	667.3	257.8	320.6

Source: Flow of Funds, Board of Governors of the Federal Reserve System.

Chart C

FOREIGN TRANSACTIONS IN U.S. BONDS
($ Millions)

	1981	1982	1983	1984	1985	1986	1987	1988	1989	1990	1991	1992	1993
Foreign Purchases	17,304	21,639	24,049	39,296	86,587	123,169	105,856	86,381	120,346	118,764	153,096	214,779	283,651
Foreign Sales	12,272	20,188	23,092	26,399	42,455	72,520	78,312	58,417	86,254	102,047	125,637	175,342	217,637
Net Purchase or sales (−)	5,033	1,451	957	12,897	44,132	50,648	27,544	27,964	34,093	16,717	27,459	39,437	66,014

Source: Flow of Funds, Board of Governors of the Federal Reserve System. These figures include corporate bonds, state and local bonds, securities of U.S. government and corporations, and debt securities sold abroad by U.S. corporations to finance direct investments abroad.

Net New Issues of Equities, Bonds, and Municipals
Chart D
($ Billions)

Period	Corporate Equities	Corporate and Foreign Bonds	Municipal Securities
1980	14.9	39.6	23.9
1981	−10.4	36.1	32.9
1982	8.2	52.1	53.1
1983	27.2	45.8	54.4
1984	−70.9	86.8	58.7
1985	−65.6	140.4	178.6
1986	−67.6	219.4	45.7
1987	−57.3	162.5	83.5
1988	−104.7	159	53.7
1989	−98.1	116	65.3
1990	−45.7	109.2	57.3
1991	60.1	149.6	69.6
1992	77.3	150.1	65.7
1993	121.6	200.7	59.4

Source: Flow of Funds, Board of Governors of the Federal Reserve System.

Corporate Debt and Equity Offerings

($ Billions)

Chart E

Period	All Corporate Issues	All Debt Issues	Corporate Debt Issues Investment Grade Non-convertible					Convertible	High-Yield
			All Investment Grade	All Non-Convertible	Mortgage Backed	Asset Backed	Other		
1980	57.7	41.6	37.3	35.9	0.5	0.0	35.4	1.4	4.3
1981	56.5	40.3	37.0	34.4	0.5	0.0	33.9	2.6	3.3
1982	66.4	44.6	40.2	38.9	1.3	0.0	37.7	1.3	4.4
1983	99.3	52.1	41.0	38.6	8.6	0.0	30.0	2.4	11.1
1984	83.4	69.3	53.7	51.2	12.1	0.0	39.2	2.4	15.7
1985	137.8	104.5	86.5	82.8	19.6	1.2	62.0	3.7	18.0
1986	284.8	227.8	187.5	185.8	57.8	10.0	117.9	1.8	40.2
1987	272.2	219.4	184.3	181.4	82.5	9.1	89.8	2.9	35.1
1988	274.0	236.7	206.7	205.8	98.9	14.3	92.7	0.8	30.0
1989	305.2	274.6	247.1	244.0	110.6	24.3	109.1	3.1	27.5
1990	311.9	288.0	285.3	281.9	134.0	42.1	105.8	3.4	2.7
1991	584.2	508.3	494.9	490.9	250.2	50.1	190.6	4.1	13.4
1992 Q1	221.0	191.8	182.7	181.5	103.3	9.0	69.2	1.2	9.0
1992 Q2	221.4	192.6	179.9	179.4	100.8	10.8	67.7	0.6	12.7
1992 Q3	231.2	210.5	199.3	199.0	107.3	13.7	78.0	0.3	11.2
1992 Q4	177.1	153.7	143.8	143.5	65.3	17.4	60.8	0.3	9.9
1992 YR	850.7	748.6	705.8	703.4	376.7	50.9	275.7	2.5	42.8
1993 Q1	268.0	239.4	224.2	223.9	97.3	12.6	114.0	0.2	15.3
1993 Q2	260.5	226.8	212.3	212.0	101.2	13.3	97.5	0.3	14.5
1993 Q3	295.6	262.2	248.8	247.9	133.9	14.1	99.8	0.9	13.4
1993 Q4	228.8	193.7	175.9	174.6	88.4	19.3	66.8	1.3	17.8
1993 YR	1052.8	922.1	861.2	858.4	420.9	59.3	378.2	2.8	60.9

Note: Firm commitment offerings only.
Source: Securities Data Company

355

Distribution of Outstanding Corporate Equities

Chart F

($ Billions)

Period	Total	House-holds	Life Insurance Companies	Other Insurance Companies	Private Pension Funds	Municipal Pension Funds	Mutual Funds	Other Domestic	Foreign
1980	1,568.9	975.4	46.3	32.3	223.5	44.3	42.4	140.1	64.6
1981	1,456.1	879.5	46.2	32.4	218.5	47.8	37.4	129.9	644.4
1982	1,642.0	941.8	52.9	38.5	282.9	60.2	49.4	140.0	76.3
1983	1,956.2	1,071.0	62.2	48.1	350.3	89.6	74.4	164.2	96.4
1984	1,887.2	994.1	60.3	44.7	359.0	96.5	80.6	155.9	96.1
1985	2,404.1	1,261.1	74.0	57.0	464.4	120.1	113.7	188.2	125.6
1986	2,794.2	1,436.5	76.4	61.2	550.9	150.2	161.2	188.9	168.9
1987	2,792.4	1,402.7	80.5	65.1	538.9	169.6	181.7	178.3	175.6
1988	3,105.5	1,528.5	89.3	71.4	609.5	219.7	187.6	198.5	201.0
1989	3,812.9	1,831.2	106.5	84.0	734.7	300.1	250.5	245.3	260.6
1990	3,543.7	1,738.7	97.9	79.9	657.6	296.1	233.2	218.6	221.7
1991	4,869.4	2,482.8	117.9	94.1	888.5	386.6	351.1	276.5	271.9
1992	5,540.6	2,884.3	134.6	97.3	962.1	448.9	451.7	261.5	300.2
1993	6,120.7	3,009.4	167.7	111.8	1,079.4	506.7	667.3	257.8	320.6

Source: Flow of Funds, Board of Governors of the Federal Reserve System.

Corporate Equity Offerings

($ Billions)

Chart G

Period	All Equity Issues	Equity Issues Common Stock All Common Stock	Seasoned	All IPOs	IPOs Not Fund 1/	Fund 1/	Preferred Stock
1980	16.1	12.8	11.5	1.4	1.4	0.0	3.2
1981	16.3	14.6	11.5	3.1	3.1	0.1	1.7
1982	21.8	16.5	15.1	1.3	1.3	0.0	5.3
1983	47.2	38.7	26.3	12.5	12.4	0.0	8.5
1984	14.1	10.0	6.1	3.9	3.8	0.1	4.1
1985	33.3	24.7	16.2	8.5	8.3	0.1	8.6
1986	57.0	43.1	20.9	22.2	18.0	4.2	13.9
1987	52.8	41.5	14.6	26.8	17.1	9.7	11.3
1988	37.3	29.7	6.0	23.6	5.7	17.9	7.6
1989	30.6	22.9	9.2	13.7	6.1	7.6	7.7
1990	23.8	19.2	9.0	10.1	4.5	5.6	4.7
1991	75.9	56.0	30.9	25.1	16.4	8.7	19.9
1992 Q1	29.2	21.9	10.9	11.1	7.9	3.2	7.3
1992 Q2	28.8	21.2	11.4	9.8	6.9	2.9	7.6
1992 Q3	20.7	14.5	4.7	9.9	4.5	5.4	6.2
1992 Q4	23.4	15.2	6.0	9.2	4.7	4.5	8.2
1992 YR	102.1	72.8	32.9	39.9	24.0	15.9	29.3
1993 Q1	28.6	22.8	10.7	12.0	7.5	4.5	5.8
1993 Q2	33.6	24.7	9.8	14.9	10.8	4.0	9.0
1993 Q3	33.4	25.2	11.6	13.6	9.3	4.3	8.2
1993 Q4	35.1	29.7	12.8	16.9	14.0	2.9	5.4
1993 YR	130.7	102.3	44.9	57.4	41.6	15.9	28.4

1/ Fund: closed-end mutual funds.
Note: Firm commitment offerings only.

357

NYSE

	Reported Share Volume (MILS.)	Value of Shares Traded ($ Mils.)	Average Daily Volume (Mils.)	Average Price of Shares Traded
1980	11,352	$374,909	44.9	$33.00
1981	11,854	389,219	46.9	32.80
1982	16,458	488,396	65.1	29.70
1983	21,590	765,275	85.3	35.40
1984	23,071	764,738	91.1	33.10
1985	27,511	970,479	109.2	35.30
1986	35,680	1,374,350	141.0	38.50
1987	47,801	1,873,597	188.9	39.20
1988	40,850	1,356,050	161.5	33.20
1989	41,699	1,542,845	165.5	37.00
1990	39,665	1,325,332	156.8	33.40
1991	45,266	1,520,164	178.9	33.60
1992	51,376	1,745,466	202.3	34.00
1993	66,923	2,283,390	264.5	34.10

Regional Stock Exchanges

	Share Volume (MILS.)	Value of Shares Traded ($ Mils.)	Average Daily Volume (Mils.)	Average Price of Shares Traded
1980	1,437	$43,485	5.7	$30.26
1981	1,595	48,390	6.3	30.34
1982	2,405	67,764	9.5	28.18
1983	3,368	106,653	13.3	31.67
1984	3,722	115,143	14.5	30.98
1985	4,709	150,252	18.7	31.91
1986	6,080	212,666	24.0	34.98
1987	7,237	248,306	28.6	34.31
1988	5,880	175,284	23.2	29.81
1989	6,708	215,523	26.6	32.13
1990	6,208	177,010	24.5	28.51
1991	7,255	204,292	28.7	28.16
1992	8,526	234,147	33.6	27.46
1993	9,809	284,569	38.8	29.01

AMEX

	Share Volume (MILS.)	Value of Shares Traded ($ Mils.)	Average Daily Volume (Mils.)	Average Price of Shares Traded
1980	1,626	$35,788	6.4	$22.01
1981	1,343	24,520	5.3	18.25
1982	1,338	21,057	5.3	15.74
1983	2,081	31,237	8.2	15.01
1984	1,545	21,376	6.1	13.83
1985	2,101	27,839	8.3	13.25
1986	2,979	45,357	11.8	15.23
1987	3,506	50,470	13.9	14.40
1988	2,515	30,922	9.9	12.29
1989	3,125	44,402	12.4	14.21
1990	3,329	37,715	13.2	11.33
1991	3,367	40,919	13.3	12.15
1992	3,596	42,238	14.2	11.75
1993	4,582	56,737	18.1	12.38

NASDAQ

	Share Volume (MILS.)	Value of Shares Traded ($ Mils.)	Average Daily Volume (Mils.)	Average Price of Shares Traded
1980	6,692	$68,669	26.4	$10.26
1981	7,823	71,057	30.9	9.08
1982	8,432	84,189	33.3	9.98
1983	15,909	188,285	62.9	11.86
1984	15,159	153,454	59.9	10.12
1985	20,699	233,454	82.1	11.28
1986	28,737	378,216	113.6	13.16
1987	37,890	499,855	149.8	13.19
1988	31,070	347,089	122.8	11.17
1989	33,530	431,381	133.1	12.87
1990	33,380	452,430	131.9	13.55
1991	41,311	693,852	163.3	16.80
1992	48,455	890,785	190.8	18.38
1993	66,540	1,350,100	263.0	20.29

SOURCE: *Securities Industry Association 1994 Fact Book*

Chart I

1993 MARKET SHARE DATA: NYSE STOCKS *				
	Average Shares Per Day (In Millions)	Average Shares Per Day (%)	Average Transactions Per Day	Average Transactions Per Day (%)
NYSE Regular Hours	264.8	78.53%	186,410	70.48%
Crossing Session I	0.2	0.06%		
Crossing Session II	4.4	1.30%		
ALL REGIONALS	34.3	10.17%	52,699	19.92%
BSE	4.2	1.25%	6,941	2.62%
CHX	13.1	3.88%	16,202	6.13%
PHLX	4.8	1.42%	7,609	2.88%
PSE	8.4	2.49%	15,602	5.90%
CSE	3.8	1.13%	6,345	2.40%
All Regionals Excluding CSE	30.5	9.05%	46,354	17.53%
THIRD MARKET Regular Hours **	19.6	5.81%	24,847	9.39%
After Hours	0.9	0.27%		
PTS Regular Hours	3.6	1.07%	543	0.21%
PTS After Hours	1.1	0.33%		
OVERSEAS BY NYSE FIRMS Program Trades	5.9	1.75%		
OTC (non–program)	1.7	0.50%		
Foreign Exchanges (non–program)	0.7	0.21%		
TOTAL	337.2	100.00%	264,499	100.00%

*   These figures are for the first six months of 1993 (125 trading days), except for non–program foreign data, which uses a daily average from May, June, and July 1993. The figures do not include trades executed in the fourth market (i.e., those directly between institutions without using an exchange or a broker dealer).

**   Regular hours refers to the operating hours of the NYSE. After hours trades are trades executed outside of the operating hours of the NYSE.

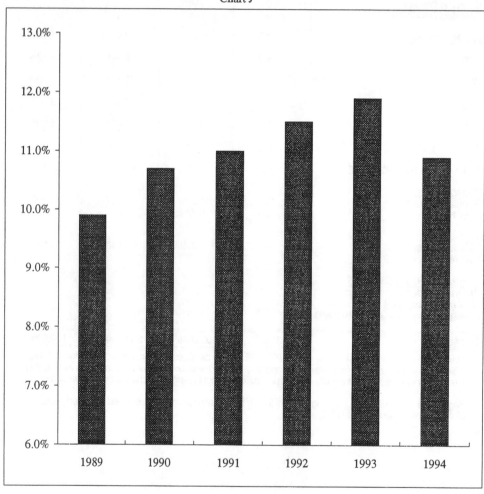

Notes: . Beginning June 1991, data includes crossing session II volume.
               1989-1993 figures revised to include data not available at time of publication of NYSE Weekly
               Program Trading Reports.
               1994 data is year to date, through 28 October 1994.
Source: NYSE.

Chart K

Foreign transactions in U.S. Corporate securities
(million dollars)

	1981	1982	1983	1984	1985	1986	1987	1988	1989	1990	1991	1992
Foreign purchase	40 686	41 881	69 770	59 834	81 995	148 101	249 122	181 185	213 778	173 293	211 207	221 251
Foreign sales	38 830	37 981	64 360	62 814	77 054	129 382	232 849	183 185	203 386	188 126	200 116	226 422
Net purchase or sales (-)	5 803	3 901	5 410	-2 980	4 941	18 719	16 272	-2 000	10 392	-15 126	11 091	-5 171

Source: **Flow of Funds, Board of Governors of the Federal Reserve System**

Chart L

Distribution of Financial Assets at Mutual Funds
($ Billions)

Period	Total	Cash	Corporate Equities	Corporate and Foreign Bonds	U.S. Government Securities	Municipal Securities	Open Market Paper	Memo Item International and Global Funds
1980	61.8	0.8	42.4	8.5	1.9	4.4	3.8	NA
1981	59.8	0.8	37.4	10.1	2.8	5.1	3.6	NA
1982	76.9	1.2	49.4	10.2	5.1	8.0	3.0	NA
1983	112.1	1.7	74.4	13.0	5.7	13.4	4.0	NA
1984	136.7	2.1	80.6	16.5	12.0	19.1	6.4	5.2
1985	240.2	3.8	113.7	20.1	64.9	33.5	4.1	7.7
1986	413.5	6.5	161.2	46.9	124.2	65.3	9.4	15.7
1987	460.1	6.9	181.7	54.2	134.1	70.7	12.6	19.5
1988	478.3	7.2	187.6	68.4	114.9	78.7	21.4	21.0
1989	566.2	8.5	250.5	74.1	120.0	93.6	19.6	26.5
1990	602.1	8.7	233.2	87.6	137.5	109.1	25.9	40.2
1991	813.9	12.3	351.1	100.5	191.4	137.1	21.5	63.6
1992	1,042.1	16.1	451.7	120.3	251.8	173.4	28.8	77.5
1993	1,429.3	22.2	668.9	176.4	293.6	217.9	50.3	152.5
1994 *	1,443.1	23.1	697.2	177.8	256.8	219.8	68.5	176.7

Distribution of Financial Assets at Mutual Funds
(Percent)

Period	Total	Cash	Corporate Equities	Corporate and Foreign Bonds	U.S. Government Securities	Municipal Securities	Open Market Paper	Memo Item International and Global Funds
1980	100.0	1.3	68.6	13.8	3.1	7.1	6.1	NA
1981	100.0	1.3	62.5	16.9	4.7	8.5	6.0	NA
1982	100.0	1.6	64.2	13.3	6.6	10.4	3.9	NA
1983	100.0	1.5	66.4	11.6	5.1	12.0	3.6	NA
1984	100.0	1.5	59.0	12.1	8.8	14.0	4.7	3.8
1985	100.0	1.6	47.3	8.4	27.0	13.9	1.7	3.2
1986	100.0	1.6	39.0	11.3	30.0	15.8	2.3	3.8
1987	100.0	1.5	39.5	11.8	29.1	15.4	2.7	4.2
1988	100.0	1.5	39.2	14.3	24.0	16.5	4.5	4.4
1989	100.0	1.5	44.2	13.1	21.2	16.5	3.5	4.7
1990	100.0	1.4	38.7	14.5	22.8	18.1	4.3	6.7
1991	100.0	1.5	43.1	12.3	23.5	16.8	2.6	7.8
1992	100.0	1.5	43.3	11.5	24.2	16.6	2.8	7.4
1993	100.0	1.6	46.8	12.3	20.5	15.2	3.5	10.7
1994 *	100.0	1.6	48.3	12.3	17.8	15.2	4.7	12.2

* second quarter

Note: Excludes money market funds and short-term municipal bond funds.

Source: Flow of Funds, Board of Governors of the Federal Reserve System, and Investment Company Institute

MAIN SALES OUTLETS OF OECD PUBLICATIONS
PRINCIPAUX POINTS DE VENTE DES PUBLICATIONS DE L'OCDE

ARGENTINA – ARGENTINE
Carlos Hirsch S.R.L.
Galería Güemes, Florida 165, 4° Piso
1333 Buenos Aires   Tel. (1) 331.1787 y 331.2391
Telefax: (1) 331.1787

AUSTRALIA – AUSTRALIE
D.A. Information Services
648 Whitehorse Road, P.O.B 163
Mitcham, Victoria 3132   Tel. (03) 9873.4411
Telefax: (03) 9873.5679

AUSTRIA – AUTRICHE
Gerold & Co.
Graben 31
Wien I   Tel. (0222) 533.50.14
Telefax: (0222) 512.47.31.29

BELGIUM – BELGIQUE
Jean De Lannoy
Avenue du Roi 202 Koningslaan
B-1060 Bruxelles   Tel. (02) 538.51.69/538.08.41
Telefax: (02) 538.08.41

CANADA
Renouf Publishing Company Ltd.
1294 Algoma Road
Ottawa, ON K1B 3W8   Tel. (613) 741.4333
Telefax: (613) 741.5439
Stores:
61 Sparks Street
Ottawa, ON K1P 5R1   Tel. (613) 238.8985
211 Yonge Street
Toronto, ON M5B 1M4   Tel. (416) 363.3171
Telefax: (416)363.59.63

Les Éditions La Liberté Inc.
3020 Chemin Sainte-Foy
Sainte-Foy, PQ G1X 3V6   Tel. (418) 658.3763
Telefax: (418) 658.3763

Federal Publications Inc.
165 University Avenue, Suite 701
Toronto, ON M5H 3B8   Tel. (416) 860.1611
Telefax: (416) 860.1608

Les Publications Fédérales
1185 Université
Montréal, QC H3B 3A7   Tel. (514) 954.1633
Telefax: (514) 954.1635

CHINA – CHINE
China National Publications Import ·
Export Corporation (CNPIEC)
16 Gongti E. Road, Chaoyang District
P.O. Box 88 or 50
Beijing 100704 PR   Tel. (01) 506.6688
Telefax: (01) 506.3101

CHINESE TAIPEI – TAIPEI CHINOIS
Good Faith Worldwide Int'l. Co. Ltd.
9th Floor, No. 118, Sec. 2
Chung Hsiao E. Road
Taipei   Tel. (02) 391.7396/391.7397
Telefax: (02) 394.9176

**CZECH REPUBLIC – RÉPUBLIQUE
TCHÈQUE**
Artia Pegas Press Ltd.
Narodni Trida 25
POB 825
111 21 Praha 1   Tel. (2) 2 46 04
Telefax: (2) 2 78 72

DENMARK – DANEMARK
Munksgaard Book and Subscription Service
35, Nørre Søgade, P.O. Box 2148
DK-1016 København K   Tel. (33) 12.85.70
Telefax: (33) 12.93.87

EGYPT – ÉGYPTE
Middle East Observer
41 Sherif Street
Cairo   Tel. 392.6919
Telefax: 360-6804

FINLAND – FINLANDE
Akateeminen Kirjakauppa
Keskuskatu 1, P.O. Box 128
00100 Helsinki
Subscription Services/Agence d'abonnements :
P.O. Box 23
00371 Helsinki   Tel. (358 0) 121 4416
Telefax: (358 0) 121.4450

FRANCE
OECD/OCDE
Mail Orders/Commandes par correspondance:
2, rue André-Pascal
75775 Paris Cedex 16   Tel. (33-1) 45.24.82.00
Telefax: (33-1) 49.10.42.76
Telex: 640048 OCDE
Internet: Compte.PUBSINQ @ oecd.org

Orders via Minitel, France only/
Commandes par Minitel, France exclusivement :
36 15 OCDE

OECD Bookshop/Librairie de l'OCDE :
33, rue Octave-Feuillet
75016 Paris   Tel. (33-1) 45.24.81.81
(33-1) 45.24.81.67

Dawson
B.P. 40
91121 Palaiseau Cedex   Tel. 69.10.47.00
Telefax : 64.54.83.26

Documentation Française
29, quai Voltaire
75007 Paris   Tel. 40.15.70.00

Economica
49 rue Héricart
75015 Paris   Tel. 45.78.12.92
Telefax : 40.58.15.70

Gibert Jeune (Droit-Économie)
6, place Saint-Michel
75006 Paris   Tel. 43.25.91.19

Librairie du Commerce International
10, avenue d'Iéna
75016 Paris   Tel. 40.73.34.60

Librairie Dunod
Université Paris-Dauphine
Place du Maréchal de Lattre de Tassigny
75016 Paris   Tel. 44.05.40.13

Librairie Lavoisier
11, rue Lavoisier
75008 Paris   Tel. 42.65.39.95

Librairie des Sciences Politiques
30, rue Saint-Guillaume
75007 Paris   Tel. 45.48.36.02

P.U.F.
49, boulevard Saint-Michel
75005 Paris   Tel. 43.25.83.40

Librairie de l'Université
12a, rue Nazareth
13100 Aix-en-Provence   Tel. 42.26.18.08

Documentation Française
165, rue Garibaldi
69003 Lyon   Tel. (16) 78.63.32.23

Librairie Decitre
29, place Bellecour
69002 Lyon   Tel. (16) 72.40.54.54

Librairie Sauramps
Le Triangle
34967 Montpellier Cedex 2 Tel. (16) 67.58.85.15
Tekefax: (16) 67.58.27.36

A la Sorbonne Actual
23 rue de l'Hôtel des Postes
06000 Nice   Tel. (16) 93.13.77.75
Telefax: (16) 93.80.75.69

GERMANY – ALLEMAGNE
OECD Publications and Information Centre
August-Bebel-Allee 6
D-53175 Bonn   Tel. (0228) 959.120
Telefax: (0228) 959.12.17

GREECE – GRÈCE
Librairie Kauffmann
Mavrokordatou 9
106 78 Athens   Tel. (01) 32.55.321
Telefax: (01) 32.30.320

HONG-KONG
Swindon Book Co. Ltd.
Astoria Bldg. 3F
34 Ashley Road, Tsimshatsui
Kowloon, Hong Kong   Tel. 2376.2062
Telefax: 2376.0685

HUNGARY – HONGRIE
Euro Info Service
Margitsziget, Európa Ház
1138 Budapest   Tel. (1) 111.62.16
Telefax: (1) 111.60.61

ICELAND – ISLANDE
Mál Mog Menning
Laugavegi 18, Pósthólf 392
121 Reykjavik   Tel. (1) 552.4240
Telefax: (1) 562.3523

INDIA – INDE
Oxford Book and Stationery Co.
Scindia House
New Delhi 110001   Tel. (11) 331.5896/5308
Telefax: (11) 332.5993
17 Park Street
Calcutta 700016   Tel. 240832

INDONESIA – INDONÉSIE
Pdii-Lipi
P.O. Box 4298
Jakarta 12042   Tel. (21) 573.34.67
Telefax: (21) 573.34.67

IRELAND – IRLANDE
Government Supplies Agency
Publications Section
4/5 Harcourt Road
Dublin 2   Tel. 661.31.11
Telefax: 475.27.60

ISRAEL
Praedicta
5 Shatner Street
P.O. Box 34030
Jerusalem 91430   Tel. (2) 52.84.90/1/2
Telefax: (2) 52.84.93

R.O.Y. International
P.O. Box 13056
Tel Aviv 61130   Tel. (3) 546 1423
Telefax: (3) 546 1442

Palestinian Authority/Middle East:
INDEX Information Services
P.O.B. 19502
Jerusalem   Tel. (2) 27.12.19
Telefax: (2) 27.16.34

ITALY – ITALIE
Libreria Commissionaria Sansoni
Via Duca di Calabria 1/1
50125 Firenze   Tel. (055) 64.54.15
Telefax: (055) 64.12.57
Via Bartolini 29
20155 Milano   Tel. (02) 36.50.83
Editrice e Libreria Herder
Piazza Montecitorio 120
00186 Roma   Tel. 679.46.28
Telefax: 678.47.51

Libreria Hoepli
Via Hoepli 5
20121 Milano   Tel. (02) 86.54.46
                            Telefax: (02) 805.28.86
Libreria Scientifica
Dott. Lucio de Biasio 'Aeiou'
Via Coronelli, 6
20146 Milano   Tel. (02) 48.95.45.52
                            Telefax: (02) 48.95.45.48

JAPAN – JAPON
OECD Publications and Information Centre
Landic Akasaka Building
2-3-4 Akasaka, Minato-ku
Tokyo 107   Tel. (81.3) 3586.2016
                            Telefax: (81.3) 3584.7929

KOREA – CORÉE
Kyobo Book Centre Co. Ltd.
P.O. Box 1658, Kwang Hwa Moon
Seoul   Tel. 730.78.91
                            Telefax: 735.00.30

MALAYSIA – MALAISIE
University of Malaya Bookshop
University of Malaya
P.O. Box 1127, Jalan Pantai Baru
59700 Kuala Lumpur
Malaysia   Tel. 756.5000/756.5425
                            Telefax: 756.3246

MEXICO – MEXIQUE
OECD Publications and Information Centre
Edificio INFOTEC
Av. San Fernando no. 37
Col. Toriello Guerra
Tlalpan C.P. 14050
Mexico D.F.
                Tel. (525) 606 00 11 Extension 100
                            Fax : (525) 606 13 07

Revistas y Periodicos Internacionales S.A. de C.V.
Florencia 57 - 1004
Mexico, D.F. 06600   Tel. 207.81.00
                            Telefax: 208.39.79

NETHERLANDS – PAYS-BAS
SDU Uitgeverij Plantijnstraat
Externe Fondsen
Postbus 20014
2500 EA's-Gravenhage   Tel. (070) 37.89.880
Voor bestellingen: Telefax: (070) 34.75.778

**NEW ZEALAND
NOUVELLE-ZÉLANDE**
GPLegislation Services
P.O. Box 12418
Thorndon, Wellington   Tel. (04) 496.5655
                            Telefax: (04) 496.5698

NORWAY – NORVÈGE
Narvesen Info Center – NIC
Bertrand Narvesens vei 2
P.O. Box 6125 Etterstad
0602 Oslo 6   Tel. (022) 57.33.00
                            Telefax: (022) 68.19.01

PAKISTAN
Mirza Book Agency
65 Shahrah Quaid-E-Azam
Lahore 54000   Tel. (42) 353.601
                            Telefax: (42) 231.730

PHILIPPINE – PHILIPPINES
International Booksource Center Inc.
Rm 179/920 Cityland 10 Condo Tower 2
HV dela Costa Ext cor Valero St.
Makati Metro Manila   Tel. (632) 817 9676
                            Telefax : (632) 817 1741

POLAND – POLOGNE
Ars Polona
00-950 Warszawa
Krakowskie Przedmieácie 7   Tel. (22) 264760
                            Telefax : (22) 268673

PORTUGAL
Livraria Portugal
Rua do Carmo 70-74
Apart. 2681
1200 Lisboa   Tel. (01) 347.49.82/5
                            Telefax: (01) 347.02.64

SINGAPORE – SINGAPOUR
Gower Asia Pacific Pte Ltd.
Golden Wheel Building
41, Kallang Pudding Road, No. 04-03
Singapore 1334   Tel. 741.5166
                            Telefax: 742.9356

SPAIN – ESPAGNE
Mundi-Prensa Libros S.A.
Castelló 37, Apartado 1223
Madrid 28001   Tel. (91) 431.33.99
                            Telefax: (91) 575.39.98

Mundi-Prensa Barcelona
Consell de Cent No. 391
08009 – Barcelona   Tel. (93) 488.34.92
                            Telefax: (93) 487.76.59

Llibreria de la Generalitat
Palau Moja
Rambla dels Estudis, 118
08002 – Barcelona
                (Subscripcions) Tel. (93) 318.80.12
                (Publicacions) Tel. (93) 302.67.23
                            Telefax: (93) 412.18.54

SRI LANKA
Centre for Policy Research
c/o Colombo Agencies Ltd.
No. 300-304, Galle Road
Colombo 3   Tel. (1) 574240, 573551-2
                        Telefax: (1) 575394, 510711

SWEDEN – SUÈDE
CE Fritzes AB
S–106 47 Stockholm   Tel. (08) 690.90.90
                            Telefax: (08) 20.50.21

Subscription Agency/Agence d'abonnements :
Wennergren-Williams Info AB
P.O. Box 1305
171 25 Solna   Tel. (08) 705.97.50
                            Telefax: (08) 27.00.71

SWITZERLAND – SUISSE
Maditec S.A. (Books and Periodicals - Livres
et périodiques)
Chemin des Palettes 4
Case postale 266
1020 Renens VD 1   Tel. (021) 635.08.65
                            Telefax: (021) 635.07.80

Librairie Payot S.A.
4, place Pépinet
CP 3212
1002 Lausanne   Tel. (021) 320.25.11
                            Telefax: (021) 320.25.14

Librairie Unilivres
6, rue de Candolle
1205 Genève   Tel. (022) 320.26.23
                            Telefax: (022) 329.73.18

Subscription Agency/Agence d'abonnements :
Dynapresse Marketing S.A.
38 avenue Vibert
1227 Carouge   Tel. (022) 308.07.89
                            Telefax: (022) 308.07.99
See also – Voir aussi :
OECD Publications and Information Centre
August-Bebel-Allee 6
D-53175 Bonn (Germany)   Tel. (0228) 959.120
                            Telefax: (0228) 959.12.17

THAILAND – THAÏLANDE
Suksit Siam Co. Ltd.
113, 115 Fuang Nakhon Rd.
Opp. Wat Rajbopith
Bangkok 10200   Tel. (662) 225.9531/2
                            Telefax: (662) 222.5188

TURKEY – TURQUIE
Kültür Yayinlari Is-Türk Ltd. Sti.
Atatürk Bulvari No. 191/Kat 13
Kavaklidere/Ankara   Tel. 428.11.40 Ext. 2458
Dolmabahce Cad. No. 29
Besiktas/Istanbul   Tel. (312) 260 7188
                            Telex: (312) 418 29 46

UNITED KINGDOM – ROYAUME-UNI
HMSO
Gen. enquiries   Tel. (171) 873 8496
Postal orders only:
P.O. Box 276, London SW8 5DT
Personal Callers HMSO Bookshop
49 High Holborn, London WC1V 6HB
                            Telefax: (171) 873 8416
Branches at: Belfast, Birmingham, Bristol,
Edinburgh, Manchester

UNITED STATES – ÉTATS-UNIS
OECD Publications and Information Center
2001 L Street N.W., Suite 650
Washington, D.C. 20036-4910 Tel. (202) 785.6323
                            Telefax: (202) 785.0350

VENEZUELA
Libreria del Este
Avda F. Miranda 52, Aptdo. 60337
Edificio Galipán
Caracas 106   Tel. 951.1705/951.2307/951.1297
                        Telegram: Libreste Caracas

Subscriptions to OECD periodicals may also be
placed through main subscription agencies.

Les abonnements aux publications périodiques de
l'OCDE peuvent être souscrits auprès des
principales agences d'abonnement.

Orders and inquiries from countries where Distributors have not yet been appointed should be sent to:
OECD Publications Service, 2 rue André-Pascal,
75775 Paris Cedex 16, France.

Les commandes provenant de pays où l'OCDE n'a
pas encore désigné de distributeur peuvent être
adressées à : OCDE, Service des Publications,
2, rue André-Pascal, 75775 Paris Cedex 16, France.

10-1995

OECD PUBLICATIONS, 2 rue André-Pascal, 75775 PARIS CEDEX 16
PRINTED IN FRANCE
(21 95 13 1) ISBN 92-64-14650-4 - No. 48288 1995